Life after Death

Life after Death

Edited by Peter Brookesmith

BOOK CLUB ASSOCIATES · LONDON

Acknowledgments
Photographs were supplied by Aldus Archive, Dennis Assinder, Associated Press, Beverley LeBarrow, Bavaria Verlag, Biblioteca Apostolica, Vatican Bibliotheque Nationale Paris, Bodleian Library, Bridgeman Art Library, British Library, British Tourist Authority, Dept. of Engineering Cambridge University, Central Press, Channel 9 – Australian TV, Jean-Loup Charmet, Colchester Castle Museum, Bruce Coleman, W.E. Cox, George E. Crouter, Culver Pictures, John Cutten Associates, E.A. Davies, Hylton Edgar, Robert Estall, Mary Evans Picture Library, Mary Evans Picture Library/Sigmund Freud, Joel Finler, FOT Library, Leslie Flint, Werner Forman Archive, John Frost, Leif Geiges, Fred Gettings, Thomas Gilcrease Institute, J. Goodliffe, Joan Grant, Anita Gregory, Robert Harding & Associates, Toby Hogarth, Michael Holford, Robert Hunt Library, Alan Hutchison, Alex Jeffry, Dr. A.G. Khan, Kobal Collection, John Lassen, Paul McElhoney, Mansell Collection, Musées Royaux des Beaux Arts de Belgique, National Maritime Museum, National Portrait Gallery, Newark Museum, Peter Newark's Western Americana, Novosti, Bob Okon, Picturepoint, Guy Lyon Playfair, Axel Poignant, Popperfoto, Psychic News, Radio Times, Scala, Paul Snelgrove, Brian Snellgrove, SORRAT, Souvenir Press, Sphere, Christian Steiner (CBS Records), A.F. Stubbs, Syndication International, Tate Gallery, John Topham Picture Library, Tyne Tees TV, UPI, Frances Vargo, Roger-Viollet, Charles Walker, York Archaeological Trust/Mike Duffy, ZEFA.

The publishers would like to thank the following authors for contributing to this book:
Paul Beard 194–201; Sue Blackmore 38–41; David Christie-Murray 108–126, 183–193; Hilary Evans 174–181; Anita Gregory 75–83; Frederick Goodman 95–106; Melvin Harris 127–138; Edward Horton 26–36; A.G. Khan 202–205; Lynn Picknett 8–11, 20–25, 140–159; Archie Roy 16–19; Roy Stemman 12–15, 42–48, 53–69, 70–74, 84–93, 161–173; Ian Wilson 49–51.

First published in Great Britain by
Orbis Publishing Limited, London 1984
This edition published 1984 by B.C.A.
By arrangement with Orbis Publishing Limited, London

Printed in Italy
ISBN 0-85613-598-4 hardback

Contents

Introduction

By any standards, the issue of whether or not there is life after death must be vitally important to all of us, whatever kind of life we have on earth. Until the 1850's however, it had been pushed into the background, partly because of the spread of materialism, promoting disbelief in the existence of a human soul or spirit, but even more because the ideas of the Church and its followers about the afterlife were becoming increasingly woolly – the conventional notions of heaven and hell were not fashionable any more, and people on the whole preferred not to think about the subject in great detail.

This peaceful co-existence of sceptics and believers was shattered around the middle of the last century when communication was established with the spirit world. This, at least, was what appeared to have happened since there could be no doubt that there were forces at work that were extremely hard to account for except on the assumption that the dead had not merely survived, but were capable of communicating with the living in a variety of ways – passing messages through mediums, moving objects, answering questions with raps, and so on.

Whatever the explanation, the evidence for the reality of the psychic (as they came to be known) forces prompted scientists to investigate them, and led to the setting up in 1882 of the Society for Psychical Research. Materialists, however, were not reassured by the scientific respectability of so many of the society's leading members, because it was perfectly clear that if the phenomena could be proved to be genuine, that would sound materialism's death knell. Orthodox Christians tended to be just as hostile because these spirits, if that is what they were – were revealed to be far from their idea of spiritual, behaving in the most eccentric fashion.

'The kind of immortality which "psychical research" endeavours to establish', asserted William Ralph Inge (Dean of St Pauls, and for many years the Church's chief polemicist against Spiritualism), would, for a Christian like himself, be 'a negation of the only immortality which he desires or believes in'.

Spiritualists and psychical researchers could reply that what Inge desired or believed in was his own business; they were producing evidence that was making it increasingly difficult to deny the reality of communications from the dead. The most influential case history, in this context, was Sir Oliver Lodge's book *Raymond*, in which he describes the messages coming through mediums from his son, who had been killed at the front in 1915. Even more striking, 15 years later, were the messages that came through the celebrated medium Eileen Garrett from Flight-Lieutenant H. Carmichael Irwin, captain of the crashed airship R101.

Both Raymond Lodge and Captain Irwin communicated through 'controls', the mediums' spirit guides who acted as a kind of door keeper, selecting which of the various 'communicators' would be permitted to pass messages, or to give them in person. But the whole concept of 'controls' was and is a controversial one; sceptics, and even those people who were far from sceptical about the possibility of life after death, found the idea of this machinery of mediumship hard to take, especially since these entities might claim to have been Red Indian braves or Arab girls, or even – as in the case of the most celebrated of them, 'John King' – pirates in their earthly lives.

Did Lodge and Irwin really communicate in this way? Or, as some researchers believe, were these spirit guides actually a dramatised fragment of the medium's own personality?

Certainly 'controls' were not necessarily what they claimed to be. 'Dr Phinuit', the 'control' of the celebrated Boston medium Mrs Piper, was able to convince the most sceptical of sitters that the information he passed on was genuine and could not have been obtained by deception. Yet he was himself a deceiver; research showed that no 'Dr Phinuit' had lived at the place or the time he claimed, and as if mortified by being caught out, he disappeared and made way for other 'controls'. Clearly there are no straightforward answers to the vexed problem of who the 'discarnate entities', as some researchers prefer to call them, really are.

Similar problems dog research in allied fields. There have been many spectacular photographs in which the image of a dead person has mysteriously appeared, even though nothing unusual was noticed when the picture was taken. Even if fraud can be ruled out, however, it is hard to eliminate the possibility that this represents some kind of extraordinary and unexplored power of the photographer's mind.

The psychic drawings of Matthew Manning and the musical compositions of Rosemary Brown strongly suggest that some mediums can be influenced by a deceased artist or composer to produce works that would be attributable to him, were he still living, but here again the possibility remains that the explanation may lie in some type of telepathic communication through what Carl Jung described as the collective unconscious, which can be held to embrace all memory, all thought, all composition – everything that has happened, in fact, since the creation. The collective unconscious, Professor H. H. Price suggested in his presidential address to the Society for Psychical Research in 1939, might resemble a submerged continent whose peaks – our conscious selves – arise out of the ocean; at deeper levels 'all personalities are in complete and continuous telepathic rapport.'

It is an ingenious idea, which can account for some of the manifestations of mediumship – and also of hypnotic regression, in which people appear to remember past lives. Sometimes episodes in these lives are 're-lived' in ways that make it hard not to accept the reality of reincarnation. Again, when individual cases are closely scrutinised, they often begin to crumble, but some remain impressive.

Some of the strongest evidence for survival comes from the 'cross-correspondences', in which messages allegedly came from the deceased founder members of the Society for Psychical Research, through mediums who were not in contact with one another, and in such a form that they could not be understood separately – they became meaningful only when pieced together. Telepathy between the mediums? This would still involve organisation 'by some diabolical intellect', as Lodge put it, 'merely with the intent to deceive' – about as likely he thought as P.H. Gosse's theory that God placed fossils in the rocks to test men's faith in the biblical story of creation.

The collective unconscious, or 'super-ESP', explanation too is inadequate to account for other evidence of survival, such as the case histories of men and women who have had near-death experiences – sometimes being actually pronounced dead – and who have encountered loved ones waiting to welcome them over to the 'other side'.

Scepticism has become so finely tuned an instrument that it is hard to claim any clear-cut, irrefutable proof of life after death, yet it is even harder to explain away the mass of evidence for the reality of life in the spirit. The physical explanations 'are easy, but miserably insufficient,' wrote the eminent mathematician Augustus de Morgan after painstaking investigations of the medium Mrs Hayden, 'the spirit hypothesis is sufficient, but ponderously difficult'.

Perhaps the last word on life after death can be given to Dr Alan Gauld, whose admirably balanced survey of the whole field, *Mediumship and survival*, was published in the SPR Centenary Series in 1982. 'I cannot dismiss the evidence *en bloc* as bad evidence,' he wrote, 'as entirely the product of fraud, misrecording, malobservation, wishful-thinking or plain chance coincidence.' Nor could he feel that the 'super-ESP' theory covered the remarkable way in which 'communicators', through mediums, often show the personality characteristics they had when living, 'distinctive purposes, skills, capacities, habits, turns of phrase, struggles to communicate, wishes, points of view'.

Yet Dr Gauld could not feel confident that the spirit explanation is the right one, for in this area, 'what we know stands in proportion to what we do not know as a bucketful does to the ocean. Certainty is not to be had, nor even a strong conviction that the area of one's uncertainty has been narrowed to a manageable compass.'

Brian Inglis

Profiles of survival

Some of the most compelling evidence for the continuation of life after death is provided in individual case studies of communication with the dead, where the motivation behind the messages is clear and strong.

Left: Anne Boleyn found a champion in Canon William Pakenham-Walsh, according to her supposed psychic communications. He believed her innocent of the adultery for which she was executed. Her real offence in the eyes of Henry VIII may have been to fail to provide a male heir

Below: Henry VIII's progress in the afterlife was allegedly hindered by the weight of his past offences. Canon Pakenham-Walsh regarded it as his life's work to help him move beyond the 'dark place' in which he found himself

The Canon and the King

Henry VIII died in 1547 at the end of a career darkened by many acts of greed and cruelty. This chapter recounts the story of a 20th-century churchman who believed he had brought Henry's spirit to repentance

IN 1917 A BRITISH MISSIONARY in China happened to read a biography of Anne Boleyn, second wife of Henry VIII, who was executed for adultery in 1536. The missionary was William Pakenham-Walsh, later a canon of Peterborough Cathedral. He was at first merely interested in Anne's life but gradually became immersed in the subject, which soon became a life-long passion. On his return to England, he determined to rescue the reputation of 'a Queen who has been much misunderstood'. But he soon found himself drawn into the afterlife agonies of Henry VIII himself, as communicated to well-known mediums and often in the presence of the clergyman.

The experiences of Pakenham-Walsh were related in *A Tudor story*, which was published in 1963, three years after his death at the age of 92. It is a bizarre yet poignant story. The author's sincerity, integrity and simplicity are strongly evident throughout. He himself had no psychic powers. He was a good-hearted, uncomplicated man who enjoyed cycling and brisk country walks. At seances, however, he broke almost every rule possible, divulging information in advance, and 'leading' the medium in obvious ways. Nevertheless, because of inner consistencies, certain circumstantial evidence and the clergyman's sense of purpose, the book is an intriguing and important contribution to psychical literature.

In August 1921 Pakenham-Walsh met a certain Mrs Clegg, a medium, at his sister's house. The first sitting set the pattern for many that followed over the next 12 years, involving several other mediums: a mixture of ingenuous 'leading' and reading between the lines by the Canon – and genuine but obscure 'evidence'. The spirit of a white-haired old man who appeared to Mrs Clegg was assumed by the Canon to be Anne Boleyn's father; a vague description of his daughter – 'with good hands, rather plump' – was, said the Canon, 'of course a perfect description of the Lady Anne' (despite the fact that Anne had six fingers on one hand).

Yet some of the information was confirmed later, after research. Queen Anne Boleyn did indeed have five brothers, whose names were correctly given by Mrs Clegg; and Anne had seriously quarrelled with her sister Mary, as the medium said. But Pakenham-Walsh then committed a major blunder by telling the medium who the spirit was – and had further meetings after that. One ended with Mrs Clegg saying that Anne foresaw how 'you will be offered a parish with the snowdrops and you will go to it with the daffodils.' Pakenham-Walsh was soon after appointed to the parish of Sulgrave in Northamptonshire, carpeted with snowdrops on his first visit and ablaze with daffodils when he took up residence. The gardener said he had 'never seen the like' in 40 years.

A need for forgiveness

If Anne Boleyn had restricted her 'visits' to Mrs Clegg the story might never have developed further. In December 1922, however, Pakenham-Walsh received a letter from Miss Eleanor Kelly, a Christian psychic. In her daily session of automatic writing, she said, she had received a message in which were mentioned both the Canon and Mr Frederick Bligh Bond, the architect and 'psychic archaeologist'. She added: 'I have had some communication now and again with souls who have died in the same period as Henry VIII, and I am very much interested in the reference [in her script] to him and the Lady Anne and the need . . . for forgiveness on her part and reparation on his.'

The chapel of St Peter ad Vincula (St Peter in chains), at the Tower of London, is Anne Boleyn's burial place. Her remains lie beneath the left-hand end of the altar. William Pakenham-Walsh prayed here that Anne, by whom he had become fascinated, 'might be to me a guardian angel'. He decided that he would write a play about her tragic life. It was not long afterwards that she first communicated with him – as he believed – at a seance

William Pakenham-Walsh was still a parson when he first received messages that he believed to come from Anne Boleyn. In due course he became a canon of Peterborough Cathedral – where, he noted, there was a shrine to Henry VIII's first wife, Katherine of Aragon. Did his devotion to the memory of Anne Boleyn cause him to misinterpret the evidence that came out of the sittings? Or did it mark him as the ideal recipient for the dead queen's urgent appeal for help?

She later received another message, this time from 'Alwyn, once a Thane of Sussex'. It spelled out the task at hand:

> As all who touch the lives of others intimately must at least remove *all* that obstructs their unity, so must these two souls be cleared each alone, and each in unison, before they too take their places in the great structure of the Body of Christ. Anne has even still some shadows to let fall before her vision is clear; he, Henry, is but now beginning to be vaguely conscious of his need of cleansing.

To this end Mr Bond arranged for the Canon to meet one of the most famous mediums of the day, Mrs Hester Dowden, at her home in Chelsea, London. The seance took the form of automatic writing with the word Katherine repeated several times. The pencil then wrote: 'I want you to help someone who needs help from your world.' They obeyed instructions to move to a nearby house so that better 'contact' could be made. There, Mrs Dowden's pencil flew violently across her writing pad: 'I am here – HENRY REX.' They had, the Canon believed, made contact with the King through Katherine of Aragon, his first wife.

Using Mrs Dowden as amanuensis, Mr Bond and Miss Kelly talked to the monarch. Asked if he knew he was dead, Henry replied: 'Yes, I know. It has been but a nightmare. . . . I want to be told exactly what has happened and why I am still in a dark place. I feel as if I was back again in the earth.' He said that his daughter Elizabeth (whose mother was Anne Boleyn) meant nothing to him. When told she had become a great ruler, he answered acidly: 'I did not expect it from her mother's child.' Reminded that the divine right of kings would carry no weight on Judgement Day, Henry erupted: 'I shall not listen to *you*. You are a fool. I would have had you executed in my time.' And the information that England's current king was George v caused a further outburst: 'I care not. You are a varlet; some knave from a tavern who is making sport of me because I lie at your mercy.' Veering from self-reproach to self-pity to outbursts of rage, he finally agreed to pray for forgiveness, but added: 'I will not pray here. A king prays alone.'

Henry, it appeared, was in the grip of great inner conflict caused by his actions as king. It seemed that he would need to forgive and be forgiven by other souls from his lifetime, such as Cardinal Thomas Wolsey and Henry's third Queen, Jane Seymour. Historians generally believe that she was his favourite wife, yet the King's spirit ranted that he detested her. This hatred seemed to be the main obstacle to his own spiritual progress. The Canon felt particularly pleased, therefore, when he and the mediums effected a reconciliation between the spirits of Henry and Jane.

Of Henry's six wives it was his first, Katherine of Aragon, who claimed him as husband and who wrote, through Miss Kelly: 'Love is guiding him along the upward, rugged path.' It is clear, however, that Henry's desire to be helped began in earnest when Pakenham-Walsh told him that if he repented his sins he would be reunited with his sons – Henry, who died after six weeks (but who, it was claimed, had since grown up in the afterlife), and Edward, who had reigned from 1547 to 1553.

The Canon's greatest day was 24 June 1933 when, in the company of two mediums, Mrs Heber-Percy and Mrs Theo Monson, he was told that he was in the presence not only of Henry and his Queens, Wolsey, Sir Thomas More, Elizabeth I and others, but also the spirits of his own daughter Helen and his son Willy. Henry wished it to be made public that he repented of his misdeeds. Anne Boleyn said that 'the manuscript [of *A Tudor story*] is one of the ladders from here to you and from you to us, by which many may climb to true knowledge.' The Canon pronounced a blessing on the gathering, seen and unseen, and then the visitors were gone.

Katherine of Aragon, the first wife of Henry VIII, had many children by him, but only one, the future Mary I, survived. Henry's anxiety to divorce Katherine in order to marry Anne Boleyn and secure the succession led to England's break with Rome and the establishment of the Anglican Church. Katherine refused to recognise the annulment enacted by Thomas Cranmer, the new Archbishop of Canterbury – and was allegedly still obdurate 400 years after her death

Edward VI was Henry's son by Jane Seymour and succeeded to the throne on his father's death. He was nine years old at the time he began his reign: by the age of 16 he had died of consumption. Henry's desire to be reunited with Edward and with his other son, also called Henry, seemed to be a strong motive for his ultimate repentance

A prayer answered

If one believes that the soul can survive death and that even the most evil man can be helped to progress in the afterlife, then the child-like honest Canon would seem eminently suitable to 'rescue' the arrogant Henry.

Critics, however, would find it all too easy to tear the story apart. Although none of the mediums knew Pakenham-Walsh before they met, they would almost certainly have heard of his obsession with the Tudors. A sensitive could, even if unconsciously, have picked up telepathic impressions of his desire to be Anne Boleyn's champion and of his exalted image of Anne. It is natural, too, that Pakenham-Walsh should have wanted to help Henry, a tortured soul in search of redemption. It is significant that Henry's first wife, Katherine, sought earthly help for him. In the Canon's eyes, she was probably Henry's only legal wife. Although a number of 'tests' set by Anne were seized upon by Pakenham-Walsh as evidence of her survival, it could also be said that they proved only that he was ignorant of the modern theory of general (super) ESP.

Anne Boleyn had said on the scaffold in 1536: 'I pray God to save the King.' Could, perhaps, a gentle ex-missionary have been chosen to answer her prayer 400 years later?

Raymond reviewed

A few weeks before the death of his son Raymond in 1915, Sir Oliver Lodge received a spirit message predicting disaster but promising comfort. Soon the bereaved family was to receive its first communications from Raymond

NEARLY A MILLION British men lost their lives in the First World War. Their courage will always be remembered, but individually most were soon forgotten except by their grieving family and friends. But for one young soldier, Raymond Lodge, death actually brought hope to the bereaved. Raymond was the youngest of six sons of Sir Oliver Lodge, the world-famous physicist, who also had six younger daughters.

Born in Liverpool in 1889, Raymond enjoyed a comfortable childhood, was educated at Bedales and then returned home to study engineering for two years at Birmingham University. After a two-year senior apprenticeship with the Wolseley Motor Company, Raymond joined a plug manufacturing company that two of his older brothers had started.

Raymond was a bright and popular boy who did not hesitate to volunteer for service, at the age of 25, when the First World War began. In September 1914 he was commissioned into an infantry regiment, the South Lancashires, as Second Lieutenant, and after training in Scotland and Liverpool he was sent to France on 15 March 1915. He joined his battalion at the front in Flanders and by the end of the month he was in the trenches.

For the next three months, Raymond was in the thick of the action in the front line, serving six or seven days at a time in the trenches, then spending a similar period in support a mile (1.6 kilometres) behind the front line but still subject to shell fire. He wrote home two or three times a week, giving graphic descriptions of the horrors of trench warfare, but somehow managing to remain cheerful.

Meanwhile, in England, Sir Oliver Lodge continued with his scientific work – and with his interest in psychical research, which had been aroused in 1883 by thought. transference experiments. A year later he had joined the Society for Psychical Research (SPR), and he had served as its president for a three-year period from 1901.

His interest in telepathy broadened to include spirit communication, and in time Lodge became convinced of the existence of a life after death. His concern for the subject was well-known, and he frequently received messages from mediums, so he was not surprised, early in September 1915, to find in his post a letter from the USA giving details of a seance by one Mrs Leonora Piper, a famous trance medium. She had apparently been given the following spirit message from one of the SPR's founders, F. W. H. Myers, for Lodge:

> Myers says, you take the part of the poet and he will act as Faunus.
> FAUNUS.
> *Protect.* he will U.D. [understand]
> What you have to say Lodge. good work, ask Verrall, she will U.D.
> Arthur says so.

There followed some confusing lines apparently trying to resolve doubt about the identity of Arthur; and the message ended with the words, 'you got mixed up but Myers is straight about Poet and Faunus.'

Lodge did not understand the meaning of the message, but he wrote immediately to Mrs Verrall of Cambridge. She was a classical scholar and an automatic writing medium who had been involved in the famous SPR cross-correspondences (see page 20). Her husband Arthur, now dead, had also been a classical scholar.

Mrs Verrall replied that the message was an allusion to the Roman poet Horace, who in one poem had described how the Roman countryside god Faunus had protected him by lightening the blow when a tree fell on him.

But what did the message mean? Lodge gave the matter little attention, except to speculate that the impending blow might be some financial misfortune, and went to Scotland on holiday.

On 15 September Lodge and a friend set out to play a round of golf. They had both been looking forward to the game, but in the event Lodge was in a state of acute depression and played so badly that after seven

Killed, like so many other young men, in the horrifying conditions of the Flanders trenches during the First World War (bottom), Raymond Lodge (below) apparently tried to comfort his family by communicating through a number of mediums. One of his messages, received by his mother in 1918, concerned the memorial tablet that his family had erected in a local church (right). Apparently highly amused, he pointed out that the day of his death was a Tuesday – not, as the inscription reads, a Wednesday. 'You can't eradicate it. . . . [It] will have to stand forever'

DUM SPIRO SPERO
Remember RAYMOND LODGE, Sec. Lieutenant
2nd South Lancashire Regiment, beloved son of
SIR OLIVER and LADY LODGE of this parish
who gave his life for his Country.
He was born Jany 25 1889, and was killed in
action in Flanders about noon on Wednesday
Septr 14 in the year of Our Lord 1915
aged 26 years.
Whoso bears the whole heaviness of the wronged world's weight
And puts it by,
It is well with him suffering, though he face man's fate
How should he die?
SWINBURNE.

holes they decided to abandon the game and return to the hotel.

Two days later Lodge received a telegram from the War Office informing him that Raymond had been killed. His young son had been leading his men back from the front line trenches when he was hit by shrapnel and severely injured in the back. He died a few hours later, on 14 September.

Raymond's death had occurred less than 24 hours before his father's acute bout of depression, and Lodge wondered, later, if there were a connection between the two. But even more significant, perhaps, was the Faunus message. Writing about Raymond's death, Lodge talked of 'the blow – which it is permissible to say was a terribly severe one.' Was this the blow that Myers had hinted, from the spirit world, that he would lighten?

If it was, it suggested that Myers knew in advance of young Raymond's death. And if that tragic event was to be cushioned, that could be done only by providing the Lodge family with irrefutable evidence of Raymond's continued existence in a new realm. And that is indeed, it seems, what the young Lodge son, aided by Myers and others in the spirit world, set out to provide – with sufficient success that Lodge published an account of these spirit messages in his book *Raymond, or life and death.*

Lodge's biographer, Professor W.P. Jolly, in his book *Sir Oliver Lodge, psychical researcher and scientist*, observes:

> Seldom can a work of research and philosophy have been more opportunely published, when almost everyone in England was mourning the loss of some friend or relative. The interest aroused by the book was quite sensational: there were six editions in little over a month, and then it settled down to a steady rate of two new editions a year for the rest of the war, going into twelve editions in all before being superseded in 1922 by a new version called *Raymond Revised.*

The book, with its verbatim accounts of seance messages received through professional and amateur mediums, as well as descriptions of the Lodge family's own table-turning sessions, was an excellent introduction to Spiritualism and gave a useful insight into the techniques used for spirit communication.

Incognito visits

As a scientist, Lodge put a heavy emphasis on the status of the communications as evidence, and it seemed that Raymond himself took pleasure in trying to provide tests to prove his survival. Lodge was a well-known public figure and would have been recognised by most mediums. Lady Lodge, however, was able to visit a number of mediums anonymously, among them A. Vout Peters. Her first seance with this medium took place on 27 September 1915. During the session the medium's guide, 'Moonstone', told her that what he was about to say was so important that he would speak sufficiently slowly that she would be able to write down every word. The message was, 'Not only is the partition so thin that you can hear the operators on the other side, but a big hole has been made.' Lodge was particularly astonished at this passage, and later described it as 'a remarkably evidential and identifying message' because of its similarity to a passage

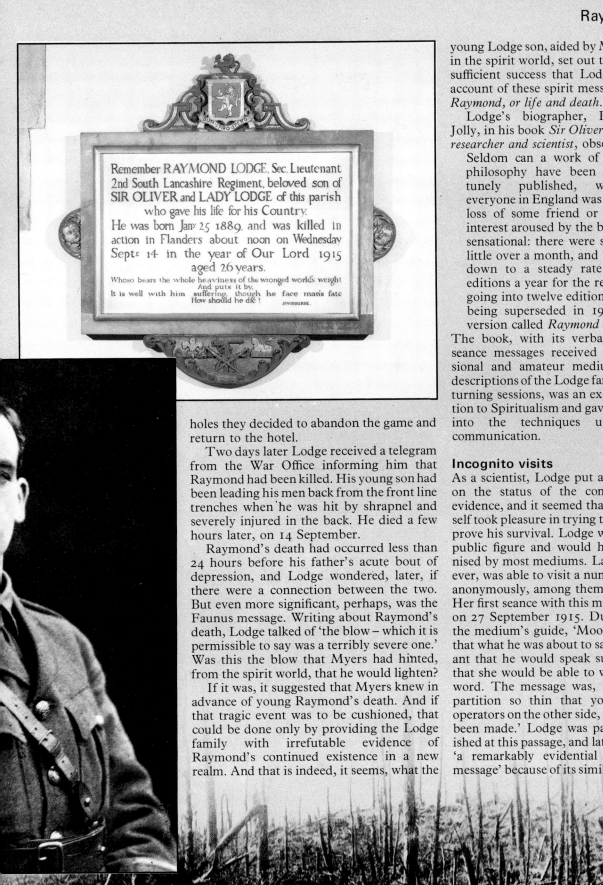

Above: Sir Oliver Lodge (1851–1940), well-known physicist and psychical researcher, and father of Raymond. In September 1914 he received a letter from an American medium containing a spirit message to him from his fellow psychical researcher, the deceased F. W. H. Myers. The message said Lodge would take the part of the poet while Myers would 'act as Faunus'. The classical scholar Mrs A. W. Verrall of Cambridge (right) – who knew both Myers and Lodge – interpreted the message as meaning that Myers would shield Lodge from some kind of blow. Less than two weeks later Lodge's son Raymond was dead – and very soon afterwards his family began to receive spirit messages from him. Could this have been the comfort Myers had promised?

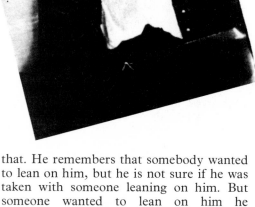

in his book *Survival of Man*:

> The boundary between the two states – the known and the unknown – is still substantial but is wearing thin in places; and like excavators engaged in boring a tunnel from opposite ends, amid the roar of water and other noises, we are beginning to hear now and again the strokes of the pickaxes of our comrades on the other side.

At the same seance, Peters said that the communicator – Raymond – was talking about photographs including one in which he was one of a group. 'He is particular that I should tell you this,' the medium said. 'In one you see his walking-stick.'

Lady Lodge could not remember a group photograph in which her son had appeared, and enquiries indicated that the medium was wrong. The matter was dropped. Then, on 28 November 1915, the Lodges received a letter from a Mrs B. P. Cheves, mother of the medical officer of the 2nd South Lancashire Regiment, saying that her son had sent her copies of a group photograph in which Raymond appeared. Did they have a copy? If not, she would gladly send them one.

While the Lodges waited for the photograph, the scientist decided to see if Raymond could communicate any more information about the group picture through another medium. Lodge had arranged a seance with the trance medium Gladys Osborne Leonard, an outstanding psychic who had a spirit child control named Feda who allegedly spoke directly to sitters.

Lodge asked Feda to ask Raymond about the photograph and how he looked. Was he standing up? 'No, he doesn't seem to think so,' said Feda. 'Some were raised up round; he was sitting down, and some were raised up at the back of him. Some were standing and some were sitting, he thinks.'

Feda said that Raymond had the impression that there were about a dozen people in the picture, if not more. Asked by Lodge if they were soldiers she replied, 'He says yes – a mixed lot.' Asked if he had a stick, the spirit control answered, 'He doesn't remember that. He remembers that somebody wanted to lean on him, but he is not sure if he was taken with someone leaning on him. But someone wanted to lean on him he remembers.'

When asked by the scientist whether the photograph was taken outside, Raymond replied, through the medium, 'Yes, practically' – a reply that amused Feda, who pointed out that either it was or it was not. Lodge suggested that it might have been a shelter and Feda then described an image she was being shown with vertical lines in the background.

On the strength of these two seance messages, Lodge built up a written description of how he thought the picture would look when it arrived. On 7 December he posted this to J. Arthur Hill, who was his unofficial secretary for psychical matters. On the same day, in mid afternoon, Mrs Cheves's package arrived to reveal a photograph of a group of soldiers, 21 in all, with five squatting in front, seven seated in the

Left: Gladys Osborne Leonard. When Raymond's brother Lionel visited her, incognito, Mrs Leonard described two spirits that were apparently in the room. One appeared to be Raymond himself; the other was tall, well-built, elderly with a beard around his chin, but no moustache, and somehow connected with the letter W – a good description of Lionel's grandfather (below), whom the family called 'Grandfather W'

Below right: a photograph of a group of officers at the front. Raymond Lodge is in the front row, second from the right. The photograph was sent to the Lodges after Raymond's death – but before it arrived, 'Raymond', speaking through Mrs Leonard's spirit guide, described it: 'somebody wanted to lean on him'. An officer seated behind Raymond is leaning his hand on Raymond's shoulder – no other officer is touching another in this way

second row, and nine standing at the back in front of a temporary wooden structure that looked as if it might be a hospital shed.

Raymond was squatting in the front row, second from right. A walking stick or regulation cane was lying across his feet and a soldier sitting behind him was resting a hand on his shoulder – the only person in the photograph to be doing so.

When Lodge's book about Raymond appeared in print, some critics dismissed it as the gullible ravings of a bereaved father. Nothing could have been further from the truth. Sir Oliver Lodge was convinced of a life after death and communication with the dead long before his son was killed. But his beliefs were not shared by the rest of his family: they sought their own proof.

On 17 November 1915 Lionel Lodge, Raymond's brother, went to London in the hope of having a seance with Mrs Leonard. He had written to her in advance, but on plain paper not from his own address, and unsigned, telling her he would be arriving at a certain time. However, he sent it to the medium's old address, and she had not received the letter when he arrived, a complete stranger who had not even apparently made an appointment.

Mrs Leonard answered the door, took him in at once when he said he wanted a sitting, drew the blind and lit a red lamp. As soon as she was entranced and Feda spoke, Lionel was told that two spirits were present. One was elderly: tall, well built with a beard around his chin but no moustache – a description that seemed somehow to worry Feda. She added that the letter W was held up. This was a very good description of Lionel's grandfather, known to members of the family as 'Grandfather W'.

The medium's spirit control then described a younger man, about 23 or 25. After giving a description, she said she could not see him. 'He won't let Feda see his face; he is laughing.' Then, whispering, she said, 'L, L, L,' adding aloud, 'This is not his name; he puts it by you.' Whispering again she said, 'Feda knows him – Raymond. Oh, it's Raymond! That is why he would not show his face, because Feda would know him.'

This, and much more, impressed the Lodge family and many of the readers of *Raymond*. Raymond's death and apparent communication from the spirit world reinforced Sir Oliver Lodge's own beliefs. And in sharing them with the public, he did much to lighten the blow of bereavement that had fallen on so many families.

'A band of eager workers is constructing a bridge, opening a way for us across the chasm,' he concluded. 'Communication is already easier and more frequent than ever before; and in the long run we may feel assured that all this present suffering and bereavement will have a beneficent outcome for humanity. So may it be!'

Not like her at all

Claiming to be possessed by the spirit of a young woman long dead, a 13-year-old girl played the role to the full – by moving in with the dead woman's parents and living as their daughter. This chapter tells of a reincarnation in a small American town

Above: Watseka, Illinois, as it looked in the late 19th century. People were very willing to hear tales of returned 'spirits' at this time, for Spiritualism was the rage in America

Right: Lurancy Vennum, who was besieged by numerous 'spirits' before one of them took up exclusive residence for a few months. It claimed to be the spirit of Mary Roff (far right), who had died 13 years before, aged 18. Mary had been subject to curious seizures, during which she allegedly produced psychic phenomena. Did she enjoy a brief reincarnation in Lurancy's body?

ONE OF THE MOST EXTRAORDINARY and best-authenticated cases of ostensible possession is that of the 'Watseka wonder'. The person at the centre of events, Mary Lurancy Vennum, was born in April 1864 in the American township of Milford, about 7 miles (11 kilometres) from Watseka, Illinois. Until the age of 13 Lurancy enjoyed good health. Then, one day in July 1877, she told her family: 'There were persons in my room last night, and they called "Rancy! Rancy!" and I felt their breath on my face.' The next night she left her bed, protesting that she could not sleep because every time she tried to sleep she heard voices calling 'Rancy! Rancy!'

This episode was followed a few days later by some kind of seizure. The next day, 12 July, she had another, which led to her announcing to her family that she could see heaven and angels and people, now dead, whom she had known. These incidents, in which she seemed almost entranced, continued and, together with her wild statements, persuaded onlookers that she was insane.

Early in 1878 two acquaintances of the Vennums, Mr and Mrs Roff, suggested that they should call in Dr E. W. Stevens of Janesville, Wisconsin. They agreed and on 31 January Dr Stevens and Mr Roff called upon the Vennums. Lurancy appeared to be possessed by a number of entities one after the other, including an old woman called Katrina Hogan and a man called Willie Canning. Dr Stevens managed with some effort to hypnotise her. The girl calmed down and claimed that she had been controlled by evil spirits. She also said that there was a spirit who wanted to control her and gave its name as . . . Mary Roff. Mr Roff exclaimed: 'That is my daughter; Mary Roff is my girl. Why, she has been in heaven 12 years. Yes, let her come, we'll be glad to have her come.'

Mary Roff had lived in Watseka for most of her life, until her death when she was still less than 19 years old, in July 1865. (Lurancy at this time was just over a year old.) From the age of six months Mary had suffered from violent seizures, which became worse during her life. Allegedly her illnesses made her notorious in the neighbourhood during her lifetime: and she was regarded as having clairvoyant powers, which were investigated by a number of the town's citizens.

After Lurancy's announcement that Mary's spirit had returned, the excited Mr Roff assured her that Mary, because of her own sufferings in life, would be able to help her. Lurancy seems to have taken the advice of some of the other spirits as well. She announced that Mary would displace the other spirits. Mr Roff made the further suggestion that Lurancy's mother should bring her to the Roffs' house '. . . and Mary will be likely to come along, and a mutual benefit may be derived from our former experience with Mary.' One can imagine

very easily the welter of emotions – fear, hope, wishful thinking, terror, bewilderment, despair – tearing at the two families. The following day Mr Vennum called upon Mr Roff to tell him that his daughter now gave every sign of *being* Mary Roff. During the next week, the girl was 'mild, docile, polite and timid, knowing none of the family, but constantly pleading to go home'.

The 'Mary Roff' personality maintained its control. About a week later, Mary Roff's mother and sister paid a visit to the Vennum household. 'Mary', seeing them coming along the street, exclaimed: 'There comes my ma and sister Nervie.' The name 'Nervie' was one that the late Mary Roff had used for her sister – by this late date now married – when she was a girl. When they entered the house, 'Mary' was overcome with emotion and pleaded to be allowed to 'go home' with them. The Vennums agreed, and on 11 February 'Mary Roff' went home.

It is on record that 'Mary' remained there for three months, behaving exactly as if she were indeed the Roffs' dead daughter, recognising everyone she had known when she had been alive, remembering scores of incidents from her past. Some of these events had happened 13 to 25 years before. When she met friends or relatives of the Roffs whom she had not seen for many years – if it is accepted that she *was* 'Mary Roff' – she would still recognise them but comment on changes in their appearance. Some days after she arrived at the Roffs' house, a Mrs Parker and her daughter-in-law, Nellie Parker, came to visit the Roffs. Mrs Parker had been a neighbour of the Roffs in Middleport in 1852 and in Watseka in 1860. 'Mary' immediately recognised them as if she had last seen them the day before, although it was 17 years since the Roffs' daughter Mary had last seen them. Particular clothes, a box of letters and a collar the dead daughter had sewn were seized on by 'Mary', in a number of cases with comments that showed she knew the exact circumstances concerning their relationship with the dead girl.

Naturally the unhappy Vennum family visited the Roffs on occasion to see how their daughter – if indeed she was still their daughter! – was progressing. The girl did not seem to recognise any member of the Vennum family or the Vennums' friends and neighbours. As the visits continued, however, she became more friendly towards them, but gave every indication that to her they were strangers that she was just coming to know.

This extraordinary situation continued until 7 May. On that day 'Mary' told Mrs Roff that Lurancy was returning. The girl sat down, closed her eyes and almost immediately opened them. She looked around and exclaimed: 'Where am I? I was never here before.'

Mrs Roff reassured her but the girl had

Below right: Richard Hodgson, a sceptic who exposed several fraudulent mediums, but was convinced of the genuineness of some. He studied the Lurancy Vennum case and believed that it had to be explained in terms of a spirit taking over Lurancy's person

now taken on the personality of Lurancy. She pleaded to be allowed to go home. She was still pleading five minutes later when a reversal took place and the 'Mary' personality took over once more. From then until 19 May the girl's body continued to be occupied by the 'Mary' personality, though more and more frequently she would be transformed into 'Lurancy'. On 19 May, for example, while Lurancy's brother Henry was present, 'Lurancy' came through and recognised Henry; then the reversion to 'Mary' again took place.

In the record kept by Mr Roff we find him writing on the morning of 21 May:

> Mary is to leave the body of Rancy today, about eleven o'clock, so she says. She is bidding neighbours and friends good-bye. Rancy to return home all right today. Mary came from her room upstairs, where she was sleeping with Lottie, at ten o'clock last night, lay down by us, hugged and kissed us, and cried because she must bid us good-bye, telling us to give all her pictures, marbles, and cards, and twenty-five cents Mrs Vennum had given her, to Rancy, and had us promise to visit Rancy often.

One of 'Mary's' last acts was to arrange that after she and Mrs Alter – her supposed sister – had said their goodbyes, Mrs Alter should take Lurancy to Mr Roff's office. By the time Mrs Alter had arrived at the office, Lurancy was firmly back in control. She obviously accepted the Vennums as her own family when she got to their house and settled in contentedly.

Lurancy Vennum's subsequent life was essentially a normal one. She married a farmer, George Binning, in January 1882 and had a family. In 1884 they moved farther west. It is on record that occasionally 'Mary' would return, in a manner reminiscent of a 'spirit control' taking over an entranced medium, but the days of full possession were over.

When Lurancy Vennum 'became' Mary Roff, she moved into the Roffs' home (above). The new 'Mary' recognised many of the family possessions. After a few months' stay 'Mary' said goodbye; Lurancy took her place and was welcomed back into the Vennum home (below). The disturbances that had once alarmed her family now virtually ceased

This extraordinary story raises a number of questions. The first, naturally, is: what authenticity can we ascribe to it?

The first account of the case was written by Dr E. W. Stevens, the man who had been called in by the Vennums on the advice of Mr Roff. Dr Stevens kept a close watch on the progress of the case, interviewed the chief witnesses and had his written account confirmed by both sets of parents. A paper by him was published in the *Religio-Philosophical Journal* in 1879, followed after a short time by a pamphlet entitled *The Watseka Wonder.*

Visit from a sceptic

The celebrated and notoriously sceptical psychical researcher Dr Richard Hodgson visited Watseka in April 1890 and questioned the major witnesses in the case still living in the neighbourhood. His account of what they told him was subsequently published in the *Religio-Philosophical Journal* for 20 December 1890.

> I have no doubt that the incidents occurred substantially as described in the narrative by Dr Stevens, and in my view the only other interpretation of the case – besides the spiritistic – that seems at all plausible is that which has been put forward as the alternative to the spiritistic theory to account for the trance-communications of Mrs Piper and similar cases, viz., secondary personality with supernormal powers. It would be difficult to disprove this hypothesis in the case of the 'Watseka

Will the real Mrs Piper . . .

Mrs Leonora Piper first discovered her exceptional abilities as a medium during her twenties, when she fell into a trance while she was being treated by a psychic healer

One of the most closely studied of American mediums was Mrs Leonora Piper of Boston, Massachusetts. While in her trance state she was ostensibly taken over by one or more psychic 'masters of ceremonies', or 'controls'. Some showed humour, wit and knowledge; others talked arrant nonsense; others seemed to be psychic confidence tricksters.

The psychical researcher Richard Hodgson was at first sceptical of the 'spiritistic hypothesis' to explain these happenings. He was inclined to the opinion of his colleague Mrs Sidgwick that the controls were 'phases or elements' of Mrs Piper's personality. But then a control appeared claiming to be George Pelham.

Pelham had been a friend of Hodgson and had promised that, if he were to die first and find himself still existing, he would devote himself to proving the fact. Two years later he *did* die, in an accident. After several years' study of the 'Pelham' control, Hodgson was finally forced to report: 'Out of a large number of sitters who went as strangers to Mrs Piper, the communicating G.P. has picked out the friends of G.P. living, precisely as the G.P. living might be expected to do . . . I cannot profess to have any doubt but that the chief communicators to whom I have referred . . . are veritably the personalities that they claim to be, that they have survived the change we call death.'

> Wonder', owing to the comparative meagreness of the record and the probable abundance of 'suggestion' in the environment, and any conclusion that we may reach would probably be determined largely by our convictions concerning other cases. My personal opinion is that the 'Watseka Wonder' case belongs in the main manifestations to the spiritistic category.

Hodgson is saying, then, and the present writer must agree with him, that there is no way that the strange case of Lurancy Vennum can be explained away by normal means. It has to be explained in one of two ways – in terms of spirits or of multiple personalities. These two types of explanation can be applied to a large body of psychic phenomena.

The spiritistic hypothesis, namely that in this case the spirit of Mary Roff took over the body of Lurancy Vennum, receives support from a similar case studied by Professor Ian Stevenson of the Department of Neurology and Psychiatry at the University of Virginia, USA. A little Indian boy, Jasbir Lal Jat, $3\frac{1}{2}$ years old, was pronounced dead of smallpox. Some hours later, however, he revived and exhibited a brand new personality. He now claimed to be a man from a different village who had been poisoned. His detailed knowledge of the man's past life convinced the little boy's parents that he was not fantasising. It was found that the man had died at about the same time that the child ostensibly died, suggesting a bizarre spirit analogue of musical chairs.

Professor Ian Stevenson, a leading American authority on cases of apparent reincarnation

This interpretation has to be studied as an alternative to the straightforward reincarnation theory in conjunction with the remarkable collection of ostensible reincarnation cases collected by Dr Stevenson and others. The 'Watseka wonder' and the case of Jasbir Lal Jat demonstrate the necessity of keeping in mind the 'possession' hypothesis.

Hodgson's other theory was that a secondary personality of Lurancy Vennum's utilised extra-sensory perception or paragnostic powers to acquire details of Mary Roff's past life from those still living and then dramatised them into a pseudo Mary Roff personality. This is also capable of fitting the facts of the case. For what reason Lurancy Vennum's subconscious should do this we can only guess. It is clear, however, that the girl was surrounded by people who were sympathetic towards the spiritistic hypothesis: if she was suffering attacks of hysteria, she might well, on the subconscious level, wish to give them what they wanted. To do this, however, she would have had to have psychic powers to gather a multitude of details from the memories of Mary Roff.

Whatever the truth of the matter, it seems certain that Lurancy Vennum, as 'Mary Roff', demonstrated that a human being can suffer psychic 'invasion' for a period measured in months, to the extent that the 'legal tenant' of the body is displaced as if he or she had never been.

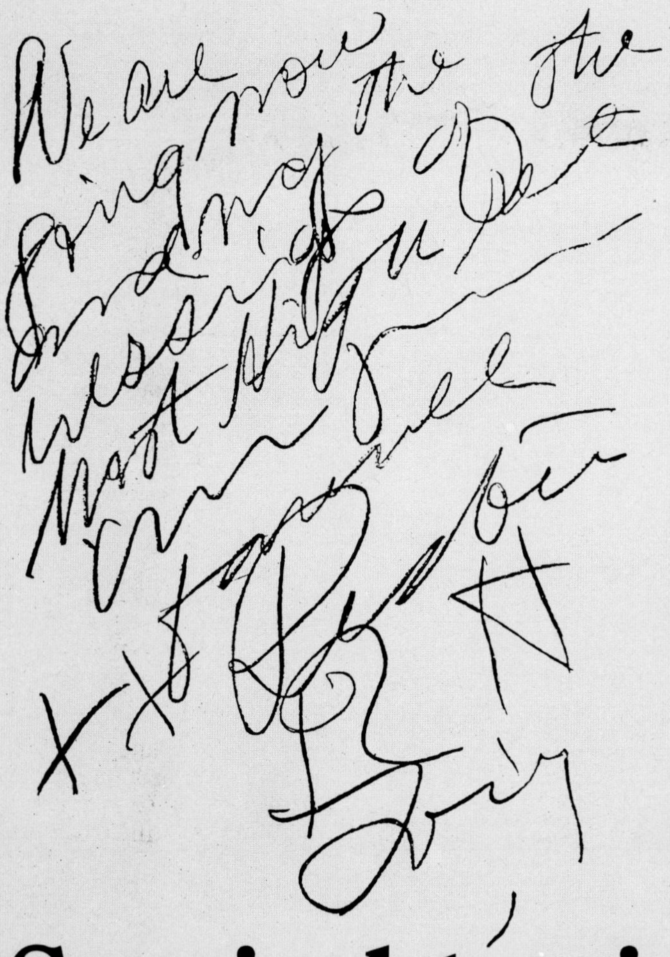

Survival: teasing out the truth

Did a group of dedicated psychical researchers plan – after their deaths – to send evidence of their survival to certain chosen mediums? A controversial set of 'communications' suggests they did

Above: Frederic Myers, a respected founder member of Britain's Society for Psychical Research, apparently tried to prove his survival after death to his living friends and colleagues. He supposedly sent messages through various mediums, in widely separated parts of the world, by means of automatic writing, which he had studied intensively in life. The fragment above is in a hand markedly different from the normal script of the medium who produced it, Mrs Leonora Piper

AN ARDENT AND VOCIFEROUS believer in the afterlife, Frederic Myers, classical scholar and founder member of the Society for Psychical Research (SPR), wished passionately to communicate his belief to others. Judging by an impressive body of evidence, he never desired it more than after his death in 1901. For the following 30 years the SPR collected and collated over 2000 automatic scripts purporting to be transmitted from Myers and other deceased members of the Society through the mediumship of several ladies. They seem to have been specifically designed to prove to the living the reality of the afterlife.

What have become known as the 'cross-correspondences' do indeed indicate that here there was some kind of intelligent communication between the living and the dead – arranged in such a way as to confound critics. Whoever thought it up, on this or the other side of the veil, was very ingenious.

Apart from Myers the purported spirit communicators were Edmund Gurney (died 1888) and Professor Henry Sidgwick (died 1900). The mediums included 'Mrs Holland' (pseudonym of Mrs Alice Fleming), who lived in India and was the sister of Rudyard Kipling; 'Mrs Willett' (pseudonym of Mrs Coombe-Tennant), who lived in London; Mrs A. W. Verrall, a teacher of Classics at Cambridge University; her daughter, Helen (later Mrs W. H. Salter); and the famous trance medium Mrs Leonora Piper, of Boston, Massachusetts.

A bold and complex plan

The purpose and plan of the cross-correspondences are bold yet complex, sometimes almost beyond belief. But it is this complexity that gives them their unique air of authenticity. The plan, as far as it can be understood, is this:

After Myers's death, he and his deceased colleagues from the SPR worked out a system by which fragments of automatic script, meaningless in themselves, would be transmitted through different mediums in widely separated parts of the world. When brought together they would prove to make sense. To make the situation more difficult these fragments would be in Greek or Latin, or contain

Below: Mrs Leonora Piper was one of the most celebrated mediums of modern times. Several of the distinguished researchers who studied her, including Myers, allegedly communicated through her after their deaths

allusions – sometimes fragmentary in themselves – to classical works. In Myers's words as dictated to Mrs Verrall: 'Record the bits and when fitted they will make the whole . . . I will give the words between you neither alone can read but together they will give the clue he wants.'

The erudition of the classical references was beyond the scope of most of the mediums, except the Verralls, showing that the scripts were not the products of their own minds. The fact that the fragments were unintelligible to the mediums themselves would rule out the possibility of joint telepathic composition by them.

It seems that Myers thought of this plan once he had the ultimate personal proof of the afterlife. None of the thoughts he recorded during his earthly life even hints at this scheme. But at least he knew how to set about proving his point: as an ex-president of the SPR he knew which mediums were genuine and competent automatic 'scribes'.

In many cases the various automatists – in England, India and the United States – were instructed to send their apparently meaningless scripts to certain investigators, whose addresses were supplied by the communicators. Each piece of automatic script was to be carefully dated and, if possible, witnessed.

An example of what H. F. Saltmarsh, in *Evidence of personal survival*, calls a 'simple' cross-correspondence is as follows. Mrs Piper, in America, heard in a trance state a word she first took to be *sanatos*. She then corrected herself (she was speaking her impressions out loud to be written down) to *tanatos*. That was on 17 April 1907. Later in the month the word came through as *thanatos* and on another occasion was repeated three times. On 7 May the whole phrase 'I want to say *thanatos*' 'came through' Mrs Piper. She did not recognise the word as the Greek for 'death'.

Meanwhile, on 16 April 1907, Mrs Holland in India received a curious opening phrase in her automatic script: 'Maurice Morris Mors. And with that the shadow of death fell on his limbs.' The two names seemed to be an attempt to get to the word *mors* – Latin for death.

The fire of life

Yet again, on 29 April 1907, Mrs Verrall in Cambridge received this cryptic communication: 'Warmed both hands before the fire of life. It fades and I am ready to depart.' Then her hand drew what she took to be the Greek capital letter delta (a triangle). Next came these disjointed phrases: 'Give lilies with full hands [in Latin] . . . Come away, Come away, *Pallida mors* [Latin, meaning 'pale death'].'

There are several allusions to death here:

Hope, star and Browning

Above: Robert Browning, whose poems include *The pied piper of Hamelin*

One of the most famous of the cross-correspondences has been labelled the 'hope, star and Browning' case. In January 1907 one of the communicators (unidentified) proposed – through Mrs Verrall – an experiment: 'An anagram would be better. Tell him that – rats, star, tars and so on . . . .'

A few days later Mrs Verrall received a script beginning:

> *Aster* [Latin for 'star'] *Teras* [Greek, meaning 'wonder' or 'sign'] . . . The very wings of her. A WINGED DESIRE . . . the hope that leaves the earth for the sky – *Abt Vogler* . . .

Mrs Verrall recognised these as fragments from poems of Robert Browning: *Abt Vogler* and *The ring and the book*. Within a week Mrs Verrall's daughter Helen produced an automatic script that included drawings of a bird, star and crescent moon, and verbal references to songbirds.

On 11 February Mrs Piper had a sitting with Mr Piddington. Myers 'came through' and said he had previously communicated something of interest to Mrs Verrall. 'I referred to Hope and Browning . . . I also said Star.'

The investigators noted that 'hope' had been emphasised by the very fact that in the quotation it had been substituted for another word; the quotation should have read 'the passion that left the ground . . .' and not 'the hope that leaves . . . '. Mrs Verrall, who knew her Browning, had remarked after reading through her script, 'I wondered why the silly thing said "hope".'

There was now a clear correspondence between the 'hope, star and Browning' reference of Mrs Piper and the texts of the elder and younger Verrall ladies. Mrs Verrall told her daughter that there had been such a correspondence but, in order not to influence her script, referred not to 'hope, star and Browning' but to 'virtue, Mars (the planet) and Keats'. Two days later Miss Verrall produced another script that included the phrase 'a star above it all rats everywhere in Hamelin town'. This was a clear reference to the poem *The pied piper of Hamelin* – written by Browning.

Frederic Myers had an extensive knowledge of the works of Browning and had always expressed a sympathy with many of his ideals. So perhaps it was natural that his disembodied mind should turn to his old literary favourites when trying to prove his continued existence.

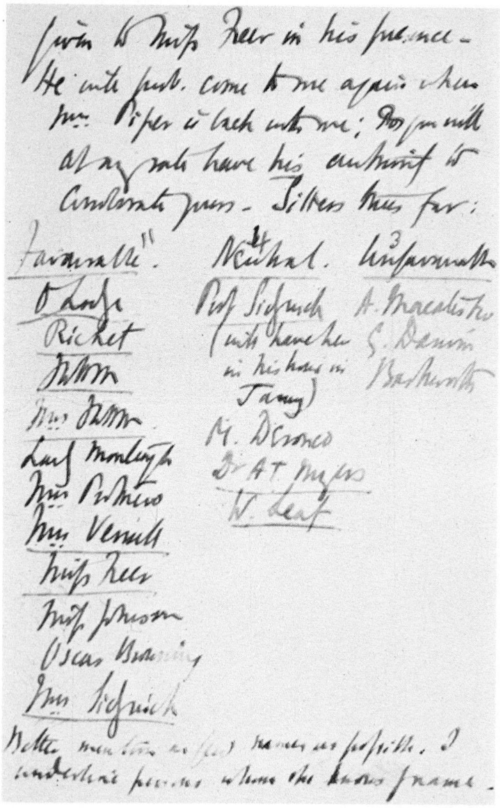
Favourable. Neutral. Unfavourable.
O Lodge Prof Sidgwick
Mrs Verrall
Oscar Browning
Mrs Sidgwick
M. Dessoir
Dr A T Myers
W. Leaf

Left: A letter from Myers to Sir Oliver Lodge. The automatic scripts allegedly communicated by him were in a different handwriting from this

Below: Mrs A. W. Verrall, key medium in Myers's elaborate post-mortem plan

Above: Mrs Alice Fleming, who was generally known as 'Mrs Holland'. She lived in India at the time the cross-correspondences were being produced

apparently Mrs Verrall had always seen delta as a symbol for death; the 'lilies' quotation is a distortion of a passage in the *Aeneid*, where the early death of Marcellus is foretold; and 'Come away . . .' is from the Shakespearean song in *Twelfth night* that begins: 'Come away, come away, death.' (The first passage, 'Warmed both hands . . .', is a slightly altered quotation from a poem by Walter Savage Landor.)

So three automatists, in three countries and in three languages, received both straightforward and allusive references to the subject of death.

Mr Saltmarsh explains how more complex cross-correspondences might work by giving this hypothetical example:

> Suppose that the topic chosen was 'Time'. Automatist A might start the ball rolling by a quotation from the hymn 'Like an ever-rolling stream'. Automatist B might follow on with a quotation from *Alice in Wonderland* dealing with the discussion concerning Time at the Mad Hatter's tea-table, e.g. 'He won't stand beating' or 'We quarrelled last March – just before he went mad, you know' and then, Automatist C gives the clue with 'Time and Tide wait for no man'. . . . Most of the actual cases are far more subtle and it was not until after much research that the connections were discovered. It is probable that even now a good many have been overlooked.

This scholarly jigsaw puzzle may seem at first glance to be a post-mortem game of intellectual snobbery. In fact, more than one critic has pointed out that the hereafter, judging by the communications of the cross-correspondences, seems to be peopled solely with upper-class Edwardians with a solid classical education and a background of SPR membership. But if the next world were to be more or less a continuation of this one, without the hindrance of physical bodies, then what could be more natural than choosing one's ex-friends and colleagues for an enormous, epoch-making venture? One does not take someone with no head for heights on an Everest expedition.

To suspend disbelief for one moment: it seems that Myers was passionately trying to 'get through', using some means that could actually constitute *proof*. On 12 January 1904 Myers had written (through Mrs Holland in India): 'If it were possible for the soul to die back into earth life again I should die from sheer yearning to reach you to tell you that all that we imagined is not half wonderful enough for the truth . . . .' Through Mrs Piper in the United States he wrote: 'I am trying with all the forces . . . together to prove that I am Myers.' And again, through the Indian connection, he wrote: 'Oh, I am feeble with eagerness – how can I best be identified?'

Sceptical challenges

The whole subject of the cross-correspondences has been analysed and is still the focus of much research. On the evidence of the examples given above there will be many sceptics who will suggest that the whole business was a kind of genteel collusion, perhaps arranged by Myers and his SPR colleagues before their deaths. Or, if conscious fraud seems unlikely, perhaps this series of bizarre word-games was the result of telepathy among the mediums – and the relationship between the two Verrall ladies was surely too close for them to keep secrets from each other. The classical words and allusions came mainly through the mediumship of the women with a classical education – they were almost totally absent in the case of Mrs Willett and Mrs Piper, who did not have this background.

Then there is the fact that the 'Myers' of, say, the Piper scripts, sounds entirely different from that of, say, the Willett scripts. And although the handwriting differed from the women's own hands, it was not actually that of Myers himself.

However, it seemed that Myers and his friends were determined to nip in the bud any such sceptical 'explanations'. In life they had known and challenged both frauds and cynics – they knew what to expect. So, marshalling their spirit forces, they began a barrage of fragmentary and intellectual cross-corresponding communications, spanning continents and decades.

The end of the experiment

Were the cross-correspondences really an ingenious plot designed deliberately to deceive psychical researchers? Or did they, as some would claim, provide the ultimate proof of post-mortem survival?

SINCE THE DEATH in 1901 of F.W.H. Myers, founder member of the Society of Psychical Research, his discarnate spirit – it is widely believed – has communicated many times through the mediumship of living people. In the first quarter of the 20th century the deceased Myers was most active, together with dead friends, in the case of the 'cross-correspondences'.

Over 2000 examples of automatic writing purporting to have come from Myers, Henry Sidgwick, Edmund Gurney and, later, from A.W. Verrall were transmitted through a large number of mediums over a period of 30 years. The scripts took the form of fragmentary literary and classical allusions – clues to a highly complex puzzle, intended by its very erudition to prove the existence of the purported communicators, all of whom had been literary or classical scholars in life. The fragments delivered to various mediums at different times made sense only when taken together, and usually meant little or nothing to the mediums taking them down.

'The sea that moaned in pain'

One of the simpler cross-correspondences was the Roden Noel case. On 7 March 1906 in Cambridge, Mrs Verrall, one of the mediums most heavily used by 'Myers', took down in automatic writing some lines of verse, allegedly from Myers, which began with the words 'Tintagel and the sea that moaned in pain'. The lines meant nothing in particular to Mrs Verrall but her investigator, Miss Johnson of the SPR, thought it reminiscent of a poem by the Cornishman Roden Noel, called *Tintadgel*. Even when Miss Johnson pointed this out to her, Mrs Verrall could not remember having read the poem or even knowing of its existence.

Four days later, in India, Mrs Holland (pseudonym of Rudyard Kipling's sister, Mrs Alice Fleming) received this automatic script: 'This is for A.W. Ask him what the date May 26th, 1894, meant to him – to me – and to F.W.H.M. I do not think they will find it hard to recall, but if so – let them ask Nora.'

The date given is that of the death of Roden Noel. 'A.W.' refers to Dr Verrall and 'F.W.H.M.' to Myers, both of whom were acquainted with Noel. 'Nora' was the widow of Henry Sidgwick, who had been much closer to the poet. But Mrs Holland had not discovered any of these pertinent facts when on 14 March 1906 – one week after the English communication, and much too soon to have received any hints from Mrs Verrall or Miss Johnson – she received this script: 'Eighteen, 15, 4, 5, 14. Fourteen, 15, 5, 12. Not to be taken as they stand. See Rev. [the book of Revelation] 13, 18, but only the central eight words, not the whole passage.'

Mrs Holland tried to make sense of the references but found it hopeless. However, when the script was sent to England, Miss Johnson seized the clue of 'the central eight words', which are 'for it is the number of a man'. The numbers cited in the script, when taken as the letters of the alphabet, translate as 'Roden Noel'.

Noel was referred to again in a script from Mrs Holland on 21 March and mentioned in one from Mrs Verrall, in England, on 26 March. On 28 March Mrs Holland's automatic writing included his name spelled out in full with descriptions of his native Cornwall and a muddled description of himself.

A complex case that took years to understand was that of the Medici tombs. It began

Henry Sidgwick (below) and Edmund Gurney (below right). Most of the scripts from 'them' containing classical references 'came through' those mediums who had knowledge of Latin and Greek – Mrs Verrall, for example, was a lecturer in Classics at Newnham College, Cambridge (bottom). It may be that the mediums were deliberately chosen because they had such knowledge. Or perhaps the communications stemmed from the mediums' own subconscious minds

in November 1906, through Mrs Holland. Her scripts were full of oblique or unexplained references to evening, morning and dawn, and death, sleep and shadows. In Cambridge on 21 January 1907 Mrs Verrall received the words 'laurel' and 'laurel wreath' repeatedly. Then on 26 February yet another medium, the American Mrs Piper, said out loud (normally she only muttered indistinctly, when coming out of her trances): 'Morehead – laurel for laurel . . . I say I gave her that for laurel. Goodbye.'

Mrs Piper then had a vision of a Negro sitting in place of Mr Piddington, one of the investigators for the SPR, who was with her. She rubbed her hands together and said: 'Dead . . . well, I think it was something about laurel wreaths.' The next day Mrs Piper received: 'I gave Mrs V. laurel wreaths' in her script.

On 17 March Helen Verrall in Cambridge received: 'Alexander's tomb . . . laurel

wreaths, are emblem laurels for the victor's brow.'

Ten days later, in India, Mrs Holland's script included: 'Darkness, light and shadow, Alexander Moor's head.'

A year and a half later, two rarely used mediums – known as 'the Macs' – received: 'Dig a grave among the laurels.'

It was two years before the topic was again referred to by the communicator. This time it was a London medium, Mrs Willett (pseudonym of Mrs Coombe-Tennant), who received: 'Laurentian tombs, Dawn and Twilight.'

A month later, on 8 July 1910, Mrs Piper in the United States spoke the words: 'Meditation, sleeping dead, laurels' when coming out of her trance.

Yet another two years passed before the investigators of the SPR discovered the meaning of the allusions: they referred to the

Above: Mrs Leonora Piper, famous trance medium of Boston, USA, who was involved in a complex case of cross-correspondences that took place between 1906 and 1910. Several mediums 'received' a series of references to shadow, death, sleep, evening, morning, dawn, meditation, Alexander and laurels. Only two years after the last communication did SPR investigators realise that the references pointed to the tombs of the Medici family in Florence. On that of Lorenzo, Duke of Urbino (right), which also contains the body of Alessandro ('Alexander') de Medici, are statues representing Dawn, Twilight and Meditation; the tomb of Giuliano, Duke of Nemours (left) bears figures representing Day and Night. The laurel was an emblem of the Medici family

Above: Helen Verrall (later Mrs W. H. Salter), one of the automatists concerned; she was also a researcher for the SPR

tombs of the Medici family, who were wealthy and powerful in Florence in the 15th and 16th centuries. On the sepulchre of Lorenzo, Duke of Urbino, are statues representing Meditation, Dawn and Twilight. On the tomb of another Medici, Giuliano, are two statues representing Day and Night.

Lorenzo's tomb also holds the body of Alessandro ('Alexander') de Medici, who was murdered; it is, therefore, as much 'Alexander's tomb' as 'Lorenzo's'. Alexander was of mixed blood and in his portraits has clearly Negroid features: truly 'Alexander, Moor's head'.

Helen Verrall had heard of the tombs, but had never visited them and had no detailed knowledge of them. She, like the others, had taken 'Alexander's tomb' to refer to that of Alexander the Great.

But, perhaps significantly, Mrs Holland did know the tombs well. And in one of her previous scripts there were references to Diamond Island, where the new Lodge-Muirhead wireless system was being tested (an experiment in which she was personally very interested). The wireless connection was linked with the tombs references by a striking pun – the fact that one of the wireless pioneers was called Dr Alexander Muirhead (Alexander Moor's head). Yet in the same script was a quotation from *Othello* that reinforced the 'Moor' connection.

So was this witty allusion created by Mrs Holland's subconscious? Knowing the tombs so well, did she perhaps unwittingly make up that particular example of a cross-correspondence? The alternative view is that the communicator deliberately chose mediums whose minds contained relevant material. Communicating through mediums was said to be extraordinarily difficult. The 'Myers' persona had this to say about the problems of communicating from 'the other side' through Mrs Holland:

The nearest simile I can find to express

> the difficulty of sending a message – is that I appear to be standing behind a sheet of frosted glass which blurs sight and deadens sound – dictating feebly to a reluctant and somewhat obtuse secretary.

One of those involved in the cross-correspondences was (it seemed) to find out for himself about the reality of the 'frosted glass' simile. On 18 June 1912 Dr A.W. Verrall, husband of Mrs Verrall, died. Six weeks later Mrs Willett received his first post-mortem communication, drawing its allusions from Christina Rossetti, Dante and the humorous magazine *Punch*. His further communications contained family jokes and extremely convoluted classical references. In combination, they proved beyond doubt, according to his 'oldest and dearest friend', the Reverend M.A. Bayfield, that they were from Verrall himself. One of his scripts ends with the wry note: 'This sort of thing is more difficult to do than it looked.'

Fragments and allusions

Most of the 2000 scripts that make up the cross-correspondences are far too complicated to examine here. H.F. Saltmarsh says in his *Evidence of personal survival*:

> The fragmentary, enigmatic and allusive nature of these communications is intentional, and their obscurity is due not solely to the deficiencies of the investigators.

Saltmarsh suggested experiments that, while they could not prove the Myers group's post-mortem existence, will demonstrate the difficulties of cheating and of constructing cross-correspondences deliberately.

Begin by choosing a book by an author you know well, and a quotation or subject from it. Then from the same book or another book by the same author pick out a quotation that alludes to the subject without directly mentioning it. Give the two quotations to someone who acts as investigator, and who must try to work out what the connection between them is. It is remarkably difficult, especially if the author's works are unknown to the investigator. Huge leaps in comprehension will have to be made.

When investigating Mrs Willett's 'Myers' scripts, Sir Oliver Lodge remarked:

> The way in which these allusions are combined or put together, and their connection with each other indicated, is the striking thing – it seems to me as much beyond the capacity of Mrs Willett as it would be beyond my own capacity. I believe that if the matter is seriously studied, and if Mrs Willett's assertions concerning her conscious knowledge and supraliminal procedure are believed, this will be the opinion of critics also; they will realize, as I do, that we are tapping the reminiscences not of an ordinarily educated person but of a scholar – no matter how fragmentary and confused some of the reproductions are.

Two of the investigators for the SPR: Eleanor Sidgwick (above), the widow of Henry Sidgwick, and Sir Oliver Lodge (below). The investigators studied each script as it was produced, comparing it with those from other automatists to find any cross-correspondences between them

Saltmarsh's second experiment concerns the improbability that chance could produce cross-correspondences between independent scripts. Simply take a familiar book and open it at random. Eyes shut, point to a passage randomly. Repeat this with another book and attempt to find a cross-correspondence between the extracts.

Despite the impressive weight of scholarly allusions, puns and quotations communicated, many modern psychical researchers regard the cross-correspondences as 'not proven'. Sceptics point out that all the people involved, including the 'investigators', were either members of the SPR or of the same social circle. They could have been in collusion. When reminded that deliberate fraud would have involved cheating on a grand scale (and over 30 years), the sceptics reply that, nevertheless, once begun, it could hardly be exposed.

The clues stop coming

When the last of the SPR's founder-members died, the cross-correspondences stopped, having accumulated to form a huge volume of scripts that any interested party can study at leisure. Cynics want to know why Myers and his group have ceased to communicate their tortuous messages. It may be because there is no one left to receive them, no medium who is – perhaps literally – on their 'wavelength'. Mediumship seems no longer to be practised in classically educated, upper middle-class circles, and there must be few automatic writers who would even recognise Greek characters or apparently nonsensical quotations jumbled together.

It is possible that subconscious telepathy took place among a group of persons, in different parts of the world and over many years. That in itself would be worth investigating. The only other explanation is that there is a life after death – at least for Edwardian gentlemen given to intellectual puns and anagrams – and that, under certain circumstances, the dead may demonstrate their existence to the living.

Although the complex cross-correspondences no longer appear, Myers is apparently still in communication. On 2 April 1972 the young English psychic Matthew Manning received this automatic script, signed 'F. Myers':

> You should not really indulge in this unless you know what you are doing. I did a lot of work on automatic writing when I was alive and I could never work it out. No-one alive will ever work out the whole secret of life after death. It pivots on so many things – personality – condition of the mental and physical bodies. Carry on trying though because you could soon be close to the secret. If you find it no-one will believe you anyway.

Death of a dream

The world was stunned when the vaunted *R101* airship crashed in flames in 1930. And the sequel was no less startling: the ship's dead captain had made contact with a famous medium

Below: the *R101* lies a charred skeleton in the fields near Beauvais, France. Miraculously, its ensign still flies

Right: within two days of the disaster, medium Eileen Garrett was 'speaking' to the *R101*'s dead captain

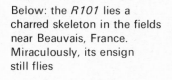

EUGENE RABOUILLE, a 57-year-old poacher, was distracted from his task of setting rabbit snares by the sound of engines overhead. He looked up into the rain-soaked night and saw a confused image of bright lights and an enormous shape illuminated by those lights. It was very low in the sky, moving slowly and falling steadily – and it was heading his way. On it came, the drone of the engines getting louder as it approached, and as Rabouille stood rooted to the spot the gigantic object suddenly pitched forward, corrected itself, and then slid almost gently into the side of a small hill about 100 yards (90 metres) from where he stood. The next moment he found himself stretched out on the ground, stunned by shock waves, deafened by noise, blinded by light.

A wall of flames shot hundreds of feet into the air, and as Rabouille picked himself up he could hear through the fire's roar terrible screams, and see in the middle of the inferno human figures rushing about, alive yet for a moment or two, but irretrievably lost. Rabouille put his hands to his eyes to shield them from the heat, and from the searing vision. Then he turned and fled. It was just after 2 a.m. on 5 October 1930.

What Rabouille had witnessed were the final moments of the British airship *R101*, and of the 48 passengers and crew who perished that rainy night near the town of Beauvais, in northern France. He had also seen the event that would crush instantly and irrevocably British faith in the whole idea of rigid airships, would spark off bitter and

lasting recriminations – and would provide the backdrop to one of the most curious episodes in the annals of psychic phenomena.

For within two days of the *R101*'s sickening destruction, no less a medium than Mrs Eileen Garrett was apparently in touch with the skipper of the enormous craft, Flight-Lieutenant H. Carmichael Irwin. Not only that, but it turned out that another airman had foretold the end of the *R101* – also from beyond the grave. And three weeks after the calamity Mrs Garrett was in contact again, this time in front of different witnesses, with the airship's dead captain.

Public fascination with these revelations was intense – naturally, as no one knew what had happened during the last few hours on board. The evidence produced by Mrs Garrett was therefore crucial not only for those who may have wanted to add ammunition to their case for survival after death, but to a question of immediate practical import. To gauge how the psychic evidence adds to both debates it is first necessary to review, in detail, the sad tale of the *R101*'s development.

In 1924 the British government had decided that the interests of a worldwide empire could be well served by the construction of a fleet of large passenger airships. Now the traditional way of going about such an enterprise would have been simply to place an order for a prototype with some suitable private firm. However, this was Britain's first Labour government, and there was strong pressure from within its ranks to give a practical demonstration of the merits of state enterprise. In the best spirit of British compromise (or fudging) the decision was reached that two airships should be built simultaneously, one by the Air Ministry itself and the other by a Vickers subsidiary, the Airship Guarantee Company.

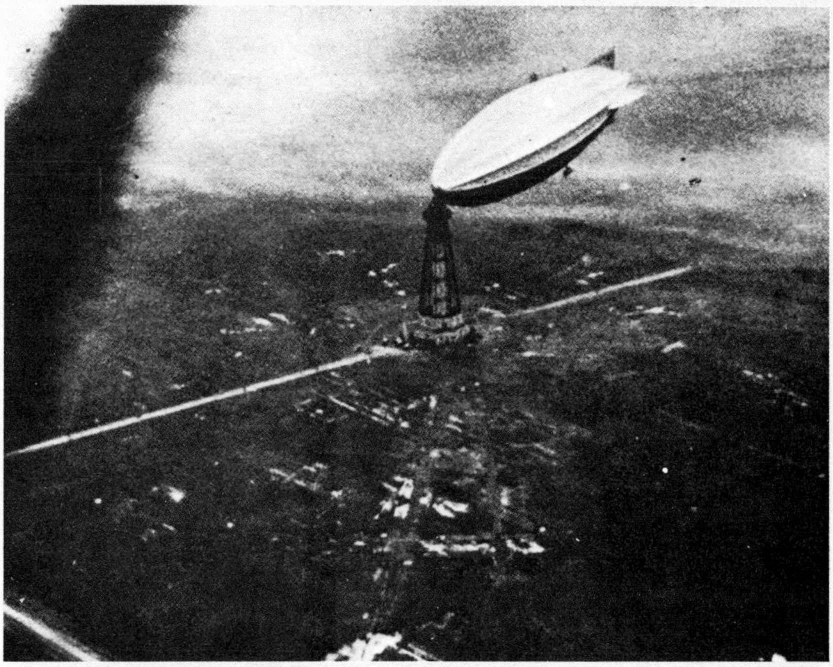

Top: the *R100* at rest after her successful flight to Montreal in July 1930

Above: Barnes Wallis, whose genius contributed so much to the success of the *R100*

Left: the *R101*, the largest airship built at that time, basks in floodlights at her mooring at Cardington. The hangar that housed her there was the biggest building in the British Empire

The specifications and standards of performance laid down for the two airships were more or less identical, and they were impressive – far in advance of any existing airship, more sophisticated even than the future *Graf Zeppelin*. They would be by a huge margin the largest airships the world had seen – kept aloft by 5 million cubic feet (140,000 cubic metres) of hydrogen. This would give them a gross lift of 150 tonnes, and with a stipulated maximum weight of 90 tonnes for the airships themselves (unloaded) they would provide a 'useful' lift of 60 tonnes – again far in advance of anything to date.

What this amounted to was a specification for a pair of airships that could transport 100 fare-paying passengers in considerable luxury to the four corners of the globe, and do so at the respectable cruising speed of 63 miles per hour (100 km/h). Altogether a grand vision, and it was by no means as fanciful as it may look in retrospect.

The Vickers team set up shop in a disused hangar at Howden, Yorkshire, and over the next five years put together an airship of the highest quality, the *R100*. They accomplished their formidable task in relative peace and quiet, away from the glare of publicity and political meddling. Meanwhile, the Air Ministry team resurrected the wartime airship base at Cardington, near Bedford. And there, unlike their rivals, they found themselves as goldfish in a bowl. How great a factor this was in the final débâcle is a matter for speculation, but what finally emerged in a blaze of public anticipation was a majestic flying coffin – the much-vaunted *R101*.

The first in the sorry catalogue of mistakes made at Cardington was probably the worst. Because of the competitive element it was

decided not to pool information with Howden. The design and construction of such advanced airships were bound to throw up problems both theoretical and practical. Original thinking would be at a premium – and there was not a lot of it in the world of British airship design in the 1920s. What the Air Ministry did – deliberately – was to dilute what little there was.

Vickers was in the enviable position of having a truly outstanding designer for the *R100* – Barnes Wallis, who was even then an acknowledged inventive genius and would later become a living legend. During the five years it took to build the two airships Wallis repeatedly suggested collaboration, but his appeals fell on deaf ears. It was almost as though the Cardington men thought they had nothing to learn from others.

Take the engines, for example. Early on it was decided in favour of a newly designed diesel type because it was marginally safer (from the standpoint of accidental fire) than the conventional petrol type. This should have been weighed against a rather more significant disadvantage of the new diesel engines: they were far too heavy. The Howden team too experimented with diesel, saw quickly that they were too heavy and reverted to proven Rolls-Royce Condor engines. Such pragmatism was out of the question at Cardington. Considerable publicity had been given to the new diesels and they would stay, overweight or not.

In a desperate attempt to make the *R101* effective, the enormous structure of the doomed craft is split in two to take in an extra gasbag

The huge gasbags inside the rigid metal frame (16 of them in all) were held in place by an elaborate system of wiring. But the wiring was such that the bags continually rubbed against the girders and rivets of the framework itself. As bad, or worse even, when the airship rolled (a natural enough occurrence) the valves in the gasbags opened slightly, which meant there was an ever-present risk of highly flammable hydrogen wafting around outside the gasbags but still inside the body of the airship.

From bad to worse

The hurried solutions to these fundamental problems were bizarre – comical even, were it not for the dreadful outcome. There were only two ways of getting more lift: reduce the weight of the airship or increase the volume of hydrogen. The former was difficult to do to any significant degree (without scrapping the diesel engines) but the latter gave scope to fevered imaginations. Why not simply chop the airship in two and stick an extra bay in the middle? And surely there was an easy way of squeezing more hydrogen into the existing gasbags. Simply loosen the wiring to allow them to expand a little more (and chafe a little more as well). And so on. If the gasbags showed an annoying tendency to puncture themselves on bits of the framework, track down the offending projections and stick a pad over them (some 4000 pads were fitted).

The immediate results (like the final result) of this kind of folly were roughly what

Captain Hinchliffe's prediction

Even while the *R101* was stumbling toward completion, there were psychic portents of catastrophe. On 13 March 1928 a dashing war hero, Captain W. R. Hinchliffe, accompanied by heiress Elsie Mackay, took off from Cranwell aerodrome in eastern England in an attempt to fly the Atlantic. They were never seen again.

Then on 31 March, one Mrs Beatrice Earl was startled by a message that came through on her ouija board: HINCHLIFFE TELL MY WIFE I WANT TO SPEAK TO HER.

Through Conan Doyle, Mrs Earl passed the message to the aviator's widow, Emilie, who in turn agreed to let Eileen Garrett (whom Mrs Earl knew) try to contact her dead husband. (He, incidentally, had once called Spiritualism 'total nonsense'.)

In the sessions that followed Hinchliffe's spirit became deeply concerned about the *R101*: 'I want to say something about the new airship. . . . the vessel will not stand the strain.' He pleaded that his old friend Squadron-Leader Johnston, the *R101*'s navigator, be told. But the men at Cardington were unmoved.

His last message was received as the *R101* headed for France: STORMS RISING. NOTHING BUT A MIRACLE CAN SAVE THEM. But by then, Eileen Garrett had begun to have visions of an airship in flames . . .

one might have expected. The 'new' *R101* was hauled out of the hangar to her mooring mast under perfectly tolerable weather conditions. At once, a gaping hole 140 feet (33 metres) long appeared along the top, where the fabric had merely given way. It was taped up. So was another, smaller tear that appeared the next day.

In defence of the beleaguered men at Cardington it should be said that they were working under intolerable pressure. In July 1930 the unheralded *R100*, having completed her trials successfully, flew to Montreal and back again a fortnight later. It was rumoured that only the more successful of the two airships would serve as a prototype for future development. To the rattled men at Cardington it was now vital that the *R101* demonstrate her superiority quickly. The destination for the maiden flight was India, a longer and more glamorous voyage than the *R100*'s to Montreal, and guaranteed to put Cardington back in the limelight.

Calendar of woe

So we come to the final grim chapter, and to the man who must bear most of the blame for the fiasco that cost his and many other lives: the Air Minister himself, Lord Thomson of Cardington. His devotion to the *R101* project bordered on the fanatical (his choice of title when elevated to the peerage provides a pointer). He combined this passion with unslakable ambition. His sights were set on becoming the next Viceroy of India, and by happy coincidence there was an Imperial Conference in London starting in late October. How better to draw attention to his claim than by descending on the conference fresh from a round trip to the Subcontinent aboard his beloved *R101*?

A September departure was impossible (Thomson accepted this but with ill-disguised resentment). Early October was the latest departure date that would get him to India and back in time to fulfil any of his commitments at the conference. The airship

Above: Lord Thomson of Cardington, whose driving ambition to get the *R101* into the air served only to hasten its end – and his own death

Below: the press immediately latched on to the strange aftermath of the disaster

must be ready by the fourth of the month because 'I have made my plans accordingly.'

Aside from the fact that the airship was unfit for such a voyage (or for a Sunday excursion) there was another hitch. It was essential to have a Certificate of Airworthiness, which could only be issued after the successful completion of exhaustive trials. But a temporary certificate was wangled, with the droll proviso that final speed trials be completed during the journey itself.

At 6.36 p.m. on 4 October the awesomely beautiful silver craft (for she was that) struggled away from her mooring mast. And it was a real struggle. Four tonnes of water (half the ballast) had to be jettisoned in those first moments, just to get airborne. Pitching and rolling, the airship that was in Lord Thomson's immortal words 'as safe as a house, except for the millionth chance' crossed low over the lights of London an hour and a half later, with one of the five engines already out of commission. At 8.21 Cardington received the laconic message: 'Over London. All well. Moderate rain.'

The last message

At 9.35 she reached the Channel at Hastings, still flying low and experiencing worse weather – hard rain and a strong southwesterly wind. Two hours later she crossed the French coast near Dieppe. At midnight Cardington received its final wireless message. After reporting the *R101*'s position as 15 miles (24 kilometres) south of Abbeville the message ended on a cosy note: 'After an excellent supper our distinguished passengers smoked a final cigar, and having sighted the French coast have now gone to bed to rest after the excitement of their leave-taking. All essential services are functioning satisfactorily. The crew have settled down to a watch-keeping routine.'

What seemed to pass unnoticed aboard the airship was her low altitude. It did not go unnoticed by some observers on the ground, one of whom was alarmed to see the gigantic craft flying overhead at an estimated 300 feet (90 metres), less than half her own length. That was about 1 a.m., and he judged her to be moving in the direction of Beauvais.

Bottom: spectators are dwarfed by the burnt-out wreckage of the 777-foot (237-metre) long airship

R101: the dead captain speaks

What exactly had brought the *R101* to its fiery end? The official inquiry could only guess – but it ignored some extraordinary evidence. For the ship's dead captain had 'come through' at an astonishing seance . . .

REPORTS OF THE CALAMITY that had befallen the *R101* began trickling into London and Cardington during the small hours of Sunday morning, 5 October 1930. At first they were guarded: even as late as 5.30 a.m. Reuters in Paris would go no further than say that 'alarm' had been caused by an 'unconfirmed report that the airship has blown up'. But this was quickly followed by the death knell: *R101* HAS EXPLODED IN FLAMES ONLY SIX SAVED.

The parallel with the sinking of the *Titanic* was inescapable – a vessel of heroic proportions, the largest and most advanced thing of its kind, safe 'but for the millionth chance' and yet hideously fated on her very first voyage. Public grief was unrestrained on both sides of the Channel.

But even in the midst of that grief some starkly insistent questions cried out for answers: how had it happened? Whose fault? A special Court of Inquiry was set for 28 October, amid angry rumours that its unspoken function would be to whitewash the Air Ministry in general and the dead Lord Thomson in particular.

As far as getting at the truth about the flight itself, and particularly what happened during those final minutes, there was a peculiar difficulty. Fate had been awkward in its selection of survivors. All the passengers were dead; so were all the officers. The only survivors were six lucky crewmen, none of whom was in the main control car (which was crushed) and none of whom was in a position therefore to know precisely how it was that the mighty *R101* kept her rendezvous with that small hillside outside Beauvais. Put together, their recollections of the final moments added little of importance to what Eugene Rabouille had seen from the ground.

Above: the *R101* cruises over the outskirts of London during her first test flight on 15 October 1929. Thousands of sightseers had crowded Cardington to see her take to the air

Right: the captain of the *R101*, Flight-Lieutenant H. Carmichael Irwin. Would the testimony of 'his' spirit voice have helped the Court of Inquiry that investigated the tragedy?

The Court of Inquiry, sitting under the distinguished statesman Sir John Simon, delivered its verdict in April 1931. As the immediate cause of the crash the Court settled for a sudden loss of gas in one of the forward gasbags; this, if the airship were dangerously low to begin with (as she undoubtedly was) and taken in conjunction with a sudden downdraught (which was plausible) would certainly spell disaster. It was as good a guess as any.

It may well be, however, that what the Court did *not* consider in evidence was of greater significance than what it *did*. There was considerable testimony that, had it been given credence, shed a much clearer light on the disaster, and, because of its nature, on issues of vastly greater significance. It was testimony of an extraordinary kind from an extraordinary source – the dead captain of the airship.

On the afternoon of the Tuesday following the crash, four oddly assorted characters assembled at the National Laboratory of Psychical Research in West London. Harry Price, who had set up the laboratory a few years earlier, was a singular man: wealthy, mercurial, an amateur magician, a passionate investigator of psychic phenomena. And, what was of great importance in the light of what was to follow, he was a savage foe of Spiritualist hokum, whether of the deliberately fraudulent variety (which as a magician he was perfectly equipped to expose) or of the innocent type (in which genuine paranormal experiences such as telepathy were wrongly ascribed to 'voices from beyond').

One of Price's guests that day was the celebrated medium Eileen Garrett, a woman of unimpeachable integrity, whose paranormal faculties continually astonished her as much as they did those who witnessed them. Despite the fact that in trances she frequently delivered weirdly plausible messages purporting to come from beyond the grave, she refused to classify herself as a Spiritualist. And she backed up her modest mystification about her strange powers with a disarming eagerness to expose them to the most searching examinations that could be devised by the Harry Prices of this world.

The other principal guest was an Australian journalist, Ian Coster, whom Price had persuaded to sit in on what promised to be a potentially fascinating seance. Sir Arthur Conan Doyle had died a few months earlier. He and Price had wrangled for years, Conan Doyle huffy about Price's acerbic views on Spiritualism, Price discerning a credulity verging on dottiness in the celebrated author.

Conan Doyle had vowed to prove his point in the only way possible, and Price had arranged the seance with Mrs Garrett to give him his chance. Coster, a sceptic, was there as a witness. Eileen Garrett, as always, did not know the *purpose* of the seance, nor did she know who Coster was. As far as she knew it was merely one of Price's clinically controlled investigations into her strange psychic talents.

Above: Harry Price, who arranged the seance at which Flight-Lieutenant Irwin's 'spirit' was first heard

Below: the bodies of those killed in the disaster lie in state in flag-draped coffins, in Westminster Hall, London. Public reaction to the crash was intense: the French provided full military honours before the bodies were brought across the Channel by two Royal Navy destroyers. An estimated half million Londoners watched the funeral procession; world leaders from Hitler to the Pope sent condolences

The three of them, along with a skilled shorthand writer, settled down in the darkened room, and Mrs Garrett quickly slipped into a trance. Soon she began to speak, not in her own voice but that of her regular 'control', one Uvani. He had first manifested himself years before and claimed to be an ancient Oriental whose purpose in establishing himself as a link between Mrs Garrett and departed spirits was to prove the existence of life after death. Sometimes he would relay messages in his own voice (deep, measured cadences, formal); at other times he would stand aside, as it were, and allow the spirit to communicate directly.

The uninvited spirit

Today, after announcing his presence, Uvani gave Price a few snippets of information from a dead German friend (of whom, incidentally, he was certain Eileen Garrett was perfectly ignorant), but nothing that excited him. And no Conan Doyle. Then suddenly Eileen Garrett snapped to attention, extremely agitated, tears rolling down her cheeks. Uvani's voice took on a terrible broken urgency as it spelled out the name IRVING or IRWIN. (Flight-Lieutenant H. Carmichael Irwin had captained the *R101*.) Then Uvani's voice was replaced by another, speaking in the first person and doing so in rapid staccato bursts:

'The whole bulk of the dirigible was entirely and absolutely too much for her engine capacity. Engines too heavy. It was this that made me on five occasions have to scuttle back to safety. Useful lift too small.'

The voice kept rising and falling, hysteria barely controlled, the speed of delivery that of a machine gun. Price and Coster sat riveted as a torrent of technical jargon began to tumble from the lips of Eileen Garrett.

'Gross lift computed badly. Inform control panel. And this idea of new elevators totally mad. Elevator jammed. Oil pipe plugged. This exorbitant scheme of carbon and hydrogen is entirely and absolutely wrong.'

There was more, much more, all delivered fiercely at incredible pace: '. . . never reached cruising altitude. Same in trials. Too short trials. No one knew the ship properly. Airscrews too small. Fuel injection bad and air pump failed. Cooling system bad. Bore capacity bad . . . Five occasions I have had to scuttle back – three times before starting.

'Not satisfied with feed . . . Weather bad for long flight. Fabric all water-logged and ship's nose down. Impossible to rise. Cannot trim . . . Almost scraped the roofs at Achy. At inquiry to be held later it will be found that the superstructure of the envelope contained no resilience . . . The added middle section was entirely wrong . . . too heavy . . . too much overweighted for the capacity of the engines.'

The monologue petered out at last, and Uvani came back to ring down the curtain on this portion of the astonishing seance. (In fact Conan Doyle did 'come through', but that is another story.)

Three weeks later, on the eve of the Inquiry, there began a sequel to this mystifying occurrence that was every bit as strange. Major Oliver Villiers, a much decorated survivor of aerial scraps over the Western Front, was badly shaken by the *R101* catastrophe. He had lost many friends in the crash, in particular Sir Sefton Brancker, Director of Civil Aviation and Villiers's direct superior at the Air Ministry. Indeed he had driven Brancker to the airship on the day of departure.

Villiers was entertaining a house-guest who had an interest in Spiritualism, and late one night, when his guest and the rest of the household had gone to bed, he suddenly had an overwhelming impression that Irwin was in the room with him (the two men knew each other well). Then he heard, mentally, Irwin cry out to him: 'For God's sake let me talk to you. It's all so ghastly. I must speak to you. I must.' The lament was repeated, then: 'We're all bloody murderers. For God's sake

The last few minutes

None of the survivors seemed to know what had caused the *R101* to dive into the ground. One had just dozed off in his bunk when he was jolted awake by the chief coxwain rushing by shouting 'We're down lads! We're down!' Another was relaxing over a drink in the specially sealed-off smoking lounge when he felt the airship dip, dip again – and erupt into flame. Two more, in separate engine cars, were no better informed.

Engine man Joe Binks, however, had glanced out of a window only two minutes before the end, and was terrified to see the spire of Beauvais cathedral, 'almost close enough to touch'. He shouted to engineer Bell, the sixth survivor, when the floor seemed to drop away, then the ship lurched. At the same moment a message was coming through from the main control car: SLOW. Then a few moments' silence. And then the holocaust.

The Air Ministry clamped down on any news of the crash, yet in the first seance two days later 'Irwin' described how he had failed to achieve cruising height: 'Fabric all waterlogged and ship's nose down . . .'

Three survivors stand near the wreck

Left: a session of the Court of Inquiry into the disaster. Though it could not ascertain the precise cause of the crash, it had no doubts that the *R101* should never have been allowed to attempt the flight to India

Right: taken shortly before the *R101* left Cardington on its last doomed flight, this photograph shows (left to right): the navigator, Squadron-Leader E. L. Johnston, whose friend Captain Hinchliffe's spirit had allegedly warned of the inadequacies of the ship through two different mediums; Sir Sefton Brancker, who was said to have agreed to join the flight only because Lord Thomson had accused him of cowardice; Lord Thomson himself; and Lieutenant-Colonel V. C. Richmond, designer of the *R101*. All died in the final holocaust

help me to speak with you.' In the morning Villiers recounted this most disturbing experience to his guest, who promptly arranged a session with Eileen Garrett.

The first of several seances was held on 31 October and it, like its successors, took a significantly different form from the Price-Coster episode. Rather than merely listen to Irwin, Villiers conversed freely with him through Mrs Garrett. Moreover, while in the first seance Irwin came through alone, in later seances he was joined by several of his colleagues and even by Sir Sefton Brancker.

Villiers was not served by shorthand, but he claimed the gift of total recall, which in conjunction with notes hastily scribbled during the 'conversations' convinced him that the transcripts he made were virtually dead accurate. They make absorbing reading, and a short extract from the first one will give their flavour:

Villiers: Now try to tell me all that happened on Saturday and Sunday.

Irwin: She was too heavy by several tons. Too amateurish in construction. Envelope and girders not of sufficiently sound material.

Villiers: Wait a minute, old boy. Let's start at the beginning.

Irwin: Well, during the afternoon before starting, I noticed that the gas indicator was going up and down, which showed there was a leakage or escape which I could not stop or rectify any time around the valves.

Villiers: Try to explain a bit more. I don't quite understand.

Irwin: The goldbeater skins are too porous, and not strong enough. And the constant movement of the gasbags, acting like bellows, is constantly causing internal pressure of the gas, which causes a leakage, of the valves. I told the chief engineer of this. I then knew we were almost doomed. Then later on, the meteorological charts came in, and Scottie and Johnnie (fellow officers) and I had a consultation. Owing to the trouble of the gas, we knew that our only chance was to leave on the scheduled time. The weather forcast was no good. But we decided that we might cross the Channel and tie up at Le Bourget before the bad weather came. We three were absolutely scared stiff. And Scottie said to us – look here, we are in for it – but for God's sake, let's smile like damned Cheshire cats as we go on board, and leave England with a clean pair of heels.

Price and Villiers did not know one another, nor were they aware of each other's seances with Eileen Garrett. They arrived independently at the conclusion that the 'evidence' they had should be placed before Sir John Simon (Price also informed the Air Ministry). Neither the Court of Inquiry nor the Ministry was prepared to accept that these unusual happenings contributed to an understanding of the *R101* tragedy.

Did the spirits really speak?

What was it that caused medium Eileen Garrett to pour out a flood of information about the crashed *R101*? Did the airship's dead captain really 'come through'? And just how accurate were the technical details of the airship that he gave?

THE R101 AFFAIR is a classic of its kind for two reasons. First, the messages purporting to come from Captain Irwin contained information about a matter of widespread general interest, and this information was couched in technical language. Everyone wanted to know what had happened to cause the catastrophe, and many were in a position to have informed opinions. Moreover, the official verdict of the Inquiry was not particularly convincing – composed as it was of a fair bit of speculation wrapped up in careful qualifications (necessarily, since there was not much hard evidence to go on). Someone really well informed about airships in general and the *R101* project in particular just might come to the conclusion that where Irwin's post-mortem account conflicts with the official verdict, 'his' has more the ring of truth. This could not by itself be conclusive, but it would be undeniably strong circumstantial evidence for spiritual survival.

Second, and as important as the contents of the messages, there is little to raise the question of spiritualism's chronic bugbear – the suspicion of deliberate fraud. There can be no field of investigation where the personal integrity of those 'on trial' looms larger, and therefore comes under closer scrutiny. Eileen Garrett went to her grave with an unblemished reputation. Further, the Price-Coster seance was held in circumstances controlled by a world-famous detective of fraudulent mediumship. To arrange a hoax, even had he wanted to, Price would have needed to enlist as fellow-conspirators Mrs Garrett and Major Villiers, a distinguished and honourable man – and indeed several others who add weight to the assertion that there was no trickery involved.

The credibility of Eileen Garrett (above) is central to the *R101* mystery. She had been in touch with the 'spirit' of the aviator Hinchliffe, who uttered warnings about the airship; had had visions of an airship in flames; and received messages from the 'spirits' of those on board the *R101* – seen here on its initial test flight in October 1929 cruising over St Paul's London

With fraud out of the way, then, the question turns on whether the information purporting to come from the dead Irwin is of such a nature that it could have come *only* from him. Put another way, is there any possible means by which the information that came *out of* Mrs Garrett could have got *into* Mrs Garrett other than by her being in contact, through Uvani, with Irwin's spirit? If not, the case for the survival of the spirit is made – a simple conclusion, but one with profound implications.

Everything hangs on the details of the messages, therefore, and it is to them that we now turn. The case for accepting the voice as being the true Irwin has been presented in considerable detail by John G. Fuller in his book *The airmen who would not die* (1979); it runs as follows.

None of those present knew anything at all about the complexities of airship design or the business of flying one, and therefore it is impossible that such startlingly specific statements as those made by 'Irwin' – at wild speed in what was to those present a language as foreign as it is to the lay reader today – could have been dredged from the conscious or unconscious mind of any of them. That rules out straightforward telepathy.

One of 'Irwin's' statements was not only highly technical, it referred to something that would not be known outside the inner sanctum intimately involved with the airship (the new hydrogen-carbon fuel mix). Another, the reference to Achy ('almost scraped the roofs at Achy'), is just as bewildering. Price tried to find Achy in conventional atlases and maps without success. But when he tracked down a large-scale railway map of the Beauvais area (a map as detailed as the charts Irwin would have had in the control

car) he found it; a tiny hamlet on the railway line a few miles north of Beauvais. Where could such a snippet of information have come from, if not from Irwin?

Finally, Price had the transcript examined, clause by clause, by an expert from Cardington (who volunteered for the job). This Will Charlton, and apparently other old Cardington hands, professed themselves astonished at the technical grasp displayed therein, and by the likelihood of Irwin's account in its essentials. Charlton reckoned that *no one* but Irwin could have been the source of this information – information that explained clearly what had happened during the fateful voyage as against the speculative account in the official report.

As far as it goes this sounds pretty convincing. But it begins to fray at the edges somewhat when it is realised that in Charlton, Price had not found an expert at all; rather a convinced Spiritualist whose claim to airship expertise rested on the shaky ground of his having been in charge of stores and supplies at Cardington. In a review of Fuller's book for *Alpha* magazine in 1980, Archie Jarman, credited by Fuller with knowing more about the subject than any living person, draws attention to some glaring examples of Charlton's ignorance, and they are certainly of such a nature as to discredit him as an expert. For example, during the Price-Coster sitting 'Irwin' made a reference to '*SL8*'. Price had no idea what it meant, and it remained for Charlton to come up with the answer: 'The *SL8* has been verified as the number of a German airship – SL standing for Shuttle Lanz.' To track down this morsel of information Charlton had had to comb through the entire record of German airships.

Experts and amateurs

Now far from being impressive (an expert having to go to considerable lengths to discover the meaning of a reference so obscure that it could emanate only from an even greater expert such as Irwin), it is utterly damning. The *SL* stands for *Schütte Lanz* (*Schütte*, not 'Shuttle' or 'Shutte' as Fuller variously has it), the Zeppelin people's German rival in airship development before the First World War, and one of whose airships was shot down in flames in a celebrated action during an airship raid on England in 1916 (a mere 14 years before). Yet Charlton, the expert, had no idea what *SL8* referred to. It is not good enough, and Fuller makes it worse by driving home the point with a sledge-hammer: 'Charlton and his colleagues of Cardington had been strongly impressed with the reference to *SL8*. No one on the staff of Cardington could confirm this designation and number until they had looked it up in the complete records of German airships.'

Further, when Jarman was compiling a report on the affair in the early 1960s he solicited the opinions of two real experts: Wing-Commander Booth, who had captained the *R100* on the Montreal flight; and Wing-Commander Cave-Brown-Cave, who had been intimately involved in the *R101*'s construction.

Eugene Rabouille, the poacher who saw the *R101* plough into the ground near Beauvais. The official inquiry into the disaster seemed, to many, to add little to his account of the great airship's final moments. The question remains: how much light does the 'spirit evidence' shed on the reasons why the *R101* crashed when she did?

Booth spoke for both when he replied: 'I have read the description of the Price-Irwin seance with great care and am of the opinion that the messages received do not assist in any way in determining why the airship *R101* crashed. . . .' Cave-Brown-Cave ended with the crushing comment '. . . the observations of Mr Charlton should be totally disregarded.'

Booth's verdict on the Villiers material was even harsher: 'I am in complete disagreement with almost every paragraph . . . the conversations are completely out of character, the atmosphere at Cardington is completely wrong, and the technical and handling explanation could not possibly have been messages from anyone with airship experience.' This latter is surely true. Just to take one example: in the passage quoted previously, 'Irwin' complains about the gas indicator going up and down. Booth's trenchant reply was: 'No such instruments were fitted.'

That technical inaccuracy is bad enough but it is mild in comparison to what the officers are said to have had in mind from the moment they set off from Cardington. They supposedly knew the airship was a dud and that they had no chance of reaching their destination. But they thought they might just creep across the Channel and tie up at Le Bourget. There were only four places on Earth with the facilities to cope with such an immense airship, and Le Bourget assuredly was not one of them.

When all was lost

Then after they crossed the Channel, according to 'Irwin' they 'knew all was lost'. So what did they do? Press on into a brutal headwind hoping to make Le Bourget (knowing all was lost), 'and try at all costs some kind of landing'. An emergency landing? Like the one they made outside Beauvais? No sane person would attempt any such thing, especially when there was an obvious alternative.

If the Captain and his close colleagues really *were* terrified about the way things were going, all they had to do was turn around and with the wind at their backs limp home to the safety of Cardington. Sane men do not accept *certain* death (and commit dozens of their fellows to the same fate) rather than admit that they have been defeated by an impossible task.

Returning to the Price-Coster sitting, Mr Jarman's view is that nothing whatever occurred during the seance that cannot be put down to Mrs Garrett's own subconscious and her telepathic powers. Take Achy, for instance, at first sight so inexplicable. Not really, according to Jarman, who knew Mrs Garrett well. Apparently she frequently motored from Calais to Paris. Achy is on that road, vividly signposted. Could not Mrs Garrett have retained the name subconsciously? Since it is more than likely that the *R101* did *not* pass directly over Achy, what else are we to believe?

And while Eileen Garrett certainly knew nothing to speak of about the technicalities of airships, the *R101* was much on her mind even *before* the crash. For she had already had visions of an airship disaster, and had discussed her fears at length with none other than Sir Sefton Brancker 10 days before the accident.

The supposedly secret nature of some of the technical information provided by 'Irwin' can also be explained. The fact is that the design and construction of the *R101* (fuel mix and all) was conducted in about as much secrecy as surrounded the building of Concorde. Anyone who cared to could have amassed immense technical detail about her during those long years of building simply by reading the newspapers. And of course the papers were full of it during the interval between the crash and the seance (Villiers had even longer to become steeped in the events that had overwhelmed his friends). As for the savage indictments of the airship that form the burden of all the seances, the Cardington follies had been notorious all along, brought to the fore, naturally, by the disaster.

Coster was a journalist, reasons Mr Jarman, and as such would be pretty well up on all this, and if we accept that Eileen Garrett had telepathic gifts we need look no further. That is a perfectly reasonable explanation, if one there be, for what Jarman himself admits is a 'mystery'.

Perhaps the final word should be left to Harry Price. In his letter to Sir John Simon, which is, incidentally, couched in the language of a disinterested research scientist, he states that he does not believe that it was the 'spirit' of Irwin present at the seance. Then he goes on: 'I must also state that I am convinced that the psychic was not consciously cheating. It is likewise improbable that one woman in a thousand would be capable of delivering, as she did, an account of the flight of an airship. . . . Where such information comes from is a problem that has baffled the world for 2000 years.'

Above: Sir Sefton Brancker, who discussed the problems of the *R101* with Eileen Garrett just before the crash

Left: the giant airship is manoeuvred by its ground crew prior to its last flight

Below: the stark, burnt-out remains of the *R101* offered no clues to the precise cause of the disaster

Born again

The doctrine of reincarnation is central to many religions. Is rebirth merely a desperate dream, or is there evidence to support it?

To be or not to be

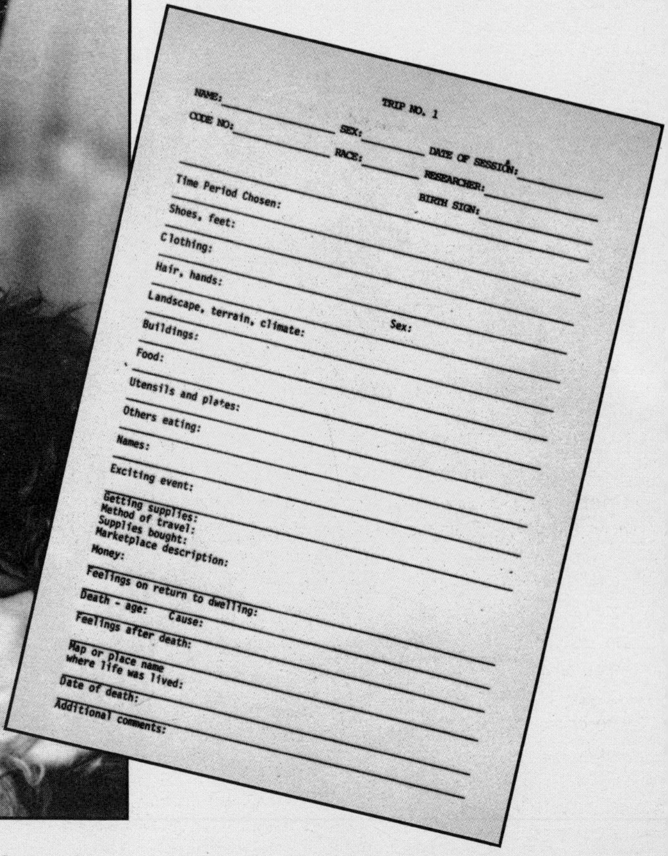

NAME: TRIP NO. 1
CODE NO: SEX: DATE OF SESSION:
RACE: RESEARCHER:
BIRTH SIGN:
Time Period Chosen:
Shoes, feet:
Clothing:
Hair, hands:
Landscape, terrain, climate: Sex:
Buildings:
Food:
Utensils and plates:
Others eating:
Names:
Exciting event:
Getting supplies:
Method of travel:
Supplies bought:
Marketplace description:
Money:
Feelings on return to dwelling:
Death - age: Cause:
Feelings after death:
Map or place name where life was lived:
Date of death:
Additional comments:

A programme of mass hypnotic regression carried out by the American psychologist Helen Wambach seems to provide strong evidence for the survival of death. But how valid are her results?

DO WE CHOOSE to be born? Do we choose our sex, the time of our birth – and even our mother? Have we chosen to live other lives before our own? Helen Wambach's group hypnotic sessions suggest that the answers to these questions may be 'yes'.

Helen Wambach is an American psychologist who, disillusioned with teaching standard psychology courses, began to explore automatic writing, table-turning and mediumship – and finally concluded that she could learn the most about human nature by using hypnosis to explore what she termed 'life before life'.

Her technique is to hypnotise large groups of people all at once. The members of the group – consisting of perhaps 40, 50 or even more people – lie on the floor and prepare themselves for a lengthy hypnotic session. Then begins the process of suggestion: Helen Wambach's voice says: 'Your eyes are closed and it feels good to close your eyes. The muscles of your face relax.' The subjects feel themselves sinking into an ever deeper state of relaxation, as Wambach guides them into the desired state.

Above: Helen Wambach, whose mass regressive hypnosis sessions have, she claims, yielded convincing evidence for reincarnation. It would clearly be absurd to ask all the hypnosis subjects in a mass session to recount their experiences while in trance; instead, Helen Wambach supplies them with data sheets (above right), which the participants are requested to fill in when they have regained normal consciousness

'Search your memory' is the next instruction, and everyone is asked to visualise a photograph of themselves as a teenager, as a small child, and as an infant. As the process of relaxation continues, Wambach suggests that each person becomes a pinpoint of consciousness floating close to the ceiling of the room; she then leads them around the building in which the session is taking place, on a kind of guided out-of-the-body fantasy. There is just one more stage, in which Wambach suggests to her subjects that their brainwaves are slowing to 5 cycles per second. She then tells them to go back to a time before they were born.

Obviously not everyone can start to recount past lives at once. A room of 50 hypnotised subjects all talking together would be chaos. Instead, Wambach asks them to remember their experiences and to fill in a data sheet after the session. Using this method, she finds that 90 per cent of her subjects recall having past lives, and just under 50 per cent can remember their existence between lives and the moments before they were born.

An advantage of this group method is that large amounts of information can be collected. Indeed, Wambach says that one of the problems is that there is too much material. She has regressed over 1000 people, who reported an average of five past lives each, from as long ago as 2000 BC right up to 1945. Some intriguing findings have emerged from these data.

One woman reported having been a middle-class housewife in 16th-century Venice, a servant girl in 18th-century Normandy, a boy who died aged eight of smallpox and a common seaman from Norway who died in 1916. Whether such people really existed is, of course, difficult to check, but reports in which specific names and dates are given or that mention historical figures can be researched. Wambach claims that, out of over 1000 data sheets analysed, only 11 showed clear historical errors. She also says that her subjects' descriptions of everyday life – the clothes they wore, the food they ate, and so on – are astonishingly accurate.

Wambach found that 49 per cent of the past lives she analysed were as females, and 51 per cent as males. This, of course, matches the actual distribution of males and females in the population very closely. She also found that the number of 'lives' reported around AD 400 was half that reported around 1600, and that the number doubled again around 1850 – matching, as she pointed out, the growth of the world's population. Could these findings have come about if the subjects were merely imagining past lives? Wambach argues that this could happen only if her subjects really had lived before.

Above: a 16th-century Greek illustration from a treatise on hunting and (left) a 15th-century illumination from a French manuscript. Helen Wambach supports her claim that her hypnosis subjects recall genuine past lives with a statistical analysis of their descriptions of life at various periods. To check her data, however, one would have to be able to say, for instance, what kind of clothes people were wearing *throughout the world* in 1450

After the subjects had recalled various past lives, they were taken to the death of each life and asked to live through it. Only around 10 per cent were upset or felt sorrow at their own deaths; indeed, over half described death as pleasant. One wrote:

> Dying was like being released, like going home again. It was as though a great burden had been lifted when I left my body and floated up toward the light. I felt affection for the body I had lived in in that lifetime, but it was so good to be free!

Unique to Wambach's work is her exploration of the period between lifetimes and before birth. The average interval between lives is apparently 52 years, and people can be taken back to remember what that time was like. Generally the sensation is likened to floating on a cloud – but at its end comes the difficult decision to be born again.

Wambach tells her deeply hypnotised group: 'I want you to go now to the time just before you were born into your current lifetime. Are you choosing to be born?' The hypnotist asks why the subjects chose the latter half of the 20th century for this life, why they chose their particular sex, what their purpose is in this lifetime and who, from this life, they have known in previous lives.

Out of a group of 54 people hypnotised in Chicago in 1978, nearly half answered these questions, and many did so with tears in their eyes. It seems that reliving birth is far more traumatic than reliving death. One woman declared:

> I felt such compassion for that baby who was me. I felt such sadness to leave the place where I was to come back into physical life. It seemed so hard to be confined in a little body, and to lose the lightness and the love I had known in the between-life state. . . . I realise that birth is not a joyous occasion. The two deaths I had in the two past lives tonight were very pleasant experiences. It's getting born that seems the tragedy.

Eighty-one per cent of subjects said that they chose to be born; for many, however, it was with reluctance, and only after consulting others.

When asked why they chose the latter half of the 20th century for their reincarnation, many were unable to say, but a large number claimed that it was a time of great potential for spiritual growth, 'an important and exciting age to be born into'. Asked about their choice of sex, many appeared to be indifferent; in fact, Wambach points out that none of her 750 subjects felt their 'true, inner

Nineteenth-century illustrations of the biblical parable of the king and his servants (above left), set in Old Testament times; of Jesus feeding the multitudes (above); and of the medieval Arthurian romances (above right). Wambach believes that her subjects' detailed descriptions of life in various periods of history cannot be the outcome of mere fantasy – but many of them tally closely with the romanticised images offered by children's books and Bible illustrations

self' to be of either sex.

Many of the subjects felt that their session under hypnosis had revealed their purpose in life. It was not to grow rich, famous or powerful but, in almost every case, to learn and to help and to love others, 'to learn patience and love of my fellow man'. Reaching this realisation during the hypnotic sessions sometimes had a profound effect on subjects, and many went away feeling that they were in some way 'better' for their experience.

Among the unexpected findings was the high proportion – 81 per cent of those who answered the questions – who claimed to have known present friends or relatives in past lives. Arthur Guirdham has publicised the notion of group reincarnation, and other hypnotists have suggested the existence of something similar. But if Wambach's findings are to be believed, this is commonplace. Fathers and mothers in this life were lovers, friends, brothers and sisters in past lives. In one case, 'I knew my mother before because we had been together at a convent in the 1200s. I saw a close friend of mine as a teenager in Russia, where I knew him.' For some people, groups of friends and relatives worked together through different lives. For others, difficult relationships had to be worked upon. 'I sensed my father and I have been working on this relationship in several past lives, and we have still not cleared it up.' Wambach concludes that it is only when we feel nothing but compassion and affection for others that we are freed from the need to live over and over again with the same spirits.

It seems that abortion cannot be called murder, if Wambach's findings are to be believed. She asked when people had entered the foetus. A few claimed it was early on in the mother's pregnancy, but the majority did not experience being part of it until at least the sixth month. A large group – 33 per cent – said that they did not join the foetus, or experience being inside it, until just before, or even during, the actual birth.

For most, the birth itself was frightening, sad or confusing. Wambach had suggested that her subjects should feel no pain, but many still found it unpleasant. One was terrified of being taken away from her mother, another felt angry at the bright lights and a third felt lost and cold. Another commented, 'This is going to be a lonely trip.'

Wambach concluded that her results could not be produced by fantasy alone. But could they?

Experience and expectation

Imagine you are one of Wambach's subjects. When the hypnotic session is over, you are presented with a sheet of paper on which are all the questions Wambach asked during the session. You are to write down all your answers. What will you write?

One possibility is that you may have 'seen' nothing during the hypnotic 'trip'. In this case, will you leave the data sheet entirely blank – or will you make something up? About 10 per cent of Wambach's subjects admitted that they experienced no past lives and, when questioned about times between lives, nearly half wrote nothing on their sheets. Wambach explained this by saying that these people had gone too 'deep' into hypnosis to be able to recall anything, but were the figures themselves right? We cannot be sure that there were not more people who made something up to please the hypnotist.

A second possibility is that you may

indeed have seen vivid images, but be quite convinced that they came from your own imagination or memory; they may even remind you of books you have read, or films you have seen. When you write all this down, will you note your feelings about where the images came from? Or will you just describe the scenes? Wambach does not mention having questioned subjects about this possibility.

Wambach argues that the fact that past lives are divided roughly equally between the sexes would not arise if people were making up those lives. But would it? What her evidence does not tell us is how many people changed sex in past lives. Other studies have found, typically, that only about 10 per cent of people change sex when regressed. If this figure is the same for men as for women, and if Wambach's sample contained roughly equal numbers of each sex, then Wambach's result would arise quite naturally – and would not prove anything about the truth of her subjects' statements.

The same can be said of the way in which the number of past lives increases as the world's population increases. Most Americans learn more about recent history than about ancient history. So the increase of reported past lives with time may be a reflection not of the increase in world population – but of the increasing knowledge of the subjects of the period concerned.

There is also the difficult question of the accuracy of descriptions of past life. Wambach gives many graphs full of analyses of different types of clothing and footwear worn in lives of different periods, types of food eaten, but it is hard to compare such findings with actual historical facts. For example, a graph shows that of those who reported lives around the year AD 500, about 50 per cent wore sandals, hides and rags, 5 per cent shoes, boots or slippers and 45 per cent had bare feet. Bearing in mind that these reports allegedly come from all over the world, how would one go about checking the data historically?

When we go on to the data on life between lives and the birth experiences it becomes even harder to check details. We can only speculate about what it is like to be a foetus, so it is difficult to assess the accuracy of the descriptions.

The typical account is of an arduous and even painful journey down the birth canal, followed by the unpleasant experience of emerging into an unwelcoming world of cold and bright lights. Some descriptions include details of the birth – but Wambach seems not to have checked whether they correspond with reality by asking the mother of the subject or by checking medical records.

Some accounts, however, are easy to dismiss as products of the imagination:

> In the birth canal I found it hard to breathe and stuffy, and I was aware of pressure all over, especially on my head. I felt like I was flailing my arms. When I emerged I felt frightened and lonely.

A foetus, of course, has no need to breathe.

These are just some of the problems arising from Wambach's work that invite scepticism as to its value. It may help the subjects to learn about themselves; it may be an educational and interesting experience. However, the evidence is far too weak to support all those claims that people really did go back to past lives. More evidence may be forthcoming to change this view, but in the meantime it seems that the most likely hypothesis is that Wambach's results can be accounted for by subconscious fabrication, compliance, imagination and her subjects' accurate memory of their experience.

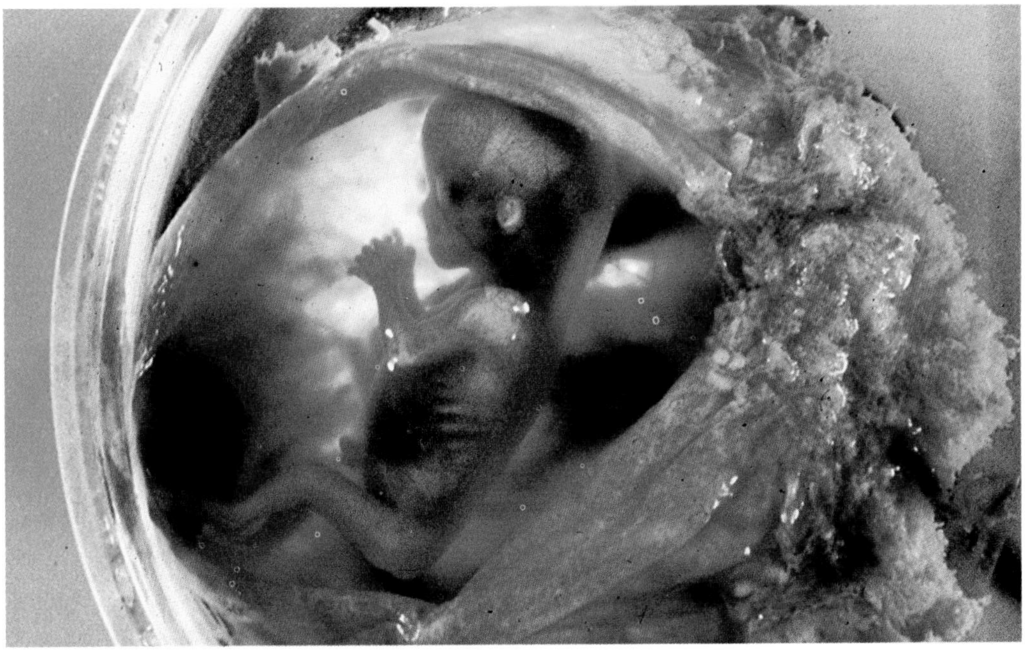

A foetus in the amniotic sac. Part of Wambach's regressive hypnosis technique is to make her subjects relive their births into various lives. One surprising finding is that most participants claimed that they entered the foetus only at a very late stage – sometimes actually during the birth process

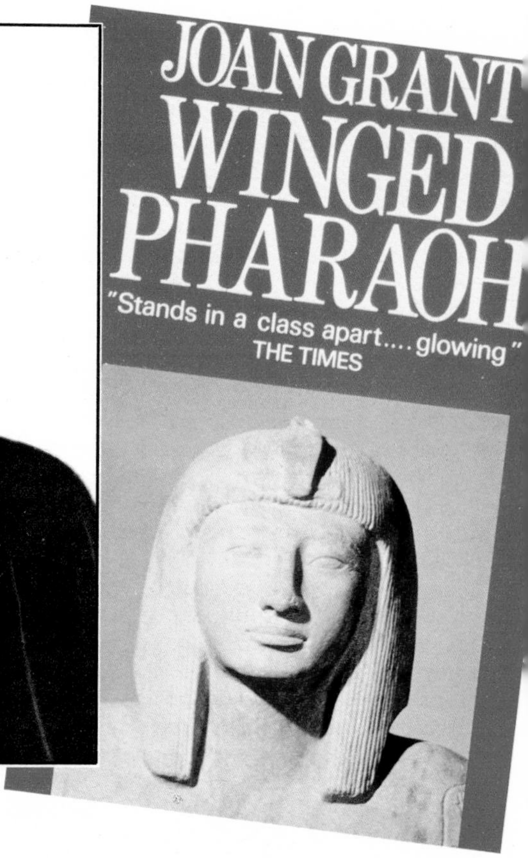

The strange histories of Joan Grant

Have we all had previous existences in many different centuries and civilisations? Joan Grant believes she has – and this chapter recounts the fascinating story of how she has learned to trace those many other lives

JOAN GRANT HIT the public eye in 1937 with her first highly praised book, *Winged pharaoh*. It was classified as an historical novel and, like others that followed, was judged by the experts to be a very accurate account of the time it portrayed. But Joan Grant did not have to research a single detail – she recorded everything from her 'far memory' of the life she had lived as a priest-pharaoh in a previous incarnation.

Joan Grant had intimations of her other lives even as a tiny child; she told stories about who she had been 'before she was Joan' – but nobody believed her. Soon she learned that it was better to keep her stories to herself, and she told nobody else until she was a teenager. Meanwhile, she struggled to unravel her strange dreams and to understand who she was. It took a great effort to train herself to wake several times a night so she could write down the events that had just occurred in her sleep.

Joan Grant was born in 1907 of a wealthy family and lived a sheltered life of comfort and plenty. Even during the First World War she suffered little physical privation. But during that time she began to have vivid war dreams in which all five senses were engaged. In fact, the smells of battlefield and hospital made her violently sick upon waking, and for weeks she tried to keep herself from sleeping by self-torture such as sitting on an icy floor or pulling hairs out. At one point during this time, when at a convent in London where she loved the nuns, she was constantly terrified for no reason. Nearly 20 years later she found out that the reason lay in a life she had lived in the 16th century.

Joan Grant, flanked by her first and best-known book and a photograph of herself as a girl. She had glimpses of other lives even as a tiny child – and *Winged pharaoh* told the story of one of them as a priest-ruler in ancient Egypt

One morning at home she came down late for breakfast after a terrible nightmare. There was a soldier with her father, and Joan said to him:

> Somehow I know you will not laugh at me. Last night I was with a man called McAndrew when he was killed. I can describe the regimental badge although I cannot remember the name of the regiment, except that it was not an English one. And I can tell you the slang name of his trench.

The visitor did not laugh because he was able to identify the regiment as Canadian. Later, he wrote to Joan's father, Jack Marshall:

> For heaven's sake don't laugh at the

child. I cannot attempt an explanation, but I have checked what she said. A battalion of that regiment went over the top on a night attack a few hours before she told me about it at breakfast. A private called McAndrew was among the killed. She was even correct about the local name of the front-line trench.

Joan was only nine at the time, and it was years before her father told her of this unexpected confirmation.

Marshall was a scientist who won a CBE for his work in mosquito research, on which he wrote the standard text. Many eminent men were visitors to his home. One, C.G. Lamb, was professor of engineering at Cambridge University and Joan's special favourite. They had long talks and she felt at ease with him, partly because of his great interest in psychical research.

Lamb had been a friend of Joan's grandmother, Jennie Marshall. One day while they were chatting, he told Joan that Jennie could have been a world-famous concert pianist if her husband had not stood in her way. 'Jennie gives me music lessons,' said Joan in reply, aware that any other adult would have scoffed at the claim, since Jennie was dead. 'Father knows I would never be a first-class pianist so there is no point in my having lessons, but Jennie knows I need music and she teaches me. Sometimes she plays the piano with me – music that is quite different from the ordinary tunes I have learned.'

Feeling that her grandmother was present, young Joan went to the piano and music began to flow. When she stopped, Lamb mopped his brow and remarked: 'Extraordinary. Quite extraordinary but completely evidential. What you have just played was often played to me by your grandmother. . . . I have not heard it since she died.'

When Joan suggested that she may have heard her grandmother play it, or have heard it at a concert, Lamb assured her that she had not.

> Only one copy of that music ever existed. It was given in manuscript to the Tsar of Russia, who sent it to your grandmother. . . . I happen to know that the manuscript of that music, together with several other manuscripts of similar value, was burned two years before you were born.

Jennie Marshall had learned that she had terminal cancer, and decided that no one else would play her music if she could not do so.

It was to the author H.G. Wells, whom she met at the age of 16, that Joan confessed all about 'the secret part of her life'. He was sympathetic, but advised her to keep it to herself until she was 'strong enough to bear being laughed at by fools'; then, when she was ready, she should write down what she knew – 'It is important that you become a writer,' said Wells.

Joan Grant broke off her first engagement because her fiancé and his family were intolerant of her belief in her dream lives. It was indeed a dream that led her to her next romance.

This dream of a man recurred over a period of time, during which she went to Switzerland for a ski-ing holiday. Alone in the hotel music room, she was playing Jennie's music on the piano when the door opened – and she looked into the eyes of the man in her dream. The stranger looked at her intently and then said, 'It really is you. I have dreamed with you for nearly two years':

Top: Seacourt, the childhood home of Joan Grant at Hayling in Hampshire

Above: C.G. Lamb, professor of engineering at Cambridge University, was interested in psychical research and gave a sympathetic ear to Joan Grant's accounts of unusual occurrences. And in one instance he was able to prove from personal knowledge that her experience was paranormal

Left: Blanche and Jack Marshall, parents of Joan Grant. Through her father's wide social contacts, Joan met H.G. Wells. The author advised her to keep her 'secret life' to herself for a while – and then to write about it later

An aerial view of the burning of the French ship *Atlantique* off Guernsey on 4 January 1933. Joan Grant had a precognitive dream about the disaster. In it she was a French sailor caught in a ship fire. She even named the ship as the *Atlantic* and knew it was sailing the Channel

within 24 hours of meeting, Joan and Esmond decided to become engaged.

Esmond had to go to France for six months on business and they planned to marry on his return. He spent the last few days before going abroad at the Marshall home. On the last night, as Esmond was walking to his bedroom, Joan heard a voice – she believes it was her grandmother's – say softly but distinctly: 'After Esmond leaves here tomorrow you will never see him again.'

On the night before he was due to return to England, Esmond died in an accident at a Paris shooting gallery with a gun he thought was not loaded.

Another dream in which a woman told her to 'Go to Leslie' sent Joan to Leslie Grant, whom she married in 1927 at the age of 20. Now she had an ally and a helper in her husband, who willingly undertook the job of writing down her dream experiences from dictation. Joan says she learned how to shift levels of consciousness between sleep and wakefulness so that she did not have to break the thread of events and was able to describe her dreams as she had them. This, she said, helped her to dip more easily into what she called her 'far memory'. Her far-memory dreams transcended space and time.

Another category of her dreams she called 'true dreams'. These depicted incidents that were later found to have occurred at about the time she was dreaming. In one such dream she was a sailor on a burning ship. On waking she told Leslie about it. There was enough detail to say with certainty that the ship was in the Channel, the sailor was French, and the vessel was going to Cherbourg. She thought the ship's name was *Atlantic.* Later that day, newspaper headlines declared '*Atlantique* burns in English Channel: many dead'.

Besides far-memory dreams, Joan Grant soon discovered another way of tuning into the past. At her husband's suggestion, she took up psychometry, and was able to receive vivid impressions of events or people connected with an object just by holding it in her hand for a short time.

A pharaoh's life

In 1936 the psychic was given a scarab and whenever she handled it she recalled events of what appeared to be a previous life in Egypt. In 200 sessions she dictated the story of her existence as Sekeeta, the daughter of a pharaoh and later a priest-pharaoh herself. It amounted to 120,000 words and was published as Sekeeta's 'posthumous autobiography' under the title of *Winged pharaoh.*

What makes Sekeeta's story particularly fascinating is its claim that far memory was known and developed in Egyptian times. Those who received training in it had to remember at least 10 of their own deaths, and their graduation examination required them to be shut in a tomb for four days and nights, during which they underwent seven ordeals.

Sekeeta passed the test and seems to have brought her ability into the 20th century, remembering along the way lives in Greece in the second century BC, in medieval England and 16th-century Italy, and various others in Egypt.

Has Joan Grant really lived all these lives? Do we all have such a continuous past, spanning many centuries and civilisations? Her series of far-memory books and three autobiographical volumes insist that there is much more to life than the existence we are currently experiencing.

What is equally interesting is Joan Grant's claim that our present ills and problems may well have their roots in previous incarnations – and can be cured by far-memory recall of them.

Have we shared previous lives with those who are close to us in this life? Can learning about traumas experienced in other lives relieve emotional problems? Joan Grant with her extraordinary insights into these matters is convinced that the answer is 'yes'

Breaking with the past

JOAN GRANT HAS SUFFERED some dreadful deaths. She has been burned as a witch, been killed by a spear through the eye during a joust, and has bled to death when she ordered her Roman court physician to cut her wrists.

Twice she has committed suicide and twice she has died after being bitten by snakes. During a lifetime in Egypt, when she was a man, she was bitten by an insect and died from the infection. Another life ended when she broke her neck in a diving accident.

Joan Grant believes that everyone has had similar past lives, with deaths that are just as traumatic and horrifying. The difference is that most people can no longer remember their previous incarnations, whereas she has had a 'far memory' since childhood. Moreover, she has developed it to the extent that she can recall her earlier lives in exact detail.

Joan Grant perfected the technique of 'shifting the level of consciousness' between sleeping and waking so that she could dictate her dream experiences of previous lives. Seven books of these experiences have been published as historical novels, though she calls them 'posthumous autobiographies'. In addition, she has written about her experiences and abilities in this lifetime (*Far memory*, 1956) and her therapy work with her third husband, Dr Denys Kelsey (*Many lifetimes*, 1969).

The book for which she is best-known is *Winged pharaoh* (1937). It is the story of Sekeeta, a pharaoh's daughter, who became co-ruler with her brother when her father died. Sekeeta spent 10 years in a temple learning to recall her previous lives, an ability she has brought with her into the 20th century as Joan Grant. Sekeeta eventually qualified to be both a ruler and a priest: a winged pharaoh.

In another Egyptian life nearly 1000 years later, Joan Grant was a man: Ra-ab Hotep. His life appeared in two books, *Eyes of Horus* and *Lord of the horizon*, which were published in the early 1940s. *So Moses was born* (1952) dealt with a life when Joan Grant was a male contemporary of Ramesses II.

Joan Grant was born in England in 1907. As well as several lives in Egypt, she had incarnations in other places. In the 16th century she was in Italy, having been born Carola di Ludovici on 4 May 1510. She became a singer with a troupe of strolling players and died at the age of 27. In more recent times, she was an English girl named

Above: Ramesses II, pharaoh of Egypt over 3000 years ago. Joan Grant believes that she lived as a man during his reign, a life she described in her book *So Moses was born*

Left: vultures savaging the carcase of a dead elephant. Vultures hovering over Alec Kerr-Clarkson in a previous incarnation created a phobia about touching bird feathers in this life. He overcame this fear when Joan Grant showed him the root cause of it by 'resonating' with his earlier self and discovering what had happened

Lavinia who broke her back in a fall from a horse. Lavinia died in 1875.

Taken at face value, it would seem that Joan Grant has lived numerous times before her present existence. But that, she says, is too simple an interpretation. She believes that our spirits are far greater than we realise and that each of the many other personalities she can recall has a soul. At death they become part of the whole spirit again. If, for some reason, the soul fails to integrate with the spirit, it produces a ghost. Joan Grant explains: 'Joan and Sekeeta are two beads on the same necklace and the memory they share is contained in the string.'

There are still wider implications to Joan Grant's far memory. She believes that many of the people who are close to us in this life have shared our lives in previous times. Sometimes they were husbands, sometimes wives. They may have been brothers or sisters, sons or daughters, lovers or friends. Our spirit, she asserts, is androgynous and therefore we incarnate in both male and female form. This makes for a wide range of personal relationships over time.

For example, one of the greatest influences on Joan Grant's early life was Daisy Sartorius, a family friend. It was while holding a scarab belonging to Daisy Sartorius that Joan Grant began recalling her previous life as Sekeeta, in the First Dynasty of Egypt about 3000 BC. In that existence, Joan discovered, Daisy had been her mother.

Similar connections were found between previous lives and her third husband, Dr Denys Kelsey. It was Denys Kelsey, a physician and psychiatrist, who cut the veins in Joan's wrists in Roman times on her orders, when he was also a physician. They later shared a life together as husband and wife in 18th-century England.

Dr Kelsey worked in the psychiatric wing at a military hospital in 1948. In trying to help the patients, he discovered the value of hypnosis, at which he became adept. In addition, 'a series of cases came my way which, step by step, extended the framework of what I believed to be fact until, after four years, a session with a particular patient forced me to the intellectual certainty that in a human being there is a component which is not physical.'

Below: witches being burned at the stake in the late Middle Ages in Germany. In one of her previous lives, Joan Grant believes she died just such a horrible death

Bottom: a group of strolling players rehearsing in 18th-century England. Joan Grant recalls leading the life of a singer with a troupe like this – but in Italy 200 years previously

Joan Grant's first book had a profound effect on Dr Denys Kelsey. He records in *Many lifetimes*: 'Before I had finished *Winged pharaoh* . . . I knew beyond any possibility of doubt, that reincarnation was a reality. . . . I would have journeyed halfway round the world to meet the author, but fortunately such a long pilgrimage proved unnecessary.' He discovered they lived only 30 miles (50 kilometres) apart. They met in 1958, and within two months 'embarked upon life together'.

Dr Kelsey had anticipated that his knowledge of hypnosis would link with Joan Grant's knowledge of reincarnation. What he did not realise, until they met, was that Joan had already worked closely with a psychiatrist during the war years and had gained a good deal of psychiatric experience. Now, working as a team, they were able to offer help to many people with a unique form of psychotherapy having its roots in past lives.

Joan Grant knew from her own experience that events in her previous incarnations, such as violent deaths, could have an effect on her present existence. On one occasion, for example, she battled unsuccessfully with herself for one hour in an attempt to pick up a slow-worm. She knew she was in no danger. But part of her was still 'resonating' to a stored memory of agonising pain in three snake-bite episodes in previous lives, two of which proved fatal.

While working in the laboratory of her

As a young woman, Joan Grant battled with herself to pick up a slow-worm, which repelled her. She later learned through her 'far memory' that this was a reaction against three very unpleasant experiences with snakes in her past lives – two of which ended in her death

father's Mosquito Control Institute, she had often given blood meals to the mosquitoes as part of her job. She had never had any ill effects. However, on several subsequent occasions, when she had mosquito bites on her eyelid, they produced a totally disproportionate amount of swelling and suffering. The reason, she discovered, was a resonance with her previous existence as an Egyptian captain. A bite on his eyelid, though from a fly, had led to what was probably septicaemia – and death.

According to Joan Grant and Denys Kelsey, once the causes of fears and anxieties are known and understood by bringing them into normal waking consciousness, the latent energy contained in them is defused. The soul can then be properly integrated and the problem usually disappears.

With the discovery that she could resonate with other people's past lives, Joan Grant found she was able to rid individuals of their apparently irrational fears when such emotion was a throw-back to previous times.

An early case, which occurred during her second marriage, concerned a psychiatrist, Alec Kerr-Clarkson. He visited her to discuss the possibility of reincarnation research. At the end of a pleasant weekend, he was about to leave the house to catch a train back to the north of England when her then husband, Charles Beatty, offered him a brace of pheasants, tied by the neck with a loop of string. The psychiatrist, looking embarrassed, backed away and asked if they could be wrapped in a parcel. Charles insisted they would travel better unwrapped, at which point Alec Kerr-Clarkson admitted, 'But I can't touch feathers.' No sooner had he said that than Joan Grant added:

> The reason you can't touch feathers is because you had a death which was very similar to one of mine. You were left among the dead on a battlefield. . . . Vultures are watching you . . . six vultures. You are very badly wounded, but you can still move your arms. Every time you move, the vultures hop a little further away. But then they hop closer again. . . . Now they are so close that you can smell them . . . they are beginning to tear at your flesh.

This account caused the psychiatrist to collapse on a sofa, sweating profusely, and he needed little persuasion to stay another night. Joan Grant spent most of the night at his bedside, during which time she realised what his problem was. He had begun to recall the episode himself quite vividly. 'Why did they leave me to die alone . . . why?' he cried out. 'Every other man had a friend to cut his throat . . . why did they betray me. . . . Me!'

It was this feeling of betrayal associated with the vultures that had created the feather phobia. Once Joan Grant was able to convince him that his comrades had not deliberately left him to a slow and painful death, having thought he was already dead, he was cured.

Using hypnosis, Dr Kelsey was able to produce similar past-life recalls in troubled patients. Joan Grant helped the therapy by resonating with the patient's experience and giving more details. Sometimes it was not even necessary for the patient to relive the experience. This happened in the case of a youth who had a severe anxiety problem. One day his parents telephoned to say he had tried to commit suicide that day. Joan Grant decided to delve into his past lives on her own to find out what was troubling him.

Dr Kelsey later was startled to find his wife in a distressed state. She was obviously in acute pain and tears were rolling down her face. He soon realised that she was reliving an episode in a previous life of the young patient. She told him:

> I can feel the blood clots in the tooth sockets. . . . It was bad enough during the first two days, after he pulled out all her teeth, but then the taste got worse and worse, not only dead blood but pus. Then the fever started . . . and she died on the fourth day.

It turned out that the woman concerned had had beautiful teeth that had been pulled out with nail pincers by a jealous husband. The youth had been that woman in a previous life and also had beautiful teeth in his present incarnation.

Dr Kelsey remembered that, in an early session, the troubled youth had said the anxiety problem had begun after an incident in a bar when another youth had threatened: 'I'm going to kick your teeth in!'

When told of Joan Grant's experience and the belief that he had had all his teeth wrenched out by a husband in the 19th century, the young man had no difficulty in accepting it. His anxiety disappeared instantly. Five years later, when Dr Kelsey and Joan Grant wrote about the case, it had not recurred.

Only a small number of people can be helped in this way, but Joan Grant believes that the message contained in her books will help many more. It is, very simply, to view this life – whatever its difficulties and sorrows – as just one of numerous others that will present us with challenges and opportunities to improve ourselves and help others.

Above: Hurtwood, in Surrey, home of Daisy Sartorius. Joan Grant lived here for a number of years following a personal tragedy. During that time, she recalled her life as Sekeeta – and found out that Daisy Sartorius had been her mother then

Below: Dr Denys Kelsey, husband of Joan Grant, in his army days. The two worked in a psychiatric practice together for many years, and Kelsey still has a practice in their home at Pangbourne in Berkshire

A tragic double act

Are the Pollock twins reincarnations of their sisters who had been tragically killed in a road accident in the late 1950s? Their father, a staunch believer in reincarnation, is firmly convinced that this is so. This chapter examines the facts

ONE OF THE MOST INTRIGUING aspects of reincarnation is the claim that many young children can recall having lived before. In the United States Dr Ian Stevenson of the University of Virginia has been collecting and studying such cases for many years. A typical example is that of a two-year-old child who will suddenly and inexplicably start talking about himself as though he were a deceased member of his own or another family. Occasionally, these children have birthmarks that resemble injuries sustained by the dead person.

Perhaps not surprisingly, a high proportion of Dr Stevenson's cases involve children who live in the East, where belief in reincarnation is widespread. It is not uncommon for poor children to claim to remember lives of wealth and influence. The cynical view of such claims is that if a poor family can convince wealthy relations that the child is the reincarnation of one of their dead, the rich relatives will pay for the child's upkeep.

However, there are a large number of case histories that do not belong to either of these categories. One such case involves the Pollock twins. The central figure in this story is John Pollock, now in his sixties and living in Humberside in northern England. For almost as long as he can remember he has been a fervent believer in reincarnation. When he was 19 he was converted to Roman Catholicism but, much to the chagrin of the priests who received him, he did not relinquish his views. On the contrary, he prayed to God to provide him with evidence that reincarnation does happen so that he could prove to his priests that this was no heresy.

When in his twenties, John married Florence, a staunch Baptist; they lived in Hexham, Northumberland, with their two daughters, Joanna and Jacqueline – both of whom attended their local Roman Catholic church each Sunday.

On 5 May 1957, Joanna, aged 11, and Jacqueline, aged 6, set out with their schoolfriend Anthony Layden to walk to church. A few miles down the road lived Marjorie

Shaftoe Leazes in Hexham, Northumberland, where Joanna and Jacqueline Pollock and their friend Anthony Layden were struck by a car and killed in 1957. Shortly afterwards twins were born to their parents – and seemed to be their dead daughters in new bodies

THREE CHILDREN DI
ON WAY TO CHURCI

SUNDAY MORNING
ROAD TRAGEDY

ON THEIR WAY TO AN EARLY MORNING SERVICE AT ST. MARY'S ROMAN CATHOLIC CHURCH, HEXHAM, ON SUNDAY MORNING, THREE HEXHAM CHILDREN AGED SIX, NINE AND ELEVEN WERE KILLED BY A CAR AT SHAFTOE LEAZES, HEXHAM.

There was no other traffic on the road at the time and the children were the only three pedestrians on the pavement.

he children who were walking
d in hand were sisters
ueline Teresa (6), and Joanna
(11) Pollock, daughters of
and Mrs Percival John
ck, of 29, Leazes Crescent,
m, and Anthony Layden
ly son of Mr and

Pupils pa
funeral
tribute

Bunches of wild
flowers from
playmates

PUPILS from St. Mar
Catholic School, Hexha
led by their headmistress
Lawrence, lined
from the

Top: the story made headlines: when a depressed woman took an overdose of barbiturates then set off in her car to commit suicide it seemed only too likely that others would die. Ironically, she survived – and the Pollock girls (above, in a happy family group) and their friend died. Yet, if their father is right, his dead daughters returned – as twins

Wynn, a wealthy widow who, for some years, had been suffering from acute depression following the loss of her husband. That same Sunday morning she swallowed an overdose of barbiturates, climbed into her powerful new car and drove off, intending to 'end it all'. Other motorists were alarmed by her dangerous and erratic driving. A farmer even tried driving after her, but in vain. At the very moment that she drove into the neighbourhood where the Pollocks lived, Joanna, Jacqueline and Anthony were walking hand in hand along the pavement. Marjorie Wynn drove straight into the three of them, in the words of one witness, tossing them 'like cricket balls' into the air. They died virtually immediately. This part of the story is incontrovertible. But John Pollock's interpretation of the tragedy makes it a very curious tale indeed – and perhaps a sinister one.

It was, he said, God's judgement upon him for asking for proof of reincarnation, and with a macabre confidence began predicting that God would now give him the evidence he wanted. When, a few months later, Florence again became pregnant, John confidently told her that she would have twin daughters who would be Joanna and Jacqueline reincarnated. Florence, recently converted to orthodox Roman Catholicism, found the ideas as abhorrent as had the priests who had received John. It was equally unacceptable to the Pollocks' doctor and gynaecologist, who firmly told John that there could be no question of Florence giving birth to twins – they could detect only one set of limbs and one heartbeat.

Yet, early in the morning of 4 October 1958, Florence Pollock gave birth not only to twins, but to twin daughters – Gillian and Jennifer. How did John know? The odds that it was a lucky guess are extremely high, for the odds against *any* twins being born are 80 to 1, and what is more there is no history of twins in either of John's or Florence's families.

In addition to this, John noticed a thin, scar-like mark on the forehead of Jennifer (the younger of the twins) that seemed to resemble the scar that Jacqueline (the younger of the two who died) sustained when she fell off her bicycle at the age of two. Jennifer also had a birthmark on her left hip, apparently identical in appearance and location to Jacqueline's birthmark.

And then other strange incidents began to happen. When the twins were only four months old, the Pollocks moved from Hexham to Whitley Bay, about 30 miles (50 kilometres) away. The twins did not return to Hexham until three years later when John and Florence took them back on a day's excursion. The twins recognised not only the house they had lived in when they were only four months old, but also Joanna and Jacqueline's school.

Uncanny knowledge

One evening, about a year later, John Pollock took out some of Joanna and Jacqueline's dolls, which had previously been kept hidden away. When Jennifer saw them she apparently exclaimed, 'Oh, that's Mary. And this is my Susan. I haven't seen her for a long time.' These were the very names that Joanna and Jacqueline had called them.

The last incident occurred when the twins were playing in a yard: someone started a car and they began screaming. As John came running out he found the two of them clutched in each other's arms, pointing at the car and shouting, 'The car, the car, it's coming at us!' And, as John later explained, the car was indeed pointing towards them at the same angle at which Joanna and Jacqueline would have seen Marjorie Wynn driving towards them.

As with so many of Dr Stevenson's cases, Gillian and Jennifer seemed to lose touch with their past lives when they were about six years old. So completely did they forget that it was not until they were teenagers that they remembered what had happened, and this was only because a schoolfriend chanced upon an article about them in an overseas magazine. Florence Pollock had, until then, managed to keep their father's theory secret from them.

Florence died in 1979. She had never accepted John's beliefs, in spite of the many 'inexplicable' incidents. In other words, we have only John Pollock's word that they occurred in the way he said they did. Take, for example, the day on which the Pollocks returned with the twins to Hexham – it was by no means an ordinary family outing. John Pollock had been in touch with Dr Stevenson who suggested that John should make the trip in search of 'proof'. Was he so determined to find proof that the twins were Joanna and Jacqueline reincarnated that he inadvertently prompted them to say they recognised the Pollocks' old house and the school they had attended?

Nor are the circumstances in which the twins saw their late sisters' toys quite as innocuous as might at first appear. By leaving the dolls deliberately outside the girls' room where they could not fail to find them, he was very much testing their reactions. Children are often much more aware of their parents' feelings and attitudes, albeit unconsciously, than the parents may realise. Since John Pollock felt so strongly about reincarnation, it is quite possible that the twins could have overheard him explaining his theories to Florence. If this is the case, one can easily argue that the twins were simply reacting to this test in the only way they knew how – by making it seem that they were, indeed, Joanna and Jacqueline reincarnated.

Right: Gillian and Jennifer Pollock in 1979, posing with a photograph of their dead sisters. According to the twins' father, as toddlers they constantly 'remembered' living as their late sisters. And Jennifer bore identical scars and birthmarks to those of Jacqueline. Not surprisingly, the Pollocks' story has achieved wide publicity: in 1966 Dr Hemendra Banerjes (below) flew from India to interview the twins and their father – whose total belief in his 'reincarnated daughters' may well be the only substance to the story

As for the apparent birthmarks, whatever the cause of the 'scar' on Jennifer's forehead, it seems to have disappeared in early childhood. Unfortunately, there is no clear photograph of it. However, while the birthmark on her hip undeniably exists – it was seen by millions on a British television programme – its significance should be set in perspective. Such birthmarks frequently run in families, sometimes spanning five generations or more.

We are left, then, to rely heavily on the credibility of John Pollock. He is as affable, open and quite obviously sincere as he is obsessed with reincarnation. Since Florence's death he has remarried. His new wife shares his ideas and the two have become very interested in Spiritualism, as has John's daughter Gillian. Perhaps significantly, her twin Jennifer, who had the birthmarks, has now married and prefers to remain aloof from her father's ideas.

The case of the Pollock twins represents one of the most remarkable of all reincarnation claims, but it still falls considerably short of the kind of proof that would settle the matter once and for all.

Mediums: between two worlds

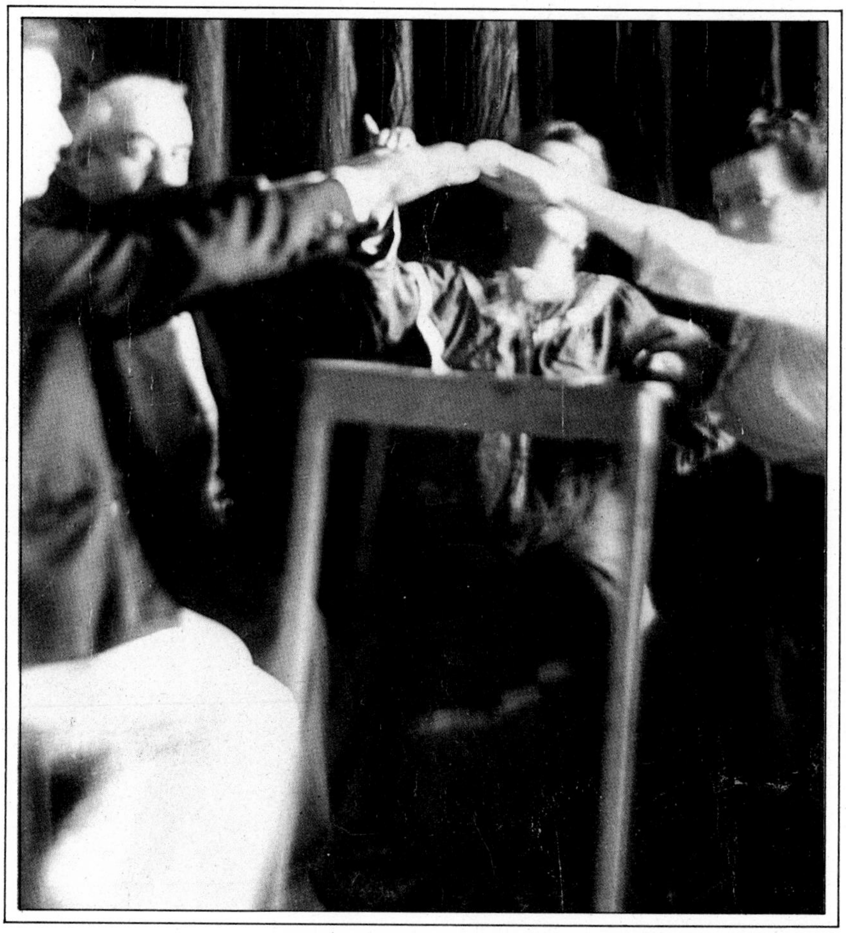

Spiritualism and mediumship are rife with fraud and abuse, but when the fakes have all been exposed, there are still people with knowledge and power that cannot be explained within the framework of our present knowledge.

Survival – the solid evidence?

Perhaps the most controversial area of psychical research is that of physical mediumship. In this chapter the reports of some classic seances are assessed – both fraudulent and apparently genuinely paranormal

ONE OF THE IRONIES of the paranormal is that often the best evidence offered for the existence of a spiritual realm is produced in a physical form. It may seem absurd that raps, moving tables and levitating trumpets are manifestations produced by spirits, but explaining such phenomena in other ways is, perhaps, no more persuasive.

Such physical phenomena do not occur in isolation: a human catalyst seems to be responsible. The birth of Spiritualism in Hydesville, in the United States, in 1848 came about through simple raps that apparently formed the basis of communication between a dead pedlar and the Fox family (see page 174). Within a few years, the three Fox sisters – Kate, Margaretta and Leah – were world-famous as mediums, and many others discovered that, under the right conditions, they too could produce physical phenomena.

Author and debunker William Marriott is surrounded by a fake medium's 'materialisation' props. In normal lighting – and without benefit of the heightened atmosphere of the seance room – these sheeted masks look laughably crude. Yet these very fabrications fooled a great many sitters

A cabin for spirits

In another American state during the early 1850s, farmer Jonathan Koons was conducting his own experiments with physical mediumship. He claimed that the spirits had told him he was 'the most powerful medium on earth' and, following their instructions, he built a small log cabin alongside his farmhouse in Ohio, so that he and his eight children – all of whom were said to be psychic – could hold seances. It was equipped with musical instruments and other items with which the spirits could play. In appearance it was like a tiny theatre, with seats for up to 30. When the audience was settled, Koons would turn the lights out and play hymns on his fiddle until unseen hands would lift the other musical instruments in the room and join in. During the noisy concert a tambourine circled above the heads of the audience, trumpets floated in the air and voices spoke. Spirit hands held phosphor-coated paper to illuminate some of the manifestations. Koons even built a 'spirit machine' – a complex piece of zinc and copper apparatus that the spirits said would help collect and focus the magnetic aura they used for their physical demonstrations. According to Koons, when this device was used the spirits could triumph over the laws of gravity and cohesion, enabling them to move heavy objects at speed and play instruments.

Just 3 miles (5 kilometres) away, and without the help of a 'spirit machine', John Tipple and his children were giving very similar performances in his spirit house, which was also said to have been built under instructions from the next world.

The Koonses' mediumship was comparatively short-lived. Jonathan Koons never charged for the seances he held and there is no evidence of fraud. But, despite Spiritualism's general popularity at that time, he encountered open hostility, particularly from his neighbours. His home was attacked by mobs, his children were beaten and his barns and fields were set alight, forcing him to leave the area. He and his family eventually became Spiritualist missionaries.

Another American family with a similar

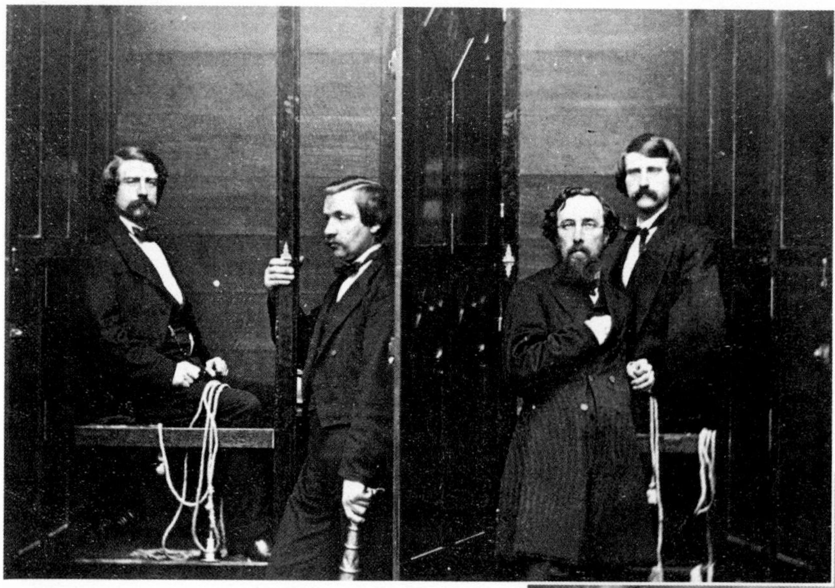

phantom, figure holding the pistol. It vanished and the gun fell to the floor.

According to the Davenport children, they were told by the spirits to allow investigators to tie them up in ropes to prove that they were not producing the noises and other manifestations that occurred in their darkened room. This they did to the satisfaction of many visitors, including sceptics.

The Davenports' mediumship was no more remarkable than that of other physical mediums in the mid to late 1800s, but what set them apart was their decision to demonstrate their powers in public. To do this, the Davenport brothers constructed a three-door cabinet that was, in effect, a portable

eventful seance room were the Davenports. Physical phenomena in the form of raps and strange noises were said to have been heard in their Buffalo, New York, home in 1846 – two years before the Hydesville episode. At that time, Ira Davenport was seven years old and his brother William was five. Four years later, the two boys and their sister Elisabeth began table turning with impressive results. The table moved, raps were heard and a spirit was said to have controlled Ira's hand and written messages. The three children are reported to have levitated simultaneously at least once. On the fifth night of their experiments Ira was told by the raps to take a pistol and shoot at a corner of the room. He did so, and at the moment it fired they saw another,

The Davenport brothers were two of the most famous mediums of the late 19th century, exciting both extreme adulation and bitter hostility. Their stage show featured what was in effect a portable seance room – a three-doored cabinet (top, from left to right: Ira Davenport, a psychical researcher, the author Robert Cooper, who was impressed by the brothers' powers, and William Davenport). When Harry Houdini met Ira Davenport in the early 1900s (above) he claimed that Davenport confessed that he and his brother had never been anything but conjurers and that they had taught the famous magician Harry Kellar (left) many of his tricks

seance room. Members of the audience were invited to tie them up securely. But as soon as the doors were closed strange phenomena occurred. Raps and bangs were heard; hands waved through a small window in the cabinet's centre door and musical instruments were played. A member of the audience was often invited to sit inside the darkened cabinet while these manifestations were produced – yet at the end of the demonstration the brothers were still found to be securely tied.

It was an impressive and entertaining display and large audiences flocked to the best theatres in town when the Davenport brothers took their 'public cabinet seance' on tour in America. But it created the same sort of controversy between believers and sceptics as Uri Geller did in the early 1970s. Certainly any competent escapologist could get in and out of tied ropes in the way the Davenports did, but that does not necessarily make them frauds. They never claimed to be Spiritualists, but they did maintain that their powers were paranormal – which was why, when the *Boston Courier* offered a $500 prize for the production of genuine physical phenomena, the Davenports applied.

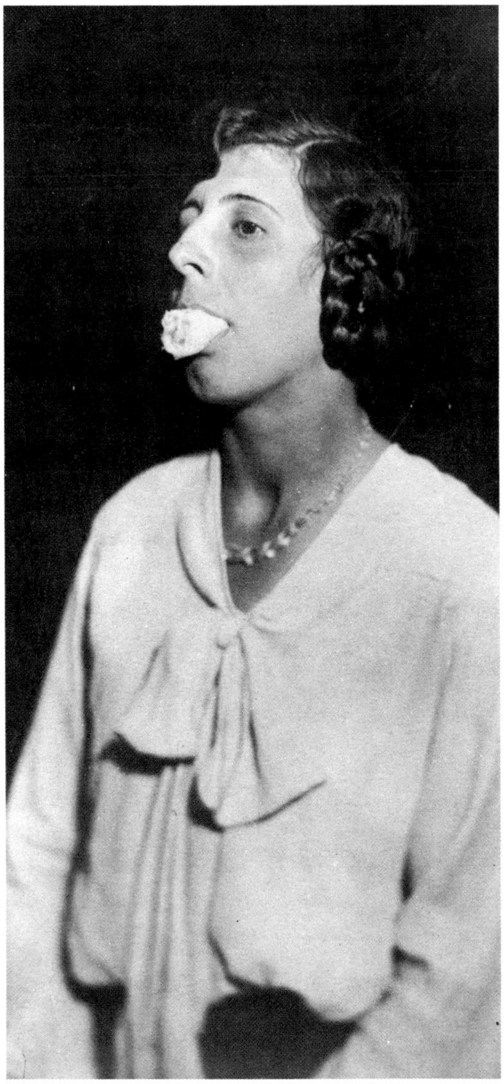

Left: Ethel Beenham, secretary to psychical researcher Harry Price, demonstrates the relative ease with which a large piece of cheesecloth can be held in the mouth – a common method of producing fake 'ectoplasm'

Below: the Polish medium Stanislawa Tomczyk levitates a table simply by lifting up her hands. Extensively investigated by the eminent European psychical researcher Dr Julien Ochorowicz, she was discovered to have extremely impressive psychokinetic powers – although some sceptics have suggested that the objects she moved, apparently through PK, were in fact attached to her hands by fine string. There seems to be no grounds for this allegation, however, wires and strings being the first things any competent investigator looks for. Since Tomczyk's day, the phenomenon of psychokinesis has been demonstrated many times, but increasingly by non-Spiritualists

A committee of professors from Harvard University tested them on behalf of the newspaper. Ira and William were tied up, and the ropes passed through holes bored in the cabinet and knotted on the outside. One of the committee members, Professor Benjamin Pierce, then climbed into the cabinet and the doors were closed.

Just what happened next is a little uncertain. We know that the *Boston Courier* denied one version of the event, which was written by T.L. Nichols, the Davenports' biographer – this was, apparently, fairly favourable. But Professor Pierce would neither confirm nor deny it. What is certain is that when the cabinet doors were opened the brothers were found untied and the professor had the rope twisted around his neck. But even so, the newspaper did not award its $500 prize to the Davenports.

The controversy over the boys from Buffalo came to a head when they took their show on the road in Europe, where they encountered hostile audiences. Their reception in London and other English cities was particularly stormy and things turned ugly in Liverpool where two members of the inspection committee selected by the audience secured Ira and William with a complicated knot. The brothers claimed that it was restricting their circulation – but a doctor who examined them disagreed. The problem was resolved by a helper who used a knife to cut the knot. A riot broke out on the following night and the Davenports left Liverpool in haste. Elsewhere in Britain they received threats that made them decide to end their tour prematurely. As they wrote at the time:

> Were we mere jugglers, we should meet with no violence, or we should find protection. Could we declare that these things done in our presence were deception of the senses, we should no doubt reap a plentiful harvest of money and applause. . . . But we are not jugglers, and truthfully declare that we are not, and we are mobbed from town to town, our property destroyed and our lives imperilled.

But Harry Houdini, the famous escapologist and illusionist, tells a different story. He befriended Ira in the early 1900s, and claimed that Ira admitted that they were no more than conjurers. There is no evidence to support that charge but it is a fact that Harry Kellar, who was also an internationally famous magician, was employed by the Davenports at one time and, in Houdini's words, 'afterwards learned to do tricks which altogether surpassed their efforts in rope-tying and escape.'

It is impossible to know now, over a century later, if the Davenports were genuine or fraudulent, and the theatricality that surrounded their 'seances' must have made it just as difficult for the eyewitnesses to decide. But experiments with physical

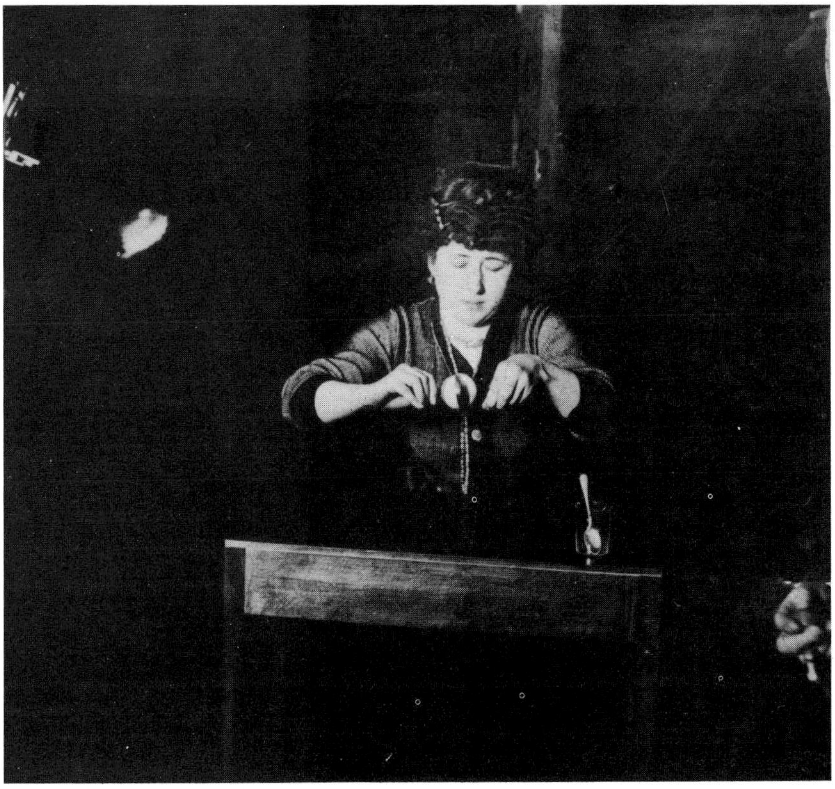

mediums under carefully controlled conditions have occasionally provided very strong evidence in favour of the genuineness of the manifestations they produce.

Sir William Crookes was one of the first physicists to explore the psychic force responsible for producing raps and movements. He tested the most famous of all physical mediums, the levitator Daniel Dunglas Home and became convinced that he possessed strong psychic powers.

Another early investigator of physical forces was Marc Thury, professor of physics and natural history at the University of Geneva, Switzerland, who witnessed the simultaneous levitation of two pianos in the presence of an 11-year-old boy, in the 1850s. Professor Thury suggested that the human body was able to exude a substance that was then manipulated by an unseen force to produce such startling effects. This was the forerunner of the ectoplasmic theory, and one that gained ground with many investigators whose observations appeared to provide a degree of confirmation.

What is puzzling in such cases as the levitating pianos is that, even if the boy had the opportunity to cheat, there is no way in which he could have lifted two such heavy items – or even one of them for that matter. Dr d'Oliveira Feijao, professor of surgery at Lisbon University in Portugal, made a similar observation with a non-professional medium, Countess Castelwitch, who discovered her powers in 1913. The doctor testified that at her seances

> blows were struck, the loudest being on the glass of the bookcase. Articles of furniture sometimes moved. Heavy chairs moved about the room . . . large and heavy books were flung on the floor (our hands being linked all the time).

Kate Goligher, an Irish medium of the 1920s, apparently levitates a table with the aid of ectoplasmic rods. These seem to be obviously fake, especially if seen in close-up (opposite, centre), yet Goligher was never proved to be fraudulent. Spiritualists believe that ectoplasm can exude from a medium and form any shape – fluid or rigid – and can thus account for any seance room phenomena from levitation of objects (or people) to full-form materialisations

Look – no hands

At one of the countess's seances a table weighing 160 pounds (73 kilograms) was raised on two legs when she touched it lightly. Another, smaller, table that was strengthened with sheet-iron was torn into 200 pieces by invisible hands that then piled the pieces into a corner of the seance room.

A few years earlier, Dr Julien Ochorowicz, an eminent European psychical researcher, carried out experiments with a young Polish girl, Stanislawa Tomczyk, who was reported to have the ability to move objects without touching them, stop the hands of a clock and even influence a roulette wheel when she chose the numbers. Dr Ochorowicz not only witnessed the levitation of small objects between Stanislawa Tomczyk's fingers, he also managed to capture the phenomenon on photographs. Sceptics, however, suggested that he had been fooled and that the medium was suspending the items with very thin thread. The researcher replied that during these demonstrations he had passed his hand between the object and the medium's fingers and the levitation was maintained. He put forward the theory that she was able to produce 'rigid rays' from her hands to cause these paranormal effects. Stanislawa Tomczyk never gave seances professionally. She confined her displays to scientific experiments and married Everard Feilding, one of the Society for Psychical Research's leading and most sceptical investigators.

Another physical medium who allowed her powers to be studied in the laboratory was Anna Rasmussen, a Danish woman who discovered her startling powers at the age of 12. A number of scientists conducted experiments with her in the 1920s, including Professor Christian Winther of the Polytechnic Academy of Copenhagen.

The professor held 116 seances with her in 1928, at each one of which some form of physical phenomenon was produced. The medium remained conscious throughout

and usually sat talking, reading or taking refreshments and apparently unconcerned and detached from the manifestations that repeatedly occurred in her presence, including the production of raps, which apparently emanated from her left shoulder, that would answer questions. What impressed the scientists most, however, was the degree of control she could exert over the phenomena. In full daylight she was able to cause the movement of pendulums suspended in a sealed glass case at a distance from her. She was even able to move one pendulum at a time, leaving the others undisturbed, and make it move in whatever direction was requested.

A spectacular career

Nearly 30 years later, the same medium – then Anna Rasmussen Melloni – was asked by modern psychical researchers if she could repeat the demonstration for them. Several successful experiments were carried out in 1956 but because her own pendulums were used to produce the most impressive results this detracted from her achievement in the opinion of some experimenters.

While the early tests with Anna Rasmussen were being conducted in Denmark, a British medium was giving the last seances of her brief but spectacular (and strictly non-professional) career. Stella Cranshaw, a young nurse, was discovered by the colourful and controversial psychical researcher Harry Price in the early 1920s. She agreed to be tested at his National Laboratory of Psychical Research in London and he devised elaborate, ingenious equipment, including a fraud-proof seance table, to test her powers, as well as imposing stringent controls.

This table was really two: one inside another. The top of the inner table was fitted with a hinged trap door that could be opened only from the underside. Musical instruments, such as a harmonica or bell, were placed on a shelf between the legs of the inner table, and a length of gauze was wrapped around the legs. The sides of each table were also enclosed in wooden trellises. These precautions made it impossible for anyone to be able to touch the objects on the inner shelf.

Stella Cranshaw sat at this table with other sitters, two of whom held her hands and feet throughout the proceedings. Soon after she went into a trance, sounds were heard coming from within the table, such as the ringing of a bell or the playing of a harmonica. The trap door in the table top was pushed up from inside and when a handkerchief was placed over it sitters felt finger-like forms moving beneath it.

The greatest achievement of Stella Cranshaw's mediumship in Harry Price's eyes was its successful manipulation of a telekinetiscope: a sensitive piece of apparatus that he had designed. It consisted of a small red light bulb, a battery and a telegraph key. When the key was pressed the light came on. To prevent this happening by normal means, Price designed it so that a soap bubble covered the key. The device was then placed inside a glass shade to prevent the soap bubble drying out. The light was turned on during a seance, apparently by psychokinesis, and when the device was inspected later the soap bubble was found to be still intact.

Stella Cranshaw was tested for a total of five years, but she had little interest or enthusiasm for psychic work. And when she married in 1928 she stopped giving seances altogether. Other physical mediums, however, continued to produce what seemed to be tangible evidence of their strange abilities.

Above left: dark, lace-like ectoplasm, said to have been produced at one of the Goligher seances in Belfast in the 1920s. Almost all such samples are said to have dematerialised, and only one specimen remains in the possession of the Society for Psychical Research – but it is indisputably cheesecloth

Below left: Stella Cranshaw, the young British nurse who was discovered to be a powerful medium by Harry Price in the 1920s. Despite her undoubted gifts, she was never really interested in mediumship and never gave public seances. When she married in 1928 she gave up this part of her life altogether

Apports: a moving story

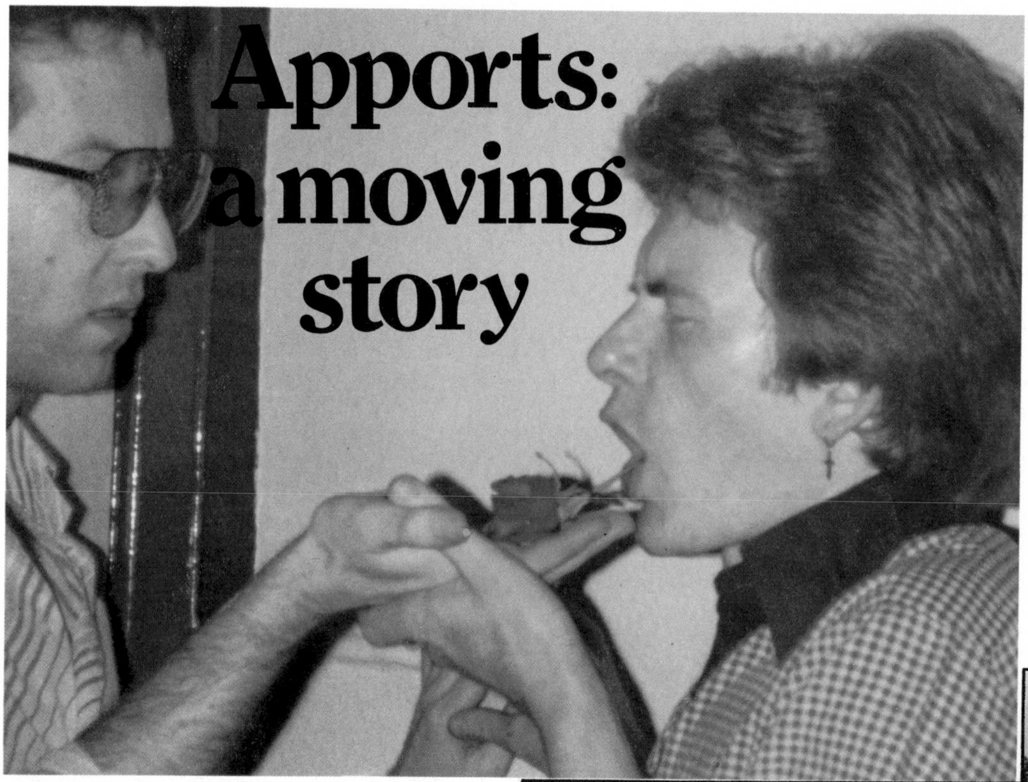

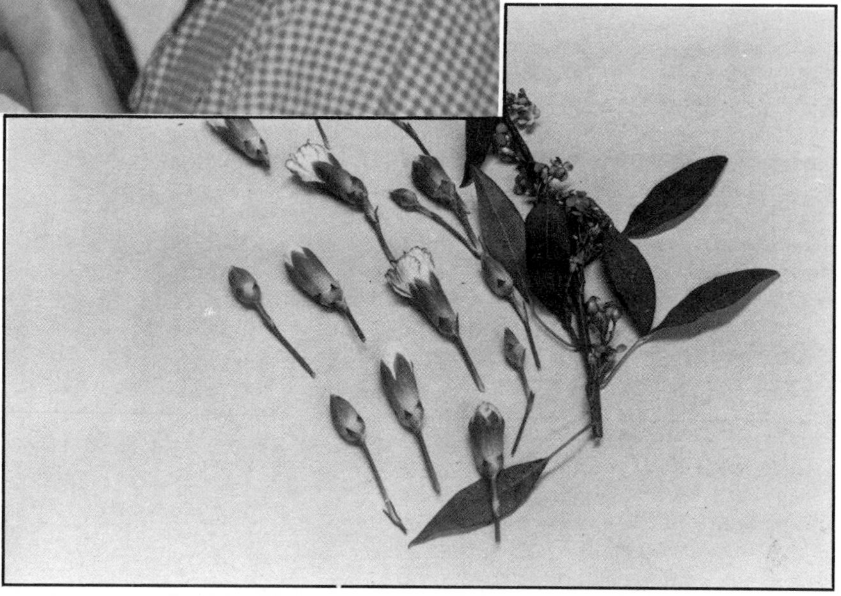

Flowers, fresh fruit, ornaments – even living animals – have been said to have materialised as 'apports' through the physical mediumship of some particularly gifted sensitives. This chapter describes some examples of a controversial phenomenon

IN THE PRIVATE home circle of London medium Paul McElhoney, objects are frequently produced 'out of thin air'. These apparent materialisations are known to psychical researchers as 'apports'. Like other physical phenomena produced by mediums they usually occur in darkness and that rouses the suspicions of believers as well as sceptics. But doubts about the authenticity of apport mediumship frequently evaporate when one considers the conditions under which they are produced, or the type of object that materialises.

In the case of Paul McElhoney, several observers have reported that flowers are apported in his mouth. Spiritualist Michael Cleary told the weekly newspaper *Psychic News* (28 November 1981) of his experience at the medium's home circle a week earlier. He had searched the medium and the seance room before the proceedings began. During the seance the medium was entranced by a spirit called Ceros. 'When Ceros brought the first flowers the lights were on,' said Cleary. 'I looked into Paul's mouth. There was nothing there. Then a [fresh] flower began to fall from his mouth. Carnations are very significant in my family. I had previously asked my mother in the spirit world to bring that kind of flower. When Ceros apported a carnation for me he said it was a present from a woman in the spirit world.'

Another witness to this phenomenon was author and investigator Guy Lyon Playfair, who also received a carnation. When he got home he put it in his mouth and tried to talk as the medium had done. 'The stalk stuck in my throat. I nearly threw up. Paul talked easily and then produced the carnation.'

Flowers have been common apports for well over 150 years. One of the earliest investigators of this phenomenon was a Frenchman, Dr G. P. Billot, who witnessed the production of flower apports by a blind woman medium in October 1820.

One of the most extraordinary accounts of an apport concerns a famous English medium, Madame d'Esperance, in whose presence a materialised spirit named Yolande was said to appear. At a seance in 1880 Yolande took a glass carafe that had been half

Top: physical medium Paul McElhoney produces an apport of a fresh flower from his mouth. There were no signs that it had been regurgitated. Although flower apports (above) appear most often at his seances, other objects have materialised, such as this cast metal model of Cologne cathedral (right), which landed in the palm of SPR council member Anita Gregory – 'from nowhere'. Ceros, McElhoney's spirit guide, said it was a gift from her dead father. Mrs Gregory discovered later that her father had spent his honeymoon in a hotel overlooking Cologne cathedral

filled with sand and water and placed it in the centre of the room, covering it with a thin piece of drapery. The sitters then watched in amazement as the drapery began rising and Yolande came out of the cabinet, in which Madame d'Esperance was seated, to inspect what was happening. When she removed the drapery it was seen that a perfect plant had grown in minutes.

Yolande told the sitters to sing quietly for a few minutes, and when they inspected the plant again they found it had burst into bloom, with a flower 5 inches (12.5 centimetres) in diameter. It had a thick woody stem, which filled the neck of the carafe, was 22 inches (56 centimetres) high and had 29 leaves. It was subsequently identified as a native of India, *Ixora crocata*, and was kept alive for three months by the gardener of one of the witnesses.

Living for the present

Ten years later, the same medium was responsible for an equally spectacular apport. This time – on 28 June 1890 – a beautiful golden lily with an overpowering perfume grew before the eyes of the sitters to a height of 7 feet (2 metres). Five of its 11 flowers were in full bloom, and in photographs taken at the time it was seen to tower above the medium. Yolande told the sitters, however, that it could not remain and became quite upset when she found she could not dematerialise it. She asked them to keep the plant in a darkened room until the next session, on 5 July, when it was placed in the centre of the room. Its presence was recorded at 9.23 p.m. but by 9.30 p.m. it had vanished. The only proof of its existence were the photographs that had been taken and a couple of the flowers.

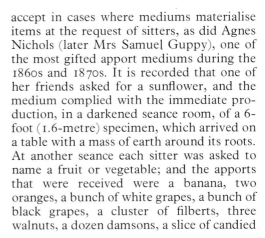

Even with such large apports, the more hardened sceptics could probably suggest ways in which they might have been produced fraudulently. But fraud is difficult to accept in cases where mediums materialise items at the request of sitters, as did Agnes Nichols (later Mrs Samuel Guppy), one of the most gifted apport mediums during the 1860s and 1870s. It is recorded that one of her friends asked for a sunflower, and the medium complied with the immediate production, in a darkened seance room, of a 6-foot (1.6-metre) specimen, which arrived on a table with a mass of earth around its roots. At another seance each sitter was asked to name a fruit or vegetable; and the apports that were received were a banana, two oranges, a bunch of white grapes, a bunch of black grapes, a cluster of filberts, three walnuts, a dozen damsons, a slice of candied pineapple, three figs, two apples, an onion, a peach, a few almonds, three dates, a potato, two large pears, a pomegranate, two crystallised greengages, a pile of dried currants, a lemon and a large bunch of raisins.

Right: Madame d'Esperance, one of the foremost physical mediums of the late 19th century, with the golden lily that – through the agency of her materialised guide Yolande – literally grew in front of her sitters on 28 June 1890 to a height of 7 feet (2 metres). Exuding a strong fragrance and with 5 of its 11 flowers in bloom, it seemed solid enough – yet at her next seance Yolande dematerialised it in seven minutes. All that remained was this photograph and a couple of the flowers

Doves and other birds are as popular with apport mediums as they are with magicians, but their materialisation is achieved under very different conditions. An Australian bootmaker, Charles Bailey, is credited with apporting an entire menagerie during his many years as a medium. To rule out trickery, he allowed himself to be stripped, searched and dressed in clothes supplied by investigators. Dr C. W. McCarthy, an eminent medical man in Sydney, imposed even more stringent test conditions. Having searched Bailey, he then placed the medium in a sack with holes for his hands, and tied him up.

On occasions the sitters were searched as well and the medium placed inside a cage covered with mosquito netting. The door to the room was locked or sealed, the fireplace was blocked and paper pasted over the window. The only furniture allowed in the room was a table and chairs for the sitters. Yet, after a few minutes of darkness, when the lights were put on Bailey was found to be holding apports, such as two nests with a live bird in each. At other seances he produced a live, 18-inch (46-centimetre), shovel-nosed shark and a crab dripping in seaweed. Many of the live apports produced at his seances disappeared as mysteriously as they had arrived.

Later in his career, Bailey's mediumship was found to be far from convincing by a number of investigators who produced evidence to show that he had purchased the 'apports' from animal dealers. But others remained convinced that some of his phenomena were genuine.

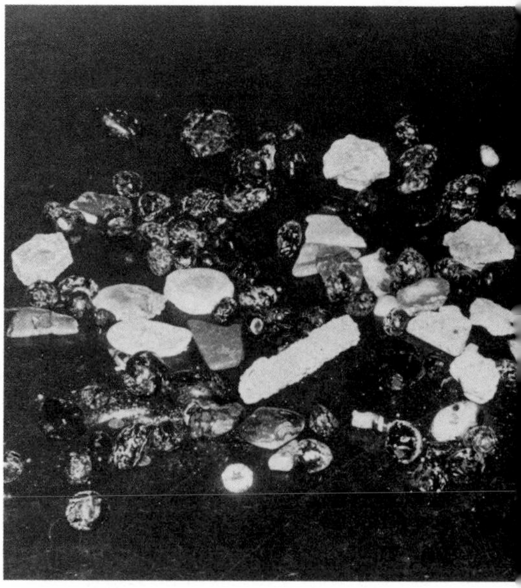

Above: the American medium Keith Milton Rhinehart, whose public demonstration in London in the 1960s provoked a guarded reaction from some members of the audience. He produced several objects (above right) from his mouth, including a prickly sea horse, but there is some evidence that he had merely regurgitated them

Below: two frames from one of the controversial films taken at Rolla, Missouri, USA, which allegedly show the paranormal movement of objects through the glass wall of the minilab. Despite several years of research, none of the minilab pioneers has managed to induce PK on the scale of the physical mediums

Accessories and allegations

But where do apports come from? The 'spirit control' of a famous medium, Mrs Everitt, refused to produce them. 'I do not approve of bringing them,' she explained cryptically, 'for they are generally stolen.' There have been well-corroborated cases, however, where an apport has been an object that has been dematerialised from one place and rematerialised in another, sometimes at a sitter's request. This account was written by Ernesto Bozzano, an eminent Italian psychical researcher:

> In March, 1904, in a sitting in the house of Cavaliere Peretti, in which the medium was an intimate friend of ours, gifted with remarkable physical mediumship, and with whom apports could be obtained at command, I begged the communicating spirit to bring me a small block of pyrites which was lying on my writing table about two kilometres [1.2 miles] away. The spirit replied (through the entranced medium) that the power was almost exhausted but that all the same he would make the attempt.
>
> Soon after the medium sustained the usual spasmodic twitchings which signified the arrival of an apport, but without our hearing the fall of any object on the table or floor. We asked for an explanation from the spirit operator, who informed us that although he had managed to disintegrate a portion of the object desired, and had brought it into the room, there was not enough power for him to . . . re-integrate it.
>
> He added, 'Light the light.' We did so, and found, to our great surprise, that the table, the clothes and hair of the sitters, as well as the furniture and carpets of the room, were covered with the thinnest layer of brilliant impalpable pyrites. When I returned home after the sitting I found the little block of pyrites lying on my writing table from which a large fragment, about one third of the whole piece, was missing.

Apport mediums seem to use different psychic techniques to produce the phenomenon, but with some the object seems to materialise

out of their bodies. T. Lynn, a miner from the north of England, was photographed producing apports in this way. Small ectoplasmic shapes were often seen extending from his body, usually near the solar plexus, and Hewat McKenzie and Major C. Mowbray tested Lynn at the British College of Psychic Science, London, in 1928. The medium was put in a bag and his hands were tied to his knees with tapes. Flashlight photographs taken by the investigators showed luminous connections between his body and the apports.

Another miner, Jack Webber, was photographed some years later producing an apport in a similar way. Webber, a Welshman, was famous as a physical medium at whose seances trumpets would levitate and spirit voices would speak to those present. At a seance in 1938, Webber was searched thoroughly by a policeman in front of all the sitters, then tied to a chair. This account of the seance is taken from Harry Edwards's book, *The mediumship of Jack Webber* (1939):

> The red light was on, sufficiently bright for all to see the medium with his arms bound to the chair. Trumpets were in levitation . . . one of these turned round, presenting its large opening to the solar plexus region and an object was heard to fall into it. It then came to the author who was asked to take out of the trumpet the article within – an Egyptian ornament. After a minute or two the trumpet again travelled to the solar plexus and another object was heard to fall into it.

In November of the same year, at a seance in Paddington, London, Webber's guide announced his intention of trying to materialise a brass ornament from an adjoining room. He asked for a photograph to be taken at a particular moment and said that this ought to record the production of the apport. The sitters then heard the sound of an object falling to the floor. When the plate was developed the small ornament – a bird weighing 2 ounces (57 grams) – could be seen apparently emerging in a white substance from the medium's solar plexus.

Above left: Sai Baba, worshipped as a modern Hindu saint, holds one of his many apports

Above: the ex-miner Jack Webber produces a cord-like string of ectoplasm. On several occasions small ornaments (top) were seen to take shape in a white cloud over his solar plexus, but when handled they were perfectly solid

American medium Keith Milton Rhinehart demonstrated apport mediumship in London in the 1960s at the Caxton Hall. In a well-lit hall, before a capacity audience, he produced a number of items from his mouth, including a very prickly sea horse. Semi-precious stones were also 'apported' *through* his body: they were found embedded in his skin and were plucked out by witnesses. Some members of the audience, however, were distinctly unimpressed: the stones were never seen to emerge through his skin and looked as if they had been deliberately implanted in his flesh. Similarly, some witnesses thought some of his 'apports' to have been merely regurgitated.

But a comparison of the best apport mediums does provide some striking similarities, which indicate that it is a genuine phenomenon. At the turn of the century, Henry Sausse recorded many instances, in *Des preuves? en voilà*, of apports produced by an entranced woman medium. Her method was to form her hands into a cup, in full light, and a small cloud was seen to form inside. This would transform itself instantly into an apport, such as a spray of roses, complete with flowers, buds and leaves.

Although there are countless similar stories of physical mediumship in the literature, the fact remains that apports are rare today. But other, no less remarkable feats of mediumship are constantly reported.

A word to the wise

The voice of the Chinese philosopher Confucius was heard over 2000 years after his death, speaking in old Chinese – but was this just a medium's clever ventriloquism? This chapter investigates this and other claims made for 'direct voice' phenomena

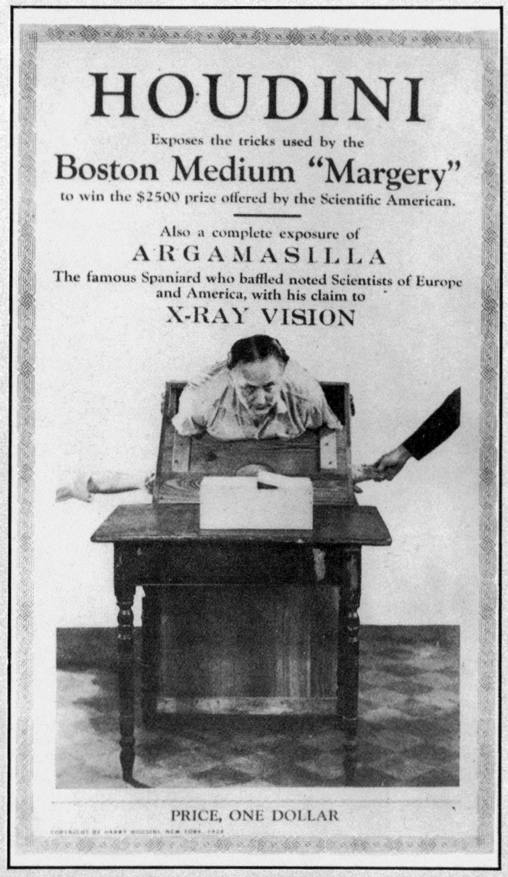

JOHN CAMPBELL SLOAN could have made a small fortune had he exploited his direct voice mediumship commercially. For in his presence the dead were said to speak in their own voices and hold long, characteristic conversations with their living relatives and friends. But Sloan, a kindly, ill-educated Scotsman, chose to be a non-professional medium. For 50 years he gave seances for which he never charged, working instead as a tailor, a Post Office employee, a packer, garagehand and newsagent.

Many of the astonishing direct voice seances that Sloan gave were recorded in a best-selling book written by Spiritualist author J. Arthur Findlay, *On the edge of the etheric*. In this, Findlay gives an account of the very first seance he attended with Sloan, on 20 September 1918. It took place, as is often the case with direct voice phenomena, in a darkened room:

> Suddenly a voice spoke in front of me. I felt scared. A man sitting next to me said, 'Someone wants to speak to you, friend,' so I said, 'Yes, who are you?' 'Your father, Robert Downie Findlay,' the voice replied, and then went on to refer to something that only he and I and one other ever knew on earth, and that other, like my father, was some years dead. I was therefore the only living person with any knowledge of what the voice was referring to.
>
> That was extraordinary enough, but my surprise was heightened when, after my father had finished, another voice gave the name David Kidston, the name of the other person who on earth knew about the subject, and he continued the conversation which my father had begun.

How do sceptics explain such occurrences? Perhaps the medium was a ventriloquist and had chanced upon the information that Findlay thought was known to no one else. He dismisses such 'normal' explanations with this answer:

> No spy system, however thorough, no impersonation by the medium or by any accomplices could be responsible for this, and, moreover, I was an entire stranger to everyone present. I did not give my name when I entered the room, I knew no one in that room and no one knew me or anything about me.

Sloan was sometimes able to produce two or three spirit voices simultaneously. On occasions he went into trance at the start of a seance, on others he remained conscious and held conversations with the spirit communicators.

One of the most gifted direct voice

Margery Crandon, a Boston medium of the 1920s, was exposed as a fraud by Harry Houdini (left), who demonstrated her tricks as part of his stage act. The medium's 'spirit guide', her dead brother Walter, allegedly left his thumb print (bottom, left) after a seance, but this was later proved to be that of a previous sitter (bottom, right). The whorls and ridges (numbered) match exactly. But was Margery always a fraud?

Below: Jack Webber produces ectoplasm. He was said to produce ectoplasmic 'voice boxes' so the dead could speak through them

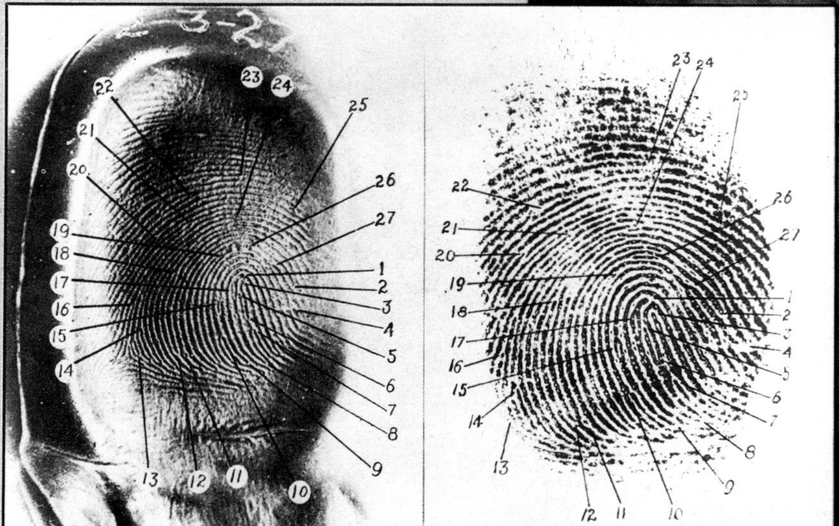

mediums of all time was Mrs Etta Wriedt of Detroit, Michigan, USA. She never went into a trance, nor separated herself from the other sitters by using a cabinet – as many mediums do. Instead, she would sit with the sitters and join in the conversations they had with the spirits. If, however, a foreign language 'came through' she would get out her knitting. She could speak only English.

A British vice-admiral, W. Usborne Moore, also had the opportunity of sitting with Mrs Wriedt when she visited England in the 1920s and testified: 'Frequently two, sometimes three, voices spoke at the same moment in different parts of the circle. It was somewhat confusing.' And at an American seance with the same medium, 'I have heard three voices talking at once, one in each ear and one through the trumpet; sometimes two in the trumpet.' These conversations were so realistic, said Usborne Moore, that he sometimes forgot that he was talking with 'those whom we ignorantly speak of as "the dead"'.

Another testimony to Mrs Wriedt's direct voice mediumship came from the Dowager Duchess of Warwick, who had been one of King Edward VII's mistresses. She first invited the medium to her home because it had been plagued with strange phenomena. On

Above: George Valiantine, American 'trumpet medium' – and accomplished fraud

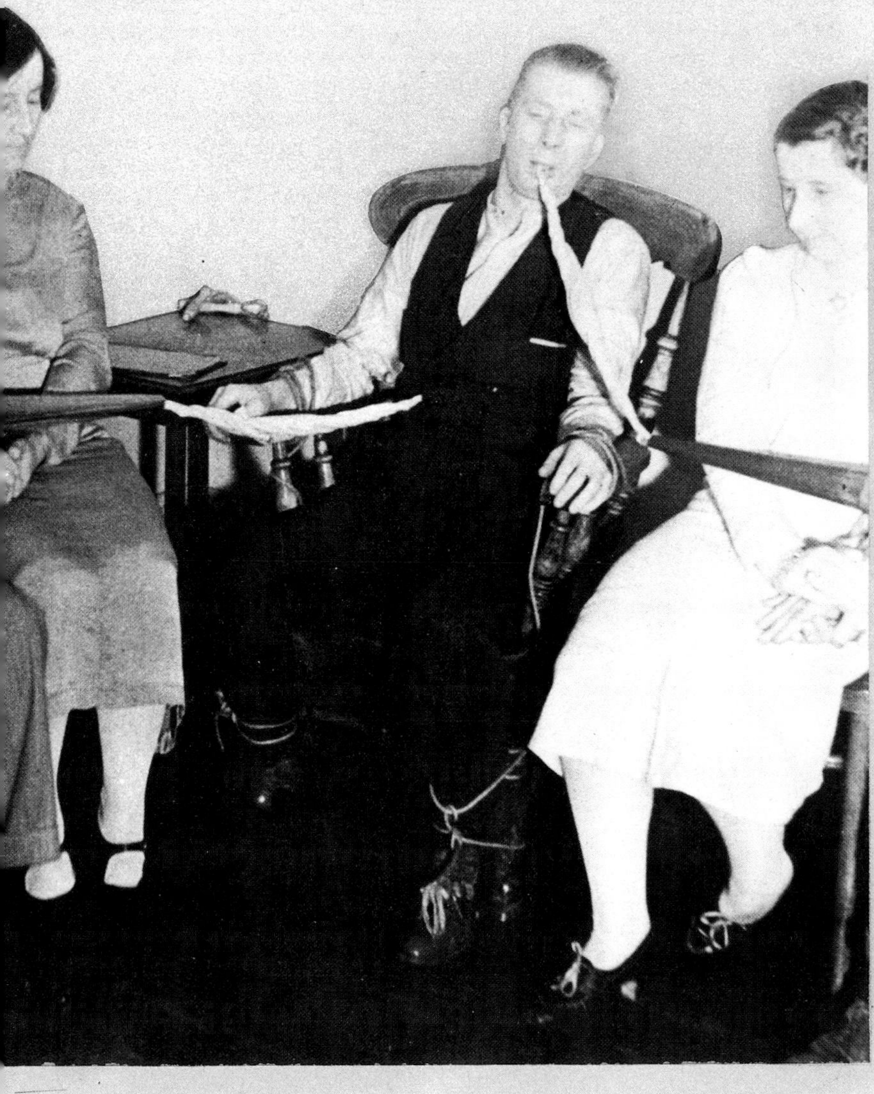

her arrival at Warwick Castle, Mrs Wriedt was shown to her room; some of her belongings, including a seance trumpet, were left in the hall outside her door. Lady Warwick, while waiting for her guest to appear, picked up the trumpet and placed it against her ear. Immediately she heard the characteristic voice of King Edward speaking to her and she was able to carry on a conversation with him, partly in German.

The king became a regular and persistent communicator at subsequent direct voice seances held at the castle – to such an extent that other communicators could hardly get a word in. In view of her former lover's apparent possessiveness from beyond the grave, Lady Warwick decided to terminate the seances with Mrs Wriedt.

A New York medium, George Valiantine, was psychically speaking a late developer. He did not discover his mediumistic powers until he was 43, but soon made an impact, particularly with direct voice seances. In 1924, English author Dennis Bradley brought Valiantine to England, where he gave seances almost every day for five weeks. The invited guests included 50 prominent people, and 100 different spirit voices were said to have communicated. Caradoc Evans, the novelist, spoke to his father in idiomatic Welsh and other spirits spoke in Russian, German and Spanish.

Confucius, he say

The most impressive communication, however, came at a seance in New York in the late 1920s. Strange and unintelligible voices had been heard previously and so Dr Neville Whymant, an authority on Chinese history, philosophy and ancient literature, agreed to attend. Dr Whymant did not remain a sceptic for long. First he heard the sound of a flute played in a characteristically Chinese way, then a quiet, almost inaudible voice said 'K'ung-fu-T'Zu', which is the Chinese version of the name Confucius. Few people, except the Chinese, can pronounce it properly. Even so, Dr Whymant did not believe it was the famous philosopher who was communicating – perhaps it was just someone else speaking his name. But when Dr Whymant began to refer to a passage from Confucius that he believed had been transcribed wrongly, and quoted the first line:

> At once, the words were taken out of my mouth, and the whole passage was recited in Chinese, exactly as it is recorded in the standard works of reference. After a pause of about 15 seconds the passage was again repeated, this time with certain alterations which gave it new meaning. 'Thus read,' said the voice, 'does not its meaning become plain?'

Subsequently, after having the opportunity of speaking to the voice again, Dr Whymant declared that there were only six Chinese scholars in the world capable of displaying

Left: Etta Wriedt, one of the most powerful direct voice mediums of all time. Often two or more voices spoke together; men, women and children 'came through' and spoke clearly, sometimes in foreign languages. When they did so, Mrs Wriedt, who understood only English, got out her knitting. On a visit to England she was invited to Warwick Castle where the Dowager Duchess (below) was experiencing strange phenomena. While showing her to her room, the Duchess picked up Mrs Wriedt's seance trumpet and was astonished to hear her ex-lover, King Edward VII, speaking to her, partly in German. He later became so persistent that the Duchess gave up her seances with Mrs Wriedt

such knowledge of the language and of Confucius, none of whom was in the United States at the time. Dr Whymant also testified to hearing a Sicilian chant at one of Valiantine's seances and he conversed in Italian with another communicator.

The man who brought him to England, Dennis Bradley, claimed that Valiantine had apparently passed on his direct voice powers to him, and another regular sitter, an Italian, the Marquis Centurione Scotto, also developed direct voice mediumship.

One of the last great British mediums to demonstrate direct voice phenomena was a Welsh miner, Jack Webber, whose powers gradually developed at weekly seances run by his in-laws. He refused to use a cabinet because he knew it would be regarded with suspicion. Instead, he allowed himself to be tied to a chair and a red light to be turned on at intervals throughout the seance to allow the sitters to confirm that he was still bound. He also allowed infra-red photographs to be taken at some of his seances, to record a number of physical phenomena including levitation, partial materialisation, and the sessions demonstrating direct voice through trumpets.

His powers were recorded by famous healer Harry Edwards in his book *The mediumship of Jack Webber*, which tells of events recorded over the 14-month period leading up to December 1939, when Webber suddenly died. In that time more than 4000 people witnessed Webber's mediumship.

Edwards heard men, women and children communicating through Webber's seance trumpets, some speaking in foreign tongues, their messages frequently containing intimate personal information. He also testified to hearing two spirit voices singing simultaneously through a single trumpet.

The photographs taken at Webber's seances seem to throw some light on the apparent mechanism of direct voice mediumship. Ectoplasmic shapes are seen to connect the medium with the levitated trumpet and in some of the pictures small round shapes, about the size of a human heart, are seen to be attached to the small end. These are said to be 'voice boxes' through which the dead are able to speak.

Off to a good start

In the United States, one of the most famous physical mediums, Margery (whose real name was Mina) Crandon, allowed some ingenious devices to be used during the investigation of her direct voice mediumship. Margery Crandon was married to Dr L. R. G. Crandon, who was for 16 years professor of surgery at Harvard Medical School. Their seances began in 1923 and a variety of physical phenomena soon developed.

One piece of apparatus used to test her powers was developed by Dr Mark Richardson and consisted of a U-shaped tube containing water, with floats placed on the surface. Margery had to blow into this through a flexible tube, causing one column of water to rise, then keep her tongue and lips over the mouthpiece throughout the seance to prevent the water returning to its original level. (Sitters could verify this in the dark because the floats were luminous.) She did as she was asked, the water level remained as it should, and yet her regular 'spirit' communicator – her dead brother, Walter Stinson – spoke as loudly as ever.

An even more ingenious piece of equipment was invented by B. K. Thorogood: a box consisting of seven layers of different materials containing a large and sensitive microphone. This was closed, padlocked and placed in the seance room to record spirit voices. Two wires ran from it to a loudspeaker in another room. People in the adjoining room were able to hear Walter's voice coming out of the loudspeaker while those in the seance room could hear nothing being spoken into the microphone.

Not all these mediums were above suspicion, however. George Valiantine was accused of fraud on a number of occasions, and when both he and Mrs Crandon allowed themselves to be investigated by the *Scientific American* – a publication that offered $2500 for a demonstration of objective psychic phenomena – they failed to convince the magazine's committee.

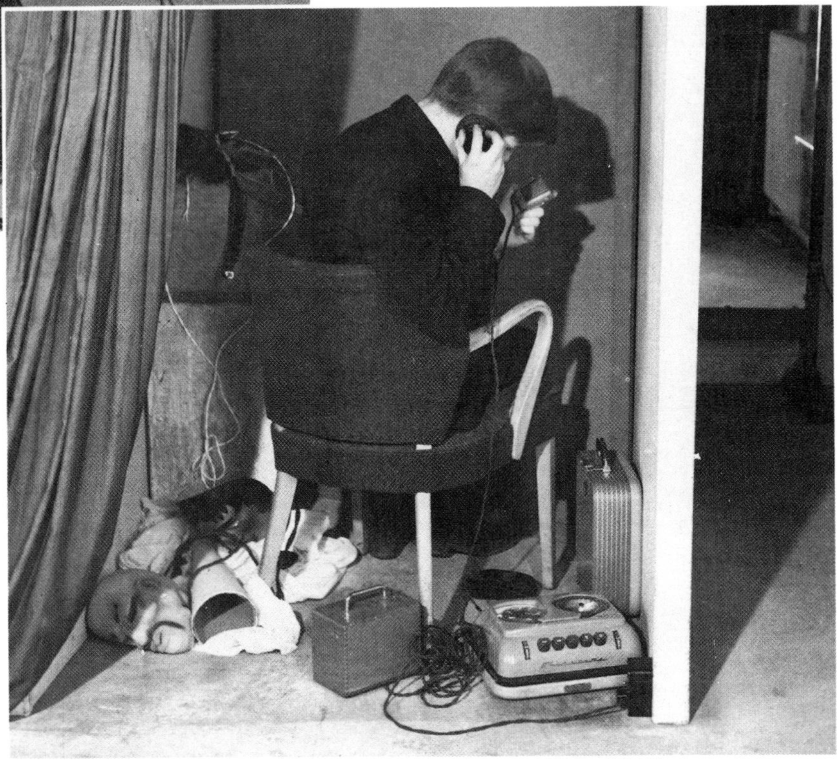

Top: William Roy, self-confessed fake, who claimed to have made £50,000 from his 'direct voice' seances. His confession in 1960 included an exposé of his tricks, such as the use of a confederate in the next room (above). Even so, he later claimed that the confession had been 'a pack of lies' and he set himself up as a medium once more under the name Bill Silver

But it was not their direct voice mediumship that was challenged. Valiantine had produced a series of wax impressions that were said to be the actual thumb prints of famous dead people. He was exposed by Dennis Bradley – the man who had championed him in two previous books – and the damning evidence was published in a third book, *And after*, in which Bradley said the prints 'were produced by Valiantine's big toes, fingers and elbows'.

Margery Crandon also ran into trouble with a thumb print, which was said to have been produced when her dead brother Walter's materialised hand left an impression in wax. In the early 1930s the Boston Society for Psychical Research showed that the thumb print was identical to that of Mrs Crandon's dentist, who had been a sitter at her early seances.

Sceptics believe that if these mediums did produce some of their phenomena fraudulently then it is more than likely that it was *all* phoney, though how they produced some of their most startling direct voice effects is difficult to imagine.

One man who did find a way, and performed successfully for many years, was William Roy – one of the most brilliant and ruthless frauds in Spiritualism's history. His real name was William George Holroyd Plowright and he was a small-time crook before he devised a fraudulent mediumistic routine to make money out of gullible people. He claimed to have made a total of £50,000 from his 'direct voice' seances.

His technique was simple. He used a confederate who searched people's coats, wallets and handbags after they were safely settled in the seance room. He then conveyed any information thus gleaned to the medium via a sophisticated communications system that came into operation when William Roy placed metal plates on the soles of his shoes to tacks in the floor that were apparently holding down the carpet. The 'medium' then used a small receiver in his ear. The same device could be clipped to the end of a trumpet so that the confederate could produce one 'spirit voice' while Roy produced another, simultaneously, using a telescopic rod to levitate the trumpet.

Roy was exposed as a fraud in 1955 and sold his confession to the *Sunday Pictorial* (now the *Sunday Mirror*) in 1960. Despite being a self-confessed fraud, Roy (who had left the country) returned to Britain in the late 1960s and began giving seances once more, using the name Bill Silver. His sitters included some of The Beatles.

It transpired that many people who were now attending 'Bill Silver's' seances knew he was William Roy, the self-confessed cheat. Yet they now believed he was genuine. And when challenged by a Sunday newspaper he claimed that his earlier published confession was 'a pack of lies', published for the money. His days of swindling the public ended in 1977 when he died.

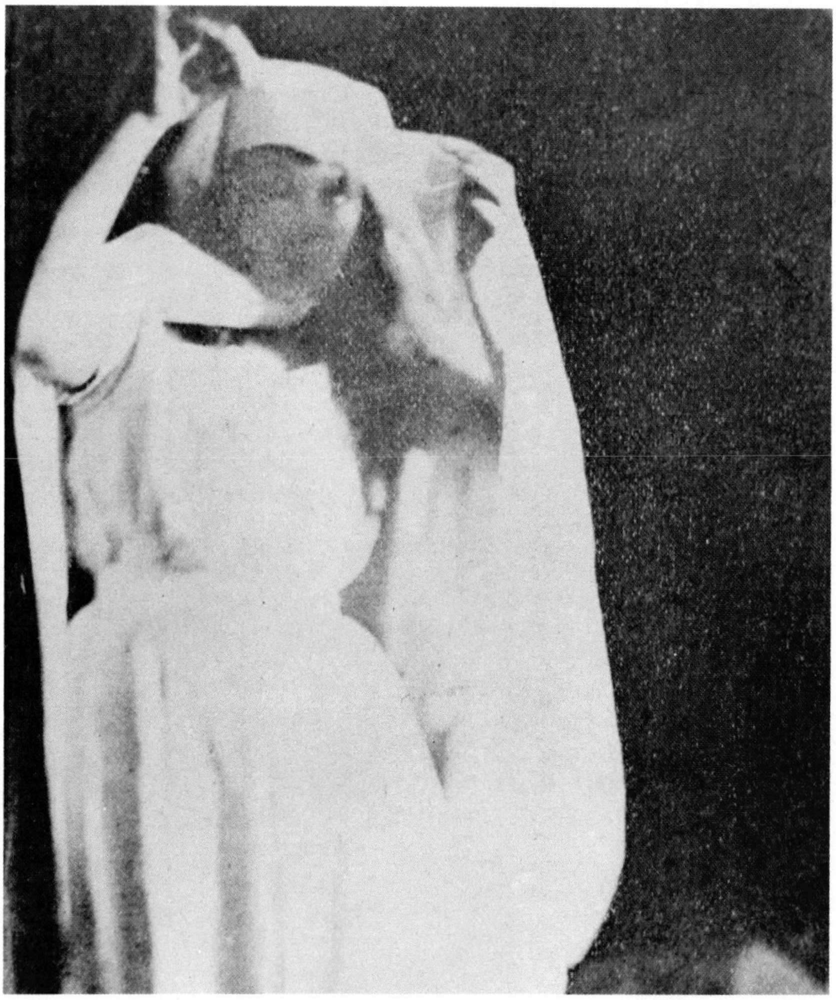

clear, however, that she did not wish to part with it.

Sometimes Yolande's spirit form would gradually dissolve into a mist, on occasions in front of 20 witnesses, and only the scarf would be left lying on the ground. 'At last she has forgotten it,' a sitter would remark. But then the scarf, too, would slowly vanish in the same manner.

Madame d'Esperance was one of the earliest English materialisation mediums and she readily co-operated with investigators who wanted to prove the spirits were not produced by fraud – even to the extent of allowing photographs to be taken. But one particular seance experience suggests that materialisation is not a straightforward phenomenon.

At a seance in Newcastle in 1880 one of the sitters became suspicious because another of Madame d'Esperance's materialisations – known as 'the French lady' – looked uncannily like the medium. He made a grab for the spirit, which promptly vanished. But the medium suffered a lung haemorrhage and was ill for a long time after the seance. On two other occasions similar incidents occurred, but Madame d'Esperance was never found to be producing the strange manifestations fraudulently.

Spiritualists say that touching a materialisation (unless permission has been granted by the 'spirits') or putting a light on during a seance can do untold damage to mediums because it causes the 'ectoplasm' – from which the spirit forms are made – to return to

This too, too solid flesh

Can the dead materialise in their physical bodies in the presence of unusually gifted mediums? There are some rare cases of materialisation where fraud can apparently be ruled out

YOLANDE WAS A 15-year-old Arab girl. She was also, allegedly, a spirit, which meant she could appear and disappear at will, in the presence of a famous English materialisation medium, Madame Elizabeth d'Esperance. Visitors to Madame d'Esperance's seances often claimed to have seen both the materialisation and the medium simultaneously. The way in which Yolande departed from the seance left the witnesses in no doubt that she was a genuine paranormal manifestation, even though she appeared to be a normal, living person while she was materialised.

Being 'only human', Yolande took a liking to a certain brilliantly coloured scarf that a sitter was wearing, and 'borrowed' it. When she dematerialised the scarf disappeared with her, but she was seen to be wearing it at her next seance appearance. She made it

Above: Yolande, alleged spirit guide of Madame d'Esperance

Right: illustration by Tissot, depicting the two materialised spirits he encountered at a seance given by London medium William Eglinton (top right) in the 1880s. It seems logical that a genuine materialised spirit would still be wearing a shroud; but the voluminous clothing would also make an ideal disguise for fake 'spirits'

the medium's body at too great a speed. Nevertheless, there have been cases where materialisations are said to have been produced in daylight.

It was London medium William Eglinton who was responsible for convincing many sceptics. After attending one of his seances, the famous conjurer Harry Kellar declared: 'I must own that I came away utterly unable to explain, by any natural means, the phenomena that I witnessed.' At one point during this seance both Kellar and Eglinton were levitated.

One of the alleged spirits who regularly appeared at Eglinton's seances was Abd-u-lah who had only one arm and was adorned with jewels, rings, crosses and clusters of rubies that were apparently worth a fortune. But another materialisation, a bearded man in a long robe, allowed one of the sitters to cut a piece of material from his clothes and a part of his beard. These were later said to match holes in a piece of muslin and a false beard found in a trunk belonging to Eglinton.

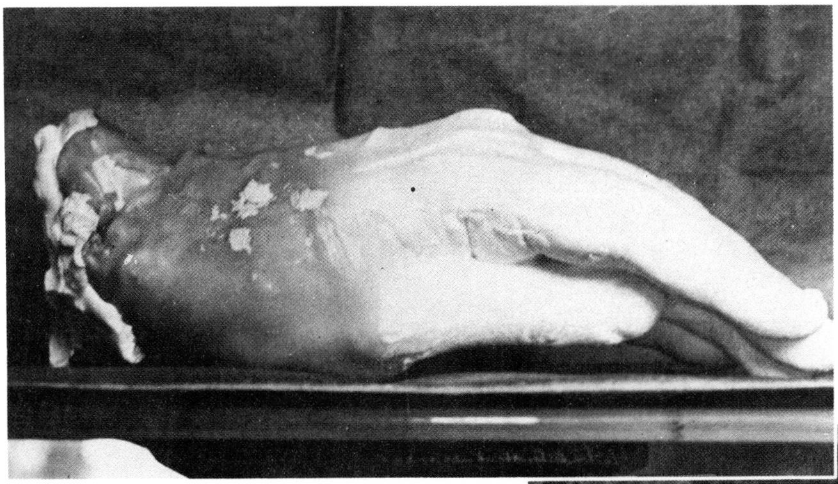

Despite this particular accusation of fraud – which was made by Archdeacon Thomas Colley – Eglinton continued to give seances and impressed many eminent people. He developed slate-writing powers: the spirits were said to write answers to questions on small black slates. William Gladstone visited him on 29 October 1884, and wrote down confidential questions in Spanish, Greek and French. The answers were given in those languages. The prime minister was so impressed that he became a member of the Society for Psychical Research.

The man who claimed to have exposed Eglinton was, ironically, no sceptic: Archdeacon Colley of Natal and Rector of Stockton, England, was a staunch supporter of another materialisation medium, an English clergyman-turned-medium, the Reverend Francis Ward Monck. Monck was not only accused of being a fraud but was sentenced to three months' imprisonment on the evidence of 'props' found in *his* room after a seance in Huddersfield in November 1876. Archdeacon Colley was in South Africa at the time but he was adamant that Monck was genuine.

The problem with materialisations is that they leave no tangible evidence of their reality. Investigator William Oxley, however, came up with an ingenious method of 'recording' the presence of Monck's materialised spirits (one that has been used successfully with other mediums). At a seance in Manchester in 1876 Oxley was able to make excellent paraffin moulds of the hands and feet of materialisations.

Waxing and waning

To make a paraffin mould, warm wax is poured onto the surface of a bowl of water and the materialisation is asked to plunge its hand into it. The spirit form then immerses its hand in a bowl of cold water, causing the wax to harden. The form then dematerialises leaving a glove-like wax cast – often with a very narrow wrist opening from which it would have been impossible for a human hand to withdraw without splitting the mould.

A Polish intellectual, Franek Kluski, was a very powerful physical medium who produced wax impressions in this way. He was never a professional medium, but he offered his services to Dr Gustave Geley and the Institut Métapsychique, Paris, in 1920. This eminent psychical researcher, and other investigators, testified that in Kluski's presence phantom limbs materialised, luminous forms glided around the seance room and brilliant lights suddenly appeared. Under strict controls they were even able to produce photographs of a phantom. And both Dr

Above left: cast of a wax 'spirit glove' made during one of Franek Kluski's seances in Warsaw in the 1920s. The materialised spirit would dip its hand in a bath of liquid wax, then into cold water to let the mould harden. The spirit would then dematerialise, leaving a hard wax cast with a tiny opening at the wrist. Harry Houdini, however, frequently demonstrated the relative ease with which the setting 'glove' could be peeled off before being hardened in cold water (left)

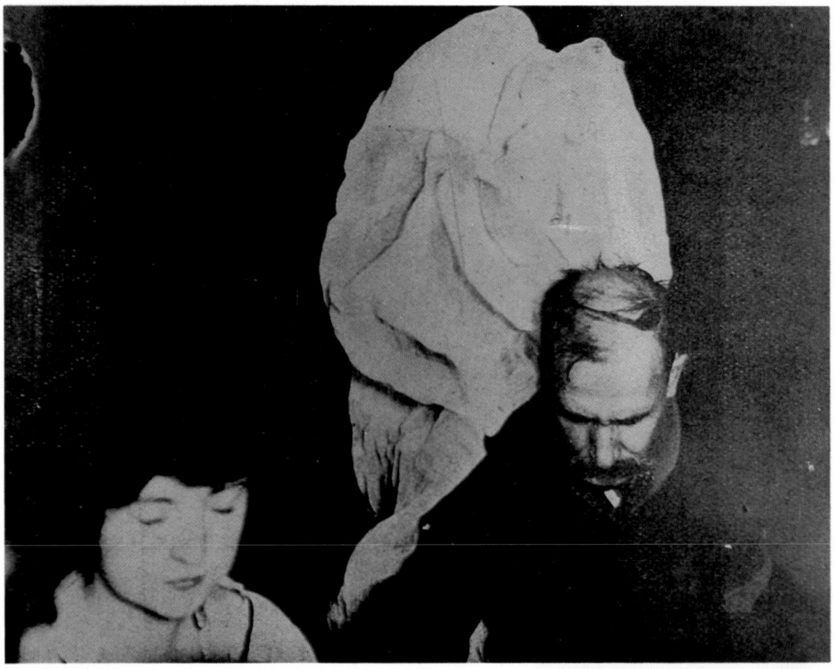

Geley and Dr Charles Richet, who was a professor of physiology in Paris, obtained excellent moulds of materialised hands and limbs with Kluski.

The full-form materialisations that appeared at Kluski's seances (see box) often arrived suddenly, though at other times they were seen to emerge from a faintly luminous cloud above the medium's head.

The materialisations produced by a Cardiff boot and shoe repairer, George Spriggs, seem almost too good to be true, but there is ample testimony from people who witnessed the phenomenon and who were all aware of the precautions that need to be taken against fraud.

Spriggs's paranormal powers developed in a Welsh Spiritualist circle in the late 1870s, beginning with clairvoyance and automatic writing – and culminating in full-form phantoms. He emigrated to Australia in November 1880, taking his psychic powers with him. A prominent Australian named Donovan, a former member of the Legislative Assembly of Victoria, attended Spriggs's seances for 18 months and wrote a book about his experiences, *The evidences of Spiritualism.*

An extraordinary incident occurred at one of the Australian seances when a man materialised and said he wanted to write a letter to a Sydney woman who had visited the seances a couple of times. He was given a pen and paper and wrote a three-page letter, which he placed in an envelope and addressed to the woman. But no one had a stamp. The spirit borrowed sixpence from a sitter and left the seance room to buy one from the shop next door. Word reached the shopkeeper that a phantom was on its way to buy a stamp and he was so flustered that he forgot to give the dead man his change. The spirit realised the error when he got back to the seance room and promptly returned to the shop for the money. The letter was posted and a reply duly received; this was kept until the spirit materialised at another seance, opened it, and read the contents aloud.

Spriggs's ability to produce materialisations faded after six years but he developed the ability to diagnose illness psychically. He returned to Britain in 1900 and between 1903 and 1905 he gave free medical advice in the rooms of the London Spiritualist Alliance.

A demand for healing

Medicine also played an important role in the mediumship of English psychic Isa Northage, and the materialisation seances she gave are perhaps the most astonishing ever recorded. She was a popular medium in the 1940s, visiting churches to demonstrate her psychic powers, which included apport mediumship, direct voice and materialisation. But it was the healing work of her spirit doctor, Dr Reynolds, that was in particular demand and eventually a church was built specifically for this work in the grounds of Newstead Abbey, Northumberland. In time – as the medium's powers grew stronger – Dr Reynolds was able to materialise and carry

Top: a phantom begins to materialise in the gloom of one of Kluski's seances. Spiritualists believe that ectoplasm – the material from which materialisations are formed – is photosensitive; which is why most seances are held in the dark

Above right: the Australian medium George Spriggs. One of his materialisations wrote a letter – and went to the post office to buy a stamp for it

The apeman cometh

Not all of Franek Kluski's materialisations would have been welcome at a party. In July 1919 an apeman made the first of several appearances at a Kluski seance. Dr Gustave Geley reported: 'This being, which we have termed *Pithecanthropus*, has shown itself several times at our seances. One of us. . . felt its large shaggy head press hard on his shoulder and against his cheek. The head was covered with thick, coarse hair. A smell came from it like that of a deer or wet dog.'

And Colonel Norbert Ocholowicz, who published a book about Kluski's mediumship in Polish, in 1926, wrote: 'This ape was of such great strength that it could easily move a heavy bookcase filled with books through the room, carry a sofa over the heads of the sitters, or lift the heaviest persons with their chairs into the air to the height of a tall person. Though the ape's behaviour sometimes caused fear, and indicated a low level of intelligence, it was never malignant. Indeed, it often expressed goodwill, gentleness and readiness to obey. . . .'

materialised form on the opposite side of the operating table. He is of small stature. The medium was deep in trance.

He first took the tweezers and swab with a disinfecting cleaner and swabbed the area. The hernia was umbilical. I collected the swab in the kidney basin. Then I saw him place his hands on the patient's flesh, and they just went in deep, nearly out of sight. He stretched out for the tweezers and swabs and I collected eight soiled ones altogether.

The materialised doctor checked that the patient was comfortable – he had felt no pain – and turned the pencil light on his flesh to inspect the area. There was no sign of a wound or a scar. Dr Reynolds then said he wanted to give the medium a rest before the next operation – and he dematerialised.

Above left: Charles Richet, French scientist and psychical researcher who was president of the SPR in 1905. He was impressed with the mediumship of Kluski, finding no natural, or fraudulent, explanation for his phenomena

Above, left and below: three stages of materialisation, based on the experiences of William Eglinton. The mist that seems to grow up from the medium's solar plexus forms a distinct shape – sometimes an object (as in the case of 'apports'), or an animal or human being. But it always disintegrates

out 'bloodless' surgery on patients. This account, written by Group Captain G.S.M. Insall, VC, is taken from a book about Isa Northage's mediumship, *A path prepared*, compiled and published by Allan Macdonald:

We prepared the room, donned white overalls and masks, as was the rule with Dr Reynolds. This was not new to me as I had been a student in the most up-to-date French hospital before the First World War changed my career to flying. . . . The two patients came in. [Both had hernias.] The first, the one with complications, was partially stripped and placed on the operating table. The other was given a chair nearby.

There was a trolley, and I checked over the instruments – tweezers, swabs, kidney basins and bowls; no cutting instruments at all except scissors to cut lint. There was also a small white pencil light. I checked the emergency door and saw that it was locked and bolted on the inside, and draught excluded by a mat placed on the threshold. I was just closing the inner door leading into the church when somebody noticed that the medium had not arrived. I opened it again, and she came in. The light was turned low and somebody opened in prayer. I could see the medium sitting in her usual chair, a curtain hanging on either side.

Immediately the prayer was over a trumpet rose and Dr Reynolds' familiar voice greeted us all. He then reassured the patients and gave them instructions. . . . I was assigned a kidney basin to collect swabs and stepped forward to the operating table.

The trumpet went down, and almost immediately the doctor appeared in

The phenomenal Palladino

Eusapia Palladino, one of the most thoroughly investigated mediums of all time, was often detected in fraud. But she had genuine powers – that convinced even her most sceptical critics

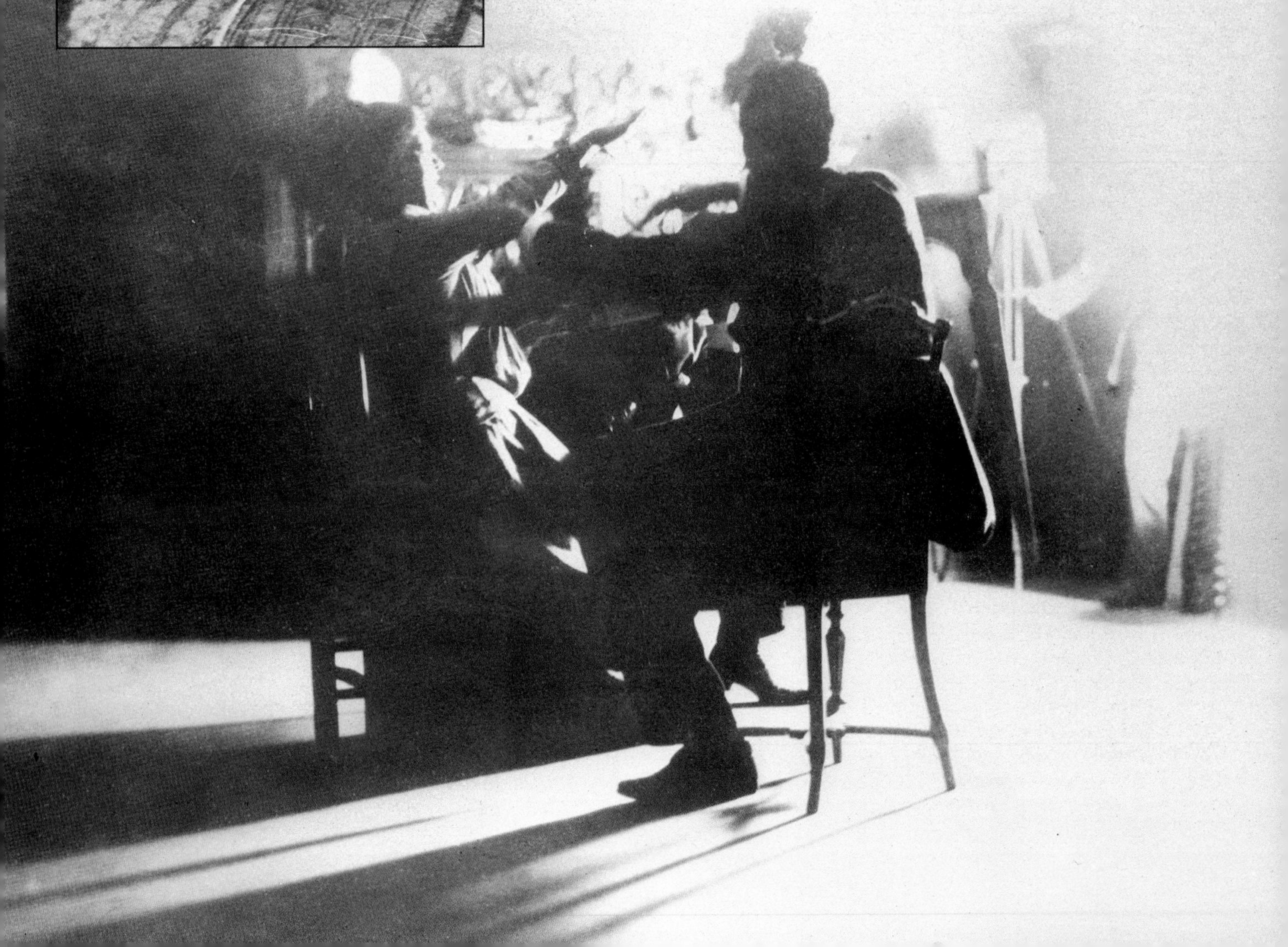

Eusapia Palladino at a Society for Psychical Research (SPR) investigation in 1909 (below) and in close-up (left). Her seances were usually noisy and full of action and variety

ANYBODY WHO SAT AT a seance with Eusapia Palladino could expect plenty of action: heavy furniture moved violently as though with a will of its own, materialised hands grabbed, clasped or stroked the sitters, horns hooted, lights flashed. Palladino produced these phenomena under extremely stringent conditions and did more than any other medium to convince psychical researchers that physical manifestations in the seance room were real – even though she was often caught out in fraud.

Eusapia Palladino was born into a peasant family in January 1854 near Bari in Italy. Her mother died while giving birth to her, and Eusapia became an orphan at the age of 12, when her father met a violent death by murder.

The centre of strange phenomena from an early age, she was only a teenager when her mediumistic powers were revealed. This came about in a remarkable way. In 1872 the English wife of an Italian psychical researcher called Damiani attended a seance in London. A spirit who identified himself as John King 'came through' and told her that there was in Naples a very powerful medium who was the reincarnation of his daughter,

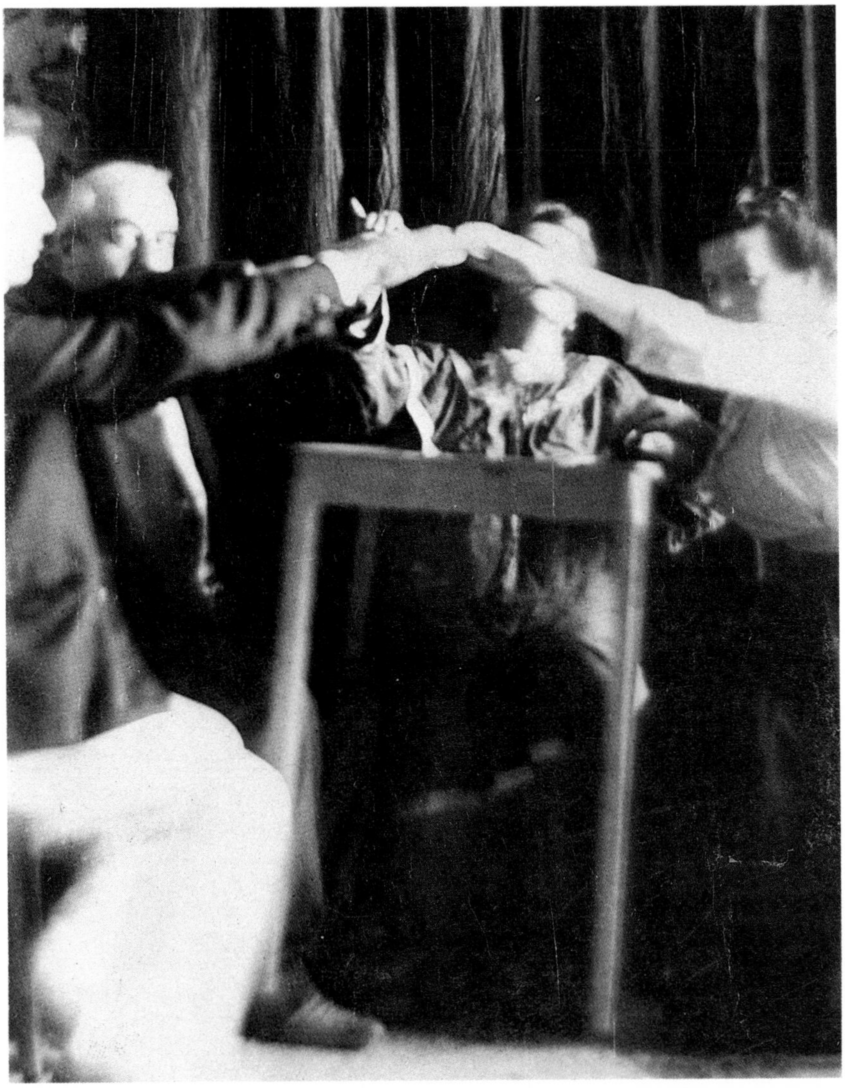

Palladino lifts a table at a seance in Genoa, Italy, in 1906. Table-turning featured heavily in this medium's production of phenomena – sometimes, in fact, the tables became quite violent and even appeared to attack sitters

the famous Katie King. He then gave the full address of the house where this unknown psychic could be found. Damiani went there and, astonishingly enough, found Eusapia Palladino. He became the young girl's mentor and helped her to develop her powers.

The first scientist to declare his belief in Palladino's genuineness was Dr Ercole Chiaia. He did so in an open letter to Cesar Lombroso in 1888, after Lombroso, a well-known psychiatrist and criminal anthropologist, had written in an article that he and his friends laughed at Spiritualism. Chiaia invited Lombroso to witness a special case – Eusapia Palladino:

> Either bound to a seat, or firmly held by the hands . . . she attracts to her the articles of furniture which surround her, lifts them up, holds them suspended in the air . . . and makes them come down again with undulatory movements, as if they were obeying her will. She increases their height or lessens it according to her pleasure. She raps or taps upon the walls, the ceiling, and the floor, with fine rhythm and cadence. . . .
>
> This woman rises in the air, no matter what bands tie her down. She seems to lie upon the empty air, as on a couch, contrary to all the laws of gravity; she plays on musical instruments – organs, bells, tambourines – as if they had been touched by her hands or moved by the breath of invisible gnomes . . . .
>
> How many legs and arms has she? We do not know. While her limbs are being held by incredulous spectators, we see other limbs coming into view, without her knowing where they come from.

When Lombroso visited Naples two years later and accepted the invitation to sit with Eusapia Palladino, he was impressed. Indeed, as a result of his experiences with the medium, Lombroso spent many years investigating the paranormal; his books on the subject show that he finally came to believe that spirits of the dead were responsible for producing mediumistic phenomena.

A staunch supporter

In 1892 a group of researchers known as the Milan Commission held 17 sittings with Eusapia Palladino. They issued a report that said, in part:

> It is impossible to count the number of times that a hand appeared and was touched by one of us. Suffice it to say that doubt was no longer possible. It was indeed a living human hand which we saw and touched, while at the same time the bust and the arms of the medium remained visible, and her hands were held by those on either side of her.

Unlike other mediums, Palladino did not sit behind a curtain during her seances. She did use a cabinet, which she claimed helped some of the phenomena build up, but she always sat in front of it. Whether she and her investigators sat in total darkness, or whether there was sufficient light to see her clearly, she always allowed the witnesses to tie her or hold her securely in the chair to satisfy themselves that she could not cheat.

Among the members of the Milan Commission was Charles Richet, professor of physiology at the Faculty of Medicine in Paris, who became one of her staunchest supporters. He conducted more than 100 seances with her and, as one of Europe's leading psychical researchers, was better placed than any other investigator to give a verdict on her psychic powers – a verdict that was favourable.

Professor Richet introduced various controls into his experiments with Palladino in order to prevent her cheating. In his book *Thirty years of psychical research* (1925), he tells of a table that was specially made for her seances:

> The legs were pointed so that it would be difficult to raise it with the foot . . . .

> We thought it much too heavy (44 pounds) [20 kilograms], but we tried it the same evening. As soon as Eusapia touched this heavy table with the tips of her fingers, it tilted, swaying about, and without the legs being touched at all, it rose up completely with all four feet off the ground.

Tables feature prominently in accounts of Eusapia Palladino's mediumship. P. Foa, professor of pathological anatomy at the University of Turin, and a team of scientists, including one Dr Arullani, held a series of experimental seances with the medium. At one of these, she advised them not to touch any levitated objects because she would not be able to restrain their movements and someone might be hurt.

Immediately, one of the tables in the room floated into the air, over Professor Foa's head, and returned to the floor where it flipped over, then stood up on its legs again. At this point Dr Arullani approached it but, says the scientists' report:

> The piece of furniture moving violently towards him, repulsed him; Dr Arullani seized the table, which was heard to crack in the struggle . . . [it] passed behind the curtain . . . . Professor Foa saw it turn over and rest on one of its sides, whilst one of the legs came off violently, as if under the action of some force pressing upon it. At this moment the table came violently out of the cabinet, and continued to break up under the eyes of every one present. Dr Arullani . . . was invited by the medium to approach the cabinet. He had hardly reached it when he felt himself hit by pieces of wood and hands, and we all heard the noise of the blows.

Top: the table used by the SPR for testing Palladino was designed specially to detect fraud

Above: Charles Richet, a French physiology professor, and Cesar Lombroso (left), an Italian psychiatrist, were both convinced of Palladino's powers, despite their knowledge that she would sometimes cheat

In 1895 Palladino, already much investigated, visited England to give a series of seances at Cambridge for the Society for Psychical Research (SPR). This was after two of its founding members, F.W.H. Myers and Sir Oliver Lodge, had attended seances with her at the home of Professor Richet and had given favourable reports.

One of the witnesses at Cambridge was Dr Richard Hodgson, who suspected that Eusapia Palladino could not do anything without cheating. Although he was supposed to be controlling her movements, he deliberately relaxed his guard – and Palladino did cheat. The SPR pronounced her a fraud, but European investigators were unimpressed by this 'exposure'. They were aware that the medium would use trickery if given the opportunity, and had said as much in their reports. Their attitude was that, had the SPR controls been stringent, the phenomena would have been genuine.

Moods of a medium

Camille Flammarion, a leading French astronomer, was another investigator of Eusapia Palladino. During one of the series of seances he conducted, he reported that the medium became very irritable and the phenomena became destructive:

> The sofa came forward when she looked at it, then recoiled before her breath; all the instruments were thrown pell mell upon the table; the tambourine rose almost to the height of the ceiling; the cushions took part in the sport, overturning everything on the table; [one participant] was thrown from his chair. This chair – a heavy dining-room chair of black walnut, with stuffed seat – rose into the air, came up on the table with a great clatter, then pushed off. . . .

Eusapia Palladino continued to produce convincing physical phenomena for Continental researchers, and eventually the SPR decided

Dr Richard Hodgson (left), a lawyer and noted psychical researcher, and Camille Flammarion (below), a famous astronomer, were among the many respected professional men who investigated Eusapia Palladino. Hodgson sat at the first of Palladino's seances at Cambridge in 1895 at which her cheating made British psychical researchers unwilling to test her again for some years

Below right: Palladino, with Everard Feilding (left) of the SPR, at the fourth of 11 seances held in Naples, Italy, in 1908. On her right is Professor Galeotti of Naples University. All the SPR investigators were particularly sceptical of Palladino – and all became convinced that the phenomena they witnessed were real

to re-open the case. In 1908 they sent a team of three to Naples to attend seances with her.

The members of that team were probably the most sceptical of all the SPR investigators – Everard Feilding, Hereward Carrington and W.W. Baggally. They concluded that the phenomena they witnessed, including levitation, movement of objects and the production of lights, raps and materialised shapes, were due to some kind of agency 'wholly different from mere physical dexterity on her part'. After the sixth of the 11 seances, which were held in a room at the Hotel Victoria in Naples, Feilding wrote:

> For the first time I have the absolute conviction that our observation is not mistaken. I realise as an appreciable fact of life that, from an empty curtain, I have seen hands and heads come forth, and that behind the empty curtain I have been seized by living fingers, the existence and position of the nails of which were perceptible. I have seen this extraordinary woman, sitting outside the curtain, held hand and foot, visible to myself, by my colleagues, immobile, except for the occasional straining of a limb while some entity within the curtain has over and over again pressed my hand in a position clearly beyond her reach.

A year later, however, Eusapia Palladino was caught cheating again, this time in the United States. She spent seven months in America from 1909 to 1910 and impressed many investigators. But at one of her seances a man managed to slip under the curtain of the cabinet and from that vantage point 'saw that she had simply freed her foot from her shoe and with an athletic backward movement of the leg was reaching out and fishing with her toes for the guitar and the table in the cabinet'.

At another American seance a conjurer who concealed himself under the seance table caught her in deceit. But another, and more famous, stage magician, Howard Thurston, testified that the table levitations he witnessed in her presence 'were not due to fraud and were not performed by the aid of her feet, knees or hands'.

Willed by the sceptics

The man who invited her to visit the United States was Hereward Carrington, one of the three SPR investigators sent to Naples, and after the unfortunate American episode he observed:

> Practically every scientific committee detected her in attempted fraud, but every one of these committees emerged from their investigations quite convinced of the reality of these phenomena, except the Cambridge and American investigations which ended in exposure.

The medium herself never denied that she

sometimes cheated. She explained that when she was in trance, she could be willed to play tricks by the sceptics among her sitters. But her defenders argue that some of the 'exposures' may have come from a mistake on the part of the observers, rather than from conscious or subconscious cheating on Palladino's part. It was common at her seances for limb-like objects to appear extending from her body, even when her hands and feet were clearly visible and being held. Perhaps, say her supporters, her detractors saw these ectoplasmic extrusions – called pseudopods – and mistook them for her own feet.

Whatever the truth about these phenomena, there is another aspect of Eusapia Palladino's mediumship that was not challenged and that, it seems, would be difficult to fake under the conditions that prevailed. At many of her seances, human-like forms or parts of bodies materialised. Sometimes they were seen clearly and sometimes they were felt through the curtain of the cabinet by the researchers.

Above: a drawing of how Eusapia Palladino was caught out in fraud at a Columbia University seance in New York in 1910. Although the medium did not deny that she occasionally cheated, the Americans never gave her another chance to prove that her powers were at least sometimes genuine

Left: Professor Enrico Morselli believed that he saw 'six phantoms' of human-like form appear at a seance with Palladino in Italy in 1902. Palladino was noted for her materialisations, some produced in fairly good light

Professor E. Morselli and eight other researchers had a memorable experience of this phenomenon at a seance in Genoa on 1 March 1902. Morselli examined the medium and then tied her to a camp bed in a way that prevented her escaping. In fairly good light he and the others present saw six phantoms appear. Each time, as soon as the materialised figure returned to the cabinet, Morselli went to it immediately and found the medium still tied up, exactly as she had been left.

Professor Richet also testified to the medium's powers of materialisation: 'More than 30 very sceptical scientific men were convinced, after long testing, that there proceeded from her body material forms having the appearance of life.'

At a seance held on 16 June 1901, attended by Dr Joseph Venzano, several phantom hands materialised and stroked the sitters. Finally, they took hold of Venzano's hands:

> When my hand, guided by another hand, and lifted upwards, met the materialised form, I had immediately the impression of touching a broad forehead, on the upper part of which was a quantity of rather long, thick, and very fine hair. Then, as my hand was gradually led upwards, it came in contact with a slightly aquiline nose, and, lower still, with moustaches and a chin with a peaked beard.
>
> From the chin, the hand was then raised somewhat, until, coming in front of the open mouth, it was gently pushed forward, and my forefinger, still directed by the guiding hand, entered the cavity of the mouth, where it was caused to rub against the margin of the upper dental arch, which, towards the right extremity, was wanting in four molar teeth.

Dr Venzano recognised in the materialisation a relative who was very dear to him and who had died some years earlier. But he was not sure which teeth that relative had had missing. When he checked this later, he found that they coincided exactly with the gaps in the phantom's teeth.

Despite the fact that most of Palladino's investigators were convinced that she had genuine powers, the American 'exposure' marked the end of the medium's international career. For the next eight years, until her death in 1918, little was heard of her. But it is known that she continued to produce physical phenomena at seances in her own country.

To this day, Eusapia Palladino remains something of an enigma, and controversy continues about her manifestations. Without doubt, however, she was of the greatest historical importance to psychical research in the 20th century. Arguably, she was also the greatest medium of modern times.

A fine pair

Willi and Rudi Schneider became celebrated mediums in the 1920s and were stringently investigated by leading psychical researchers of the day. Yet doubts remain about their authenticity

IN THE SPRING OF 1919 rumours began flying around the small Austrian city of Braunau. It was said that spirits were being conjured up in the flat of Herr Josef Schneider. Twenty years later the psychical investigator Harry Price was to write of Braunau as 'a charming frontier old-world village which is famous as the birthplace of three distinguished persons – Adolf Hitler, and Willi and Rudi Schneider, the Austrian physical mediums.'

Josef and Elise Schneider had 12 children altogether, nine boys and three girls, but only six boys survived: Karl, Hans, Fritz, Willi, Franz and Rudi.

Rudi, the youngest, was born on 27 July 1908. His parents, disappointed that he was a boy, put him in girls' clothing, curled his hair and even called him 'Rudolfine' for a time. He seemed to have survived the ordeal, taking up the traditionally boyish pursuit of football and showing a special interest in cars and aeroplanes – a preoccupation he shared with his brother Willi who was five years older.

There are slight variations in the stories of how the mediumistic activities began. The most widely told version is that in the early spring of 1919, officers stationed at Braunau

Willi Schneider in a state of trance during a seance in Munich in 1922. Two German psychical researchers are acting as controllers

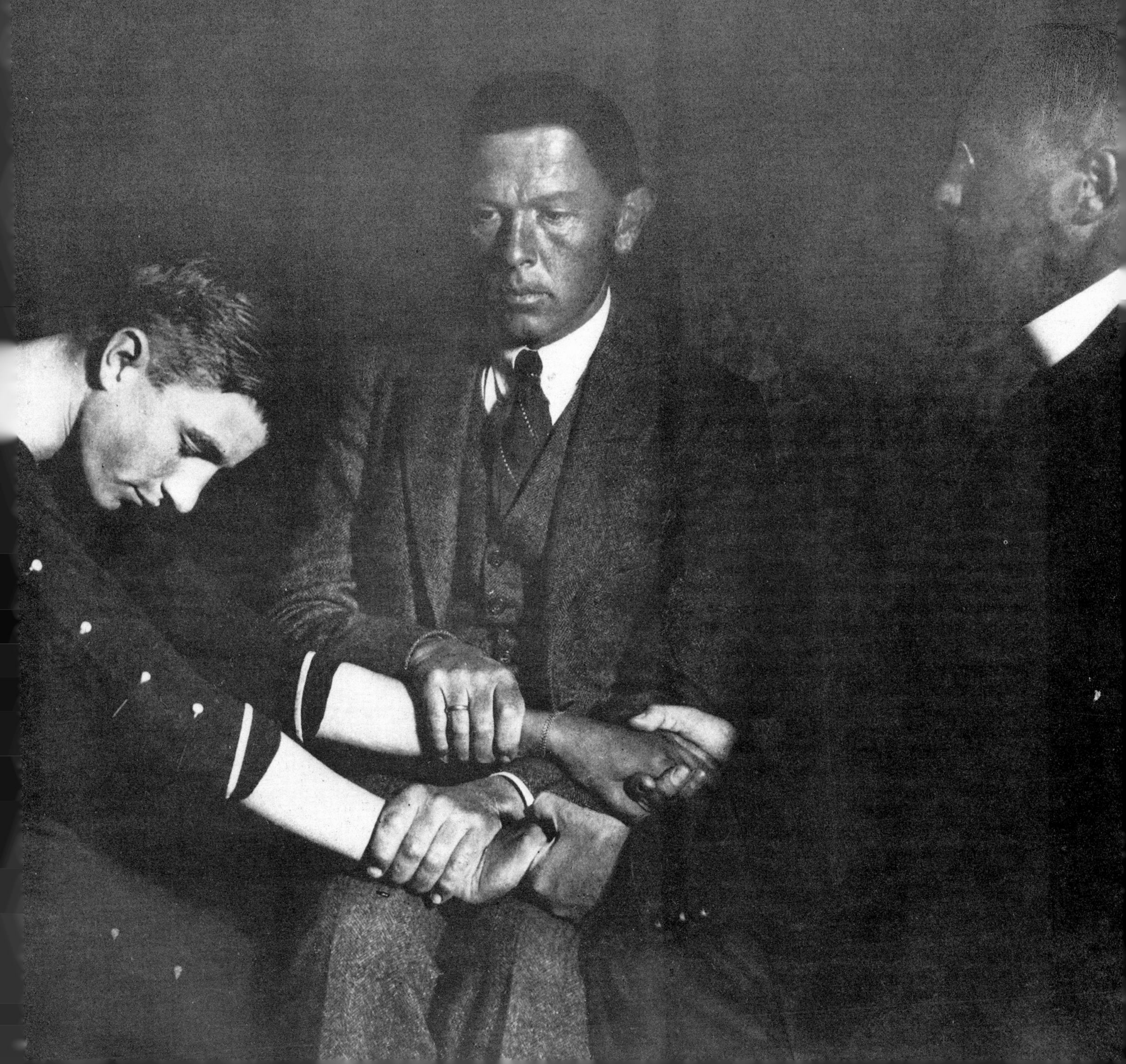

Left: Elise and Josef Schneider with their psychic sons Rudi and Willi. Josef, who worked as a typesetter in a local printing house, kept a detailed record of Rudi's seances in two thick exercise books that became known as Vater Schneider's ghost books

Right: Lola Montez, the dancer and famous beauty who lived from 1818 to 1861 and had a notorious liaison with King Lugwig I of Bavaria which may have cost him his throne. At first Olga, Willi Schneider's spirit guide, claimed to be Lola; but Olga could not understand English even though Lola had been the daughter of a British army officer; nor could Olga give any details of Lola's life

began buying large quantities of paper from the print shop below the Schneider flat. The family discovered that the officers were holding spirit seances, and the paper was needed for recording spirit messages being spelt out by a planchette – a small board mounted on castors, and with a pencil attached.

Mrs Schneider and some friends decided to experiment with a planchette themselves, but without success. When some of the Schneider boys returned home one afternoon they also tried but the planchette would not move. It was only when Willi arrived and took a turn that the planchette began to slide across the paper. Josef Schneider, who was affectionately known as Vater ('Father') Schneider, explained what happened:

> It began to write 'Olga' in beautiful handwriting. Everyone was astonished and someone from the circle called out 'Well, what sort of an Olga are you then?' The reply was 'I was the mistress of the King of Bavaria, called Lola Montez.' Now the questioning began and every day until midnight we did table turning and writing.

Initially, the planchette appeared to move most fluently when Willi's hand was resting on it. Then one day, it apparently moved when his hand was not on but above it. As the questioning continued, Olga does not seem to have repeated or insisted upon her claim that she was Lola Montez, a colourful and tempestuous Irish-Spanish dancer, created Countess von Landsfeld by King Ludwig I who had to abdicate his throne in 1848, some claim, because of his liaison with Lola. History tells how Lola could speak English fluently whereas Olga could not even understand it. And, indeed, on later occasions when Olga was asked to give details about Lola's life she was unable to do so. It seems likely that her identity was wished on her by the seance participants, but not by Willi, nor by Olga herself.

Vater Schneider asked Olga if they could help her in any way. She wrote that they could indeed: would they have some masses said for the repose of her soul, please? The family were devout enough Catholics to comply with her request, though not sufficiently obedient members of their Church to desist from having seances. The masses were said, the seances continued. Olga was apparently grateful for their help and she promised that in return for their kindness she would make their name famous throughout the world. This promise she kept: the events that took place that day were to signal the beginning of a series of paranormal phenomena that were to startle the world.

Olga instructed the family to cover a kitchen stool with a large cloth and to place objects – including handkerchiefs and a basinful of water – near it. Willi sat next to the stool and, apparently, within a short time strange things started to happen. The water splashed out of the bowl, two tiny hands appeared to materialise, the sound of clapping was heard, objects placed near the stool were said to move; a handkerchief, for instance, was drawn beneath the cloth and then thrown out again with knots tied in the four corners, and sometimes the hands seemed to tap those of the onlookers. Throughout the activities Willi seemed unconcerned and appeared to be enjoying the chaos that was being created around him.

One of the witnesses was a Captain Kogelnik, a man not naturally predisposed to believe in occult goings-on and rather inclined to dismiss them as antiquated, medieval rubbish. However, that first encounter with Willi Schneider's mediumship was to transform his outlook. According to Kogelnik, in those early days before Willi became an international celebrity, his ability to produce phenomena was at its height:

> Not even the slightest attempt was made by him to support the supernormal phenomena through normal means. He never fell into trance: he himself watched the manifestations with as much interest as any other person present.

Kogelnik describes how, on one occasion, the cloth over the stool lifted and a small hand emerged: 'I quickly and firmly grasped it and was just about to draw out from the table what I thought must be there – when I found my closed fist was empty and a heavy blow was dealt against it.'

Below: the small Austrian city of Braunau, where Willi and Rudi Schneider were born and brought up

Below right: Willi producing ectoplasm at one of his early sittings. Witnesses who saw the ectoplasm described it as a cobweb-like substance, or like an undulating, phosphorescent fog emanating from the boy's head

Increasing conviction

As Kogelnik returned to the Schneider household and regularly witnessed Willi's skills, he became increasingly convinced that he was observing genuine physical phenomena. They were, he wrote, splendid:

> A zither was put on the floor, close to the table cloth, and out from under the table there came a small hand with four fingers stroking the strings and trying to play. This hand was well visible, looked like that of a baby and was very well developed in every detail as far as the wrist, above which it passed off into a thin . . . glimmering ray which disappeared behind the table cloth. . . . A large brush was put before the table cloth. The hand grasped it and began energetically to brush the floor in front of and behind the cloth. . . .

To begin with, Olga had written out her wishes and instructions while Willi was fully awake. After a time, however, she began to speak through him while he was in a trance; when this happened his voice came out as an unfamiliar hoarse whisper. Also at this stage, another phenomenon occurred: Willi began producing ectoplasm. Kogelnik described it as being a cobweb-like substance, first wrapped around the medium's face, then materialising on one shoulder, then the other. The

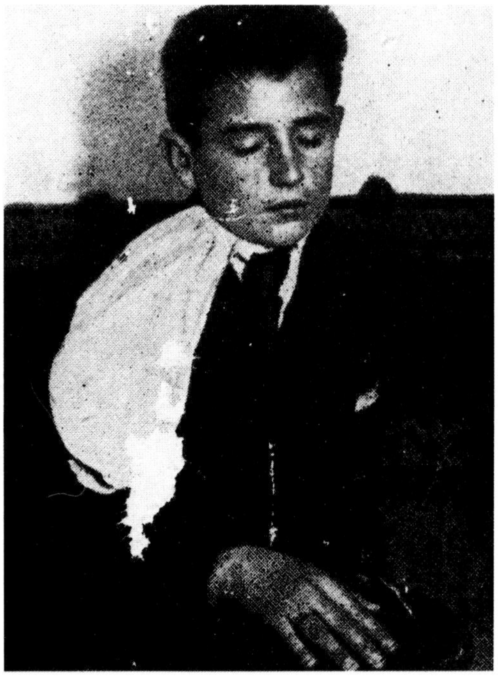

substance seemed to disappear without a trace. One day Olga invited Kogelnik to take a closer look. From a distance of about 10 inches (25 centimetres) he saw a faint undulating phosphorescent fog being emitted from the boy's head. It eventually appeared to settle on Willi's hair like a cap, before being withdrawn into the body through his nose.

Neither was this the most extraordinary occurrence. On one occasion a phantom 5 feet (1.5 metres) tall gracefully danced a tango for the delighted onlookers before disappearing, perhaps in search of a partner.

Not surprisingly, Willi's phenomena soon attracted local and then international attention. Various scientists went to Braunau to investigate. Among the most important figures in psychical research in Europe at that time was Baron von Schrenck-Nötzing. Kogelnik contacted him, aware that he would be interested in Willi.

Schrenck-Nötzing began systematic experiments with the boy in December 1921; these were to continue for several years, and altogether he had 124 seances with Willi. He published his findings in 1924. Twenty seven university teachers and 29 other interested people, including doctors and writers, participated in these experiments, the results of which were claimed to be strongly positive, with the phenomena reported as happening in the Schneider household being repeated in the laboratory.

The flashlight picture (below) of one of Willi's sittings reveals a fake 'phantom' pinned to the curtain. But many people, including the novelist Thomas Mann (above), were convinced Willi's powers were genuine

The eyes have it

Vater Schneider's ghost books, a complete record of Rudi's seances, helped Rudi when an accusation of fraud was levelled against him. Two Viennese professors, Stefan Meyer and Karl Przibram, who had attended a seance with Rudi, later claimed that the controller had been influencing the sitting. Vater Schneider was able to defend his son's integrity by producing the very page (right) on which the two professors had endorsed the seance record, one of them adding for good measure the words '*Die Kontrolle war einwandfrei*' – 'the control was perfect.' They were obliged to retract the claim that they had caught Rudi cheating, and had to content themselves with asserting that they had found a 'natural' way of producing the phenomena.

Among those who carried out investigations were Dr E.J. Dingwall and Harry Price who together visited Munich in May 1922. It was apparently with 'some amusement' that Schrenck-Nötzing allowed the two Englishmen to search for trap doors and false walls. Having satisfied themselves that intruders could get in only through the front door, this was locked and sealed for the duration of the experiments. Unaffected by these conditions, Willi produced some extraordinary phenomena, including the levitation of a table, which rose with such force that Dingwall was unable to hold it down. After a series of tests Dingwall thought the evidence was strong enough to point to phenomena that were, indeed, the work of unexplained 'supernormal agencies'. At that point he felt he could 'scarcely entertain with patience' the idea that all involved were engaged in a hoax. Unfortunately, however, Dingwall was not to maintain his conviction: he suggested, some time later, that Schrenk-Nötzing must have somehow been responsible for what they had witnessed, though it is difficult to see how the Baron could have achieved such a feat.

Willi's mediumship gradually began to wane and by the time he came to be investigated in London in 1924 the phenomena he did seem capable of producing were very disappointing. However, in 1919, before the decline had become firmly established, Olga

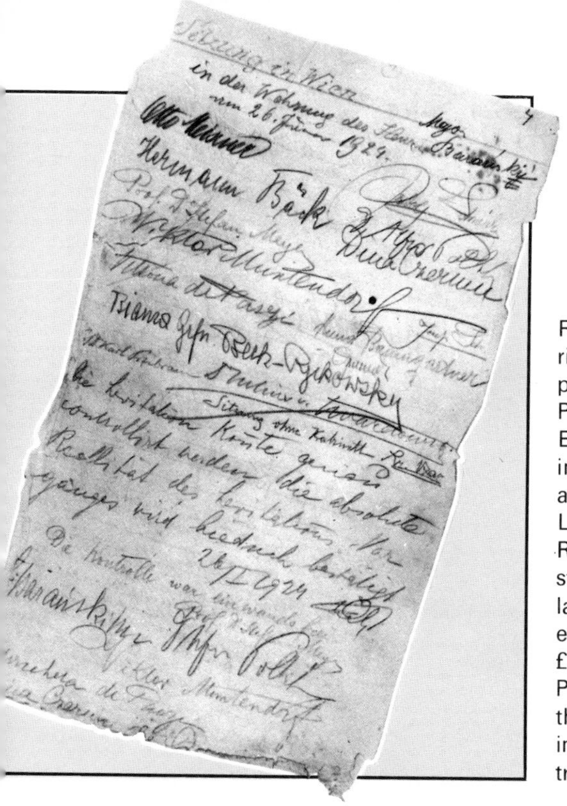
Sitzung in Wien
in der Wohnung des Herrn ... am 26. Juni 1924.

made one of her strangest announcements to date. In the hoarse hurried whisper that was characteristic of Willi in trance, she stated that she wanted Rudi, that he was a stronger medium than Willi. The Schneider parents objected: Rudi was only 11 years old, he could not stay up late, he would be frightened. Olga was adamant. 'He will come!' she said. And he did for, as the Schneiders were arguing with Olga, the door opened and Rudi entered the room. He looked as if he were sleepwalking: his eyes were tightly closed and his hands outstretched. The moment he sat down, phenomena started to occur.

Rising star

Rudi went into a trance and spoke as Olga. Willi, meanwhile, appeared to take on a new personality who announced herself as 'Mina' and spoke in a voice quite distinct from the one previously used by Willi when in trance. Olga was never again to speak through Willi and, with the phenomena he could produce already in decline, his younger brother now became the focus of attention.

Schrenck-Nötzing took an interest from the earliest days of Rudi's mediumship and experiments were begun at once. At first they were held in Braunau but later the boy was investigated at the Baron's own laboratory in Munich. The powers Rudi seemed to possess were equal to those of his brother.

From the outset Vater Schneider decided to keep a record of his second son's progress. He quickly learned what was needed by way of documentation and evidence. His long experience with Willi helped to convince him of the need to keep a systematic account of every seance in which he participated. In the case of Rudi this was a substantial number.

Every time there was a sitting he entered the names of those present, the date and the place in an exercise book. Then he – or someone appointed to do so – gave an account of what had happened at the sitting. And finally all those participating were asked to sign the record alongside any comments they cared to make.

The two thick exercise books that Vater Schneider managed to fill make fascinating reading. They were always described as Vater Schneider's *Geisterbücher* – or ghost books. He refused to be parted from them in his lifetime, but Rudi's widow gave them to this author when she learned that I was interested in Rudi's mediumship.

These books are fading now; the binding is extremely frail, but the accounts of sittings can still be read quite easily. Altogether they contain reports of 269 sittings, from 8 December 1923 to 1 January 1932. These painstakingly collected data provide good evidence for the genuineness of Rudi Schneider's psychic powers.

Rudi being subjected to rigorous tests by the English psychical researcher Harry Price, who invited him to England for a series of investigations under the auspices of the National Laboratory of Psychical Research. While Rudi was staying in London the laboratory paid his hotel expenses plus a stipend of £3 a week, which, as Harry Price observed, was more than he would have earned in Austria at his apprenticed trade of motor mechanic

Rudi Schneider (below) grew up in Braunau, Austria (left), and was only 11 when his psychic powers were discovered. His first seances were held in a room (bottom) in his parents' apartment in the Stadtplatz

A hard price to pay

Although rigorous investigation had convinced sceptics that the Austrian medium Rudi Schneider was genuine, his reputation was to be ultimately destroyed, ironically enough, by the person who had become his staunchest supporter

OVER A PERIOD of about eight years the paranormal powers displayed by the young medium Rudi Schneider were painstakingly recorded by his father. Known as Vater Schneider's *Geisterbücher* – 'ghost books' – these documents chronicle the events at 269 seances that took place between 8 December 1923 and 1 January 1932.

Analysis of the records shows that Rudi could produce four distinct types of phenomenon: psychokinesis, materialisations, levitations of his whole body, and producing in the sitters the sensation of being touched.

To an extent the seance data are incomplete. They do not record how vigorous the movements of objects were, how often they

The phenomenon that occurred most often in Rudi's seances was the movement or manipulation of objects, such as knotting a handkerchief (right). To determine whether the medium was moving objects by fraudulent means the French investigator Eugène Osty devised an apparatus for his laboratory in Paris (below) that emitted an infra-red beam to monitor target objects. If an object was tampered with, a camera would be triggered to take a flashlight photograph. In several of Rudi's seances the infra-red beam triggered the camera – yet the resulting picture showed no evidence of fraud

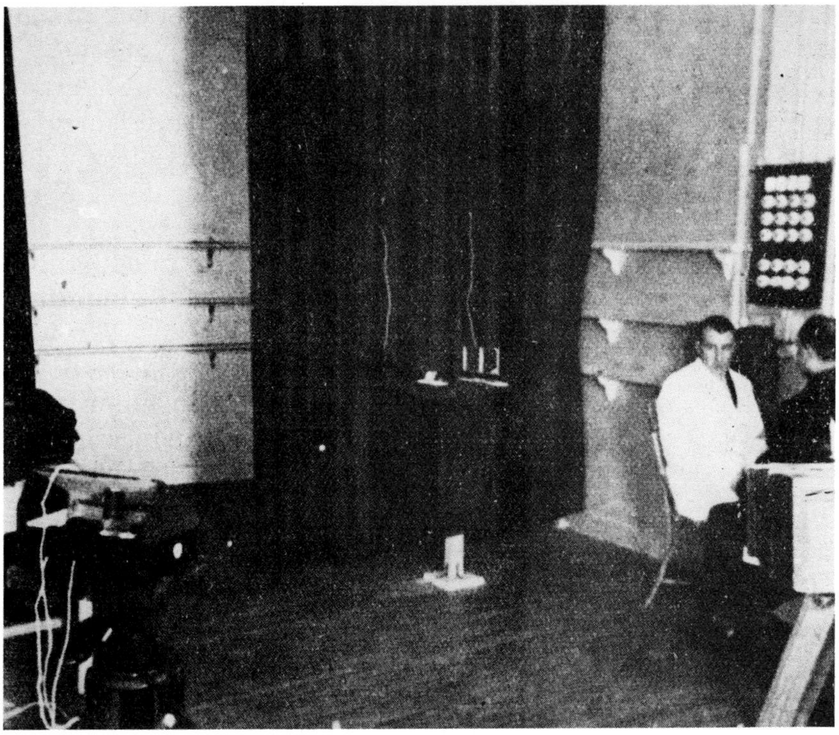

occurred at each sitting, how long the materialisations lasted, and so on. However, despite this, it has been possible to collate some interesting information that seems to indicate that Rudi was very definitely not a fake.

The most common sittings were those at which only psychokinesis was observed. This happened at 28.2 per cent of the seances and became more frequent over the period. It is interesting that there is not a single sitting at which only materialisation is recorded; whenever it took place so did the movement of objects. And it is significant that the sensation of being touched, probably the most easily imagined and faked phenomenon, was experienced relatively infrequently: at 9.7 per cent of the seances.

Home and away

To establish whether different types of seance took place at the Schneiders' home in Braunau as opposed to elsewhere, the sittings were classified rather like football matches, as either home or away. It would have been suspicious if whole classes of phenomena happened only at home. However, this was not the case: although seances seemed rather less successful when conducted away from Braunau, *all* types of phenomena reported at home also happened elsewhere.

Negative seances at home were 6.4 per cent of those recorded; negative ones away were 18.7 per cent. But the percentage of the extremely impressive seances at which all types of phenomena occurred was much the same regardless of where they were held: those at home accounted for 5.3 per cent; those away 5.1 per cent.

Levitations of Rudi's body occurred least often, though this did happen in Braunau and elsewhere, including in the laboratory, where some experimenters held the medium's hands while others passed their hands underneath his body.

Another question that arises is whether the phenomena – or given sets of them – happened only in the presence of certain people. Of the 796 people whose names appeared in the seance records, 557 attended once only, and 174 participated in two to four sittings; the rest, 65, attended appreciably more often.

It does appear from a careful examination of the data that the participation of some of the most frequent sitters led to richer and more varied seances, and that few totally negative seances occurred when they were there. The presence of Rudi's brother Karl and his wife Rosa seemed to encourage phenomena, but they were also present at uneventful seances, so this does not necessarily mean they were in collusion with Rudi. In addition, all the phenomena reported also took place when these special sitters were not there.

Vater Schneider's books are not the only evidence of Rudi's mediumship. He was also

investigated outside his native Austria, in London and in Paris.

The psychical researcher Harry Price invited Rudi to London in 1929 for a series of seances at his National Laboratory of Psychical Research. According to the records, Price's seances produced much the same phenomena as had those at Braunau and Munich, when Rudi's elder brother Willi had been the medium under investigation. Handkerchiefs knotted themselves, a handbell sailed through the air, a cardboard cut-out painted with luminous paint flew about the room, sitters felt as if they were being touched by unseen hands, mists and snowman-like apparitions were seen, and objects were forcibly pulled out of the participants' hands.

A great many of the witnesses were impressed by what they saw, and Price himself was triumphant. In his book *Rudi Schneider*, in which he described the seances, Price claimed that it would not matter how many times in the future Rudi were exposed since he, Price, had now demonstrated the reality of physical phenomena.

However, this is not how things turned out and, ironically, it was Price himself who, more than anyone else, was to destroy Rudi's reputation and cast doubts on the authenticity of his phenomena.

The trouble started because Rudi was much in demand among psychical researchers, and Harry Price had come to regard him as his own property. In fact, Baron von Schrenck-Nötzing, who had earlier investigated Willi Schneider, had been one of the first to champion Rudi; but when Schrenck-Nötzing died, Price immediately tried to take charge of the medium. It was Price's possessiveness that was to ruin Rudi's career.

Among those who tested Rudi was the French researcher Eugène Osty. It was during one of his tests in Paris in 1931 that Osty made an extremely important discovery in the field of paranormal study.

While Eugène Osty (above) was devising his infra-red system for monitoring seances, English psychical researcher Harry Price had produced his own apparatus for recording phenomena. This consisted of a box table with a loose top balanced on knife edges (right) any movement of a handkerchief or other object placed on it triggered a flashlight camera. It was this equipment that produced, in a sitting with Rudi held on 25 February 1932, the picture (above left) of a handkerchief apparently moving by psychokinesis

One of the most obvious and important issues in any case of mediumship is the question of control. A medium has to be secured or monitored in some way, particularly if sittings are held in darkness, to ensure he does not produce the phenomena in a 'normal' manner. When a medium is in a trance he may not be wholly aware of what he is doing. If he is expected to move a table he may do just that, using a foot say, but without being conscious of the fact.

During experiments with Rudi, he was either held by two people, one on either side, or he was connected to an electrical device that would signal any movement on his part. Osty hit upon the idea of laying the emphasis of control not on the medium but on the objects to be moved paranormally: the bell, handkerchief and so on. Osty and his son Marcel, an engineer, devised a system of infra-red rays that monitored these target objects; if a hand or any device were to reach out and seize any of the objects a beam would be interrupted and a camera triggered to take a photograph (this is a common monitoring technique today).

What actually happened in the course of the investigations was a surprise to all concerned. Rudi went into a trance, the spirit guide Olga, who had first appeared in the early days of Willi's mediumship, manifested and announced she would pick up the handkerchief. Immediately the infra-red beam triggered the flash of the camera and the camera clicked. But the ensuing photograph revealed nothing.

Initially it was thought that the instruments had failed. The apparatus was set up again, Rudi went into a trance, and the whole

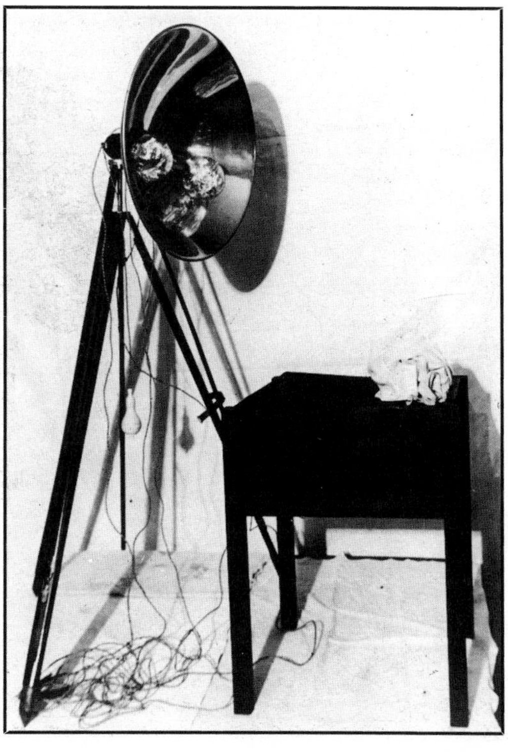

sequence was repeated. Again the camera revealed nothing. Olga, incidentally, complained that the flash had disturbed her, and prevented her picking up the handkerchief.

The equipment was tested and the experiment repeated several times but always with the same result. Osty began to suspect the interference with the infra-red rays was itself paranormal, since the tripping of the switch always followed Olga's announcement that she would move some object. And it would seem that Osty was right for Olga was eventually persuaded to interfere with the infra-red on demand. It was as if some tenuous form of matter were emanating from the medium when his trance personality tried to reach the objects on the table. This matter, invisible in white light, was yet sufficient to interrupt or absorb infra-red radiation.

These observations – perhaps some of the most important ones of physical mediumship ever made – were repeated the following year in London in the course of experiments organised by Lord Charles Hope, using apparatus constructed under the supervision of C. C. L. Gregory, then director of the University of London Observatory.

Price war

Harry Price re-enters the story at this point. He investigated Rudi again, this time using infra-red equipment; the results were good. Price, however, was not happy. He resented the boy being investigated by researchers other than himself, and he mounted a smear campaign against Osty and anyone else engaged in 'rival' investigations of Rudi. Price spun an extensive and complicated web of lies around Rudi's activities and finally published a photograph supposedly showing Rudi with one of his hands free during a seance. This was supposed to reveal how the boy could cheat without the experimenter's knowledge. The experimenter in the photograph was none other than Price himself.

Arguably, this photograph could have been a fake; but it really explained nothing since Rudi could not, even with a free hand, have reached the target objects and therefore could not have been responsible for the partial blocking of the infra-red beam that occurred.

There can be no doubt that Price acted in bad faith. He knew the effect publication of such a photograph would have on the public and on psychical researchers: the scandal would cast doubt on the whole issue; scientists would be reluctant to become involved; and Rudi Schneider would be discredited in the way other physical mediums had been in the past.

In the event, by the time Price issued the photograph, one year after the said seance had taken place, Rudi's phenomena had begun to wane. Most seances produced no phenomena; only very occasionally were slight movements of objects observed; even the interference with infra-red radiation was detected infrequently.

In 1957 Rudi died of a cerebral haemorrhage at the age of 49. His brother Willi outlived him by some 10 years.

The importance of Rudi's mediumship is due to the extensiveness and care with which he was investigated, to the excellence of some of the documentation, and to the infra-red experiments masterminded by Osty. Despite the accusations of fraud levelled against him, Rudi impressed and convinced many people; years later the accounts of his seances still have the ability to do just that.

The photograph that discredited Rudi, taken on 28 April 1932 at a sitting at Harry Price's National Laboratory of Psychical Research in London. The picture shows Rudi (left of the group, back to camera) with his left arm stretched out behind him, free from control. Price's ostensible object in publishing the picture was to discredit other researchers who had investigated Rudi, by showing how easy it was for the medium to evade his controller (in this case, Price himself). But publication inevitably undermined Rudi's own credibility and irrevocably damaged his reputation. His psychic powers were, in any case, on the wane; he returned to Austria, married, and set up a driving school

A thoroughly modern medium

Few Spiritualist mediums have questioned the otherworldly origin of their powers, but Eileen Garrett, one of the most gifted, had her doubts. She was an unusually objective psychic

EILEEN GARRETT has been described as 'probably the most thoroughly investigated medium of modern times'. The reason, quite apart from her exceptional psychic talents, was that she devoted most of her life to encouraging research into mediumship and its meaning, frequently offering herself as the first psychic guinea-pig in experiments.

Her powers ranged from clairvoyance and astral projection to physical mediumship. But it was as a trance medium – apparently allowing the dead to speak through her lips – that she made the greatest impact. It was in this manner that she was used as a channel for communications allegedly from the captain of the British airship *R101*, Flight-Lieutenant H.C. Irwin, in 1930: a remarkable case that many still regard as among the best in providing evidence for life after death (see page 30).

Eileen Garrett as a young woman. Brought up against a background of sectarian strife in Ireland she soon rejected religion, and even after she became a famous medium she was frequently irritated by the dogmatic assertions of many Spiritualists. She was eager to be scientifically investigated in the hope that more could be discovered about the human psyche

But Mrs Garrett was more reticent about her mediumship than others. She accepted that the content of her trance communications was paranormal in origin, but she was open-minded about 'the dead' who spoke through her. This ambiguous approach to her mediumship extended to the spirit 'controls' who worked through her, each of whom had a distinct personality. There was Uvani, who claimed to have been a soldier in India centuries ago, and Abdul Latif, a 12th-century physician from the court of Saladin, whose particular interest was healing. In the early days of her mediumship Mrs Garrett accepted them as spirit helpers, but in time she began to doubt this and believed, instead, that they might be secondary personalities produced by her own subconscious.

Split personalities?

In an attempt to find the truth Mrs Garrett willingly participated in experiments designed to compare these trance personalities with her own waking personality. The investigators spent many hours talking to Uvani and Abdul Latif – even using word association tests on the spirit controls and the medium. However, these tests were inconclusive. One investigator decided that Uvani was probably a 'split-off' personality from the medium – indeed, Uvani himself said he manipulated a split-off portion of Mrs Garrett's unconscious. Another researcher concluded that the two spirit controls were independent personalities.

Mrs Garrett's own opinion in later life, given in her autobiography *Many voices* (1968), was:

> I prefer to think of the controls as principals of the subconscious. I had, unconsciously, adopted them by name and during the years of early training. I respect them, but cannot explain them. . . . The controls are well aware that I have maintained an impartial, but respectful, attitude towards my own work and theirs, and so the search continues.

Later, she added, 'I have never been able wholly to accept them as the spiritual dwellers on the threshold, which they seem to believe they are.'

The mystery deepened with the surfacing of two more controls. One, named Tehotah, claimed to be an entity that personified the Logos or divine word, while Rama was said to be the personification of the life force.

Left: New York psychologist Lawrence LeShan was impressed with Mrs Garrett's psychic gifts and her analytical intelligence. He investigated her thoroughly; during one psychometry experiment LeShan was amazed when Mrs Garrett, picking up an envelope containing the target object – an ancient Babylonian tablet (below) – not only described it accurately but proceeded to give a detailed description of the secretary who had originally parcelled it up

Neither had incarnated as an individual.

Eileen Garrett was born in County Meath, in the Republic of Ireland, on 17 March 1893, the daughter of Anne Brownell and a Spaniard named Vancho. Two weeks later her mother drowned herself and a few weeks after that her father also committed suicide: the double tragedy created, apparently, by the pressures of Protestant and Catholic conflicts. As a result, Eileen was brought up by an uncle and aunt – who were Protestant, but no bigots.

A late uncle's advice

Like so many other sensitive children – and in particular natural psychics – Eileen had playmates who were invisible to others. But the most impressive paranormal experience of those early years concerned her uncle, who had been extremely kind and understanding to her. A couple of weeks after his death Eileen saw him standing before her 'looking young, erect and strong'. He said that he understood the difficulties of her present life. Then he predicted that she would go to London to study in two years – which is exactly what happened. He then vanished before she could ask any questions. It was from that moment that Eileen became interested in the question of survival of death.

In time she encountered Spiritualism and began developing her psychic gifts – particularly trance mediumship – under the guidance of James Hewat McKenzie at the British College of Psychic Science. As a result, she provided many bereaved people with impressive evidence for survival.

In 1931 the American Society for Psychical Research invited her to New York to give sittings, and she also worked with Professor William McDougall and Dr J.B. Rhine at Duke University, North Carolina, in experiments into ESP.

New York psychologist Lawrence LeShan spent more than 500 hours questioning Mrs Garrett about her psychic abilities, then designed several experiments to test them thoroughly. One was a psychometry test in which the medium was asked to hold various objects and give her clairvoyant impressions about them.

The objects included a fossil fish, a scrap of bandage, a piece of stone from Mount Vesuvius, an old Greek coin and an ancient Babylonian clay tablet. Each was wrapped in tissue, then placed in a box that, in turn, was put inside a manila envelope and numbered. Another person then put these numbered envelopes inside larger envelopes, marking them with a different number. As a result, no one knew which object was inside which envelope.

During preparations for this experiment a secretary picked up the Babylonian tablet and examined it. Two weeks later, when LeShan conducted the experiment with Mrs Garrett 1500 miles (2400 kilometres) away in

Right: Professor William McDougall who, together with Dr J. B. Rhine, conducted experiments with Eileen Garrett at Duke University in North Carolina, USA

Left: Cecil B. de Mille, director of epic films and a notoriously tough character; nevertheless he was reduced to tears when Mrs Garrett described an old lady she 'saw' standing next to him. It was a perfect description of his dead mother

Florida, she picked up an envelope and said immediately that there was 'a woman associated with this'.

It was later found that this envelope contained the clay tablet, and Mrs Garrett's description of the woman so perfectly matched the secretary who had handled it that, according to LeShan, it would have been possible 'to pick her out of a line-up of 10,000 women'. The medium even mentioned two scars that the woman had.

During the experiments with her, LeShan learned indirectly of a man who had vanished from a mid western city in the USA. He gave Mrs Garrett, in New York, a square of cloth cut from one of the man's shirts and asked for her impressions. The medium gave a fairly accurate description of the missing man, whose appearance was, at that time, unknown to LeShan, adding that he had had a loss in his family between the ages of 13 and 15. It was discovered that his father had deserted the family when he was 14 and had not been heard of since. She also said that the man was in La Jolla, California, and it was confirmed later that he had gone there after leaving his home.

A spontaneous phenomenon of a physical kind occurred in 1931 when Mrs Garrett was lying on an operating table in hospital. Just after she succumbed to the anaesthetic, the doctors and nurses in attendance heard a voice. Her physician, who had been in India in his youth, told her later that he recognised certain definite words of command, as spoken in Hindustani. Because of the way Mrs Garrett had been prepared for the operation the doctor knew that it was quite impossible for her to utter a sound. He was so impressed by the experience that he sent a letter to various Spiritualist leaders putting the circumstances on record.

Eileen Garrett was far removed from the popular, otherworldly, image of a medium. She had a vivacious personality and a questing spirit, and in addition to her psychic work she also ran a tea room, a workers' hostel and eventually a literary magazine, *Tomorrow*, which she later changed to deal entirely with psychic matters.

She married three times, lost three sons – one at birth and two through illness. Her daughter continues her work through the Parapsychology Foundation, which Eileen Garrett founded in New York in 1951.

Eileen Garrett died at Le Piol, France, in 1970, having made an enormous personal contribution to psychical research. She had no doubt about the reality of paranormal phenomena. What she *did* doubt was the spirit hypothesis of mediumship that so many accept blindly. And by setting up the Parapsychology Foundation she ensured that the search for some understanding of the nature of psychic phenomena would continue long after her death.

Below: Eileen Garrett was a prolific writer and a dynamic personality. Here she surveys some of the books written by or about her

Below right: after Mrs Garrett's death in 1970 her daughter continued her work through the Parapsychological Foundation, which Eileen founded in 1951

Doris Stokes is, she says, a perfectly ordinary, down-to-earth person. But she has a special gift, which enables her to hear the dead speak. This chapter looks at the life and work of the woman whose exceptional psychic powers have brought comfort to thousands of people

The medium and the message

DORIS STOKES'S appearance on Australian television caused a sensation. The switchboard was flooded with calls, letters poured in, and Channel 9 took off *Starsky & Hutch* to make room for a second hour-long programme about this daughter of an English blacksmith.

No other personality had had such an impact on Australian viewers, yet Doris Stokes is not a superstar. She lives with her husband John in a modest London flat and regards herself as a very ordinary person. But she has an unusual gift that sets her apart from others: she is a medium who claims to be able to speak with the dead.

After being interviewed by Don Lane on his popular television variety show, Doris Stokes was invited to give messages to members of his studio audience. It is something she does regularly in Spiritualist churches in England without creating much of a stir – but for most Australian television viewers the spectacle of a woman 'speaking' to spirits was astonishing. They demanded more and Australian television was happy to oblige. 'A [psychic] star was born', her visit to Australia was extended, and soon a tour of major cities was organised during which the largest halls – including the Sydney Opera House – were packed with people eager to see her in action and perhaps receive a personal message.

Doris Stokes appears on Australian television in the *Don Lane Show* (right). As a result of the programme Doris received thousands of telephone calls and hundreds of letters, and went on a whirlwind tour of Australia. She was staggered at this response from the public and told the crowds: 'I'm nothing special. Please don't get the wrong impression. I'm just the same as you are'

What is it about Doris Stokes that created such a reaction? It is the direct and confident way in which she acts as a 'go-between', relaying names and information that she says are given to her by the dead. Much of this she hears as voices – different in accent and intonation – and so she is known as a *clairaudient*, rather than a *clairvoyant* (a medium whose impressions are visual).

In the television studio her down-to-earth, good-humoured manner ensured that there was nothing 'spooky' about her performance. She simply stood in front of her audience and waited for the voices to give her information.

'The lady over there,' she said, pointing to one of Don Lane's studio guests. 'I've got a man here called Bert.'

'That's my brother-in-law,' the woman gasped.

'He says he went over very quickly.'

'That's right.'

'Who's Wyn?'

'I'm Wyn.'

The messages she gives are usually made

up of such trivia, but the accuracy of the names and details leave her recipients in no doubt that they are witnessing a paranormal phenomenon. Guesswork alone would not explain the content of the messages. But is it really communication with the dead or is she just using extra-sensory perception (ESP)? That is something that each person has to decide for himself, just as Doris Stokes had to decide in her early days.

Her psychic gifts were apparent from an early age when she found herself describing – or predicting – things that she could not have known normally. This worried her mother, but her father – a natural psychic like his daughter – understood and did nothing to discourage her. It was not until after Doris was married and her father had died that her psychic powers grew stronger: and her experiences left her in no doubt that she was in contact with people who had died.

A visit from the dead

Her most dramatic personal experience occurred during the Second World War. Her husband was reported 'missing in action' and a medium at a local Spiritualist church in Grantham, Lincolnshire, 'confirmed' that he had been killed. Doris Stokes returned home to her baby son in a state of shock. She describes what happened next in her autobiography, *Voices in my ear*:

> Then the bedroom door flew open so sharply I thought it was mother bursting in and there stood my father. My mouth dropped open. He looked as real and as solid as he did when he was alive . . .
> 'Dad?' I whispered.
> 'I never lied to you, did I, Doll?' he asked.
> 'I don't think so,' I said.
> 'I'm not lying to you now. John is not with us and on Christmas Day you will have proof of this.' Then as I watched, he vanished.

Three days later came a letter from the War Office telling her that John was dead. But while everyone else mourned, the 'widow' refused to believe it. Her dead father was proved right, however. Just as he had predicted she learned that John was still alive, though wounded and a prisoner of war, on Christmas Day.

Doris was never trained as a medium, although she once attended a Spiritualist 'development circle' – and was appallingly embarrassed. First, she was shown into a room of 'cranky old dears clucking admiringly about a bossy medium.' They all then sat quietly, with their eyes shut, waiting for the spirit world to communicate with them. But Doris's eyes flew open again when a large lady stood up and majestically announced, in a deep voice, but still unmistakably her own, that she was 'Chief Sitting Bull'. Doris could hardly believe it – all these people taking this patent nonsense so seriously! And then

'Chief Sitting Bull' addressed some very stern words to her; she had to uncross her legs and keep her feet on the ground 'to earth the power'. Doris remarked that she was made to feel like a human light bulb and found it all quite ridiculous. She never went back.

However, she had no need for training. It soon became apparent that her special, psychic gifts could give comfort and practical help to the bereaved and the despairing. She began to give 'seances' – although that rather spooky and old-fashioned word sounds very odd in conjunction with Doris – both on public platforms and in private houses. She never promises to 'get through' to any particular person on the 'other side', but settles the audience down, confident that the spirits will eventually speak to them through her. They have very rarely let her down.

She has found that the longer a person has

Top: Tom Sutton, Doris's father. He died when Doris was a young girl, but 'visited' her twice several years later during the Second World War. On the first occasion he told her that her husband John (above) – reported missing in action – was alive and would return. The second time he warned her that her healthy infant son was soon to die. Both 'predictions' were accurate

been dead, the stronger his or her voice seems to be – those newly 'passed over' tend to sound faint. Sometimes the voices fade away altogether. She has now learned to cope with these silent phases but in her early days she was tempted to cheat. Doris Stokes must be one of the few practising mediums to admit to it.

She was young and felt very 'special' because of her strange abilities and was therefore inclined to show off. When the voices stopped, leaving her alone and unaided on a platform in front of a packed house, she was eager to heed the advice of an experienced 'circuit' medium. Get to the meetings early, he suggested, and listen in to the conversations of the audience. You're bound to pick up a few hints, names, dates and so on. People will always talk about their hopes – in this case the spirits they hope to 'hear' from through Doris. Take down some notes surreptitiously, he said, then if your voices stop abruptly you can consult them and 'fudge' the messages. That way your audience will leave happy.

Doris admits that she tried cheating in this way, twice. The first time she slipped her notes into her hymn book, hoping she would not have to use them. But gradually – in the middle of a message for a lady in the audience – the voices stopped. White-faced, Doris fumbled for her notes – but they had disappeared. Somehow, remembering bits of what she had overheard and making up the rest, she finished the 'communication' but noticed that the lady seemed a little bewildered – it was such a muddle. But the worst was yet to come.

Just as abruptly as they had departed, the voices came back. Doris managed two real messages then was aware that her spirit guide – whose name approximates to the English spelling Ramononov – had taken over and was saying 'Now we'll go back to Mrs . . .' (the lady whose message had just been faked) 'and you'll apologise to her and tell her that the last part of the message didn't came from the spirit world'.

Horrified at being faced with a public humiliation, Doris hesitated, then plunged in: 'I'm terribly sorry. I've got to tell you the last bit of your message didn't come from the spirit. That was me.'

Advice from the other side

People who seek help from mediums are mostly the grief-stricken bereaved. What raises Doris Stokes above the run-of-the-mill Spiritualist medium is her extraordinary down-to-earth attitude. To her the spirit world is as real as this one – and her firm conviction of survival after death communicates itself to her audience. Her specific and often deeply personalised messages purporting to come from the dead frequently offer urgent advice: one deeply depressed widower was told by his wife not to take the overdose he was planning. He was impressed by the fact that no one knew of his intentions except himself – that, and the anger Doris conveyed from his wife. 'Your wife is very anxious about you. She says that is not the way. You must not do it. She's waiting for you and if she's gone on she'll make sure of being there to meet you when your time comes, but you must wait until your time comes, or you will regret it.'

Many a medium could have trotted out that advice – for almost all religious people are opposed to suicide – but Doris backed this up by 'proving' the continued existence of the man's wife through conveying many personal pieces of information that only the widower and his wife could have known.

There are occasions, however, when Doris herself needs the help of psychics. One such time was when she was 33, and, her first child having died, she was hoping to become pregnant again. One day she was talking to a friend, Walter Brookes, a well-known Yorkshire medium, when he suddenly asked if she had just come out of hospital. No, said Doris, who was feeling fit and well.

'Just a minute,' he said. 'This is serious. I'm afraid you're going into hospital – July I think, something to do with your right side. They'll say you're going to die, but your father wants you to write this down. It's the name of the person you must ask for. Mrs Marrow.'

That July Doris Stokes was suddenly stricken with agonising pain in her stomach. She was rushed to hospital where it was found that pregnancy had occurred in one of her Fallopian tubes. John Stokes was told there was nothing that could be done for her. She was dying.

Remembering the message from Doris's dead father, John Stokes asked the doctors if they knew a Mrs Marrow. When he learned they did and that she was a gynaecologist at a Nottingham hospital he insisted that his wife be transferred. There, under Mrs Marrow's expert care, Doris recovered. And soon she was able to resume her work as a medium, relaying messages that may well have saved the lives of others.

Following the success of her first visit to Australia, Doris returned in 1980 for an equally triumphant tour, with television and radio appearances.

Spiritualism's critics, of course, are not pleased that mediums such as Doris Stokes are allowed to demonstrate their powers to such a wide audience. But Doris is happy to be judged by the results of her work – and they speak for themselves.

Below: Walter Brookes, the medium who gave Doris a message warning her of a forthcoming illness

Above: Doris 'performs' before the studio audience of Tyne Tees Television's *Friday Live* programme in December 1979

The voices of celebrities could often be heard at seances held by Leslie Flint, for show business personalities seemed to favour him as a channel of 'direct voice communication'. This chapter describes the long career of an outstanding psychic

In a manner of speaking

LONG AFTER THEY DIED, Rudolph Valentino, Lionel Barrymore and Leslie Howard continued to 'perform' before appreciative audiences. Not on stage or film, of course, but in the darkened seance room of the London direct voice medium Leslie Flint. They are but a few of the famous dead – the full list reads like a *Who's who* of the arts, with an additional sprinkling from other notable professions – who communicated through Flint during the 42 years that he worked as a professional medium.

It has to be said at the outset that claiming spirit contact with the famous usually arouses suspicion. Their lives, likes and loves are usually public knowledge and a gifted impersonator would have no difficulty in posing as a medium and 'communicating' in a voice similar to that of the late celebrity

But Leslie Flint's spirit visitors were not always famous. At the height of his career many ordinary people were able to pay a fee to sit with him and some later testified to speaking to their relatives and friends. Flint, in such circumstances, could have known nothing about the dead who returned, and faking their voices and speech mannerisms is seemingly out of the question.

This account, however, will concentrate on the celebrities who have apparently returned from the grave to hold long conversations at Leslie Flint's seances. His spirit links with show business stars took him to the United States and to the Hollywood homes of legendary figures. The wealth he encountered on those visits was in stark contrast to the poverty he experienced as a child.

Leslie Flint's parents parted when he was young and he was brought up in a Salvation Army home. At an early age he was credited with the ability to 'see' the dead, but this served only to separate him from other children. When he left school he had a number of temporary jobs, including one as a gravedigger, before being drawn into a Spiritualist group where he developed his direct voice mediumship.

It took Flint seven years to develop this rare gift, sitting twice a week. At first he went into a deep trance and trumpets were used to amplify the voices of the spirits attempting to communicate with the living. As his powers

Leslie Flint (above) was a professional medium for 42 years, during which time his seances were closely scrutinised by scientists and psychical researchers, and the 'spirit voices' that were heard were recorded on tape. Many sitters testified that the voices were those of deceased persons, both famous and obscure, personally known to them. Rudolph Valentino (right, in *The sheik*), though a silent star in life, proved to be one of the most frequent communicators; Flint was, in turn, one of Valentino's most ardent fans

grew stronger, however, he was able to remain conscious during the seances and eventually to dispense with the trumpets. Sitters would assemble in the seance room, the lights would be put out and voices would address them from thin air. Flint occasionally joined in the conversation.

Rudolph Valentino came into Flint's world at an early stage. Another medium told him that a man with the initials R.V. 'wants to help you in a psychic way and work through you to help mankind'. The spirit then appeared to the medium dressed as an Arab. Valentino was the only person Flint could think of who fitted the bill – he had read a book about him as a teenager – but he could not understand why the great screen lover should want to help him.

Confirmation soon came from a totally unexpected source. A letter came to Flint from a German woman, saying that Valentino had communicated at a seance in Munich. He gave Flint's name and address and asked the medium to tell Flint that he was trying to make contact. Over a period the Munich seances produced items of information that corroborated statements made by Valentino to Flint through other mediums.

When Flint developed his direct voice mediumship, the film star was one of the first people to speak through him. Sometimes he spoke in his native Italian.

Valentino made a striking prediction. He said Flint would visit Hollywood, stay in

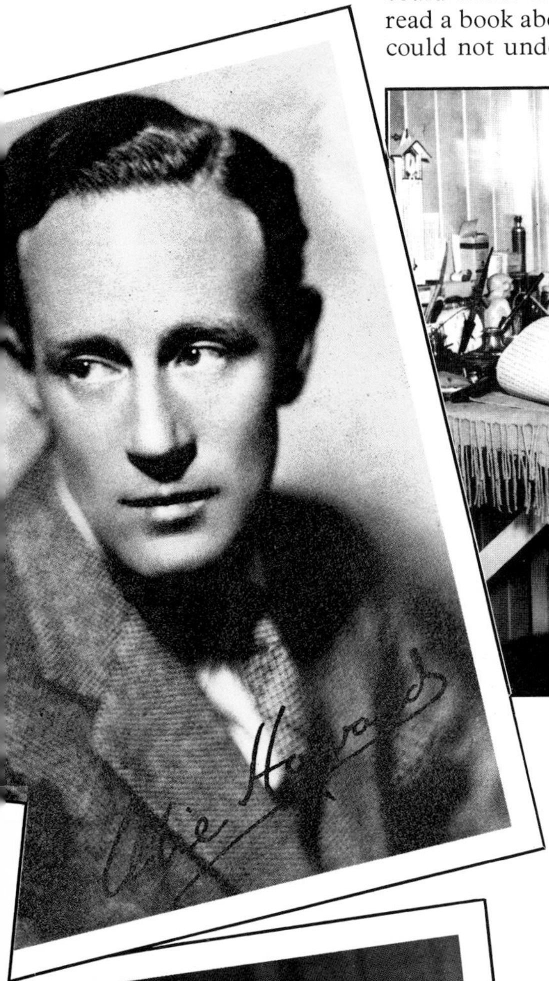

Some eminent visitors from the 'other side' who made guest appearances at Leslie Flint's seances: Amy Johnson (above right) reported that there were no aeroplanes in the afterlife for her to fly; George Bernard Shaw (above) continues to write, however. Leslie Howard (above left) and Lionel Barrymore (left) are two giants of the stage and screen who have allegedly spoken using Flint as a channel

Valentino's Beverly Hills home and hold seances in his bedroom. Unlikely as it seemed, it all came to pass. Some years later, while visiting Hollywood, Flint was invited to visit a psychical researcher. As soon as Flint was given the address he realised it was the former home of Valentino. And the room in which the seances were held was the star's former bedroom.

Leslie Howard, Lionel Barrymore and Mrs Patrick Campbell are other actors who are said to have reappeared at Flint's seances. Rupert Brooke and George Bernard Shaw have returned to reveal that they are still writing. Amy Johnson said she was no longer flying: there are no aeroplanes in the spirit world. But they have pianos, and Frédéric Chopin is still playing and composing. Shakespeare continues to write plays 400 years after his works were first performed.

Mahatma Gandhi and Cosmo Gordon Lang, former Archbishop of Canterbury, have spoken at length on spiritual matters from their new vantage points in the next world. Marilyn Monroe has returned to say she did *not* commit suicide but died from an accidental overdose of drugs. Queen Victoria sent messages to her last surviving daughter, Princess Louise, and King George V communicated to two members of his household.

How strong is the evidence that the voices are real and the communicators are who they say they are?

Flint has described himself as the 'most tested' medium in Britain and has apparently always been willing to take part in experiments. An early investigator of his direct voice mediumship was Dr Louis Young, who had exposed several doubtful mediums in the United States. He made Flint fill his mouth with coloured water before a seance started. The lights were put out. Spirits chattered away as usual. And at the end Flint returned the water from his mouth to a glass.

The Rev. Drayton Thomas, a member of the council of the Society for Psychical Research, conducted a more severe test in 1948. He placed a strip of sticking plaster across Flint's mouth and then covered it with a scarf. The medium's hands were tied to the arms of his chair and another cord ensured that he could not bend his head down, thus preventing him loosening the plaster with his hands.

Once again, spirit voices spoke with their usual clarity, often very loudly. This would have been impossible if Flint were faking them. But at the end of the seance the medium was found to be bound and gagged just as he was at the start, and the clergyman had considerable difficulty in removing the sticking plaster without causing pain.

In 1972 the *Sunday Express* science correspondent, Robert Chapman, assisted by Professor William R. Bennett, former head of the Department of Electrical Engineering at Columbia University, New York, and Nigel Buckmaster, an SPR member, devised an even more elaborate means of establishing the authenticity of the spirit voices. Flint was gagged and bound firmly to his chair. He was also fitted with a throat microphone, which would show whether he was producing the sounds by ventriloquism. Two television cameras were used, together with an infrared detector so that Flint could be observed in the dark.

Yet the voices spoke, and the investigators saw the ectoplasmic voice box, which is said to be used by spirit communicators, as it formed about 2 feet (60 centimetres) from the medium's head. 'There could be no question of these voices coming from some hidden tape recorder furtively switched on by Flint,' Chapman concluded, 'because there was question-and-answer dialogue with the "other side".'

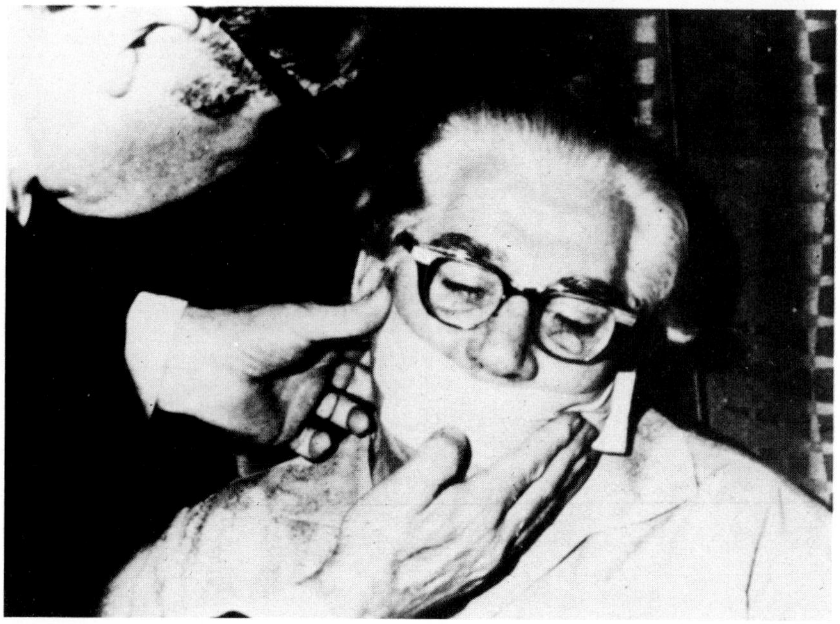

Top: the Rev. C. Drayton Thomas, an SPR member, tested Flint in 1948. He was satisfied that during the test Flint remained bound and gagged, even though 'spirit voices' were heard clearly throughout

Leslie Flint's mouth was sealed with sticking plaster (above) in a test conducted by the *Sunday Express*. To prevent any tampering with the gag, his hands and his head were restrained (right). The investigators heard the voices, and also saw the 'ectoplasmic voice box', supposedly responsible for producing them, as it materialised in thin air, just a little way from the medium's head

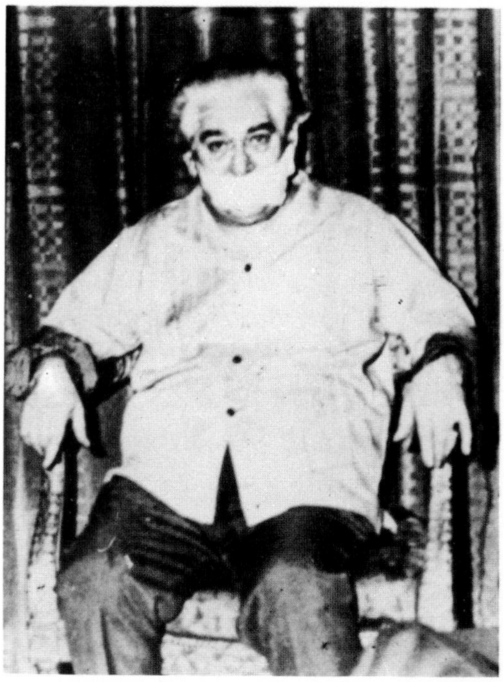

Spirits on tape

Many of the celebrated spirit visitors were tape recorded by two researchers, George Woods and Betty Greene. They kept regular appointments with Flint for more than 15 years, during which they compiled a library of 500 tape recordings. Valentino appears on 60 of them.

The flavour of Flint's seances can be gained from this brief excerpt from a session held on 20 August 1962. A rich male voice began speaking, and Betty Greene gave him encouragement – which, however, was taken amiss by the communicator:

'Come along friend. You are doing very well.'

'Since I am doing precisely nothing at the moment, I can't see how you can consider I'm doing extremely well,' the voice replied, mockingly.

'We thought you were saying something and thought we hadn't heard you,' Betty Greene explained.

'I have never been known to say nothing.'

'Please, may we have your name?'

'If I couldn't say something of value,' the

Above left: George Woods and Betty Greene tape recorded Leslie Flint's seances over a period of 15 years, building a library of 'voices from the dead'

Left: 'Mickey', Leslie Flint's control or spirit 'master of ceremonies'. He was an Irish boy who had lived in Camden Town, north London, until he was killed by a lorry. This drawing was made by a 'psychic artist' at one of Flint's seances

voice continued, 'then I would rather say nothing.'

'Who is it speaking please?' Betty Greene persisted, but the voice chose to ignore the question in its next utterance.

'This is most extraordinary! Then again, being dead is an extraordinary business, especially when you are talking to people on Earth who are supposed to be alive and are very much dull and dim in consequence! What an extraordinary business this is!'

George Woods muttered 'yes' in agreement, and the visitor continued with a clue to his identity:

'There seems to have been a great deal of interest in my works, lately. . . .'

'Friend, may we have your name please?' Betty Greene asked again.

'My name got me into a great deal of trouble when I was on your side,' he responded and avoided the question for a while longer. Eventually, and grudgingly, he told the couple: 'Oh, you might as well know. My name is Wilde.'

'Oh,' said George Woods with evident delight, 'I've read your books.'

'How fortunate you are! I suppose I should be highly flattered. Not that I'm getting any royalties. No doubt you belong to a very good library.'

'Oscar Wilde' went on to talk about his new existence, which, he said, was not unlike his earthly life: 'I live a life of delicious sin, but only as the world sees sin. It is no longer sin here to be human and to be natural.'

Other voices that came through Flint could be judged by people who had had direct knowledge of the deceased person. Charles Loseby, QC, who had been a student under Lord Birkenhead, sometime Lord Chancellor, at Gray's Inn, testified that it was Lord Birkenhead's voice that Woods and Greene recorded at one of their seances. A retired physics teacher, J. Croft, who studied under the famous physicist and psychical researcher Sir Oliver Lodge, said that the voice on another tape recording

> had the qualities which we had associated with the voice of Sir Oliver Lodge. . . . There was a characteristic sibilance, an easy fluency of expression, and a choice of the apt word and phrase which we remembered were a feature of Sir Oliver Lodge's speech.

Mrs Alys F. Watson, god-daughter of Lilian Baylis who founded the Old Vic theatre in London, listened to another seance recording, after which she declared to George Woods: 'I shall be only too happy to confirm that it was Lilian Baylis's voice that I heard, which I am sure it was.'

Leslie Flint decided to retire in December 1976. The recordings made by Woods and Greene and by many other sitters provide a lasting reminder of his mediumship – and, doubtless, will continue to cause controversy for years to come. Despite many glowing tributes, sceptics have found it easy to pick holes in some of the seance conversations. The words and mannerisms of some famous speakers are not always what we would expect.

Flint himself, after all those years of listening to spirit voices in a darkened seance room, still finds some aspects of his own mediumship puzzling. He cannot explain, for example, why some voices spoke only in a whisper, whereas others spoke loudly.

One other aspect of his work, often overlooked in the articles about him, is worth recording. Very often sitters would sit and chat for an hour in his seance room and nothing would happen at all. Flint may have been one of the most gifted direct voice mediums of all time, but his powers could not be turned on at will.

Spirit photography

Images have appeared on developed film which were not visible to the photographer when the pictures were taken. These are often images of people related to the subjects of the photographs. Can they all be the result of extensive and complex trickery?

Unexpected developments

A spectral figure has often turned up on a photograph when nothing of the kind was visible at the time it was taken. How do these 'extras' appear? Are they genuine? Where do they come from?

THE EASE WITH WHICH 'EXTRAS' may be imposed upon photographs has led most people to believe that all spirit photographs are in some way fraudulent. However, the evidence suggests otherwise. While the greater number of so-called psychic pictures are indeed intended to amuse or defraud, a few spirit photographs have been made in circumstances that place them on a level beyond ordinary understanding. What makes the discussion of spirit photography so difficult is that no one knows how genuine images come to be on plates and film. And no one knows exactly what these spirit images are.

The most extraordinary spirit photographs have been made in seances, often under rigid test conditions, but a few interesting ones have been made unexpectedly by amateurs. People take a snapshot of a friend, or of an interior, or of a pet, and afterwards find, to their astonishment, the image of a face or figure – sometimes recognisably that of a deceased relative or friend – on the print. This happens rarely, but it does happen; and many examples, with written accounts, have been preserved by archivists and librarians interested in psychic phenomena. The earliest preserved examples of spirit photographs were of this order: they were taken by amateur photographers who had no specialist interest in psychic effects, and who indeed were disappointed that their portraits and landscapes were 'spoiled' by extra images.

It is generally accepted that spirit photography as such began in Boston, Massachusetts, USA, on 5 October 1861, when William Mumler accidentally produced his first spirit picture. But this date may not be entirely accurate. For, according to an early pioneer of Spiritualism in Boston, Dr Gardner, a few portraits exhibiting a second figure that could not be accounted for had been made before that at nearby Roxbury. The Roxbury photographer was an 'orthodox Christian' who, after hearing about Mumler's pictures, refused to print any negatives containing 'spirits' on the grounds that 'if it had anything to do with Spiritualism, it was the work of the Devil.'

The fact is that, well over a century later, we still do not know how spirit photography

An embracing couple not seen by either the photographer or the subject (far left) appeared on this picture taken in a churchyard in 1928 by a Mrs Wickstead. The 'spirits' could not be identified – and the Society for Psychical Research, who investigated the matter, could not explain them

actually works. The majority of psychical researchers involved with spirit photography claim it occurs by the direct intervention of the spirits themselves. By such reasoning, of course, the result is not so much 'spirit photography' as 'photography by spirits'. The famous journalist W. T. Stead was an early champion of spirit photography, and many portraits of him show images of recognised extras alongside. After he died in the *Titanic* disaster in April 1912, he continued to converse in spirit with his daughter Estelle, as she reported. And then the matter went further, for his image began to appear as an extra alongside her in pictures. When Estelle asked him to say something about the actual production of such psychic photographs, Stead insisted that the spirits were themselves involved with producing the images – mainly in order to convince people of the reality of life after death.

The spirit photographs made by professionals and participants in seances are fascinating enough. But it is the innocence and the element of the unexpected that permeate the accidental spirit photographs of amateurs that intrigue the historian of the genre more.

Perhaps the most famous of the early

Above: a spirit portrait of William T. Stead, who had died in the *Titanic* disaster, with his living daughter Estelle. According to her, she asked him how psychic photography actually came about; he replied that the spirits themselves were involved in producing the unexpected images

Above right: the ghostly heads of two drowned sailors photographed by a passenger on the boat, *Watertown*. The spectres were seen in the waves for several days after the drowning and the photographer deliberately took the picture to record this psychic phenomenon

Negative findings

The faking of spirit photographs seems to have begun almost as soon as the genuine product appeared in the 19th century. One of the common faking techniques was the double exposure – marginally easier with the large plates then in use. A more cunning method involved the painting of a background screen with a special chemical invisible to ordinary sight, but which showed up on photographic film. This screen was pre-painted and placed behind the sitter. Still other techniques were devised by ingenious and unscrupulous photographers.

The case called the 'Moss photographic fiasco' is among the most interesting of the proven frauds. In the early 1920s, G.H. Moss was employed as a chauffeur by a man who was interested in the paranormal. Moss was an amateur photographer, and one day he brought a print with a ghostly 'extra' to his employer. The employer showed interest and, after some experiments on his own, introduced Moss into the British College of Psychic Science. About 1924, Moss was given a year's 'contract' to work under test conditions at the college, on a fixed salary. His work there was impressive and well-received – until he was exposed as a fraud.

Moss produced a number of spirit images that were recognised as the likenesses of dead relatives and friends by sitters. In one of these (below) the sitter was a trance medium. She recognised the extra as her dead sister. A cut-out photograph of that sister was mounted alongside the extra to illustrate the resemblance. In another (right), the image was recognised by a person observing the photographic session, though it was not clear whether the recognised spirit was dead or alive.

A third example of Moss's work (far right) was made in a seance with the well-known medium Mrs Osborne Leonard on 5 January 1925. The sitter was informed by 'a voice from beyond' that he would be sitting for a photograph in 8 days. The invisible speaker promised that she would reveal herself then.

examples of amateur spirit photography is the intriguing 'Lord Combermere's ghost' picture. The circumstances surrounding the taking of this photograph have been well-recorded and documented. The picture was a study of the splendid library in Combermere Abbey, Cheshire, taken by Miss Sybell Corbet in 1891 as a souvenir of her visit. She was surprised, if not disappointed, to discover on the plate the transparent image of an old man sitting in a chair at the left of the room.

Only the head, the body and arms of the figure are relatively clear – the legs are missing. Subsequent research by psychical investigators revealed that at the precise time that the plate was being exposed, the body of Lord Combermere was being buried in the local churchyard at Wrenbury, a few miles away from the abbey. Lord Combermere had died in London a few days previously as a result of a road accident. In this accident his legs had been so badly damaged that, had he lived, he would never have walked again.

The touch of drama that characterises this photograph came to light well after it was taken. Indeed only rarely do amateur photographers take pictures in the knowledge that they are recording psychic phenomena. One of the few exceptions is the case of the *Watertown* pictures, which contain images of drowned seamen. These were deliberately taken by one of the passengers on board a boat, the *Watertown*, from which two seamen had been swept overboard and drowned during the course of the journey. For several days afterwards, passengers and crew insisted that the seamen's spectral heads could be seen in the waves and spray.

Much more typical is the account of the curious extras on a snapshot taken by Mrs Wickstead in 1928. The snapshot – now quite faded, but never of first-rate quality – was one of two taken at the church in the village of Hollybush, not far from Hereford. Mrs Wickstead was on a car tour with friends and had stopped to see the church. She decided to take a photograph of her friend Mrs Laurie, who, in the event, can barely be seen in the photograph. After the picture had been taken, Mrs Laurie drew Mrs Wickstead's attention to the grave of a soldier who had died in service. Alongside this grave was one of a girl who had died shortly afterwards.

'I wonder if they were lovers?' Mrs Laurie had asked.

In a letter to Sir Oliver Lodge, later

That sitting, which had already been arranged without Mrs Leonard's knowledge, did indeed produce an extra – and some of the sitter's friends insisted that the image bore a strong likeness to his recently deceased wife. A portrait of her was pasted alongside so that a comparison could be made.

Moss was unmasked by the astute F. Barlow, at that time the Honorary Secretary for the now defunct Society for the Study of Supernormal Pictures. While Barlow was examining a group of Moss's negatives containing extras, he noticed a roughness on the edges of certain plates. Closer examination showed that each negative bearing a spirit image had one edge filed. Detailed examination of the plate wrappings revealed that they had been skilfully opened by steaming and resealed.

Moss vehemently denied fraud and even signed a statement declaring his innocence. However, when faced with the filed plates, he made a confession. He had secretly opened certain plates and superimposed an image on them, marking them for later use by filing the edges.

Emile le Roux in 1909, and is one of the very few stereoscopic spirit photographs.

The instructions came from a spirit who claimed to be the uncle of le Roux's wife. The spirit made contact through her when she was practising automatic writing in le Roux's presence. Through the automatic script, the 'uncle' said that he could be photographed at a later point in the day and gave instructions as to the time and the exposure. Le Roux, a keen amateur photographer, considered the exposure to be far too long; but he followed instructions and took the picture with his stereoscopic camera at the time indicated. The image of the deceased uncle not only appeared but was quite recognisable. In its day, the plate became very famous – but time after time le Roux had to defend himself against the usual charges of fraud. His own simple words reveal the recurrent story of the amateur caught up in a process that he or she cannot explain:

> In reality, this photograph was made under the most simple circumstances, and I would say that except for the strangeness of the spirit head, there were so few difficulties both before and after its execution that, in spite of the

president of the Society for Psychical Research (SPR), Mrs Wickstead wrote that Mrs Laurie had seemed impressed by the two graves and had made a point of showing them to her husband. 'We thought no more about it until about six weeks later when the film was developed and came out as you see with these two figures on the path in the shadow of the yew tree,' Mrs Wickstead wrote. The two figures were in an embrace. The picture was investigated by the SPR, but the mystery of the extras was never solved.

Invisible spirits

There have been rare cases of sensitives seeing and photographing spirits that have remained invisible to others present. One famous example of this is known as the 'Weston' photograph.

The Reverend Charles Tweedale and his family lived in Weston vicarage, a much haunted house in the town of Otley in West Yorkshire. While having lunch on 20 December 1915, Mrs Margaret Tweedale saw the apparition of a bearded man to the left of her son. The others around the table could see nothing. However, her husband immediately fetched the camera and took a picture of the area indicated by his wife. When the negative was developed, a portrait of the apparition appeared on the print.

One extraordinary picture session that took place in Belgium seems to support the belief that the spirits intervene directly in psychic photography. In this instance, a spirit actually instructed an amateur photographer in the most precise manner how and when to take a picture in which the spirit would manifest. The picture was taken by

Above left: the spirit of a dead child appears with her father on a portrait taken by Dr Hooper, a clairvoyant. Hooper claimed that he saw the girl when he took the picture, though she was invisible to others present

Above: an 'extra' of Madame le Roux's uncle appeared on this picture of her, taken by her husband during an automatic writing session. Through the script, the spirit gave instructions on taking the photograph

Left: an unidentified extra in Gloucester Cathedral taken about 1910

Above right: a picture of a bottle allegedly made by the direct transfer of a thought onto a photographic plate in 1896 – called a 'thought-photograph' before the word 'thoughtography' came into use. It was made in France by a Commandant Darget

Right: the ghost of a woman, dead a week, is seen in the back seat in a picture taken by her daughter. Experts said the photograph had not been tampered with

scepticism which arose within me, and which has not yet quite vanished, I am forced to admit that in order to explain this negative it is necessary to look in another direction than 'fraud' or the double exposure of the plate.

This tantalising image of the deceased uncle is stereoscopically adjusted for depth – an indication that, photographically at least, the psychic entity is subject to the same optical laws as a living being.

The subject of spirit photography greatly excited psychical investigators in the 1870s and 1880s, but no organised and sustained study seems to have been made. There are many references to the phenomenon in the *British Journal of Photography* and a number of articles in the *Journal* of the SPR. But the issue was clouded by the controversy over Spiritualism and no undistorted and full treatment of psychic photography itself has come down to us.

In any event, psychic photography did not end with the unexplained appearance of spirit forms on prints. One new form that has emerged in recent times is the manifestation of UFOs. And, since the main question is whether images on film can be produced without optical processes, thoughtography is of relevance too.

The term 'thoughtography' came into use in Japan in 1910 following a series of tests by Tomokichi Fukurai of a clairvoyant who accidentally imprinted a calligraphic character on a photographic plate by psychic means. Later the sensitive was able to do this by concentrated effort. Fukurai's work was

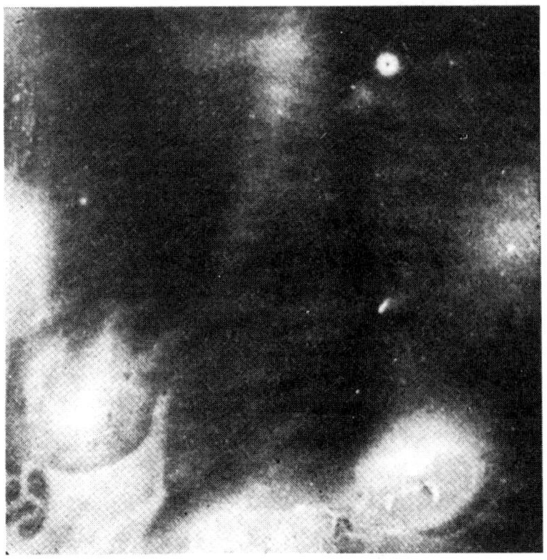

published in English 20 years later and some experiments similar to his were then undertaken in Europe and the United States. But it was not until 1962 that interest in thoughtography was activated by Pauline Oehler, of the Illinois Society for Psychic Research, through her work with the American psychic Ted Serios

Serios was much investigated under strictly controlled conditions, particularly by Dr Jule Eisenbud who was a psychical researcher working mainly in Denver, Colorado, USA. In many experiments planned by Eisenbud over a period of two years, Serios could at will produce pictures of what he was thinking about – an old hotel, cars, a corner of a room, and many other mental images. He could also produce an image of a target set by himself or others. For example, one day he glanced casually at a travel magazine in Eisenbud's waiting room. The next day he decided to produce a picture of Westminster Abbey, which he had noticed in the publication. And he did so.

Thoughtography has since become an integral part of modern psychical research. And although Serios's ability to transfer his thoughts onto film has never been explained, neither has it ever been proved fraudulent.

Among the professional spirit photographers of the late 19th century, however, there were undoubtedly frauds – and a number of them were exposed. But does that negate the important fact that many photographic images have been produced by paranormal means?

Ghostly 'extras', spirit messages and materialisations of people and objects – these were the hallmarks of the professional psychic photographer. Were the spirit manifestations they produced genuine? This chapter weighs the evidence

An enterprising spirit

BY ITS VERY NATURE, psychic photography has from its beginnings been open both to the accusation of fraud and to fraud itself. Not a single established spirit photographer was free of taint – all, at one time or another, were the object of bitter intrigue, legal action or both. Yet many had genuine psychic abilities.

The Bostonian William Mumler was almost certainly the first person in the United States to earn a living as a professional spirit photographer. He became very well-known, and it is clear from surviving pictures that his mediumistic abilities were quite remarkable. Several investigations failed to unearth any fraud on his part. Nonetheless, Mumler fell foul of the law in 1869 – but it was as a result of a journalistic campaign whose aim was to create scandal. The spirit photographer was eventually charged as a swindler, but the evidence brought to the court was so overwhelmingly in his favour that the case was dismissed.

Mumler's most famous spirit picture is one taken towards the end of 1865, about four years before his trial. The sitter, who visited Mumler incognito, was no less a person than Mary Todd Lincoln, then recently widowed by the assassination of President Abraham Lincoln. In the print is a recognisable image of Lincoln, standing behind her and laying his hands upon her shoulders.

After Mumler's death in 1884, another spirit photographer came to notice on the west coast of the United States. This was the Californian Edward Wyllie. Dr H.A. Reid, who was a specialist in the history of 19th-century psychic photography, said of him:

> As to the work of Edward Wyllie, the medium photographer, the proofs and testimonies that the phenomena were genuine and not trickery, were all so open, untrammelled, fair and conclusive that to reject them is to reject the validity of all human testimony.

Wyllie led an adventurous life of travel in India and New Zealand before settling in Pasadena, California, in 1886 as a photographer. He had been psychic since childhood and his psychic leanings came to the fore rapidly with the appearance of unwanted 'extras' on his photographs. These spirit forms at first threatened to interfere with his business, but when he realised that the extras were often recognisable to his sitters, he changed his line of business accordingly. Wyllie was able to photograph spirit forms 60 per cent of the time. The number of 'recognitions' among these was substantial. His highly distinctive style is characterised by several extras upon a single plate. For example, a portrait of J.R. Mercer contains the spirit forms of his mother and his wife, a bunch of flowers and a spirit message signed 'Elisabeth B. Mercer'.

In the decades in which Wyllie was the foremost of spirit photographers in the United States, the most famous and versatile of English mediums was William Eglinton. Though it is true Eglinton was from time to time unmasked as a fraud, he had undoubted psychic powers. Unlike the majority of Spiritualists of his day, he was able at times to work in daylight. He would often permit photographs to be made and one

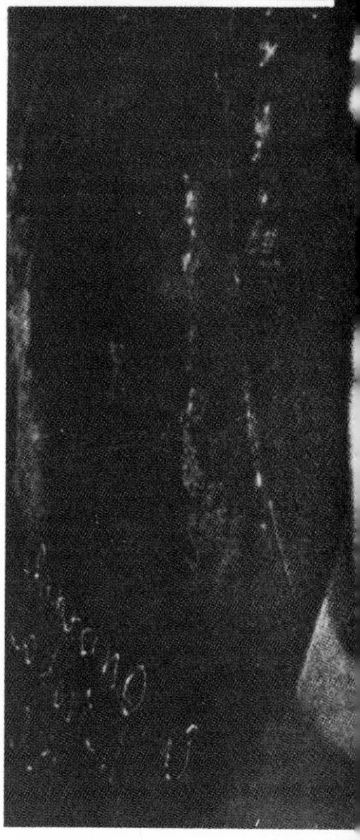

remarkable picture shows a complete materialisation. This was witnessed and described by Eglinton's biographer, John S. Farmer:

> At this time his breathing became increasingly laboured and deep. Then, standing in full view, by a quick movement of his fingers, he gently drew forth, apparently from under his morning coat, a dingy white-looking substance. He drew it from him at right angles and allowed it to fall down his left side. As it reached the ground it increased in volume and covered his left leg from the knee downwards. The mass of white material on the ground increased in bulk and commenced to pulsate, move up and down and sway from side to side. Its height increased and shortly afterwards it quickly grew into a form of full stature, completely enveloped in the white material. The upper part of the medium then drew back and displayed the bearded face of a full-length materialised spirit, considerably taller than himself. . . .

The only method of making photographs of materialised figures in the seance room was by means of the magnesium light, which was said to have a deleterious effect on the medium as well as on the spirit. Even so, some of the most impressive of 19th-century spirit photographs were made by means of the magnesium flare. Among these pictures is a series made during the seances of the Spiritualist Madame d'Esperance, who left fascinating memoirs of her dealings with leading Victorian mediums, investigators and spirit photographers. In her archives there is a picture taken in March 1890 of the fully materialised form of a beautiful 15-year-old Arab girl called Yolande, who, it appeared, would materialise frequently. Indeed she became the medium's most constant spirit companion. Yolande would take approximately 15 minutes to materialise into human form. A description of the process has been left by one of the members of the d'Esperance circle:

> First a flimsy, cloudy, patch of something white is observed on the floor, in front of the cabinet. It then gradually expands, visibly extending itself as if it were an animated patch of muslin,

Left: the widowed Mary Todd Lincoln with the spirit of President Abraham Lincoln. The picture was taken in Boston, Massachusetts, USA, by William Mumler, the first professional spirit photographer, the year that Lincoln was assassinated

Below: the English medium William Eglinton (right) seen with the remarkable materialisation he produced in full view of witnesses and a photographer

Below right: the sitter's mother and wife, a spirit message and some flowers are the kind of 'extra' that typify Edward Wyllie's distinctive style of psychic photography

Left: a spirit, perhaps of a Spanish girl called 'Ninia', taken during one of the many successful photographic seances conducted by Madame d'Esperance in the 1890s

Right: a spirit portrait of the American poet Walt Whitman (right) compared with his living likeness. It was taken by the English medium William Hope

Below: this ghostly nun is a partial materialisation photographed in 1918 by the medium Castelwitch

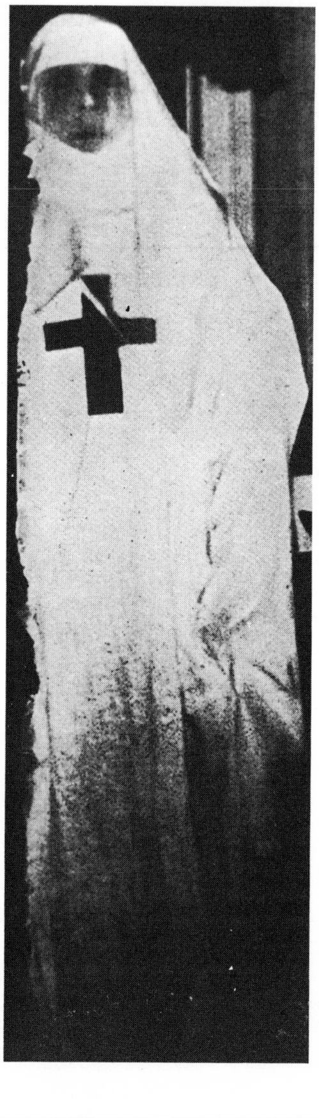

> lying fold upon fold, on the floor, until extending about $2\frac{1}{2}$ by 3 feet [75 by 90 centimetres] and having a depth of a few inches. . . . Presently it begins to rise slowly in or near the centre, as if a human head were underneath it, while the cloudy film on the floor begins to look more like muslin falling into folds about the portion so mysteriously rising. By the time it has attained two or more feet [60 centimetres], it looks as if a child were under it and moving its arms about in all directions. . . . Presently the arms rise considerably above the head and open outwards through a mass of cloud-like spirit drapery, and Yolande stands before us unveiled, graceful and beautiful, nearly 5 feet [1.5 metres] in height, having a turban-like headdress, from beneath which her long black hair hangs over her shoulders and down her back.

The dematerialisation was no less dramatic, though it took only between two and five minutes. The form suddenly fell 'into a heaped patch of drapery'. The drapery – Yolande's clothes – 'slowly but visibly melt into nothingness', said the witness.

The picture of Yolande is pleasant to the eye, but not all materialisations are quite so lovely to behold. They can be repulsive, both in the process of formation by the medium and in their final form.

The material by which spirits are given visible form is the mysterious substance called ectoplasm. It is exuded from the medium's body, most usually from one of the orifices, and the extrusions from the mouth of the medium – or, in one case, from the nipples – are often repellent. Even when a materialised form has the power to walk in the manner of a living being, it may be only partially formed. One example of an unpleasant partial manifestation was photographed by the medium Castelwitch during seances in Lisbon in 1918. The spirit form was that of a nun, and it was so ghastly in appearance that one of those taking part in the seance actually broke down, begging the spirit not to come closer. A description by one witness to these seances and the nun's several materialisations captures something of the atmosphere:

> We saw at first a kind of vapour, through which it was possible to distinguish the picture on the wall. This vapour grew a little longer, became thicker, and took the form of a spirit which gave us the impression of being a monk [*sic*] dressed in white. It advanced and drew back three times towards the red light, on its way it knocked on the table. Three times it disappeared and then reappeared, making the same movement.

Even the clinical description of this spirit nun by the psychologist and psychical researcher Baron von Schrenck-Nötzing carries a sense of the macabre into the textbooks:

> The phantom is flat, in spite of the very vivid facial expression. The face of the nun is veiled, and the upper body draped in a white fabric. It is remarkable in the fact that in this figure the whole right side (including the right ear, shoulder and arm) is entirely

missing, as if this part had, from top to bottom, been ripped off a life-sized portrait.

The hallmark of the professional spirit photographer is the ability to capture images of the dead that are recognisable to living relatives or friends. The professional with the highest record of such recognitions was the Frenchman Jean Buguet. While Mumler could claim 15 recognitions, and the Englishman Frederick Hudson 26, Buguet could claim 40 recognitions in his spirit photographs. Even had Buguet miraculously discovered a new way of making double exposures that would fool the photographic experts of his day, fraud on that scale would have been almost impossible. For many of the Buguet spirit forms were of people who had died before the invention of photography, so there were no originals to use for double exposures.

Buguet was, like Mumler, brought to trial. And as in Mumler's case, hundreds of favourable testimonials poured into the court. The trial was almost certainly rigged. Buguet was found guilty but, as one writer later commented, this 'did not and could not efface the facts of genuine psychic photography'. No more did it efface the fact of Buguet's ability as a spirit photographer.

Above right: Charlie and the 'extra' of his son, taken by Edward Wyllie as a test for psychical researchers. They wondered if a spirit would appear when the sitter was completely ignorant of Spiritualism – and Charlie, who was Chinese, filled the bill

Left: a typical early photograph by the Frenchman Jean Buguet, who produced a high percentage of 'extras' that were recognised by the living as being of the dead. Buguet was brought to trial and convicted of fraud, but still has many defenders of his abilities as a true psychic photographer

Some of the stories attached to recognition photographs are extraordinary. A particularly interesting one concerns the production of a picture of a Chinese man and his son, made by Wyllie for one of the psychical research societies on the west coast of America. The society had expressed a hope that Wyllie might be able to obtain a spirit form on a photograph of someone who was wholly ignorant of Spiritualism. Accordingly, when Charlie, a Chinese laundryman, came in on his usual round, Wyllie asked him if he would like to sit for his portrait.

> He was very much scared. I made his mind easy and asked him to come in a few days, and I would give him the picture. When I developed the negative, there were two extras on it – a Chinese boy and some Chinese writing. When Charlie came round I showed him the print, and he said, 'That my boy; where you catchee him?' I asked him where his boy was, and he said, 'That my boy. He's in China. Not seen him for three years.' Charlie did not know that his son was dead.

Such pictures and such stories point strongly to the genuineness of spirit photography, whether by amateurs or professionals and in spite of the fact that the mysterious extras have never been fully explained. And the phenomenon is not limited to human spirit forms, for animal extras appear regularly - if less frequently – in psychic photography.

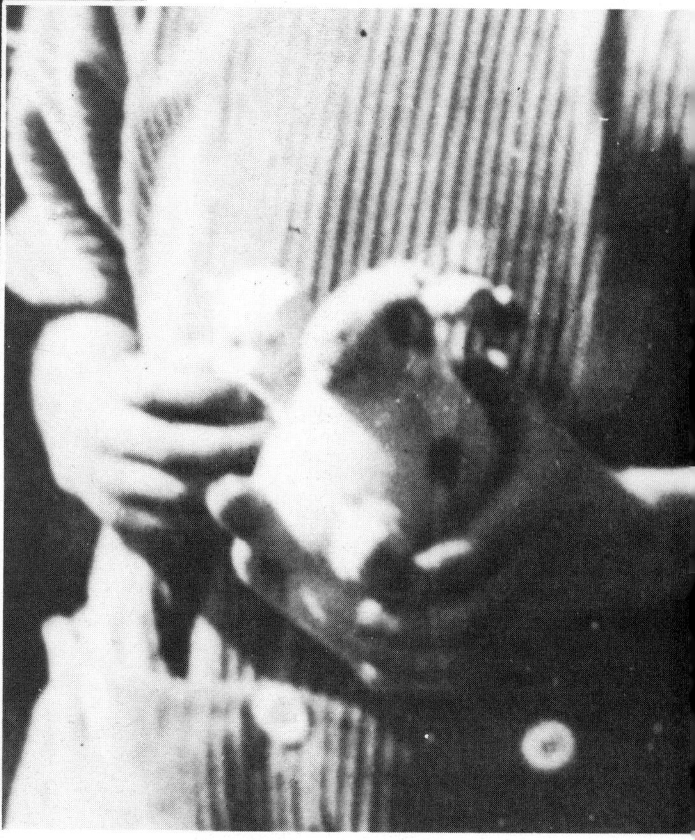

An animal lover's album

Spirit photography, whether by amateurs or professionals, has its gallery of ghostly cats, dogs and other animals – usually pets – that appear as unexpected and fascinating 'extras'

THE MAJORITY OF SPIRIT photographs in which there are animal 'extras' have been made unintentionally. They have generally been taken by amateur photographers who have been most surprised to find the curious images on their films, but who have usually recognised the identity of the unexpected spirit forms.

An interesting example of this is a picture taken by Major Wilmot Allistone at Clarens, in Switzerland, in August 1925. At first glance it seems a somewhat badly composed family snap, but on closer inspection it reveals itself as a remarkable psychic photograph. The Major was surprised and intrigued to discover that the developed print bore a faint image of a white semi-transparent kitten, nestling above the right hand of his son alongside the furry toy animal that the child held in his left hand. The boy had held no such kitten when the picture was being taken. But what astonished the Major was the fact that this ghostly kitten resembled the boy's pet, which had died a few days previously, having been mauled by a St Bernard dog.

The Allistone family and a surprising 'extra' in the form of a kitten, which showed up as though nestled in the boy's hand along with the toy he held (seen clearly in the detail). The most astonishing thing about the spirit animal was that it resembled the child's recently killed pet

The negative and prints of this fascinating photograph were later submitted to extensive investigation by experts, who even studied the negative under a stereoscopic microscope. The appearance of the dead pet was never explained.

Another example, though in some respects even more peculiar, is the picture that was submitted to the British College of Psychic Science in 1927. This was an ordinary photograph of Lady Hehir and her Irish wolfhound Tara taken by a Mrs Filson. The picture proved to be far from ordinary, however. The extra in this case is no semi-transparent wraith but a very substantial puppy head, curiously misplaced at the rear end of the wolfhound. Both Mrs Filson and Lady Hehir recognised this disjointed extra as the Cairn puppy Kathal, which had been a close companion of the wolfhound. It had died in August 1926, about six weeks before the picture was taken.

In her signed declaration submitted to the college, Lady Hehir remarked, 'I feel convinced that he [the Cairn puppy] is often in the room with Tara and me, as she talks in a soft cooing way to something she evidently "sees".'

One cannot have pets for very long without observing that they appear at times to see visitants invisible to the human eye – and whether these are ghosts, elementals, or some other sort of being is open to discussion. However, one unusual photograph shows a pet actually watching a form that was invisible to the photographer at the time. It was intended to be an ordinary flash picture of Monet, the pet cat, taken by his owner Alfred Hollidge in 1974. The Hollidge family had only one cat and there was certainly no other cat in the house when the picture was being taken. But the developed negatives showed a dark animal running in front of Monet – a small kitten, or a large rat, with a curiously long tail-like attachment trailing behind. There is no way of being sure what Hollidge himself saw, for he left the negatives for some months before sending them off for processing, and he died before they were returned – so he never examined the final prints. But it is more than likely that he would have remarked on anything strange when taking the photograph, and would have been anxious to see the prints had he observed the dark intruder. Perhaps the most interesting thing about this spirit photograph is that Monet seems to be watching something in the area in which the extra appeared on the print.

A number of spirit photographs with animal extras have been taken by professionals. The well-established American psychic photographer Edward Wyllie took a picture in which the spirits of both a woman and a dog appeared. It was taken in Los Angeles, California, in 1897 for J. Wade Cunningham, who later sent the English journalist and Spiritualist William T. Stead a long account of its making.

Above: a pet cat and a ghostly dark intruder that apparently was unseen by the photographer – but the cat seems to be watching it with intense concentration

Below: a Cairn puppy, dead about six weeks, makes a curiously out-of-place appearance on this picture of its mistress and the wolfhound that was its close companion in life

According to Cunningham, a female medium would often tell him of the beautiful woman who would sometimes appear when he was present. This spirit woman was frequently accompanied by a dog that barked and jumped 'with delight' at the sound of Cunningham's voice. One day the medium asked the spirit if she would be prepared to bring the dog and sit for a photograph. Wyllie, not knowing what was expected of him, was commissioned to make this spirit picture. The print he produced revealed both the beautiful woman and the dog, which Cunningham happily recognised as a pet he had owned many years before.

The English medium and psychic photographer William Hope rarely took open-air pictures, but while on holiday in Exmouth, Devon, in 1924, he took some snapshots of his assistant, Mrs Buxton, and her family on the steps of their caravan. The print is badly faded now, but it is still possible to see a number of curious extras. Mrs Buxton herself is all but blotted out by an ectoplasmic cloud, and above her, swathed in this mist, is an image of the face of her son, who had died in the previous year. She later said that, while the picture was being taken, she was 'wishing that he could have been one of the group'.

Alongside the son's head to the right is a form that clearly resembles the head of a horse or pony. The family recognised this as the son's white pony Tommy – which had died a short time before the son.

A third extra is harder to see. This is superimposed over Mr Buxton's waistcoat, and is the image of an old man. Mr Buxton reported that it was a portrait of his brother, who had died some time previously.

The faded quality of this Hope picture is a reminder that very few spirit photographs survive the ravages of time. It is a pity that the one made by the little-known psychic photographer Dr Stanbury in the 1880s could not be preserved.

It seems that a certain Mrs Cabell had

Left: both the woman and the dog in this photograph were allegedly spirits, captured on film by the psychic Edward Wyllie. He was commissioned to take the picture without knowing what was expected of him

Right: a number of 'extras' crowd this picture taken by the English medium William Hope. There is the woman's dead son (in the cloud of ectoplasm), a pony's head to the right of the boy's head (recognised as a dead pet) and the image of an old man to the left of the boy's head (recognised as the boy's dead uncle)

Below: a strange animal form obtained during a series of experimental seances in the studio of a photographer

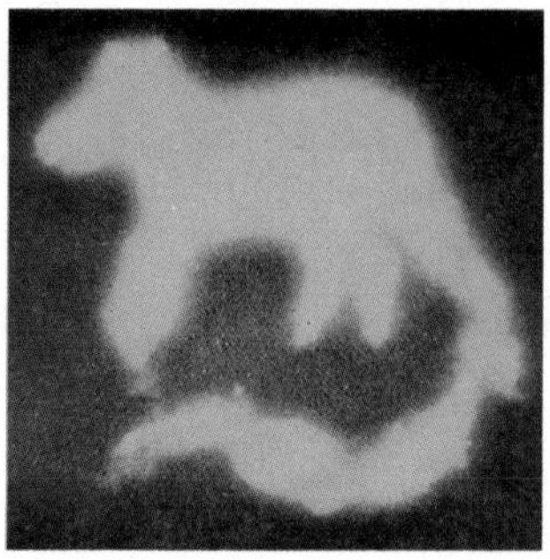

owned two dogs, one an old carriage dog with the grandiloquent name of Secretary Stanton, the other a small black-and-tan named Fanny. The two dogs were close friends, and died of old age within a few hours of each other. Some four years after their deaths, Mrs Cabell was spending the summer at Onset Bay in Massachusetts, USA, and was invited to a seance.

The medium observed on the psychic plane a 'little wee bit of a dog' jumping around Mrs Cabell, and when she examined the collar, she found the name 'Fanny' inscribed upon it. Mrs Cabell was of course very excited, and took up with interest the suggestion that they visit Dr Stanbury, who was nearby, to see if he could take a picture of her old pet. Mrs Cabell later told this story:

> Imagine my surprise at seeing my little pet cuddle up under my arm. And my surprise I cannot express at seeing the old coachdog, Stanton, also. He occupied the most prominent position, and had almost crowded out of sight his little friend in his eagerness to get there himself. . . . The dogs' pictures have been recognised by hundreds of people who knew them when in life. . . . It was four years after their death, or passing away, when this photograph was taken, which I prize beyond all price.

Animals at times appear in the seance room as well. A sort of ape creature appeared on a photograph of the famous Polish medium Franek Kluski, who was also photographed with an owl-like bird hovering over his back. This bird, which seems almost to be attacking Kluski, was not seen in the room before or after the seance. A totally unexplained image of a bat-like creature appeared above a cloud of ectoplasm in a picture taken by Staveley Bulford, a member of the British College of Psychic Science, in 1921. The cadaverous humanoid face of the bat appears to have been built out of a special kind of ectoplasm, which Bulford himself described as 'a quite different kind of ectoplasm, very dense and quite non-luminous'.

The series of seances that produced the ectoplasmic bat were conducted in the photographic studio of a Mr Scott between May and July 1921. They produced some extraordinary psychic pictures, as well as later 'communications' from the photographed spirits.

Pictures obtained during these experimental seances were varied in subject matter, though they included the 'standard' portraits of spirits, swathed in ectoplasmic cotton wool or curiously unrelated ectoplasmic structures. One was of the plant, rather than the animal, world. It was extremely clear and detailed, in the form of a spray with thick velvety leaves, and flowers reminiscent of an edelweiss. But the animal world was represented, in a photograph taken of Scott himself: above his head there appeared a quaint animal with a long, winding tail within a cloud of shiny ectoplasm.

While many psychic photographers tried deliberately to catch human spirits with the camera, few made a conscious effort to photograph animal spirits. Perhaps this is why animal spirit photography occurs so rarely.

The study of spirit photography, and of its fakery, is fascinating. And study reinforces the evidence that many psychic photographs are genuine – whether of 'extras', thoughts, or other manifestations.

Hypnosis and regression

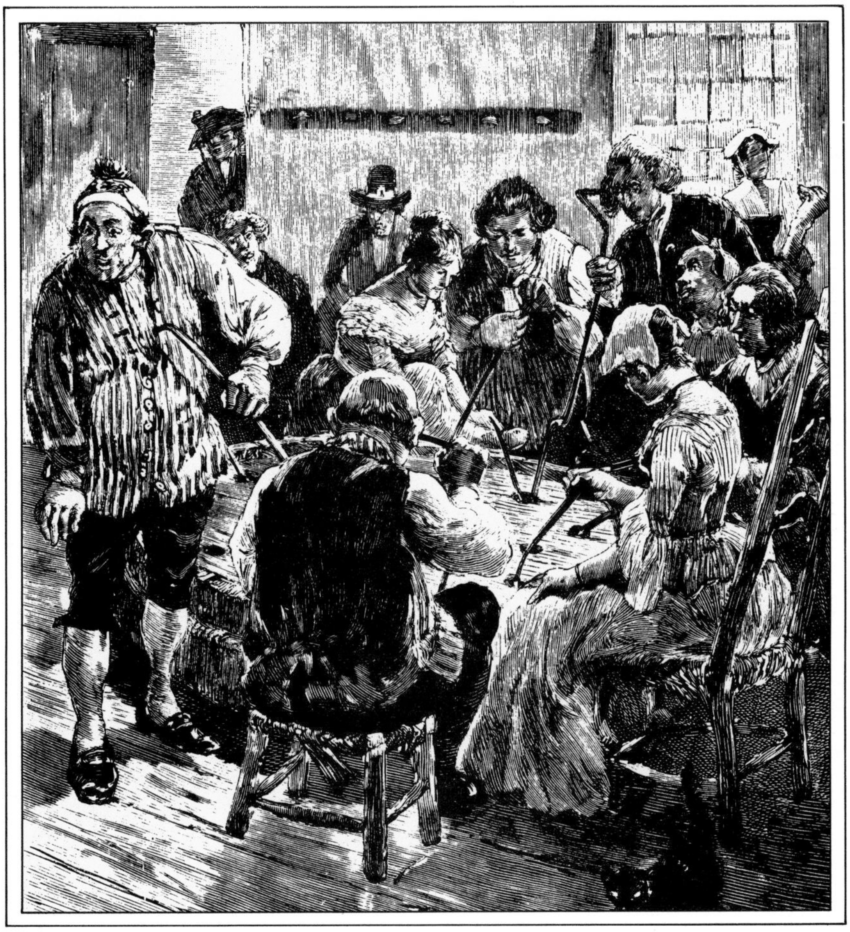

People under hypnosis have regressed back through childhood to the point where they appear to recall an earlier life or lives. They can describe them accurately, bringing forth information unknown and seemingly inaccessible to their present personalities. Is this clinching proof of reincarnation?

Other voices, other lives

It has long been known that under hypnosis some people regress to what appears to be a previous life. They not only assume another personality, but they can describe details from the past that are completely unknown to them outside of the trance state

Hypnotherapist Joe Keeton (top) has conducted more than 8000 regressions. One of his subjects, Ann Dowling (above), went back over 100 years and became Sarah Williams, who lived in Liverpool in the 1850s (top right). Among the facts recalled by Mrs Dowling was the visit of Swedish singer Jenny Lind (below)

HYPNOTIC REGRESSION into alleged previous lives is one of the most exciting and fascinating of psychic phenomena – and one of the most frustrating. During the past 20 years it has been brought to the attention of the general public every so often by programmes on radio and television, articles in the press and books written either by hypnotists themselves or by collaborators working with them.

Morey Bernstein's *The search for Bridey Murphy*, published in 1965, is still remembered if the small talk veers towards the occult; Arnall Bloxham's tapes, featured on radio and television programmes, and given a longer life by Jeffrey Iverson's *More lives than one?*, are widely known. Recently, Peter Moss has collaborated with Joe Keeton, prodigious in his expenditure of hypnotic man-hours, in the book *Encounters with the past*, which describes recordings of extracts from sessions with chosen subjects.

It is not generally realised that hypnotic regression into previous lives is not a recent discovery and has, in fact, been studied for nearly a century. The work of pioneers in this field, much of it lost because it was done long before the advent of the tape-recorder, is nevertheless valuable to students of reincarnation, whether they believe in it or not.

Travelling back in time

Part of the fascination of hypnotic regression lies in the very frustration that it engenders. Its revelations are both positive and negative, some bolstering the faith of reincarnationists and puzzling sceptics, others bewildering believers and encouraging doubt. Regression is positive in that the dramatisations of former existences are vividly portrayed far beyond the acting abilities of subjects in their waking condition, so that observers repeatedly say: 'If this be acting, neither an Olivier or a Bernhardt could better it.'

Positive, too, is the consistency with which many subjects, regressed repeatedly to the same historical period, take up the previous life, so that the same personality, outlook and intonation of speech appear without effort or hesitation. The same incidents and facts are remembered even when trick questions are introduced to try to trap the speakers. This happens even when years separate the sessions.

Regression is positive in two further ways. The first is that obscure historical facts, apparently completely unknown beforehand to either hypnotist or subject and confirmed only after considerable research, are revealed in reply to general questions. An example of this is shown by one of Joe Keeton's subjects, Ann Dowling, an ordinary housewife who, during over 60 hours of regression, became Sarah Williams, an orphan living a life of utter squalor in a Liverpool slum in the first half of the 19th century.

When asked what was happening in Liverpool in 1850, Ann Dowling mentioned the visit of a foreign singer whose name had 'summat to do wi' a bird'. Research showed that Jenny Lind, the 'Swedish Nightingale', on her way from Sweden to America, sang for two nights in Liverpool's Philharmonic Hall in August 1850.

The second positive aspect of hypnotic regression is found in the tiny details of past usage that slip naturally into the subject's conversation while reliving the past life. These details *might* have been picked up by the subject in his present lifetime and held in his subconscious memory, but they are unlikely to have been formally taught or known to people of ordinary education.

David Lowe, a member of the Society for Psychical Research, lectures about a woman whom he has regressed into a number of lives, some of them in different generations of the same family (an unusual feature), illustrating his talks with copious tape-recordings of her conversations in previous existences.

During a 17th-century regression, David Lowe asked the woman how a certain word containing a 'w' was spelt. Her spontaneous answer was 'double v' – the common pronunciation of the letter at that time. This

The belief in reincarnation

The belief in reincarnation – that man's soul is reborn over and over again in another body or form – stretches far back into the past. The doctrine appears in primitive religions such as those of the Indian tribes of Assam, Nagas and Lushais, who believed that after death the soul took the form of an insect. The Bakongs of Borneo believed that their dead were reincarnated into the bearcats that frequented their raised coffins. The Kikuyu women of Kenya often worship at a place 'inhabited' by their ancestral souls in the belief that to become pregnant they must be entered by an ancestral soul.

According to Buddhist and Hindu thought man or the soul is reborn in accordance with merits acquired during his previous lifetime. But some sects of Hinduism hold that a man does not necessarily assume a human form in the next life. If he has been involved with vice or crime it is possible he may return as a cactus, toad, lizard, or even as poison ivy! The Buddhists believe that man is made up of elements: body, sensation, perception, impulse, emotion and consciousness, which fall apart at death. The individual, as such, ceases to exist and a new individual life begins according to the quality of the previous life, until at last achieving perfection and nirvana – eternal bliss.

Although reincarnation is not mentioned in Western texts until the late Greek and Latin writers, the idea dates back to at least the 6th century BC. It appears in the Orphic writings, which appear to have played a great part in the thought of Pythagoras. He believed that the soul had 'fallen' into a bodily existence and would have to reincarnate itself through other forms to be set free. He himself claimed to have had previous existences including one as a soldier in a Trojan war.

Plato was greatly influenced by the Orphico-Pythagorean views and mentions reincarnation in his concluding part of the *Republic*. The soul, according to Plato, is immortal, the number of souls fixed, and reincarnation regularly occurs. Although discarded by Aristotle and other Stoic views, Plato's derivation was taken up by later schools of thought such as the Neoplatonists. Within the Christian church the belief was held by certain Gnostic sects during the first century AD and by the Manichaeans in the fourth and fifth centuries. But the idea was repudiated by eminent theologians at the time, and in AD 553, the Emperor Justinian condemned reincarnation, at the Second Council of Constantinople, as heresy.

Today the Westerner does have some difficulty in identifying with the Eastern idea of reincarnation. Most Western religious denominations share the view that the individual retains individuality after death, and finds the idea of returning as an animal or plant distinctly foreign. In 1917 the Roman Catholic Church denounced the idea as heresy.

Most adherents of reincarnation are now claiming the evidence from regressive hypnosis as proof for their case.

Tibetans believe that their spiritual leader, the Dalai Lama, is the reincarnation of a previous Dalai Lama whose soul enters the body of a child born at the precise moment of his death

trivial detail was more telling to some listeners than all the researched dates and genealogies that substantiated the woman's story, remarkable as these were. When asked if she were engaged (to be married), the subject failed to understand the modern expression, but later talked happily of her recent betrothal.

Fact or fiction

The negative side of hypnotic regression is nevertheless considerable. There are many anachronisms, occasional historical howlers, instances of extraordinary ignorance and, with some subjects, inconsistencies (although much rarer than, and more balanced by, the consistencies).

One 19th-century character mentioned her 'boyfriend' in the modern sense of someone with a sexual love-interest in her. Another, regressed to the early 1830s and asked who ruled England, replied 'Queen Victoria', although four years of William IV's reign had still to run and Victoria's accession could not have been known for certain.

A common difficulty in substantiating historical facts is the scarcity of records of ordinary folk before the 19th century. Even when subjects mention landowners and comparatively important people, there is often no record of their existence in local archives. It is therefore sometimes extremely difficult to separate fact from fiction, especially as there may be a great deal of 'role-playing', the incubation in the subconscious mind of an imaginary personality around a nucleus of fact read in a history book or a novel.

Origins of modern hypnosis

Hypnosis is still so misunderstood and thought of as occult in the minds of many that it is as well to describe its place in modern thought.

Modern hypnosis began with Franz Mesmer, an Austrian physician who became a fashionable figure of Parisian society in the 18th century. He mistakenly believed that human beings emitted a force that could be transferred to objects such as iron rods. He 'magnetised' the rods by stroking them, then placed them in tubs filled with water in which his patients immersed their legs. Many and various were the ills allegedly cured by this method.

The extravagance of Mesmeric theory and its claims, together with the undertones of occultism that went with them, aroused intense opposition and throughout the 19th century, serious investigators into hypnosis and the few medical men bold enough to experiment with its use met the kind of hostility once reserved for witches.

The Society for Physical Research, which was founded in Britain in 1882, set up a committee to investigate hypnosis that continued to exist until a few years ago. Its findings, however, were not easily communicated to the general public and the phenomena it showed to be genuine were remarkable enough to maintain hypnotism's occult reputation, in spite of the Society's careful, objective and scholarly approach. But the therapeutic value of hypnosis was slowly established, especially in the treatment of psychological disorders.

After much investigation, it was discovered that subjects under hypnosis could be told either to *remember* what had happened on, say, their fifth birthday, or to *be* five years old again and to relive the day.

In the latter case, subjects would be led back to that day, write as they wrote at that age, relive the opening of their presents and each incident of the birthday party. They would have no knowledge of anything that happened after their fifth birthday until led forward by the hypnotist. It was as if all the layers of experience from five years old onwards had completely disappeared. The first man to attempt this age regression is said

The founder of modern hypnosis, Franz Anton Mesmer, believed that people emitted a force that could be transferred to iron rods. Parisians of all classes flocked to his salon in the 18th century where they sat round a large wooden tub called a *baquet*. This was filled with water, iron filings and bottles of 'magnetised' water. Projecting from the tub were iron rods, which patients held against their afflicted parts

to have been a Spaniard, Fernando Colavida, in 1887.

Further discoveries led to the investigation of pre-birth experiences in the womb and within a few years Dr Mortis Stark was studying the possibility of actually regressing subjects to a life before the present. At about the same time, in 1911, a Frenchman, Colonel Albert de Rochas, published an account of regressions that he had collected over several years.

A therapeutic role

The method employed in hypnotic regression is simple. After hypnotising the subject, the operator takes him back step by step to the beginning of his present life, then into the womb, and then instructs him to go back and back until he comes to some experience that he can describe. This is sometimes an 'existence' in the intermission between death ending a former life and birth beginning the present, sometimes experience of the former life itself, the period and circumstances of which the hypnotist can elicit by careful questioning.

The process is not merely used for interest's sake or to prove reincarnation – it can be therapeutic. Neuroses and other psychological disorders may be caused by traumas, the existence of which has been caused by shocks or other experiences in childhood or youth apparently too horrible for the conscious mind to face. To cure the neurosis, the trauma must be discovered and faced by the patient, and hypnosis is one technique able to dig it out.

By an extension of the process, neuroses and phobias may be caused by traumas experienced in alleged former lives that are revealed under hypnosis. Thus, one woman's terrible fear of water was caused by her having been bound with chains as a galley-slave in a previous existence, thrown into a river and eaten alive by crocodiles. A man terrified of descending in lifts had been a Chinese general who had accidentally fallen to his death from a great height. A young American girl about to dive from a high board was suddenly paralysed with fear after a moving bystander had been reflected in the water. Hypnosis revealed the hideous end of a former life in which she had been a girl in Florida who, just as she was jumping into the water, had seen the shadow of the alligator that was to devour her moving below the surface.

Whether or not these are memories of genuine previous experiences, they are convincing to many who have them. Much of the investigation into this particular aspect of hypnosis challenges the sceptics to find an explanation other than that of reincarnation. There *are* alternative explanations, which will be presented in future chapters.

Ten more lives to remember

Madame J, a soldier's wife and mother of one child, was delicate in health and as a girl had 'hated history'. She was regressed by Colonel de Rochas to 10 previous lives, some extremely detailed.

In the first she died at eight months. She then lived as a girl named Irisée in the country of the Imondo near Trieste. She next became a man, Esius, aged 40, who was planning to kill Emperor Probus in revenge for taking his daughter, Florina.

The fourth life was that of Carlomée, a Frankish warrior chieftain captured by Attila at Châlons-sur-Marne in AD 449. Abbess Martha followed, born in AD 923, who tyrannised young girls in a Vincennes convent as late as 1010. The Abbess was succeeded by Mariette Martin, aged 18 in 1300, daughter of a man who worked for the king – 'le beau Philippe'.

Madame J. then became Michel Berry, who was killed at the age of 22 in 1515 at the Battle of Marignano. This life was extremely detailed, Michel's career developing from his learning the art of fencing at 10, through his life as a page at the courts at Versailles and the Sorbonne and sundry love affairs to his presence aged 20 at the Battle of Guinegatte in Normandy.

Top: Colonel Albert de Rochas caused a sensation in 1911 with an account of hypnotic regression

Centre: the Emperor Probus, who was hated by Esius, the third personality in Madame J's previous lives

Above: the Battle of Marignano, in which Michel Berry died

After an eighth life as a wife and mother aged 30 in 1702, Madame J again became a man, Jules Robert. Jules was aged 38 in 1776 and a 'bad' worker in marble. Nevertheless one of his sculptures reached the Vatican.

Jules Robert reincarnated as Marguerite Duchesne, born in 1835, daughter of a grocer in the rue de la Caserne, Briançon. She went to school in the rue de la Gargouille. Research showed that the school existed, but there had never been a grocer Duchesne in the rue de la Caserne. Otherwise Madame J's description of places was accurate.

The case for Bridey Murphy

Have our lives been shaped not only by experiences and impressions gained since birth, but also by those from some other, previous existence? This question has vexed people for centuries. Here, the remarkable case of an American, Mrs Virginia Tighe, who, under hypnosis, regressed over a hundred years to become an Irish woman – 'Bridey Murphy' – is considered

IN 1956 AND 1957, Emile Franckel conducted a series of live experiments for a Los Angeles television programme called *Adventures in Hypnotism*. Franckel's aim was to bring to the public's attention the possibility that individuals under hypnosis can relive previous lives. His attitude was sceptical: he believed that recollections of previous lives arose from promptings from the hypnotist or deep subconscious memory. Some of the experiences he was able to draw from his subjects, however, seemed unaccountable by this explanation. Since the hypnotist did not know his subjects, he could scarcely have induced their responses except by a series of coincidences too remarkable to be statistically acceptable as mere chance.

Yet Franckel was right to have remained sceptical. For although some of the results were so remarkable as to seem almost miraculous, hypnosis is a mental state that almost anyone may experience given the right circumstances and which almost everyone can produce in at least some subjects – provided, of course, that he has mastered a few simple techniques – techniques that should never be used merely as a party game nor for exhibition purposes, nor by anyone who is unaware of its dangers. This does not mean that hypnosis is fully understood by the medical profession. The following cases illustrate some of the areas where our knowledge is still inadequate in explaining regression into previous lives under hypnosis.

Assuming that the human personality consists of potentialities derived from a combination of factors – parents' genes, plus, perhaps, racial memories and other elements, if belief in reincarnation is to be established as fact, these 'other elements' will include memories of previous lives.

What appears to happen under hypnosis is that the layers of experience we have all acquired during our lives – experiences that have pushed our memory of previous existences deep into the subconscious – come to the surface. When the hypnotist suggests, for example, to a 30-year-old subject: 'It is now 1970. You are now 20—you are waking up on your 20th birthday. Tell me where you are, what is happening', the subject's life and development of the past 10 years are as if they had never been.

Practising hypnotists know that no two subjects ever behave exactly alike, for all human beings are unique in some way, and with many subjects there seems to be a 'shadow' personality—a fantasy personality

Below: King Richard II (1367–1400) and courtiers at Conway Castle, Wales. In 1906 a clergyman's daughter claimed while under hypnosis, to have lived a previous life in the court of Richard II and to have known his mother, the 'Fair Maid of Kent'

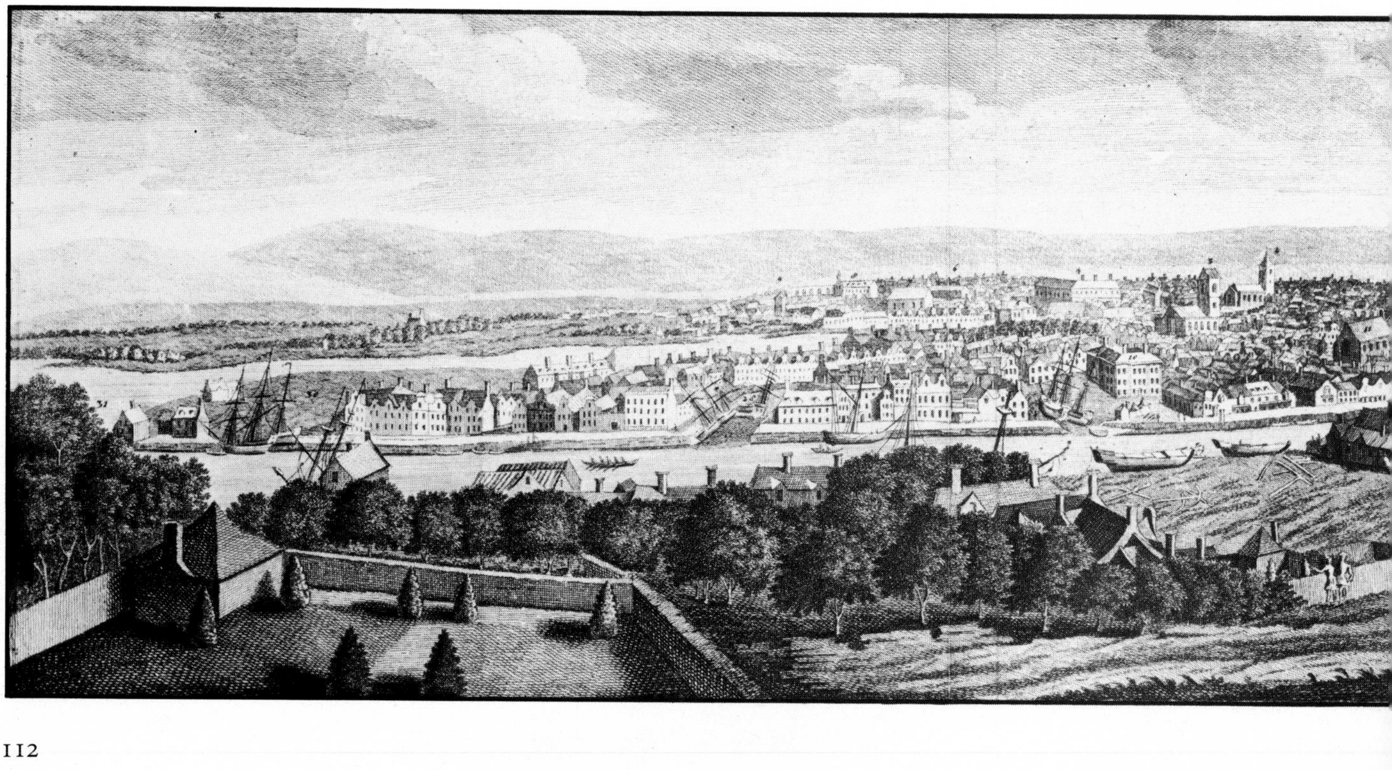

that is only revealed sometimes in dreams or under hypnosis. And, the suggestion is, it is this 'fantasy personality' that is revealed, not recollection of a previous life.

How are we to distinguish between what may be mere fantasy and a true account of a previous life? As early as 1906 the Society for Psychical Research reported the case of an unnamed clergyman's daughter who, under hypnosis, recounted her life during the reign of Richard II. In that life she was no great lady herself – despite the claim by cynics that *all* cases of regression imagine themselves to be famous people – but an acquaintance of Maud, Countess of Salisbury, her friend Blanche Poynings, née Mowbray, and Richard's mother, 'Fair Maid of Kent'.

In this case, almost every historical fact stated under hypnosis was found to be true, as were details of the dress and food described by the girl. Moreover, she had no recollection of ever having read about either the period or the people.

Some early psychical researchers into hypnotic phenomena awoke their subjects and placed their hands on a planchette board, usually screened from the subjects' view, and proceeded to interrogate them. The planchette – it is claimed – wrote down true answers to the questions from knowledge in the subjects' subconscious minds. Under these conditions the girl revealed that she had just read an historical romance in which every person and fact, except for some minor details, had appeared, though she had devised a new setting for them.

If all cases were as straightforward as this, there would be no need for further investigation, and believers in reincarnation would have to look elsewhere for evidence. How complicated the majority of cases are, however, is shown by the celebrated case of

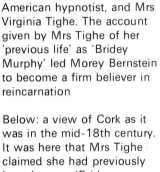

Right: Morey Bernstein, the American hypnotist, and Mrs Virginia Tighe. The account given by Mrs Tighe of her 'previous life' as 'Bridey Murphy' led Morey Bernstein to become a firm believer in reincarnation

Bridey Murphy. This is no more remarkable than a hundred other cases of hypnotic regression, but was brought to the public's attention by a heated debate in a number of American newspapers and a film shown widely in English-speaking countries.

In a number of sessions from November 1952 to October 1953, Morey Bernstein, an amateur American hypnotist, regressed Mrs Virginia Tighe to a life in early 19th-century Ireland. Mrs Tighe, 29 years old at the time, a native of Madison, Wisconsin, and resident in Chicago from the age of three until her marriage, had never visited Ireland, nor had much to do with Irish people (she

Below: a view of Cork as it was in the mid-18th century. It was here that Mrs Tighe claimed she had previously been born as 'Bridey Murphy' in 1798

Right: kissing the Blarney Stone in the manner described by Mrs Tighe. Today, all one does is to lie on the back, hold on to two bars attached to the wall, lower the head and kiss the underside of the Stone. The earlier method, used at the time of 'Bridey Murphy', would not have been known by Mrs Tighe without her having done a great deal of research

Below: to counter the claim that he had in some way rigged his experiments, Morey Bernstein hypnotised Mrs Tighe only in the presence of two witnesses

Bottom: uillean pipes of the type 'Bridey Murphy' claims were played at her funeral in Cork in 1864

strongly denied allegations to the contrary, and the evidence supports her denials). Under hypnosis she began to speak with an Irish accent, said she was Bridget (Bridey) Murphy, daughter of Duncan and Kathleen Murphy, Protestants living at the Meadows, Cork. Her brother Duncan, born in 1796, married Aimée, daughter of Mrs Strayne, who was mistress of a day school attended by Bridey when she was 15.

In about 1818 she married a Catholic, Brian MacCarthy, whose relatives she named, and they travelled by carriage to Belfast through places she named but whose existence has never been found on any map.

The couple worshipped at Father John Gorman's St Theresa's Church. They shopped at stores that Bridey named, using coins correctly described for the period. In addition, Bridey produced a number of Irish words when asked, using some as they were used then, though their meaning had changed since: 'slip', for example, referring to a child's pinafore, not petticoat – the more common modern word. Bridey Murphy had read some Irish mythology, knew some Irish songs and was a good dancer of Irish jigs. At the end of one sitting, Mrs Tighe, aroused from her trance, yet not fully conscious,

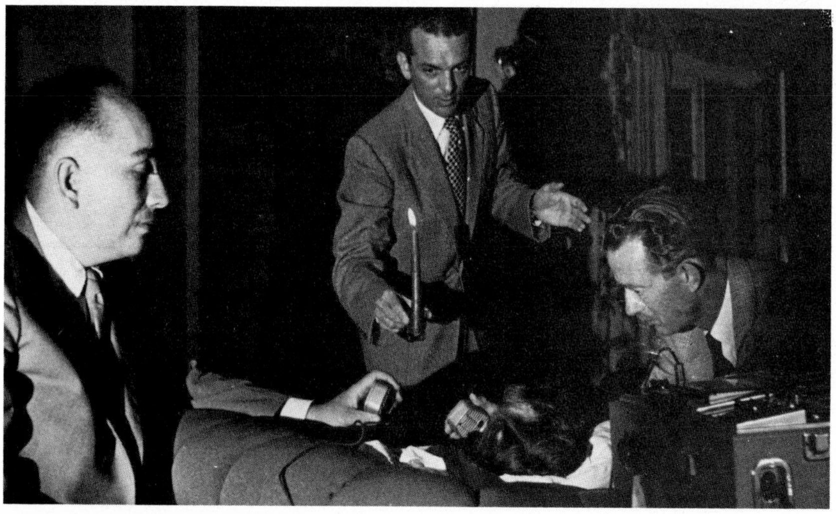

danced 'The Morning Jig', ending her performance with a stylised yawn. Her description of another dance was confirmed in detail by a lady whose parents had danced it. Another telling detail was that she described the correct procedure for kissing the Blarney Stone used in Bridey's day.

Bridey's story was investigated by the American magazine *Empire*. William Barker was commissioned by the magazine to spend three weeks in Ireland checking the facts 'Bridey' had given. His visit resulted in a 19,000-word report. Barker's account is typical of regression cases. Some facts were confirmed, others unconfirmed, others proved incorrect. Memories of insignificant detail proved true, while Bridey displayed total ignorance of other important events.

Confirmation of facts proved impossible in many instances. There was no possibility, for example, of confirming dates of birth, marriages and deaths, as no records were kept in Cork until 1864 and if the Murphy family kept records in a family Bible, a customary procedure, its whereabouts are not known. No information could be discovered concerning St Theresa's Church or Father Gorman in Belfast, but the two shops mentioned by Bridey, Carrigan and Farr, had both existed. Bridey had said that uillean pipes had been played at her funeral and these were found to have been customarily used at funerals because of their soft tone.

So the neutral enquirer is left puzzled. Where did Mrs Tighe learn about uillean pipes, kissing the Blarney Stone and the names of shops in Belfast whose existence was only confirmed after painstaking research? Why should she have created a vivid picture of life in Ireland at the beginning of the 19th century, if this was simply a creation of some part of her subconscious? From where did she – along with many other regressed subjects with no pretence at acting ability – draw the talent to dramatise so effectively a life in another age and another country?

Yet, if reincarnation is a fact, why should trivialities be remembered and great emotional experiences that one would have expected to have contributed to one's development in this life be forgotten or go unmentioned? The questions are as bewildering as they are intriguing.

Remembrance of things past

Believers in reincarnation find the details of everyday life recalled under hypnosis are proof of previous lives. This chapter discusses whether these are more important than a knowledge of major historical events

The Jews of York met a violent end as a result of persecution by Christians, in the massacre of 1190. One of Arnall Bloxham's subjects, Jane Evans, regressed to the previous life of Rebecca, one of the Jews who was murdered

IF THERE WERE a place in the *Guinness book of records* for the greatest number of past lives one individual was able to recollect, it would probably go to a patient of Dr Blanche Baker of San Francisco. This patient, born in Utah of Scots-English-American ancestry, boasted a total of 47 previous lives – 23 as a man, 24 as a woman. Historical details revealed by this patient were later found, it is claimed, to be accurate.

But the recollection of past lives aroused in Dr Baker's patients resulted not from a direct suggestion that they should return to previous existences, but by a light, hypnotic free association technique first used in 1950. Under this form of hypnosis, Dr Baker's patients experienced scenes of violence, death and curious personal relationships, in which the senses of sight, smell, taste and touch played important parts, accompanied sometimes by physical pain and acute emotional anguish.

The feeling of pain and grief experienced by many patients under hypnotic regression answers in many ways the oft-asked question, 'If we have lived before, why do we not remember past lives?' There would seem to be a natural tendency for the mind to suppress memories of events or scenes that have caused pain and distress. So it would not be surprising for people to forget or positively wish to forget previous lives that were painful or unpleasant. And under hypnotic regression it is those events that have caused extreme physical and mental pain in previous lives that are often the most vivid memories recalled.

Traumas from the past

Take the case, for example, of Jane Winthrop, a name assumed by another of Dr Baker's patients. Under hypnosis, Jane became Mary Dunlap, a settler in 18th-century Massachusetts who lost her husband, Allan. 'Certainly,' said Jane Winthrop, 'I have never consciously known such overpowering grief as I relived each time I spoke of Allan's death,' adding: 'That which comes from any of us must be first within us.'

Here Jane Winthrop touches upon an important element in the belief in reincarnation. Just as in this life much of what we are is the result of forgotten or unconscious schooling and instruction, so, our present selves, reincarnationists believe, are similarly made up of experiences from previous lives, which we have also forgotten. As in this life a neurosis may be caused by a childhood trauma and cured by its being uncovered under hypnosis and brought to the patient's conscious memory, so a trauma from a past life may be revealed and its discovery heal the present-life neurosis it has caused.

Whatever the explanation of former 'lives', the vividness of them and the emotions they arouse are convincing to those undergoing the experience and to some observers as well. Yet vividness and conviction do not in themselves guarantee truth. Barbara Larson, a university graduate, a teacher until her marriage and mother of three, was hypnotised in middle age and became Sam Sneed (1853–96), a cocky young gambler and cardsharp. Sneed's whole career was portrayed from a 19-year-old gamester, swaggering across America, hopping trains one jump ahead of the lawmen of the towns in which he played, through salesman and entrepreneur to solid citizen, selling advertising and writing editorials for the Sacramento *Bee*. Shot by a Frank Jordan, whom he had accused of corruption, he was buried in Sacramento cemetery.

Such a bare narrative cannot do justice to the intense vividness of the regression;

Above: part of the Ontario landscape in Canada that Joanne McIver claimed to recognise from her previous life, some 100 years before, as Susan Ganier

Right: a model of Eboracum, the Roman city of York. This was the home of Livonia, one of the previous lives of Jane Evans

Below: Arnall Bloxham, a distinguished British hypnotherapist, has tape recorded over 400 cases of regression. Some of his subjects have regressed to as many as 14 quite separate former lives spread out over many centuries

as one observer wrote: 'To watch the transformation of swaggering Sam Sneed into a charming, attractive Californian matron was an astonishing experience. For two hours I had been so caught up with the life of this Personality Kid that I felt I knew him better than most of my friends, because this seemed to be the inner man speaking. Those who have since heard the tape recording capture this same intensity of feeling, and roar with laughter at his broad sallies.'

Yet there is no evidence that Sam ever lived, and many errors were discovered in his story. Mrs Larson, rehypnotised and challenged in Sam's person about the proved errors, insisted his story was true. It is a principle of hypnotic theory that subjects under hypnosis do not lie if specifically told to tell the truth. One would have expected Sam to lie, and in this he was 'true' to his character. What the hypnotist does not seem to have done is to have hypnotised Mrs Larson in her own person and asked her for the source of her fantasy – if it was one.

More probable was the study by Jess Stearn, published in 1969, of Joanne McIver's previous life as Susan Ganier. Joanne, who lived at Orillia, some 80 miles (129 kilometres) north of Toronto, was regressed by her father during her teens, and produced some half dozen former lives, of which five were fragmentary compared with that of Susan Ganier. Her story was that she was born about 1835 in St Vincent Township, Ontario, some 90 miles (145 kilometres) from Sydenham Township, later Owen Sound, near where the McIvers live today. Susan married Thomas Marrow, a tenant farmer, in July 1849, the ceremony being conducted by an itinerant preacher called McEachern, and they settled at Massie village. Thomas was killed in an accident in 1863, and Susan died after a completely uneventful existence as farmer's wife and widow, in 1903.

The search for proof

Though 19th-century provincial records of births and deaths are incomplete, some confirmation of the Ganier story was found. Ganier's farm was shown on a contemporary map issued by the Ontario Department of Lands and Forests. Massie exists, though it does not appear on most maps, and a Vail's Point, mentioned by Susan, also exists. The tombstone of her close friend, Mrs Speedie, a postmistress, who died in 1909, can still be seen in Annan, a nearby village. Arthur Eagles, an octogenarian in 1969, remembered the Ganier family, knew Susan Marrow, whom he used to drive as an old lady into Owen Sound, and recalled that his parents had told him that Thomas and she were man and wife. The Toronto Department of Public Records confirmed the existence of people previously named by Joanne: Mrs Speedie, Robert MacGregor, the blacksmith in Massie, Joshua Milligan, storekeeper, and William Brown, miller.

Susan's knowledge of details of contemporary life was correct. Sugar came in packages at 10 cents a box, saddles cost from $7.50 to $12, oranges were greatly prized and a Democrat was a kind of wagon, peculiar to that time and place (this last item, however, seems known generally to Canadians). Joanne claimed to recognise places known to Susan, including the churchyard, a barn and her old home, and identified a well where none had been known to exist. At one period during the investigation she felt herself to be Susan Ganier, as if she were moving in two worlds simultaneously, with confusion of memories of past and present lives. When regressed her voice changed from its normal huskiness to a lighter, musical treble, and the depth of her emotions under hypnosis, especially her joy after marrying Tommy, her recreation of scenes delineating her relationships and the vivid pictures she gave of the Canadian wilderness were beyond acting or

The medieval home (above left) of a wealthy merchant prince, Jacques Coeur (inset), at Bourges in the Loire Valley, where Jane Evans lived as Alison, a teenage servant. Under hypnosis, Mrs Evans gave a remarkably accurate description of life in France at the time of Charles VII

any impression given by reading books.

The majority of the 400 regressions achieved by hypnotherapist Arnall Bloxham were of lives as uneventful as that described by Susan Ganier. Some, however, detailed in Jeffrey Iverson's books, *More lives than one?* (1976) and featured in broadcasts and on television, are intensely dramatic. One of the best known of his subjects is Jane Evans, who has been regressed to six previous lives.

First she was Livonia, living in AD 286, wife of Titus, tutor to Constantine, later Roman Emperor, son of Constantius and Helena, living at Eboracum (York). Livonia and Titus were converted to Christianity by a woodcarver named Albanus and died violently in Diocletian's reign. Professor Brian Hartley, an expert on Roman Britain, stated that Livonia knew 'some quite remarkable historical facts, and numerous published works would have to be consulted if anyone tried to prepare the outline of such a story.'

Where the facts could be checked, most of them proved correct. It was possible that Constantius could have been Governor of Britain from AD 283 to 290 because historians know nothing of these 'missing' years of his life. Hartley, however, questioned some details such as Livonia's statement that Roman ladies rode on horseback.

Mrs Evans' second life as Rebecca, a Jewess, showed an entirely different personality. She was massacred in 1190 with many other Jews in the crypt of St Mary's Church, Castlegate, York, where no crypt was known, until it was discovered in 1975, several years after the regression. Professor Barrie Dobson, author of a book on the massacre, commented that Jane's story was true to what was known of the events and the times, that much of the detail was impressively accurate, that disputed facts could well be true and some could have been known only to professional historians. There are some anachronisms where memories of the present life and a previous life may have become confused. But Rebecca's terror when the murderers enter the crypt is, as usual, beyond acting.

Her third life, as Alison, the teenage servant of a French merchant prince, Jacques Coeur, has been criticised on the grounds that all the facts about Coeur are readily available to British readers. Mrs Evans' knowledge included a description of the merchant's mansion at Bourges in the Loire Valley with its courtyard and style of architecture in the year 1450. She also showed a detailed knowledge of medieval French history and the life of her master, though she omitted obvious facts such as he was married and had five children.

Yet if Jane Evans' knowledge had been gained only from books she would have known these facts, and, if she had been faking, would have produced them. She

Left: one of Mrs Evans' brief regressions was as lady-in-waiting to Catherine of Aragon (1486–1536), when the young princess was about to depart from Spain in 1501 to marry Prince Arthur, eldest son of Henry VII of England

Below left: Queen Anne, who reigned from 1702 to 1714, with her son William, Duke of Gloucester. In her fifth life, Mrs Evans was a London sewing-girl, Anne Tasker, who referred to the death of the young prince, though she inaccurately described him as the Queen's only son

referred to the king, Charles VII, by his nickname of 'Heron Legs' – his thin shanks looked ridiculous in yellow tights – gossipped about his mistress, Agnes Sorel, and other personalities, and repeated the rumour that Louis, the Dauphin, had murdered his wife. Alison also mentioned a golden 'apple' containing jewels, listed as a 'grenade' (that is, pomegranate) in a catalogue of items confiscated by the Treasury from Coeur.

Mrs Evans' fourth remembered incarnation was as Anna, lady-in-waiting to Katherine of Aragon at the time she was about to leave for England to marry Henry VII's son, Arthur. She again gave correct historical details but revealed nothing remarkable. Nor did she reveal much in her fifth life, as Anne Tasker, a London sewing-girl in Queen Anne's time at the turn of the 17th and 18th centuries. She made one reference, however, which illustrates a difficulty for researchers in this field. She referred to the death of William, the Queen's 'only child', an allusion which critics fasten upon as an obvious inaccuracy. Yet it is true in the sense that Anne's son, upon whom all her hopes rested, was her only *remaining* child. Hit or miss?

Mrs Evans' last incarnation before her present life was as Sister Grace, born in 19th-century Des Moines, Iowa, and a member of an enclosed order. The nun has not been identified, because no registration of birth in Iowa was required until the 1920s and although censuses existed, they were not accurate. All that is known is that Sister Grace showed a knowledge of contemporary events that Jane seemingly did not have.

It is reasonable to expect that Mrs Evans would have spoken the languages of her incarnations, and a considerable research has been carried out on paranormal speaking in foreign tongues. However, most subjects, when regressed to previous lives in other lands, do not adopt the language of the time or the country. When Arnall Bloxham was asked if any of his subjects spoke in a foreign tongue, he replied no, for if they had he would not have understood them. But his subjects pronounced the names of cities and people correctly according to the pronunciation of the country (not Munich, for example, but 'München').

The language of the dead

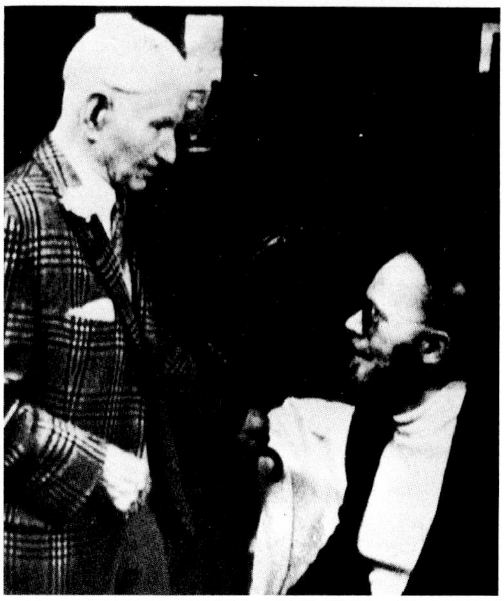

Under hypnosis, people blind from birth have described how they could see in former lives. Others have broken into foreign tongues that they have never heard or read. Is this proof of reincarnation?

Two frigates of the Royal Navy pursue a French warship during the Napoleonic wars. Graham Huxtable (inset, right) recounted similar experiences as a gunner's mate when he was hypnotised by Arnall Bloxham (left)

GRAHAM HUXTABLE, a 'charming, soft-spoken' man from Swansea, Wales, was one of the most extraordinary cases ever encountered by Arnall Bloxham. Under hypnosis, Graham Huxtable regressed to become a 'swearing, illiterate gunner's mate with a hacking cough and an earthy chuckle' in the Royal Navy at the time of the Napoleonic Wars. His voice became deeper, his Welsh accent changed to that of rural southern English, he used archaic naval slang and his descriptions of life on board an English frigate at the turn of the 18th century were later confirmed as accurate by naval historians. But neither the ship's name, which Huxtable called the '*Aggie*', or the ship's master, 'Cap'n Pearce', have been identified.

The case highlights many of the problems encountered by researchers into hypnotic regression. An illiterate sailor, unable to read his ship's name, ignorant of any information not communicable by word of mouth, whose horizons were limited by the neighbourhood in which he lived and the ship on which he served, whose social intercourse was with people as ill-educated as himself, is inevitably unable to supply the kind of information historians look for. Yet, as in other cases, Graham Huxtable adopted a persona that was able to provide information of which Huxtable himself was ignorant, vividly describe events that had happened to him and speak in a voice that was beyond any reasonable possibility of fraud. His screams of agony as he relived the experience of his leg being shot off in a naval engagement convinced even the most hardened sceptic that there was nothing false about Graham Huxtable.

Edna Greenan, a middle-aged housewife, hypnotised for over 80 hours by Joe Keeton, presents similar problems to the researcher. Under hypnosis, Mrs Greenan consistently 'became' Nell Gwyn (1650–1687), the illiterate actress and mistress of Charles II. The material she supplied through Mrs Greenan is of six kinds: historically correct, definitely incorrect, fresh information of great historical interest if it could be corroborated, half-truths, informed guesses, and small talk and gossip of the time.

It might be suggested that so much has been written and is known about Nell Gwyn that Mrs Greenan could have created her character either consciously or subconsciously. But when questioned about whether she had read anything about Nell she answered, both when conscious and under hypnosis, that she had not. Her whole manner and her speech, liberally sprinkled with nicknames and items of gossip, were entirely convincing to witnesses.

Nell Gwyn (left) was at the centre of Charles II's court in the late 17th century. Three hundred years later Joe Keeton hypnotised Mrs Edna Greenan (right) who gave an intriguing account of a former life as Charles II's mistress – none other than Nell Gwyn

Sceptics who demand historical accuracy from regressed subjects and knowledge of events that were happening at the time of a 'previous life' might listen to the conversation held in a modern bus queue or shopping centre before they condemn the simplicity, naiveté and lack of general knowledge of the common people in past centuries.

Where, then, might we find hard evidence to substantiate the claim that cases of hypnotic regression 'prove' that reincarnation takes place? One way is suggested in cases of regression with the congenitally blind, who in alleged previous lives were apparently able to see. If under hypnosis they are able to describe objects, events and experiences in the same way as a sighted person, where could they have acquired this ability other than in a previous life?

Work done by Paul Palmer and Dr James E. Parejko of Chicago State University with six blind subjects, of whom four were regressed, indicates that those born blind 'gave essentially the same life reports as sighted persons', and described events during regression as if they were sighted. Their reports may, of course, merely denote a manner of speech, as when one says 'I see' meaning 'I understand'. Alternatively they might be experiencing the kind of thing, for which there is a large body of evidence, as subjects who are able to 'see' with their elbows or some other part of the body. Or it could be a case of some other form of paranormal ability that we have yet to identify.

Whatever the cause, the blind subjects under hypnotic regression usually relied upon touch, taste and smell to describe their experiences. Only occasionally did they use expressions one would expect of a sighted person, and expressions like 'rosy cheeks that looked warm if you touched them' were common. One subject was able to describe a wooden lion's mouth, the shape of the carved teeth and how the whole thing appeared water-stained. Another subject claimed to be able to 'see' a clean-shaven man with blotches like pimples all over his cheeks and with a little tuft of whiskers growing on his throat.

Other descriptions were of a sloppy woman in a dirty blouse, windows reflected in a mirror, curtains with sunlight behind them and jewellery so dazzling in sunlight that it caused the subject to avert his eyes. Objects tended to be described three-dimensionally and at a distance – an old piano across a room, lips in a half-pout, a distant girl with red hair that was not a wig, clothes looking as though they had been slept in.

These blind subjects did not dream visually. In their regressions, however, they saw in colour and also not in colour. Like sighted people they distinguished between 'seen' objects and 'felt' objects, but the blind found that seeing objects was more of an effort than it was for those who are normally sighted. Yet they certainly spoke as if they saw and, when they returned to the same 'previous life' several times, their surroundings remained the same and more details were related. This phenomenon, which can be repeated under experimental conditions, is perhaps the best evidence there is for reincarnation.

This promising line of enquiry, however, could possibly be handicapped by lack of suitable subjects or opposed on the grounds that it is cruel to 'give sight' to someone who has never been able to see. The blind person must, of course, be given the choice of being hypnotised. But there is another line of criticism that is more damaging. It has been suggested that rather than giving an accurate description of things 'seen' the blind person is really describing things as he *imagines* a sighted person *would* describe them.

The gift of tongues

Another phenomenon that some have claimed provides proof of reincarnation is that of 'xenoglossy' or 'xenolalia'. This is the ability of some subjects, while under hypnosis, to speak a foreign language of which they are totally ignorant when conscious.

Dr Ian Stevenson relates the case of T.E., a 37-year-old American, whose doctor husband hypnotised her for therapeutic purposes. Under hypnosis she regressed to become Jensen Jacoby, speaking broken English or Swedish in a deep male voice. Jacoby, a peasant, appeared to have lived some centuries ago either in Sweden or New Sweden (present-day Philadelphia) in America. Eight scholars, seven of them Swedish-speaking, studied T.E. and her tapes, and since exhaustive research into her background showed that there was no time in her life when she could have learned Swedish or had contact with Swedish-speaking people, they agreed that it was a true case of responsive xenoglossy.

Another case investigated by Dr Stevenson is that of Dolores Jay. Hypnotised by her husband Carroll Jay in May 1970, Dolores regressed to become 'Gretchen', replying to Dr Stevenson's English in German. In 22 sessions between 1971 and 1972 Dr Stevenson, a German speaker, interviewed Gretchen in the presence of three Germans.

Gretchen responded well to Stevenson and two of the Germans but not well to the third. She gave her family name as Gottlieb, said that her father, Hermann, had been Mayor of Eberswalde, that her mother was dead and her close friend was called Frau

El Greco's painting of the Pentecost (now in the Prado, Madrid) shows the disciples of Christ receiving the gift of tongues. The miracle has been repeated in modern times, as hypnotised subjects have spoken languages that they have never been taught

Schilder. She could name no political leaders or heads of state living at the time. A Roman Catholic, Gretchen named Pope Leo and was obviously afraid of the *Bundesrat* – a word which entered Germany's political vocabulary in 1867. This was a repressive measure that discriminated against German Catholics. Gretchen died at the age of 16. Research showed that the only Eberswalde known did not have a mayor.

In the transcripts 237 German words appeared, of which 120 were spoken before any German words were spoken to her. The German spoken by Gretchen was modern, though with some archaisms. Her pronunciation was generally excellent though sometimes grossly wrong, and her grammar was sometimes faulty. In April 1971, Dolores wrote 38 words in a mixture of correct and phonetic spelling. She had not studied German nor attended a school where German was taught. Nor had she had any contact with German speakers. A lie detector confirmed her statements.

Less than a year before Gretchen manifested herself under hypnosis, she had appeared in a dream to Dolores. In 1971 and 1972, a series of nightmarish dreams and a sense of Gretchen's presence in Mrs Jay's house culminated in a brief hallucinatory flash in which she appeared. This appearance, combined with a general sense of strain, caused Mrs Jay to end the sessions.

Possessed by a spirit

A spontaneous case of either regression or possession involving xenoglossy, again investigated and reported by Dr Stevenson and a colleague, Dr Satwant Parsricha, may be included here because, though not hypnotic, it belongs to the same family of phenomena.

'Miss A', a university teacher, lived with her mother at Nagpur, Maharashtra, in India. She and her family had always lived there, speaking Marathi, with some Hindi and English. Miss A had studied Sanskrit and during her high school days had taken at most just a few lessons in reading Bengali script. Her father had Bengali friends but she had never spoken Bengali with them.

From early 1974 until 1978, a personality known as Sharada intermittently 'occupied' Miss A for periods varying from a day to seven weeks on about 30 occasions. She was quite unable to speak Marathi and spoke fluently in Bengali, contrasting markedly with the halting Swedish and German spoken by Jacoby and Gretchen. Sharada's possession of Miss A came on gradually, over a period of several hours, sometimes overnight while the latter slept, and appeared particularly on the eighth day of the waxing or waning Moon.

Sharada dressed, acted and spoke like a married Bengali woman of the early 19th century. Her speech was that spoken by Bengalis of that time. Modern Bengali contains some 20 per cent of words derived from English. These did not appear in Sharada's conversation. Nor did she show a knowledge of modern inventions and technology.

Spending her days indoors and indulging almost exclusively in devotional activities and singing, Sharada showed a marked preference for, and unusual knowledge of, the foods of Bengal and a familiarity with its small towns, villages and rivers. She gave details of the family to which she belonged, whose present head has a genealogy that includes six of the men named by Sharada. From these details her life, which was ended by a snakebite, can be dated to the years between 1810 and 1830. Sharada remembers 'fainting' after the snakebite, but could not explain how she came to be in Nagpur, 750 miles (1200 kilometres) west of Bengal.

Reincarnation or possession are alternative explanations for all cases in which one personality appears to occupy or take on the personality of another person. The difference between 'true reincarnation' and possession cases is that, in the former, a personality *remembers* his previous life while retaining consciousness of his present life, in the same way as one remembers past events in this life: 'I am now six years old; I recall my fifth birthday last year; *and* I remember when I was grown up 10 years ago.'

The 'possessed' person is not conscious of having an identity other than the one he is aware of at that moment. He is either himself ('non-possessed'), or he is the possessed personality. Each is distinct. But the possessed person does have memories, memories of the personality he has assumed while possessed. And they have been shown to be memories of real events and situations. How knowledge of these events and situations is gained, remains a mystery.

Right: Pope Leo XIII, who was correctly named by Dolores Jay during her regressions to a former life as a young Roman Catholic girl in 19th-century Germany

During the 1970s an Indian university teacher was possessed by the spirit of a Bengali girl. Not only did she dress like an early-19th-century Bengali woman (below) but spoke the language fluently

Under hypnosis a person can assume an entirely different personality. But is this an echo of a past life or a creation of the subconscious mind? This chapter sums up the evidence hypnosis offers for – and against – reincarnation

Memories, dreams or inventions

FEW ACCOUNTS of 'previous lives' recalled by people under hypnosis are free of inconsistencies or historical inaccuracies. But these in themselves are not sufficient to destroy the possibility that some cases of hypnotic regression are true reports of events that happened in a previous life. Psychologists have developed their own theories to account for hypnotic regression. And some, while denying that reincarnation is involved, accept that something outside the range of normal scientific explanation is at work. Broadly, then, there are two views taken of hypnotic regression: the 'normal' and the 'paranormal'.

Suggestibility plays a large part in the relationship between the hypnotist and his subject. The knowledge that the hypnotist is conducting an experiment in regression may be enough for the subject to respond by being provided with a past life manufactured for the purpose. There is evidence that the subconscious creative capacity of human beings – their mythopoeic ability – is extraordinarily powerful. Under hypnosis the subject may display a talent for acting, drawing, painting, writing or musical performance or composition far exceeding not only his own conscious ability but also the ability of most other people. The manufacture of a past life to gratify the hypnotist may therefore be carried out and enacted at short notice and with startling conviction.

The material for such 'lives' may come from many sources. A veridical or recurring dream that is felt to be significant because of its vividness or recurrence can provide the foundation, although the dream may originally have been due to a physical event, such as a traumatic birth experience. There may have been some subconscious imprinting by parents or other people in the subject's childhood, or even earlier, for there is evidence that the foetus can hear and register impressions in the womb during the months immediately prior to birth.

A subject widely read in historical material could use this knowledge to create a number of different lives, each focused on a different period of history. Ideas that are communicated, either consciously or subconsciously, by the hypnotist can be picked up and elaborated, while even someone unversed in hypnosis can elicit a response from the subject through quite innocently posing leading questions.

Hypermnesia, the arousal of acutely detailed memories, and cryptomnesia, the tapping of hidden memories, also provide reincarnation material. Events recalled in this way may be stage-managed by the subject's subconscious mind to create a fantasy past life based on experiences in this life. There are instances of hypermnesia, for example, in which a reader in a library glances at a printed page of, say, some archaic language for a few minutes and, decades later, is able to reproduce the same text to the minutest detail.

State-management by the subconscious mind may provide an explanation for the case of 'Bridey Murphy'. Mrs Virginia Tighe, an American, regressed under hypnosis over 100 years to become Bridey Murphy. The *Chicago American*, in its 'exposé' of the case, argued that certain facts disproved the theory of reincarnation.

Above: automatic painting by London housewife Madge Gill, who died in 1961. She ascribed such drawing to the intervention of a spirit called Myrninerest – but could it have been the work of her subconscious mind?

Overleaf, top: the 17th-century Little Prophets of Cévennes preached sermons before they could even prattle; genetic memory or some unexplained power of the mind may have been at work

As a child, Mrs Tighe had lived in Chicago opposite an Irish family called Corkell. One of her childhood friends was Kevin Corkell. Bridey Murphy said she had lived in Cork and had a friend called Kevin. More revealing, the newspaper claimed, was the fact that Mrs Corkell's maiden name was Bridie Murphy; and Mrs Tighe's sister had fallen down a flight of stairs in circumstances similar to the fall that caused Bridey's death.

But this evidence, according to Professor C. J. Ducasse of Brown University, does not succeed either in disproving or establishing the argument that Bridey Murphy is just the childhood memory of Mrs Tighe or that Virginia Tighe is the reincarnation of Bridey Murphy. That case remains open.

The recall of genetic, racial and 'folk' memories provides another possible explanation of regression phenomena. We undoubtedly inherit some traits from our ancestors, but whether we inherit their memories is another matter. The claim that genetic memory can account for such cases as the Little Prophets of Cevennes – French Huguenot children who, in times of persecution in the 17th century, preached Protestant sermons with ecstatic fervour even before they could normally prattle – is usually countered by the argument that, even if you accept the considerable contempory evidence of their ability, there are still too few cases to justify the theory. If, however, all the cases of extraordinary recall of this type were looked at together, there might then be sufficient evidence at least to make the theory feasible.

There is, however, a strong argument against genetic and racial memory. Some former lives described by subjects under hypnosis are too close to the present for such memory to take effect. Sister Grace, the last of Jane Evans' six recorded lives, was not only too close to her in time, but she was also a celibate nun; there could be no physical bridge across which her memories could have been passed to Jane. But there may be, in all of us, archetypal 'folk fears' – of being burnt as a witch or heretic, for example, or of suffering from chronic poverty – which under hypnosis are expressed as events in a 'previous life'. A Jewish girl, too young to have known of concentration camps except as a fact of history, nevertheless dreamed vividly and recurrently as a child that she was immured in one.

'Dissociated personalities' – cases well-known in the psychology of abnormal behaviour in which the human body may be inhabited in turn by up to a dozen or more 'individuals' – are a rare form of mental illness. But sometimes, when apparently normal people are hypnotised for therapeutic purposes, such a personality or personalities may emerge whose existence would otherwise never have been suspected.

It may be that some people harbour

Cayce's cosmic knowledge

Born 18 March 1877 on a Kentucky farm, Edgar Cayce was to become America's most famous clairvoyant. An active churchgoer all his life, he was inclined to dismiss reincarnation as un-Christian – but one day in 1923 a small boy climbed upon his lap and said: 'We were hungry together at the river.' This shook Cayce, as he had had a dream, known only to his immediate family, of fleeing from Indians on the Ohio river and being killed. An old friend and religious thinker, Arthur Lammers, persuaded Cayce to use the trance state to investigate the possibility that he had lived a former life.

Cayce was reluctant at first, baulking at such an unorthodox idea. But examining the results (he appeared to have been a high priest in ancient Egypt, an apothecary in the Trojan war and a British soldier during the colonisation of America), Cayce began to believe.

Cayce said that his readings were called from a 'universal record' or '*Akashic* record' (from the Sanskrit *akasha*, meaning the fundamental etheric substance of the Universe). These are complete records of everything done and said since the beginning of time.

with his grandfather's enemy, the real O'Malley; the 'bad blood' presumably accounted for the string of mistresses.

Another subject became Dick Wonchalk (1850–76), who led a solitary life after his family was massacred by Indians when he was a child. This 'life' characterised the subject's real feelings of isolation in childhood, concern about loneliness, fear of not being accepted by people and self-blame for his inadequacies.

There may be a purpose behind incubating such lives. The physical body, when attacked by disease, produces antibodies that counterattack the invaders and, in a healthy body, eventually gain supremacy. It is conceivable that the mind produces mental antibodies, which, by 'explaining' some present weakness in terms of a past life, heal the patient psychologically and psychically. Thus, the American high-board diver discussed on page 111, who was unaccountably panic-stricken by a shadow in the water as she was about to dive and could not go in the water, may have neutralised her irrational

Left: a Nazi concentration camp – the scene of vivid and recurrent dreams for a girl too young to know about them

Below: a witch being burnt at the stake in France in 1680. Deaths like this are frequent in 'former lives' described under hypnosis, and may be a reflection of a commonly held fear of a violent end

Bottom: Alexander Cannon was a spiritualist whose hypnotic subjects also used a spiritualist vocabulary to describe 'intermission' periods between their former lives

compensatory personalities in their subconscious, either as a means of expressing a personality whose fulfilment has been denied them by circumstances or as a compensation for some quality missing in their conscious lives. An argument against this is that the majority of regressed lives are dull, many unhappy and most end in violent death.

The same argument may be raised against the psychological explanation of subconscious role-playing. When we daydream consciously we see ourselves as happier, more fulfilled people than we really are. Why should so much subliminal role-playing emphasise the dull, the sordid and the wretched?

Students of psychodynamics – the examination of personality in terms of past and present experiences with regard to motivation – believe that regressed lives are based on unconscious memory, revealing relations between the subject's conscious personality and that or those that emerge under hypnosis.

In real life one Timothy O'Malley ran the subject's grandfather out of Ireland and was later killed in an accident with his horse. The grandfather disliked his grandson and told his parents that their son had bad blood in him, which the grandson overheard; the grandson had once borrowed his grandfather's mare without permission, arousing the old man's fury. Under hypnosis the subject became Brian O'Malley, claiming to be a British officer in the Irish Guards, born in 1850, who had a number of Irish and French mistresses and was killed in 1892 by a fall from his horse.

Apart from the historical inaccuracy – the Irish Guards were not formed until 1900 – E.S. Zolic, who investigated the case, ascribes the 'life' to the subject's identification

fear under hypnosis by 'explaining' it as the result of an event in a former life, in which just as she was about to jump in the water she saw the shadow of an alligator that then killed her. This 'explanation' removed the fear, which was no longer irrational.

Paranormal explanations include the telepathic tapping of the hypnotist's beliefs and outlook to the subject, although often facts known to the hypnotist are not communicated to the subject. Thus Albert de Rochas' subjects recount intermission experiences between lives in terms of his own Roman Catholic beliefs, whereas those of Alexander Cannon, who was a Spiritualist, used a Spiritualist vocabulary.

Above: Indians attacking a wagon train – one subject told of his loneliness after his family had died at the hands of the Indians. Psychologists think this 'life' dramatised his own deep sense of loneliness and social inadequacy

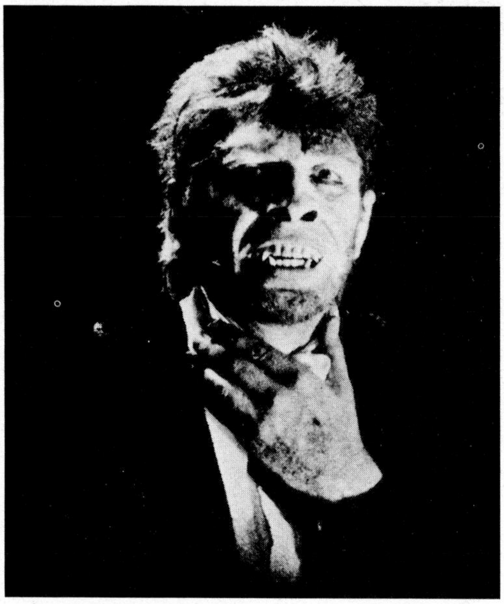

Below: the two faces of Dr Jekyll. Fredric March in the 1931 version of *Dr Jekyll and Mr Hyde* characterises conscious and subconscious forces inside us all that can come to the surface under hypnosis

Clairvoyance – the obtaining of information from, for example, closed books in libraries the subject has never visited – is another possibility; and this may be combined with extra-sensory perception (ESP) of knowledge in other human minds. There is a theory of General-ESP or Super-ESP, which suggests that the mind of the hypnotised subject can have access to information in books or in other people's minds and, by selecting and arranging this from many sources, may present an accurate account of an actual life once lived.

Those Spiritualists who reject reincarnation ascribe the accuracies reported in regressed lives to efficient spirit communication, and inaccuracies to the communicative difficulties; it is just as hard, they say, for spirits to communicate with us as we find it to break through to them. Finally there is the conception of the Akashic records (see box), which are repositories of everything that has been said and done since the world began and to which certain human minds can have access. Some people claim that it is from these that regressed lives are obtained, although why particular lives should be selected and why the subject usually fails to show any other psychic ability are not explained.

Despite all attempts to explain hypnotic regression in terms of conventional psychology, there remains a core of case histories that does not fit the various theories devised. Indeed, with our present state of knowledge there is no one theory that fits all the facts. It is difficult to say whether anything could prove, conclusively, that hypnotic regression gives us a glimpse into previous lives and so this phenomenon remains, at least partly, unexplained.

Many people have a fantastic ability to discuss their past lives in vivid detail – but all too often it turns out, to their own surprise, that they are merely reciting something they once read or heard

THE SUBCONSCIOUS MIND can be regarded as a vast, muddled storehouse of information. This information comes from books, newspapers, magazines, from lectures, television and radio, from direct observation, and from overheard scraps of conversation. In normal circumstances most of this knowledge is not subject to recall, but there are times when some of these deeply buried memories are spontaneously revived. And some of these revived memories re-emerge as baffling examples of cryptomnesia: memories whose origin has been completely forgotten.

As a result, the material can sometimes seem to have no ancestry and can be mistaken for something newly discovered or created. The late Helen Keller, blind, deaf and mute from infancy, was tragically deceived by such a cryptomnesic caprice. In 1892 she wrote a charming tale called *The frost king*. It was published and applauded, but within a few months it was revealed that the piece was simply a modified version of Margaret Canby's story *The frost fairies*, published 29 years earlier. Helen had no conscious memory of ever having heard the story, but it was established that a friend had read a batch of Miss Canby's stories to her in 1888 – and *The frost fairies* was among them. Helen Keller was devastated. She wrote:

> Joy deserted my heart . . . I had disgraced myself . . . yet how could it possibly have happened? I racked my brain until I was weary to recall anything about the frost that I had read before I wrote *The frost king*; but I could remember nothing.

In the same fashion a number of cases of automatic writings – allegedly from discarnate spirits – have been traced to published works. For example, the famous 'Oscar Wilde' scripts, produced by two psychics in the 1920s, were gradually shown to be derived from many printed sources, including Wilde's own *De profundis* and *The decay of lying*. One of the writers of the automatic scripts, Dr S. G. Soal, was led to remark: 'The variety of sources from which the script is drawn is as amazing as the adroitness with which the knowledge is worked up into

Hypnotic regression was fashionable in the earlier years of the century. The subject went into a sleep-like state and revealed information that he had acquired when younger but that had since been lost to his conscious mind

Plumbing the depths

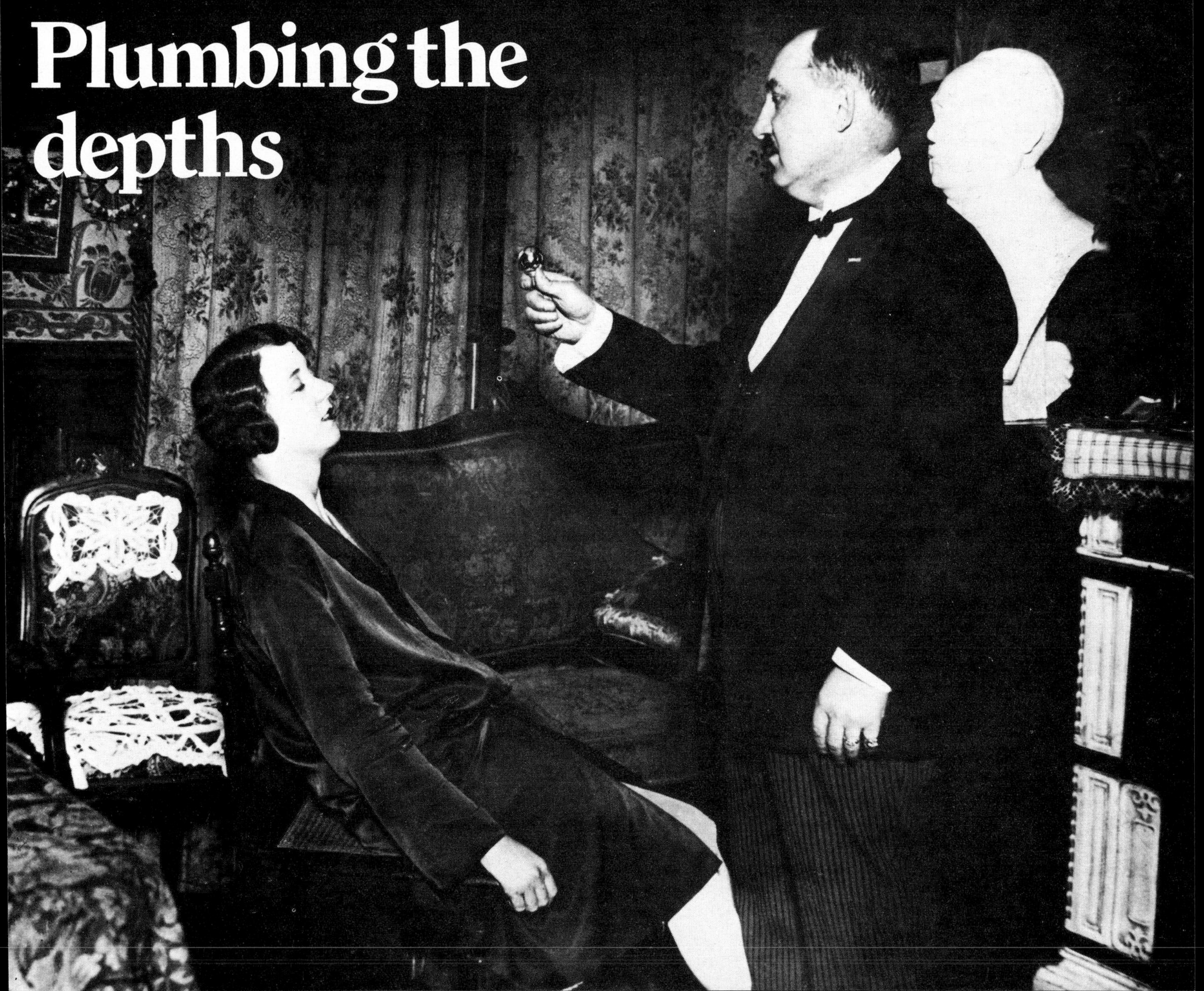

In the 1920s two psychics claimed that they had been used by Oscar Wilde (left) for transmitting new literary pieces. Later investigation suggested that these examples of automatic writing were actually rearrangements of passages from his other works

Below: a self-portrait by Hélène Smith (left) with her guardian angel

sentences conveying impressions of the different mannerisms of Wilde's literary style.' This is a significant verdict indeed, for very often the cryptomnesic material emerges not in a pure form, but in an edited, or paraphrased version. And this may mislead investigators in search of the primary sources.

Such unconscious plagiarisms are certainly intriguing, but most baffling of all are surely the vivid memories of 'past lives' that emerge under hypnosis or trance conditions. To some, these have always smacked of cryptomnesia, but to many others this explanation seems ruled out by the great wealth of detail – often obscure – provided by such 'regressionists'. Here the use of tape recorders has proved invaluable. Before their introduction all such research was costly and time-consuming, since everything the subject said had to be taken down in shorthand – with the inevitable loss of any accents, nuances and subtleties in the voice. Sound tapes, by contrast, provide lively and more convincing case records than any of those furnished by the pioneer researchers. Even so, there are two classic cases from the turn of the century that still command respect. The most famous involved the Swiss medium known as Hélène Smith.

Hélène was investigated by Theodore Flournoy, professor of psychology at Geneva University. His major findings were published in his *From India to the planet Mars.* He records that Hélène laid claim to a previous existence as the ill-fated Marie-Antoinette. She also claimed a much earlier reincarnation as the wife of the Hindu prince Sivrouka Nayaka, a 15th-century ruler of Kanara. Her Indian memories were enriched with descriptions of ceremonies and palaces, but complicated by her insistence that Flournoy had also been present in Kanara – as her husband!

Later research seemed to show that Hélène's obscure Indian knowledge was drawn from an inaccurate history by De Marles, published in 1823, but she '. . . dug down to the very bottom of her memories without discovering the slightest traces of this work'. However, the real proof of her ability to resurrect and restructure unconscious knowledge came with her most extravagant romance – one involving contact with the inhabitants of Mars.

During her Martian episode she produced a small album of exotic drawings of Martian landscapes, houses, people and plants. But these were all typically childish fantasies with superficial oriental touches. Much more impressive was the emergence of a spoken and written Martian language. Yet an analysis of 'Martian' showed that the sounds were those of the French language; the order of words was absolutely the same as in French; while its crude grammar was simply a parody of French grammar. The vocabulary alone was her invention. Even so, the whole affair

involved a remarkable feat of construction and memory, for Hélène was always consistent in her use of the 'Martian' words on different occasions. And all this was apparently the work of her subconscious.

Although not everyone was satisfied by Flournoy's explanation of the Hélène Smith case, the Blanche Poynings case of 1906 was neatly solved within a few months.

Blanche Poynings was a woman who had lived during the reign of Richard II. Ostensibly she began in 1906 to communicate through a clergyman's daughter, known as Miss C., while she was under hypnosis. Blanche had been a friend of the Countess of Salisbury and proved to be a garrulous gossip. She poured out details of the Countess's affairs, correctly naming her two husbands, children, in-laws and retainers. She also chatted about her own four marriages and her time at court.

A rich, detailed account

Everyday events were not neglected either, for Blanche tattled away about the fashions: 'Men wore shoes with long points which were chained to their knees. They had long hair cut straight across the forehead.' And she '. . . used to wear brocaded velvet, trimmed with ermine, and a high-peaked cap of miniver'. Among other tit-bits was mention of the three types of bread eaten by the different classes, namely simmel, wastel and cotchet. In all, she provided a rich and convincing account of life in the late 14th century. By contrast, Miss C. claimed to know nothing at all of this period.

These sessions greatly puzzled Lowes Dickinson of the Society for Psychical Research (SPR). He followed up all the statements of names, relationships and events and to his surprise was able, in almost every case, to verify the truth of Blanche's assertions. This simply increased his puzzlement, for 'some of the facts given were not such as even a student of the period would naturally come across.' Blanche Poynings, for instance, was a relatively unimportant figure, merely referred to by two chroniclers as one of the Queen's attendants. So he concluded that the most likely explanation was that the facts were drawn from an historical novel. But Miss C. could recall reading only one novel set in that period: *John Standish*. But this work did not contain the material found in the Poynings messages.

Further research by Lowes Dickinson only increased his bewilderment. More and more facts came to light that confirmed Blanche's story, but some were drawn from such obscure genealogical data that he began to feel that they would never have been incorporated in a novel. For a while he came to 'think it possible that Miss C. was really

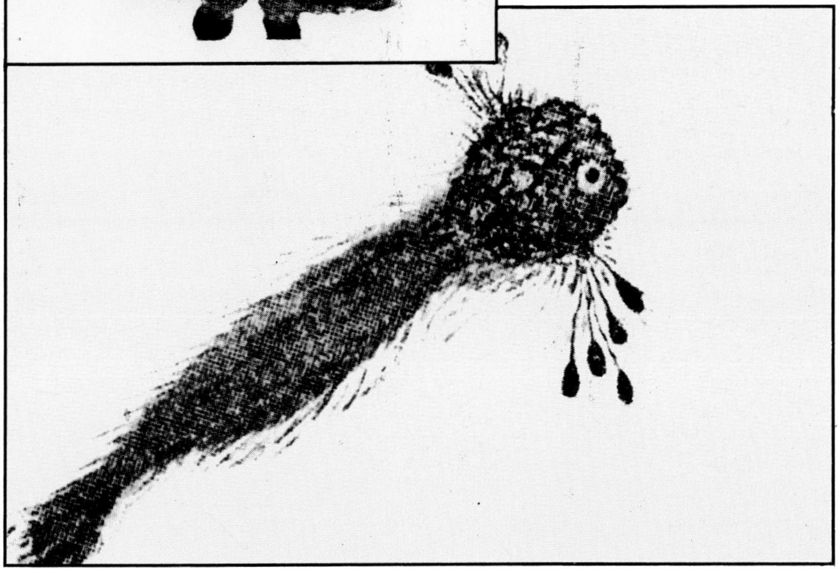

Swiss medium Hélène Smith claimed to have contacted Martians: she drew one of them, Astané (left), his house (above left), and his 'ugly beast' (below), whose body is covered with pink hair, and who has a black head and a green eye

communicating with the departed Blanche Poynings.'

The first stage of a solution to the mystery came at a tea party at Miss C.'s house. Her aunt and brother were present and they began talking about the then current craze for planchette readings. Lowes Dickinson was amused by Miss C.'s claim that she could draw faces with the planchette and he asked for a demonstration. The faces appeared but he found them uninteresting, so he went on to use the device for the traditional questions and answers. At one point he suggested that Blanche should be asked for, and the 14th-century lady immediately obliged.

A string of questions and answers brought out the unexpected name 'E. Holt'. This meant nothing to anyone present, but further answers revealed that 'Mrs Holt . . . wrote a book. . . all the people are in it. . . I am there . . . *Countess Maud* by Emily Holt.' Once the name of the novel was out in the open, Miss C. remembered having read a book with that title, and her aunt confirmed it. Yet neither of them could remember anything else about the book – not even the period it dealt with!

So a final hypnotic session was arranged, and Miss C. was asked to picture herself when young. When asked about her aunt reading *Countess Maud*, she was now able to describe the cover of the book and its main subjects. She went on to say: 'I used to turn

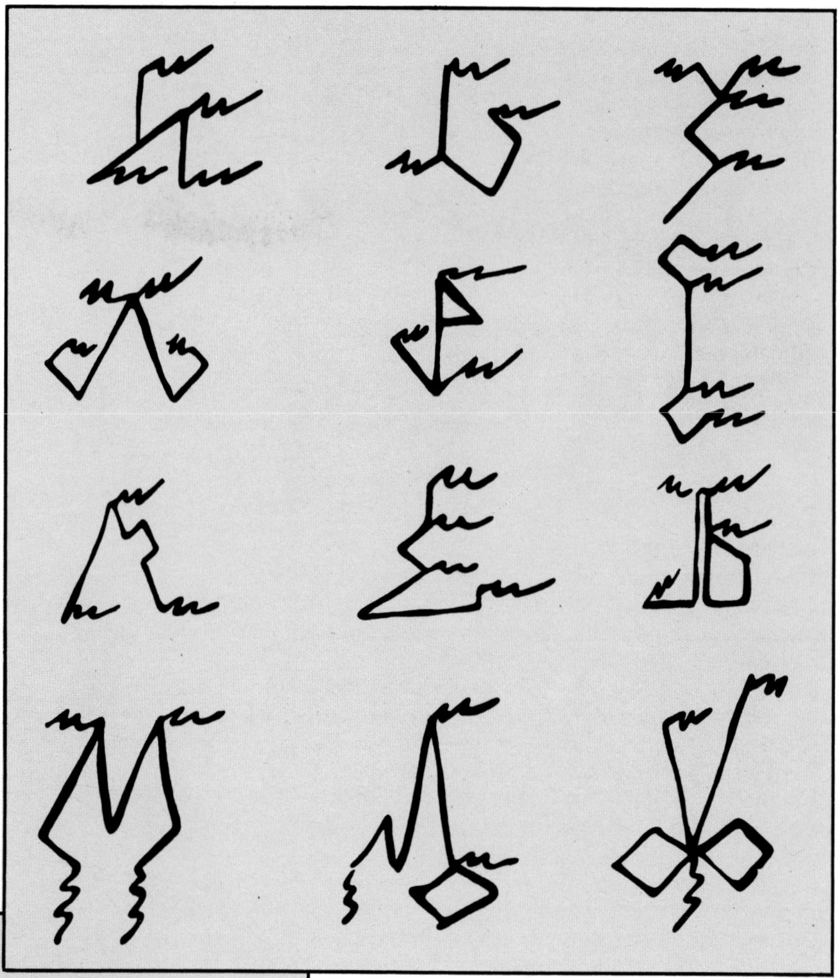

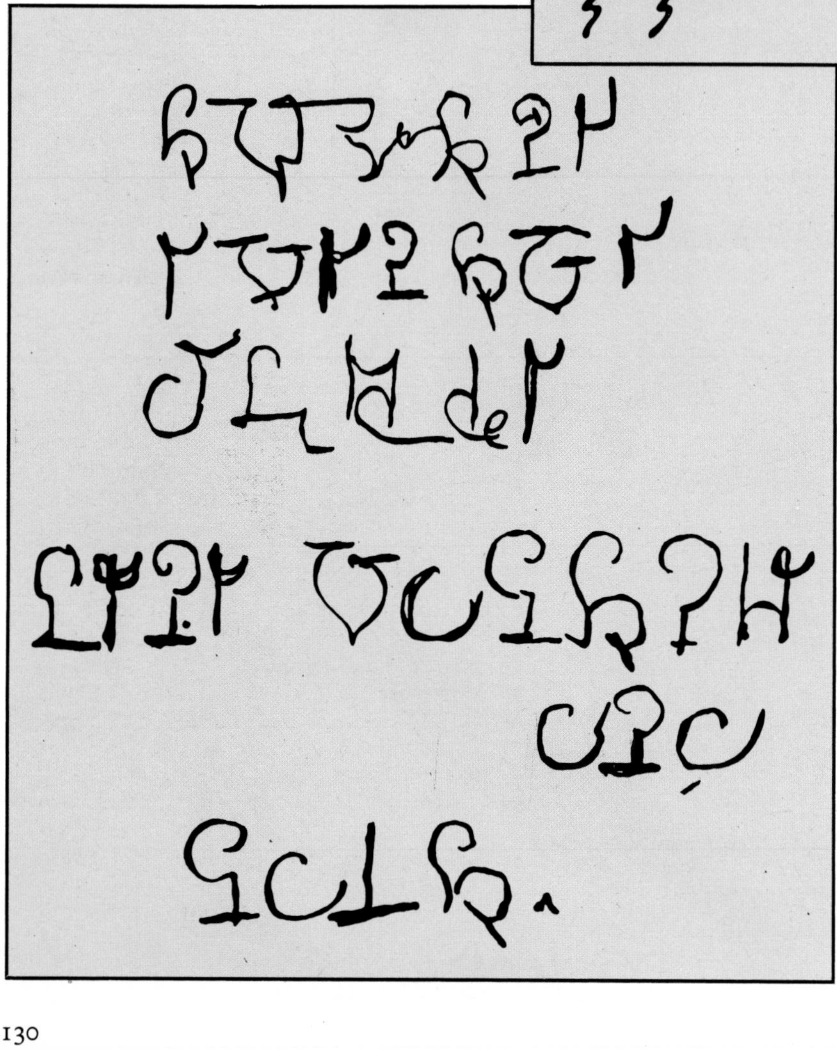

over the pages. I didn't read it, because it was dull. Blanche Poynings was in the book; not much about her.' Then she confessed that Blanche now seemed to her to have no existence apart from the printed page: 'Nearly all the events [are] from the book, but not her character.'

Lowes Dickinson scrutinised the novel thoroughly and, with trifling exceptions, discovered in it every person and every fact referred to in the hypnotic sessions. But he also noted that Miss C. had exaggerated the importance of the minor character Blanche, and had ignored the order of events in the book and substituted her own plan. In this way the whole of the borrowed material was skilfully presented in a natural way. He concluded:

> Her subconscious self showed in fact remarkable invention and dramatic power . . . so that if we had not happened to light upon the source of the information . . . it might have seemed a plausible view that Miss C. really did visit a real world and hold conversations with real people. As it is, the discovery . . . throws discredit on everything else, and especially on the elaborate details about her past lives with which Miss C.'s subconscious self favoured us.

Much of the genealogical information that so

In 1906 a clergyman's daughter known as Miss C. claimed she had received communications from a woman calling herself Blanche Poynings. Allegedly, Blanche had lived during the reign of Richard II (right), and had been a friend of the Countess of Salisbury. She spoke convincingly of the Countess's private life and of contemporary court events

Left: during seances, Hélène Smith wrote down these two pieces of 'Martian' script, translating some of the symbols

impressed Lowes Dickinson occurs not in the main text of *Countess Maud* but in an extremely detailed appendix. Yet when Miss C. was asked under hypnosis whether she had ever read the appendix she said 'no' and also denied that her aunt had read her this part of the book. And yet it is clear from a comparison of the appendix with the accounts given by 'Blanche Poynings' that this must be false. This confirms the necessity of treating testimony given under hypnosis with great caution.

Seventy years later another young woman startled and impressed people with 'memories' of a past life. This time thousands were convinced by her dramatic testimony, for it was recorded on tape and even 'relived' before television cameras, before becoming the subject of a best-selling book.

The sleep of reason

Cases of somnambulism, or sleep-walking, fascinated the Victorians. They believed that when people sleepwalked information that had long been lost in the subconscious tended to resurface. Fortunately, this interest has provided us with some fascinating case histories.

One, recorded by Dr Dyce of Aberdeen, involved a servant girl who was subject to bouts of 'hypnotic sleep' during the day. In one of these sleeps she carried out her everyday duties without being in any way aware of what was going on around her. In another sleep she repeated the entire baptismal service of the Church of England – although she was unable to do so when awake. And, on one occasion, she sat through a church service in a trance-like state and was so moved by the sermon that she burst into tears – although she could not afterwards remember anything about it. However, in her next sleep she did manage to give an accurate account of that service.

Dr Dyce's contemporary, Dr Abercrombie, recorded a much more remarkable case involving the strange powers of a very dull and awkward servant girl who, once she went into a sleep-like trance, became gifted and erudite.

Dr Abercrombie noted that her language was always fluent and exact, and that her imagery was always appropriate and eloquent. Her most amazing feat, however, was giving a remarkable imitation of a violin playing. First the sound of the instrument being tuned up, then a practice session and finally a more elaborate piece.

It turned out that she had grown up in a farmhouse in which her sleeping quarters had had one very thin wall. The bedroom on the other side belonged to an itinerant fiddler. Each night he went through his repertoire while she slept. The music had obviously lodged in her subconscious, but it surfaced only during a trance-like sleep. Her ability to speak articulately and fluently was traced back to the conversations she had overheard in the schoolroom of the main house. This 'remarkable affection' lasted at least 10 years.

The frontispiece to the novel *Sylvester Sound the somnambulist* by Henry Cockton, published in 1841. The story drew on many well-attested cases of actual somnambulism

When some people are hypnotised they can, apparently, easily recall past lives – often in surprisingly vivid detail. But what if they never lived those lives – where did they discover such a wealth of material? This chapter examines some classic cases

THE BRIDEY MURPHY case of 1952 can now be seen as a landmark in reincarnation research. Bridey was supposedly an Irish woman who lived in the early 19th century and whose life was 'recalled' under hypnosis by a 29-year-old American woman, Virginia Tighe (see page 112). The case captured people's imaginations and raised hopes at a time when traditional faiths were being questioned in Europe and the United States. And, since it involved an exciting use of the newly available domestic tape recorder, it seemed to point the way for anyone who wanted to study regression. Some of the emulators found it relatively easy to find subjects who could regress to what seemed to be previous existences.

A few hypnotists were bewildered, though, to find that the same subjects could, apparently, be *advanced* to old age or even to future existences. Were these nothing but subconscious fantasies provided to please the hypnotists? And if so, was the same true of the ostensible *past* existences? Were they simply a *mélange* of buried memories, made gripping by the sincerity that accompanies cryptomnesia?

In 1956 Dr Edwin S. Zolick of Marquette University in the United States set out to answer these questions. He designed a two-part experiment involving an undergraduate volunteer whom he called 'Jamie O'Toole'. In the first session Jamie was regressed in stages from his first day in high school to his third birthday. Jamie was then instructed: 'Go back slowly to the time before you were Jamie O'Toole, and tell . . ., if you can, who you were and what you did before you became Jamie O'Toole.' In a short while Jamie announced that he was Brian O'Malley, born in the year 1850. He lived in County Cork and was an officer in Her Majesty's Irish Guards. He was unmarried, but had a mistress – in fact 'many different ones, but only one at a time . . . pretty . . . pretty girls, French and Irish girls.' His life had ended at the age of 42, when he fell from his horse while jumping hurdles.

The second session was held a few days later, but this time hypnosis was induced without any attempt at regression. Instead the subject was asked 'Do you know who Brian O'Malley is?' After a brief period of confusion Jamie recounted all the essential details of his previous session. He was then asked where the name Brian O'Malley came from. At first he claimed not to know, so he was asked if it was part of a story he had read or part of a film he had seen – but he still could not recall the origin. Zolik's next move was to ask whether the story might have been told by Jamie's parents.

This led to a swift reply: 'Yes, yes . . . yes, my grandfather – from my grandfather.' The simple question 'Can you tell me the story?' produced the enlightening reply:

> . . . not Brian. His name is Timothy O'Malley . . . Timothy O'Malley was an English soldier . . . I remember now. He and my grandfather fought. O'Malley was an Irishman. Grandfather and O'Malley fought. O'Malley was killed – he was killed in an accident with a horse later . . . Yes, grandfather

Virginia Tighe, one of the most sensational of hypnotic regression subjects, as she was at the age of seven (far right): she 'returned' to her infancy in her first hypnotic sessions, conducted when she was a young woman in her twenties (right). Then she went on to 'recall' a previous life as Bridey Murphy, an Irish girl of the 19th century. But it was later claimed by critics that the incidents of Bridey's life suspiciously resembled details of Virginia's own childhood

Under hypnosis, a 15-year-old schoolgirl described how she had once been a young boy who had wanted to become a fish to swim out into Lake Issykjokul (below). The boy, imagining that he *was* a fish, jumped in – but drowned. It later turned out that the subject had once read a novel containing a very similar incident

Life before life?

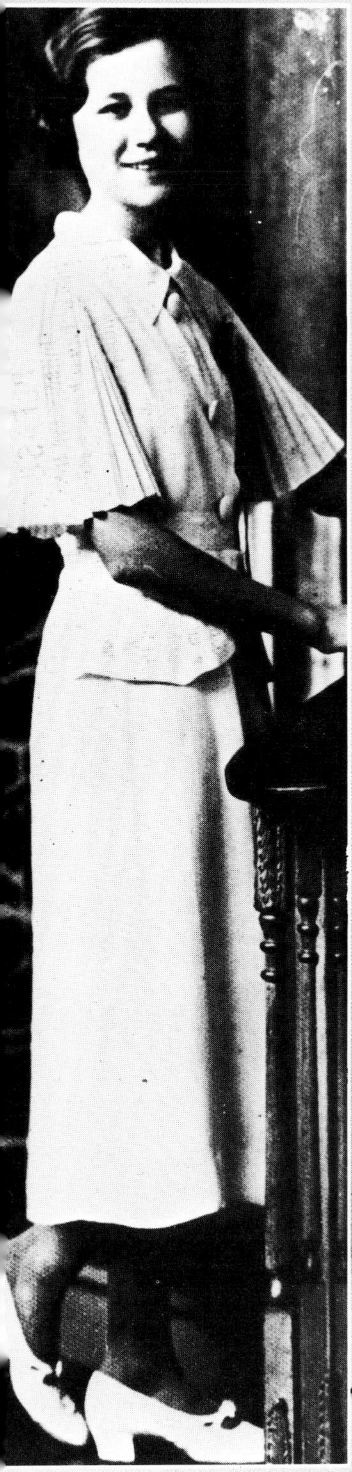

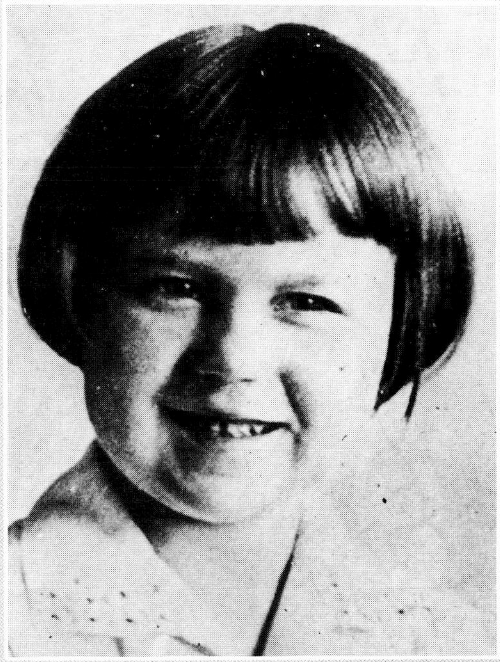

fought and hurt him . . . I think O'Malley was responsible for my grandfather being run out of Ireland . . . Grandfather hated him – *hated him*.

Here Jamie O'Toole dried up, perhaps overcome by emotion, but after a short while the session resumed and he was asked if the grandfather had mentioned O'Malley's mistress. He replied: 'Grandfather said O'Malley was a blackguard' – far from a definite answer, and vague enough to cover the category of a loose-living womaniser. Further questions revealed that Jamie had heard these tales while living on his grandfather's farm. He was about seven years old then.

In later answers he stated that he had liked stories about the army. He said:

I wanted to grow up and be a soldier – grandfather had been a soldier . . . he never liked me . . . he was not really my grandfather . . . I wanted to please him . . . he said I had bad blood in me . . . Mom cried – Dad told grandfather he could not say that – big argument – I just wanted to go.

At this point Jamie was so moved that he began to sob softly; Zolik waited until it seemed proper to continue and then probed to find out why a small boy would be thought of as a villain. Jamie then said:

Grandfather was mad . . . I didn't hurt the mare . . . he told me not to ride her . . . I took her out . . . she was very high-spirited and I let her have her head . . . she was not hurt, just enjoyed being out . . . He was very mad and bawled me out . . . After that I wanted to please grandfather so that he would like me, but never felt that he did. . . .

Since Jamie O'Toole was evidently disturbed by recalling this unhappy time, Zolik decided to end the session. But he was fully satisfied that the answers had provided enough data for a valid analysis of the case. In his view Jamie had identified with the 'blackguard' O'Malley because both of them were in conflict with the grandfather, and Jamie, after all, had 'black blood' too.

Another important reason for this identification lay in the experience with the horse – a horse had been responsible for O'Malley's death and for Jamie's 'psychological annihilation by his grandfather'. In brief, Zolik's detailed analysis showed that past-life memories could easily be nothing more than a mixture of remembered tales and emotionally coloured symbolic events.

Zolik's method of probing for the real-life origins of 'reincarnationist' material was

something he recommended to anyone seriously interested in reaching the truth. Unfortunately few, if any, of the enthusiastic hypno-regressionists took any notice of his advice, and session after session was committed to tape and marvelled over without any effort being made to verify the origins or meaning of this material. The hypnotherapist Arnall Bloxham, for one, recorded over 400 'past-life' regressions without even once digging for the possibly mundane origins of these alleged lives.

The Finnish psychiatrist Dr Reima Kampman, by contrast, has devoted years to the systematic investigation of the cryptomnesic origins of 'past-life' accounts. He began his work in the 1960s in the Department of Psychiatry at the University of Oulu. He found his subjects among large groups of volunteers drawn from the highest grades of the secondary schools in Oulu. All those who could enter a deep hypnotic state were selected for closer study. Kampman found it relatively easy to induce 'past-life' recall as a response to his instruction: 'Go back to an age before your birth, when you are somebody else, somewhere else.'

In one case, a 15-year-old girl spoke of a previous life in 1780. She was then known as Malina Bostojevski. She lived during a time of war and spoke about the disasters caused by the conflict. She also gave an accurate account of people's attitudes and living conditions in those times. Subsequent regressions brought a further five different personalities to light.

Seven years later, the same girl produced a completely different batch of previous lives. The most striking of this new group involved her past life as a seven-year-old boy who lived at the foot of a huge mountain. His father was the captain of a boat that sailed on Lake Issykjokul. The father's name was given as Aitmatov.

This boy led a lonely life, seeing little of his father, though yearning to be with him. And his bleak life reached a grim end when he grew to envy the fish that swam so freely in the river: he longed to become one and to swim to the lake to rejoin his father. In a wild fantasy he felt that he really was a fish, leapt into the lake and was drowned.

When not under hypnosis the girl had no memory of the boy, the lake or the father, so a further session was arranged. This time she was asked to remember where she had first heard the tale of the sad little boy. At once the girl brought out the name of a novel, *Valkoinen laiva* ('The white ship'). An examination of the book showed that it was set

An unnamed 19-year-old student claimed that she had once lived in the ancient city of Babylon (below). She also gave a vivid account of contemporary life in 13th-century England (above), and of her life in revolutionary Russia (above right)

around Lake Issykjokul; it involved the life and death by drowning of a forlorn little boy; and the name of the author was, in fact, Aitmatov!

Perhaps even more amazing were the eight 'past lives' conjured up by a 19-year-old student. In one life she lived in ancient Babylonia; her next life began in the Chinese city of Nanking; then she moved on to Norway, before re-emerging in Norwich in England. After that followed a life in Paris, another in England and a final existence in revolutionary Russia. Her 13th-century English life – as Dorothy, an inn-keeper's daughter – brought to light 'a very explicit account of contemporary happenings.' And she astonished everyone by singing a song that none of the listeners was familiar with; she called it 'the summer song'. The language used in the song was later studied by a student 'with high honours in the English language'. He had no difficulty in identifying the words as examples of an old form of English – possibly Middle English. But this meant nothing to the girl, who had no memory of ever having heard the words or the music of the song before.

The solution to this riddle came during a later experiment. The girl was asked to go back to a time when she might have seen the words and music of the song, or even heard it sung. She then regressed to the age of 13 and remembered taking a book from the shelves of a library. It was a casual choice and she merely flicked through the pages. Yet she not only remembered its title but was able to state just where in the book her 'summer song' could be found. The book was '*Musiikin vaiheet*', a Finnish translation of *The history of music* written by Benjamin Britten and Imogen Holst. And the mystery music was, of all things, the famous round *Sumer is icumen in*, with the words rendered in a simplified medieval English.

Another of the girl's 'previous lives' gave up its secret origins under hypnosis. In this 'life' she had been Karin Bergström, a seven-year-old girl who had died in an air raid in 1939. She was able to supply an address for her old home and she knew the names and occupations of her former parents. Enquiries showed that there had indeed been an air raid on the date she had given. Moreover, the address she had given had, indeed, been hit. But the population records showed that no real Karin Bergström, nor any relatives of such a person, had died in the raid.

So the girl was asked to regress to the time when she had first heard of the Bergströms or the bombing. She soon remembered herself as a little girl, turning over the pages of a patriotic book. In it there were photographs of streets and houses hit by bombs and something about the people made homeless. The exact date of the raid was given, and one picture showed two of the victims killed that day – significantly, a mother and her seven-year-old daughter. Thus the complete 'past life' memory had been assembled from nothing more than the disjointed material found in this one book, seen when she was a very young child.

A spate of similar successes led Kampman to conclude that he had demonstrated:

> that the experiences of the present personality were reflected in the secondary personalities, both in the form of realistic details and as emotional experiences. The recording of a song from a book simply by turning over the leaves of the book at the age of 13 is an outstanding example of how very detailed information can be stored in our brain without any idea whatever of it in the conscious mind, and how it can be retrieved in deep hypnosis.

Below: the 19-year-old student also described her past life as Karin Bergström, who died when only seven years old, in 1939, in an air raid in the Russian–Finnish conflict. Contemporary records show that the house that she claimed she had died in had indeed been hit in an air raid at that time

Past lives: an open book?

Vivid, detailed and accurate – the tape-recorded narratives of numerous 'past lives' recounted by a young woman under hypnosis were all of these. But are these accounts actually historical romances?

'THE MOST STAGGERING EVIDENCE for reincarnation ever recorded'. That was the claim made for Jeffrey Iverson's book *More lives than one?*, which was based on transcripts of tape recordings made by hypnotically regressed subjects. Iverson had been the producer of a BBC Television programme called *The Bloxham tapes*, screened in 1976 and based on the work of the Cardiff hypnotherapist Arnall Bloxham. Many thousands of readers must have been induced to believe the claim made for the book.

For over six years there was no effective challenge to the publicity claim that the taped accounts were 'so authentic that they can only be explained by the certainty of reincarnation'.

Fortunately, the extravagance of these claims led the present writer to investigate the programme and the book. He decided to concentrate on the six past lives claimed for a young Monmouthshire woman, Jane Evans, since Iverson considered this to be 'the most consistently astonishing case in Bloxham's collection'.

The investigation soon showed that the claims made for the tapes were false, the result of misdirected and inadequate research. Jane Evans's three major accounts proved to have the clearest origins – in her *present* life. Her testimony as Alison, a teenage servant to Jacques Coeur, a French merchant prince of the 15th century, was said to prove that she 'knew a remarkable amount about medieval French history', while in her waking state she said: 'I have never read about Jacques Coeur, I have never even heard the name.'

Jeffrey Iverson even concluded that she could not have picked up the many facts that she produced from the standard histories, such as A. B. Kerr's *Jacques Coeur, merchant prince.* After all, she knew so much about such matters as the intrigues surrounding the King's mistress, Agnes Sorel. Among other things she was able to describe fully the exterior and interior of Coeur's magnificent house – even giving details of the carvings over the fireplace in his main banqueting hall. More surprisingly, she spoke of the carved tomb of Agnes Sorel, which was housed in a church. According to Iverson, this tomb 'had been cast away by French revolutionaries and spent a hundred and sixty-five years, until its rediscovery in 1970, out of sight in a cellar.'

But these claims do not stand up to scrutiny. The truth is that the Sorel tomb has been a tourist attraction since the 1920s at least. It is mentioned in H. D. Sedgwick's *Short history of France* of 1930, and a number of photographs of it have been published.

It is very much the same with Jacques Coeur's house. In fact, this is one of the most thoroughly photographed and filmed houses in all France. Fine, explicit photographs are included in Dame Joan Evans's *Life in medieval France.* There one can see the stone carvings over the fireplace and gain a clear idea of how the place looked, both inside and out. There can be little doubt that Jane Evans has seen these or similar pictures.

And there is strong evidence that the rest of Jane's material was drawn from a source not mentioned by Iverson: a novel called *The moneyman*, by T. B. Costain, published in 1948. It is based on Coeur's life and provides almost all of the flourishes and authentic-sounding touches included by Jane Evans in

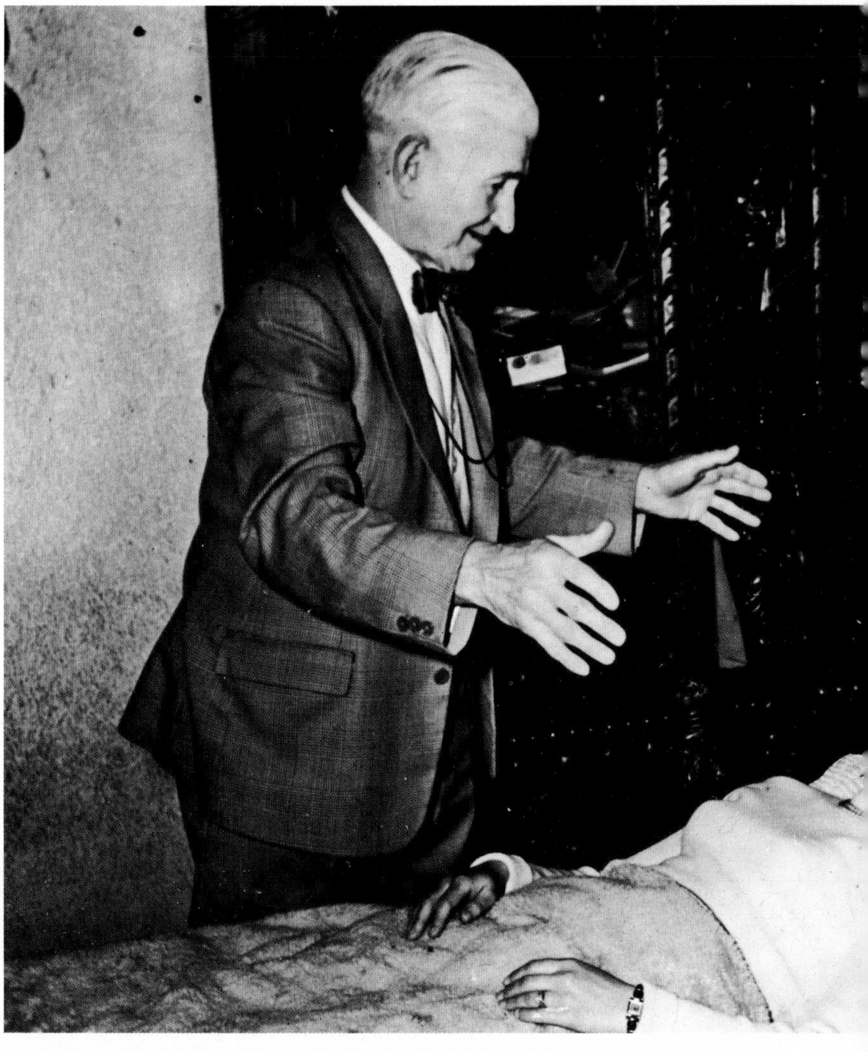

Arnall Bloxham, a hypnotherapist practising in Cardiff, at work. He came to national attention when a television programme and a book described the hypnotic regressions that he conducted and his claims that they represented genuine past lives of his subjects

Below: Agnes Sorel, here depicted as the Virgin, was mistress of Charles VII of France. She figured in Jane Evans's 'recollections' of the 15th century

Below right: Louis de Wohl's novel *The living wood* is undoubtedly the source of the details in Jane Evans's 'memories' of her life in Roman Britain. She would most probably have encountered the British edition, *The empress Helena*

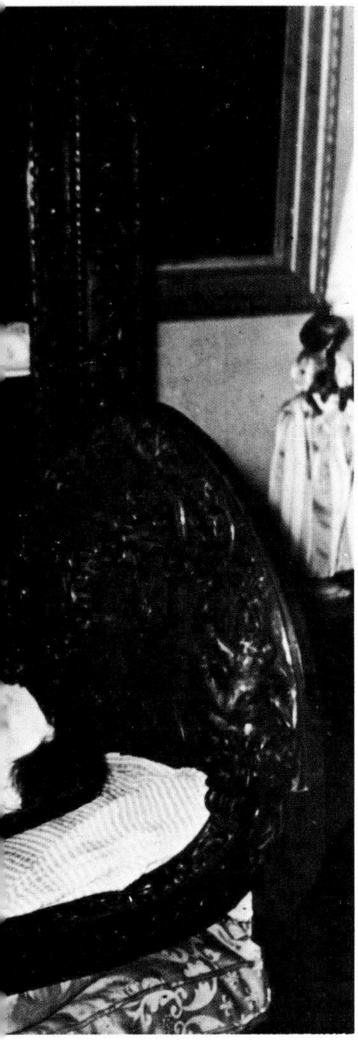

her 'past life memories'. Furthermore, the novel avoids all mention of Coeur's wife and family – and Jane Evans does exactly the same.

The view that Jane Evans's tapes were simply the result of cryptomnesia could still, perhaps, be brushed aside as mere speculation, if it were not for the confirmation provided by the vetting of her two remaining major accounts of past lives.

As Rebecca, the Jewess of York, she was supposed to have met her death during the massacre of 1190. At that time, most of the Jewish community died in the York Castle keep, but Rebecca's death came in the cellar of a church where she had taken refuge. A formidable legend has grown up around this cellar episode. It has been claimed that the church was positively identified as St Mary's, Castlegate, and that a crypt was actually discovered there after Jane's regression.

The truth is that the original television programme script stated that there were *three* possible churches that could qualify as the place of refuge. St Mary's was shown, but it was chosen as the place in which to film simply because it was the most convenient: at the time it was being converted to a museum. It was this conversion that led to the uncovering of an aperture under the chancel. For believers this was, naturally, a medieval crypt and proof of Rebecca's story. But it is likely that this small vault in fact dates from well after the massacre of the Jews.

In any case, the furore over the 'crypt' is irrelevant, since the Rebecca regression is clearly a fantasy. It is an amalgamation of at least two different stories of persecution taken from widely separated centuries.

The proof that we are dealing with a fantasy lies in the historical inaccuracies found in the tale. Rebecca repeats four times that the Jewish community in York were forced to wear yellow badges – 'circles over our hearts'. But the Jewish badge was not introduced until the following century, and even then the English pattern consisted of two oblong white strips of cloth, representing the tablets of Moses. The yellow circle was, in fact, the badge worn in France and Germany after 1215. This is one aspect of Jewish history over which there are no legitimate doubts whatsoever.

Ghetto that never was

Then a group of absurdities were discovered in passages from the tapes that were *excluded* from both the book and the film. In these revealing passages Rebecca repeatedly speaks of living in the ghetto in the north of York. This ghetto was a quarter without street names, where only the rich Jews lived, and she pointedly mentions a poor Jew who could afford to live only in 'the middle of York in a street called Coney Street'.

Now there never was a special Jewish quarter in York: the Jews were scattered in Micklegate, Fossgate, Bretgate, Feltergayle and near the centre in Jewbury. And the idea that a Jew would live outside the ghetto because of poverty is ludicrous. Even if he did, he would not live in Coney Street, which was, in truth, the choice place for many of the rich Jews – including Josce, the head of their community.

This means, inevitably, that Jane Evans has the ability to store vivid accounts subconsciously and combine and edit these creatively – to the point where she becomes one of the characters involved. The clinching proof that this is so is provided by her regression to the life of a Roman wife, Livonia – for this is the purest of all, based on one source only. On hearing this tape Professor Brian Hartley, an authority on Roman Britain, commented: 'She knew some quite remarkable historical facts, and numerous published works would have to be consulted if anyone tried to prepare the outline of such a story.' The professor is right: careful

Left: English Jews were made to wear a badge representing the tablets of Moses during the 13th century. But Jane Evans, as 'Rebecca, Jewess of York', described the badge as a circle and ascribed it to the 12th century

Right: Micklegate Bar, at the entrance to one of the areas of York where Jews lived in the 12th century. But there was no true ghetto – contrary to Jane Evans's account

research had gone into the making of Jane's story, but it was undertaken by Louis de Wohl, author of the novel *The living wood*, published in 1947. Jane's life as Livonia is taken direct from that novel. Two brief comparisons will show just how.

Livonia's tale opened in Britain during the late fourth century AD. She described the garden of a house owned by the legate Constantius. She named his wife as Lady Helena, his son as Constantine. She described his son being taught the use of shield, sword and armour by his military tutor, Marcus Favonius Facilis. This entire sequence is taken from the novel: Constantine trains in the use of arms and armour under his military tutor Marcus Favonius, called Facilis 'because everything was easy to him'.

Livonia then described a visit by the historical character Allectus. He brought Constantius an urgent message from Rome, but despite the urgency he had 'stopped at Gessoriacum to see Carausius, who is in charge of the fleet'. This section too is drawn from the novel: there the visit leads up to the take-over of rule in Britain by Carausius, aided by Allectus. In the same way *every single piece of information* given out by Jane Evans can be traced to de Wohl's fictional account. She uses his fictional sequences in exactly the same order and even speaks of his fictional characters, such as Curio and Valerius, as if they were real people.

Below: this figure of a Roman centurion called Facilis, at Colchester, was Louis de Wohl's inspiration for his character of the same name in *The living wood*

There are two minor differences worth noting: these involve her editing faculty.

First she takes a slight character, Titus, a Christian soldier willing to die for his faith, and recasts him as a tutor to Constantine. But all Titus's feelings and actions are those of de Wohl's character Hilary. Hilary is converted to Christianity, ordained as a priest and killed during a violent campaign against his faith.

Second, Jane Evans takes Livonia, an insignificant character in the book, described as 'a charming creature with pouting lips and smouldering eyes', and amalgamates her with Helena. A composite Livonia, recast as the wife of Titus, then emerges. This new character is able to act both as an observer and as someone who voices Helena's sentiments – thus making the story that much fuller and much easier to relate.

This feat of editing reveals a little of the psychology behind these fantasies. For Hilary is the eminently desirable male in the book, described as having 'a beautiful honest face with the eyes of a dreamer'. He is also secretly in love with Helena. As Titus he becomes the lover of Livonia of the pouting lips and smouldering eyes – in other words of Jane Evans herself. And there we have the combustible material that warmed a young girl's daydreams – all inspired by an exciting historical novel.

Regrettably, Jane Evans has refused to cooperate in any way in this re-investigation. But all those who have studied the files of source material (including Professor Hartley and another academic consulted in the television programme, Professor R. B. Dobson of York University – and, to his credit, Jeffrey Iverson) now accept that the once impressive tapes are proof of cryptomnesia – and nothing more remarkable than that!

Psychic art

Are Beethoven and Van Gogh still producing works of art, long after the end of their earthly lives? The idea seems incredible, yet it is difficult to explain how untrained mediums write symphonies and paint pictures in the styles of long dead artists.

The latest works of Beethoven, Brahms and Liszt

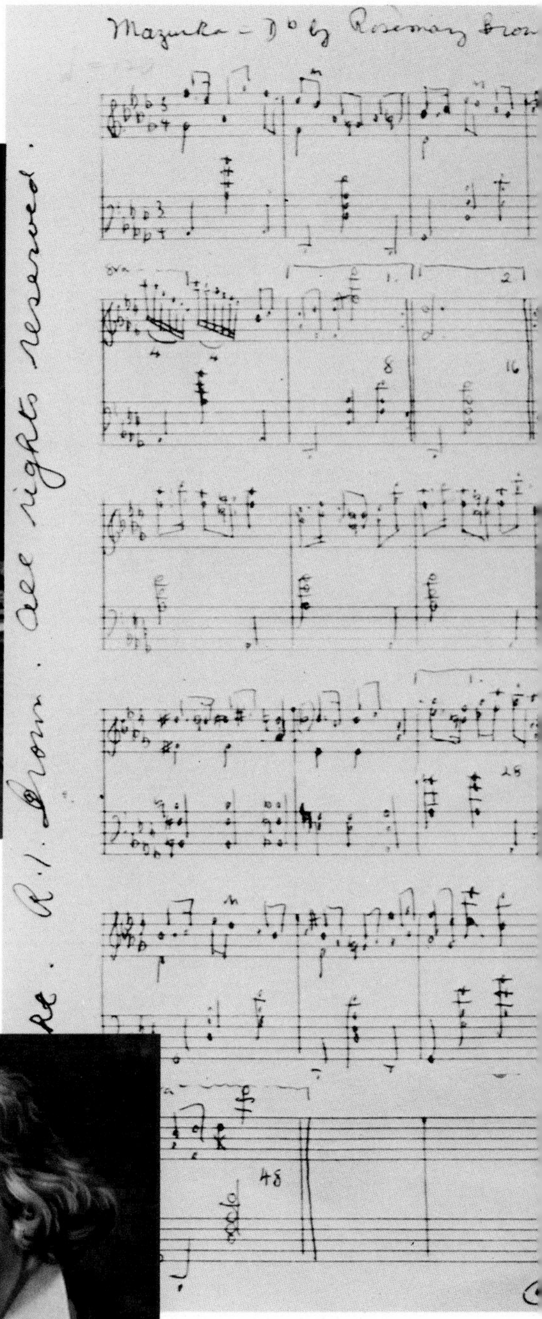

Many sensitives claim to receive works of art from long-dead artists – composers, authors, painters. But are these works truly from beyond the grave, or do they come from the subconscious mind?

BEETHOVEN IS STILL WORKING on his 10th Symphony. This extraordinary concept – that musicians and other creative beings can still produce works of art years, even centuries, after their death – is as natural as breathing to many spiritualists and psychics.

The best known of the mediums who claim to be amanuenses for long-dead composers is London housewife Rosemary Brown, who acts almost as an agent for Liszt, Beethoven, Brahms, Debussy, Chopin, Schubert and, more recently, Stravinsky. She is an unassuming, middle-aged lady with only a rudimentary musical background and she is the first to acknowledge that the works 'dictated' to her are beyond her everyday musical capacity. Mrs Brown sees herself merely as the humble scribe and friend of the late composers – the ultimate polish must come from the professionals in performance.

The idea of survival beyond death is not, however, strange to this Balham housewife. As a young girl she had visions of an elderly man who told her repeatedly that he and other great composers would befriend her and teach her their wonderful music. It

Above left: Rosemary Brown being filmed by an American television company in October 1980. During the filming Rosemary 'wrote' *Mazurka in D flat* (above), which she claims was inspired by Chopin (above right)

Left: Beethoven contacted Rosemary Brown in 1964; he told her he was no longer deaf and could once again enjoy listening to music

Below right: American composer and conductor Leonard Bernstein. Rosemary Brown sought an interview with Bernstein on the advice of her 'spirits'. He was most impressed with the music Rosemary showed him

was only many years later, when she was a widow concerned mainly with the struggle of bringing up two children on very limited means, that she saw a picture of Franz Liszt (1811–1886) and recognised him as her ghostly friend.

In 1964 she was contacted by other great composers – including Beethoven and Chopin – and her life work began in earnest: taking down their 'unfinished symphonies' and sharing her belief that there is no death – the great musicians are still producing.

The pieces transmitted to her are no mere outlines: they are full compositions, mainly for the piano but some for full orchestras. Mrs Brown says the music is already composed when it is communicated to her: the musicians simply dictate it as fast as she can write it down.

Indeed, observers of the process are amazed at the speed with which Rosemary Brown writes the music – and the standard is far beyond her conscious capacity or even her conscious knowledge. During the writing sessions Mrs Brown chats familiarly with her unseen guests, so sincerely and normally that it is difficult to be embarrassed, despite the bizarre circumstances. Pen poised over the music sheets, she listens. 'I see . . .', she says to Franz Liszt, 'these two bars go here . . . no, I see, I'm sorry. No, you're going too fast for me. If you could just repeat . . .' With pauses for checking and some conversation with the composer, she writes down the work far faster than most musicians could possibly compose.

Sometimes communications are interrupted as she gently chides Liszt for becoming so excited that he speaks volubly in German or French. Chopin occasionally forgets himself and speaks to her in his native Polish – which she writes down phonetically and has translated by a Polish friend.

So are these posthumous works recognisably those of Liszt, Chopin, Beethoven, Brahms? Concert pianist Hephzibah Menuhin said 'I look at these manuscripts with immense respect. Each piece is distinctly in the composer's style.' Leonard Bernstein and his wife entertained Mrs Brown in their London hotel suite and were very impressed both by her sincerity and by the music she took to them purportedly from the long-dead composers. British composer Richard Rodney Bennett said: 'A lot of people can improvise, but you couldn't fake music like this without years of training. I couldn't have faked some of the Beethoven myself.'

Since that memorable breakthrough in 1964 Mrs Brown has also, she says, been contacted by dead artists, poets, playwrights, philosophers and scientists. Vincent van Gogh (1853–1890) has communicated his current works through her; at first in charcoal ('because that's all I had') and then in

Right: Franz Liszt, who first appeared to Rosemary Brown when she was a young girl. He told her that, when she grew up, he and other composers would contact her and teach her their music.

oils. Debussy has chosen to paint through Mrs Brown, rather than compose because his artistic interests have changed since he has 'passed over'.

Bertrand Russell, philosopher, has had to reconsider his atheism and disbelief in a life after death, for, as Rosemary Brown points out, he is very much 'alive' these days and wants to pass on the message of hope in eternal life. Albert Einstein also communicates, patiently explaining any difficult jargon or concepts, reinforcing the belief in further planes of existence.

Sceptics point out that the music alleged to come from the minds of the great composers is less than their best, being often reminiscent of their earliest, rather than their mature, works. This, says Mrs Brown, is not the point. Her first introduction to Franz Liszt was 'more than a musical breakthrough.' The late Sir Donald Tovey is believed to have explained the motivation behind the communications in this posthumous statement:

> In communicating through music and conversation, an organized group of musicians, who have departed from your world, are attempting to establish a precept for humanity, i.e., that physical death is a transition from one state of consciousness to another wherein one retains one's individuality . . . We are not transmitting music to Rosemary Brown simply for the sake of offering possible pleasure in listening thereto; it is the implications relevant to this phenomenon which we hope will stimulate sensible and sensitive interest and stir many who are intelligent and impartial to consider and explore the unknown of man's mind and psyche. When man has plumbed the mysterious depths of his veiled consciousness, he will then be able to soar to correspondingly greater heights.

Rosemary Brown's contacts are not confined to the field of music: Van Gogh inspired this drawing (right) in 1975, and Debussy (below), now more interested in visual art, also paints 'through' her. She was contacted by Albert Einstein (bottom) in 1967, and by Bertrand Russell (below left) in 1973

Mrs Brown has many friends and admirers outside the spiritualist circle, notably among distinguished musicians, writers and broadcasters. Whatever the source of her mysterious music, this modest and religious lady inspires respect and affection, so obvious is her sincerity.

She is, however, not unique in her musical communications. The British concert pianist, John Lill, also claims an other-worldly inspiration for his playing. This winner of the prestigious Tchaikovsky Piano Competition had a tough beginning, playing the piano in pubs in London's East End. As he says 'I don't go around like a crazed fellow with my head in the air . . . [I'm] neither a nutter nor some quaint loony falling around in a state of trance.' But, as he added thoughtfully, 'because something is rare it doesn't mean that it doesn't exist.'

The 'something' began for him when he was practising in the Moscow Conservatoire

Right: concert pianist John Lill is convinced that he has had spiritual help in his career. He believes that Beethoven watched him practising for the Tchaikovsky Piano Competition in Moscow, and has since held several conversations with him. And Beethoven has dedicated a piece of his own music to him – the *Sonata in E Minor* communicated to Rosemary Brown in 1972

Below: Clifford Enticknap, who has written an oratorio entitled *Beyond the veil* 'under the inspiration' of G. F. Handel (bottom)

for the Tchaikovsky Piano Competition. He became aware of a figure watching him – someone wearing unusual clothes. He believes he was being observed by Beethoven, who has since held many conversations with him. However John Lill does not consider himself a special case. This sort of direct inspiration, he says, is available to everyone who achieves a certain frame of mind:

'It is very difficult to conceive inspiration unless it is something you receive. I don't see it as something from within a person. When I go on stage I close my mind to what I have learnt and open it fully in the expectation that inspiration will be received.'

But sometimes it is difficult to achieve this state of mind 'if it's a particularly muggy day, or the acoustics are dry. Even the attitude of the audience makes a difference. A quiet mind is essential.'

Inspiration, says Lill, is an infinite thing: 'music begins where words leave off – where music leaves off the "force" begins'.

The composer of, among other magnificent works, the *Messiah* is still 'writing' grand oratorios through his medium Clifford Enticknap, an Englishman who has always been obsessed with Handel and Handelian music. Handel taught him music in another incarnation, says Enticknap, and their relationship as master and pupil dates back to the time of Atlantis where Handel was a great teacher known as Joseph Arkos. Yet before that the soul we know as Handel lived on Jupiter, the planet of music, together with all the souls we know as the great musicians (and some we may never know for they will not be incarnated on Earth).

In his personality as 'the master Handel', the musician communicated to Enticknap a four-and-a-half-hour long oratorio entitled *Beyond the veil*; a 73-minute excerpt of this has been recorded by the London Symphony Orchestra and the Handelian Foundation Choir and is available on tape through the Handelian Foundation as 'proof' of Handel's survival beyond death.

In BBC-TV's programme *Spirits from the past*, shown on 12 August 1980, snatches from the oratorio were played over scenes of Mr Enticknap playing the organ in Handel's favourite English church. Television critics found little fault with the music – which did indeed sound to the untutored ear to be very similar to Handel's more familiar works – but the words provoked widespread ridicule. One critic compared them with the unfortunate poetry of William McGonagall (1805–1902) whose poetic sincerity was matched only by his total lack of talent and sheer genius in juxtaposing the risible with the pathetic. (Another critic went so far as to exclaim: 'Fame at last for McGonagall – he's teamed up with Handel beyond the veil!')

However, mediums warn against judging spirit communications in a state of flippant scepticism. As John Lill says of the difficulties the spirits have in 'getting through': 'It's all to do with cleaning a window, and some windows are cleaner than others.'

If, as many serious researchers into the paranormal have believed, the music does not in fact come from the minds of deceased musicians, then where does it come from? Certainly not from the conscious mind of Mrs Brown, who obviously struggles to keep up with the dictation.

Some psychics believe that our deeper inspirations are culled from the 'Akashic records' or 'Book of life', wherein lies all knowledge. In certain states of mind, and in some especially sensitive people, this hidden knowledge becomes available to the human consciousness. Mrs Brown could well be one of these specially receptive people and the music she believes comes from Chopin or Beethoven may come instead from this 'pool' of musical knowledge. Because of her personal humility her conscious mind may dramatise her method of receiving the music as direct dictation from the masters.

The late Mrs Rosalind Heywood, researcher into the paranormal and author of *The sixth sense*, has another suggestion. Mrs Brown is, she guesses, 'the type of sensitive whom frustration, often artistic, drives to the automatic production of material beyond their conscious capacity.'

To those who believe in the omniscience of the human subconscious the compositions given to the world by Mrs Brown and others like her raise more questions than they answer. But it is all so beautifully simple to the mediums – there is no death and genius is eternal.

A galley of psychic art

Does artistic genius die with the artist – or does it survive, to find expression through the hands of living sensitives? Extraordinary claims have been made that past masters have produced modern paintings

Above: the style is unmistakably Aubrey Beardsley's but this pen-and-ink drawing was produced through the hands of English psychic Matthew Manning

Above right: a posthumous Picasso. Matthew Manning remarked on the 'energy and impatience' of the artist. Picasso was one of the few artists who chose to use colour

PABLO PICASSO, who died in April 1973, produced several drawings in both pen-and-ink and colour, three months afterwards. Perhaps it would be more accurate to say that Picasso-style drawings were transmitted through British psychic Matthew Manning, who had been trying to 'get through' to Picasso. While concentrating on him he had found his hand being controlled – apparently by the spirit of Picasso, or whatever signed itself 'Picasso' on the drawing.

Psychic art presents many of the same questions to the psychical researcher that are posed, for instance by the prize-winning literature of Patience Worth or Beethoven's 1980 symphony. Is the painting, poetry or music, believed by many to be evidence of the artists' survival beyond the grave, merely an exhibition of the medium's own repressed creativity, finally finding expression? Or is it really as simple as the psychics would have us believe – that the world's great musicians, writers and artists are 'proving' their continued existence by carrying on their arts through selected 'sensitives'?

But some examples of 'automatic' or psychic art are impressive, both in their own right and, more significantly, as examples of the styles of the great painters. Some collections of psychic art are also impressive in their diversity of style and their sheer quantity.

It was Matthew Manning's enormous collection of sketches, paintings and drawings,

Above right: a Manning Monet. The style seems to be consistent with that of the great French Impressionist

Right: when this sketch of a hanged man began to take shape Matthew felt physically ill and wanted to stop the drawing, but his (anonymous) communicator compelled him to finish it

produced psychically by him as a teenager in the early 1970s, that convinced his publisher that he was a very special young man.

Matthew Manning's intelligent, articulate and objective approach to all the strange phenomena in his life makes fascinating reading. In his first book, *The link*, he discusses his method of 'contacting' dead artists. He simply sat quietly with a pad and pen in his hand and concentrated on the artist. He never went into a trance and was always aware of everything going on around him. Almost immediately the pen would begin to move, usually starting in the centre of the page and finally filling the page with what seemed like a well-planned work of art. Almost always the result was recognisably in the style of the artist he had been concentrating on – sometimes it was even signed. Occasionally, although bearing a strong resemblance to the style of the artist he had wanted to 'get through' to, the pictures were not signed. It seemed to Mr Manning that some other discarnate artist, perhaps even a pupil of the greater one, had intervened.

The communicators showed very distinct personalities. 'No other communicator tires me out as much as Picasso does,' said Mr Manning. 'After only a few minutes, the time it takes him to do one drawing, I feel worn out and cannot continue for at least 24 hours . . .' When Picasso first came through in 1973, Matthew Manning says his hand was 'moved with excessive force' and two of his finer pen-nibs were snapped. When the drawing suddenly stopped, completed, and Matthew looked at the picture objectively he could see that it 'was unmistakably in Picasso's style; it was bold and strong.'

Also, Pablo Picasso was one of the few

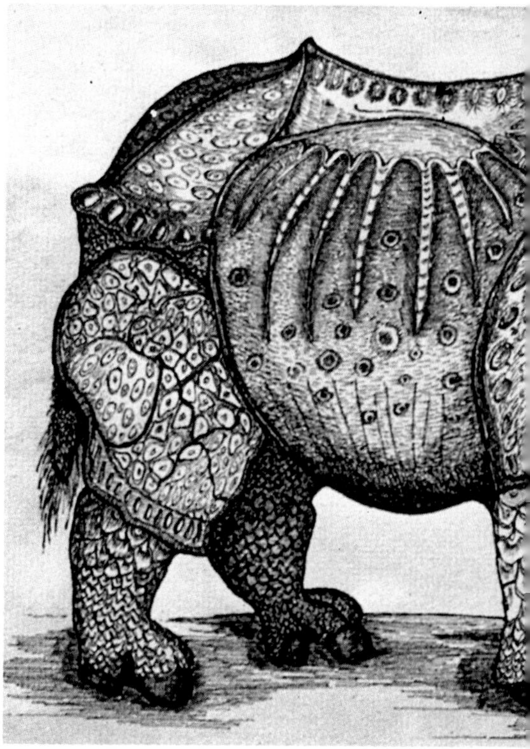

– were any mistakes made and covered over. It took between one and two hours to produce a finished work, whereas most living artists would take perhaps six or eight hours to produce a painting of similar size and complexity – and then not necessarily of the same high quality. More time would also have been spent in planning and sketching.

But one psychic artist has produced new 'old masters' at the rate of 21 in 75 minutes. In March 1978 the Brazilian Luiz Gasparetto appeared on BBC-TV's *Nationwide*

communicators who was not confused about using colour – he directed Matthew Manning's hand to pick out certain felt-tipped pens from a box of mixed colours. Most of his other discarnate artists used pen-and-ink.

Among the signed works in his collection are drawings recognisably in the styles of Arthur Rackham, Paul Klee, Leonardo da Vinci, Albrecht Dürer, Aubrey Beardsley, Beatrix Potter, Pablo Picasso, Keble Martin and the Elizabethan miniaturist Isaac Oliver.

Sometimes a finished picture would be very similar to a famous work by that particular artist. Matthew Manning often recognised them as 'copies' but occasionally the remarkable similarities had to be pointed out to him. A virtual reproduction of Beardsley's famous *Salome*, for example, took place under his eyes as he concentrated on Beardsley. But what value did these copies have – except to prove perhaps that the artist was alive and his style unchanged? Were they meant, in fact, to establish his identity?

The 'new' work came at an incredible speed. There was no preliminary sketching, nor – except in the case of Aubrey Beardsley

Above: four centuries after his death Isaac Oliver, the Elizabethan miniaturist, executed and signed such detailed – and typical – work via Matthew Manning

Albrecht Dürer (1471–1528), inventor of engraving and true son of the Renaissance, was another of Matthew Manning's alleged communicators. The rhinoceros (above right) and the study of human hands (right) – 'transmitted through' Matthew Manning – are characteristic of Dürer's minute observation and the scope of his interests

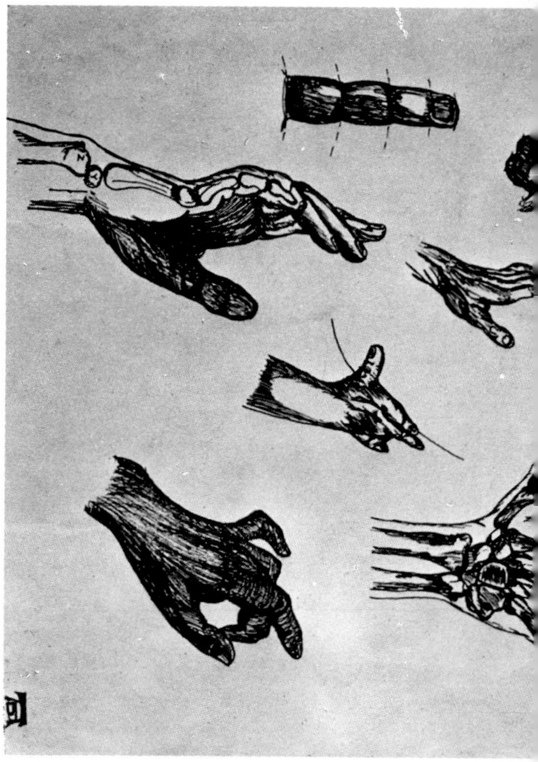

Right: a crayon drawing by Brazilian trance artist Luiz Antonio Gasparetto in the style of Henri de Toulouse-Lautrec (1864–1901). Whereas most of Luiz's paintings take only a few minutes to complete, this one took several hours. The drawing was made in 1978 while the medium was living in London, studying English

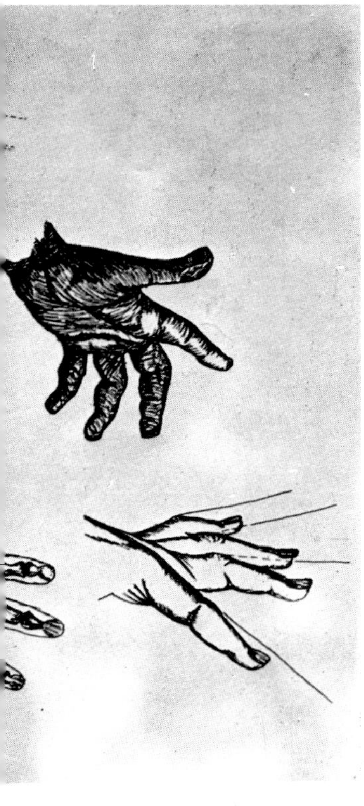

Spiritualist medium Coral Polge presented this psychic sketch of 'a little girl' (right) to a sitter. In fact 'she' bears a striking resemblance to Dag Hammarskjöld when young (far right): the sitter was researching for a book about him at the time

Two of Luiz Gasparetto's crayon drawings in distinctly different styles: one very reminiscent of Modigliani's style (below) and a charming study (below right) that is actually signed 'Renoir'

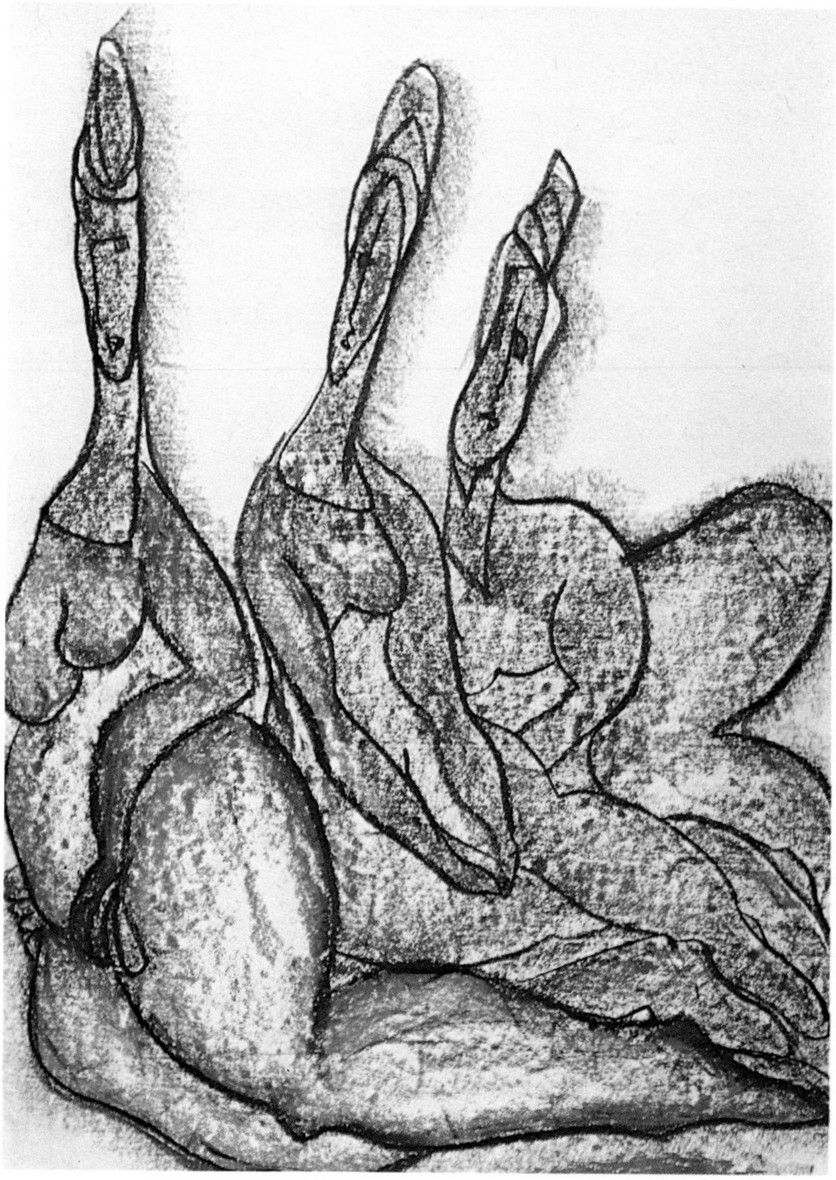

and was seen by millions to go into a trance and produce 21 pictures – sometimes working with both hands simultaneously on two separate pictures, sometimes producing perfect paintings, but executing them upside down – and all so fast that many viewers believed the BBC had accelerated the film. And the results were apparently 'new' Renoirs, Cézannes and Picassos.

Senhor Gasparetto found working under the harsh studio lights very trying, because he normally paints – in a trance – in the dark or, at the most, in a very weak light. As he is also a psychologist by profession, he views what he produces with some objectivity. But, although familiar with others who write or

Sometimes painted with both hands simultaneously, sometimes with his toes and almost always within a few minutes, Luiz Gasparetto's trance-paintings bear striking resemblances to the works of famous, dead artists. Often the 'spirit' paintings are signed, such as this typical Van Gogh (right) – signed 'Vincent' – and this slightly unusual Picasso (far right). Others need no signature; the style is sufficient. Who else could have painted this closely-observed portrait of a *demi-mondaine* (below) but Toulouse-Lautrec?

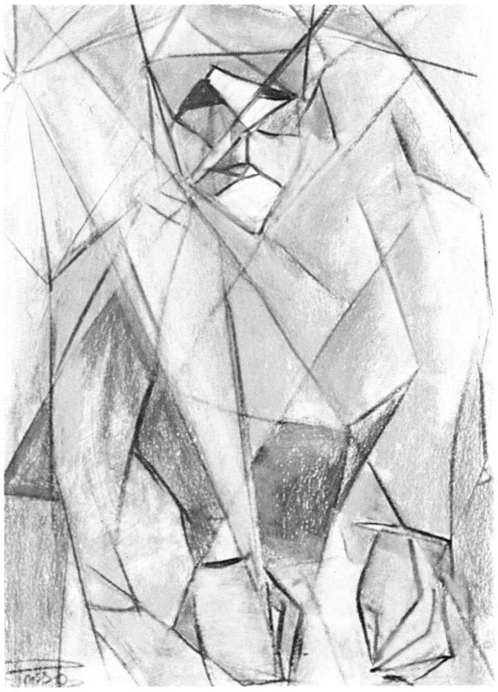

paint by psychic means, he says: 'I've never seen anyone else who can draw with both hands in the dark – in 30 different styles.' In a state of normal consciousness he says he cannot paint at all.

The Brazilian says he sees, senses and talks to all the great artists who 'come through'. Interestingly, in view of Matthew Manning's experience, Senhor Gasparetto said: 'Picasso sometimes used to be violent. If anyone whispered he would throw the paper away.'

Luiz Gasparetto travels extensively with journalist and fellow Spiritist Elsie Dubugras, giving demonstrations of psychic painting. After each session the paintings are auctioned and the proceeds go to charity.

Although Senhor Gasparetto is still producing vast numbers of psychic paintings, Matthew Manning has done little automatic art or writing since adolescence. At first he did it because he found it quelled the poltergeist activity that seemed always to surround him, but now the power, whatever it is, has been harnessed for healing.

There are some mediums, such as Frank Leah, Coral Polge and Margaret Bevan, who have produced drawings of the spirits who come to comfort the bereaved; in many cases these 'spirit portraits' of loved ones are startling likenesses.

Researchers and sceptics alike have come up with theories of repressed creativity, or even a secondary personality, to account for the strange phenomenon of psychic art. Perhaps we will never know how or why it happens, but out of all the vast array of paranormal phenomena this threatens no one – and often produces works of great beauty.

The riddle of Patience Worth

The ouija board has picked up many strange messages from the spirit world, but when 'Patience Worth' came through she produced literature of remarkably high quality.

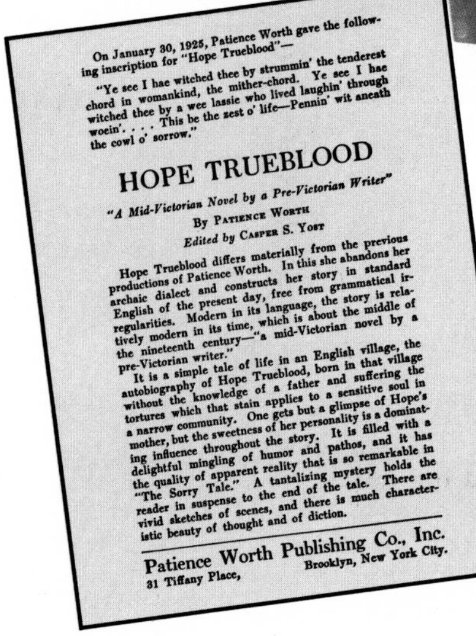

On January 30, 1925, Patience Worth gave the following inscription for "Hope Trueblood"—

"Ye see I hae witched thee by strummin' the tenderest chord in womankind, the mither-chord. Ye see I hae witched thee by a wee lassie who lived laughin' through woein'. . . . This be the zest o' life—Pennin' wit aneath the cowl o' sorrow."

HOPE TRUEBLOOD

"A Mid-Victorian Novel by a Pre-Victorian Writer"

By PATIENCE WORTH

Edited by CASPER S. YOST

Hope Trueblood differs materially from the previous productions of Patience Worth. In this she abandons her archaic dialect and constructs her story in standard English of the present day, free from grammatical irregularities. Modern in its language, the story is relatively modern in its time, which is about the middle of the nineteenth century—"a mid-Victorian novel by a pre-Victorian writer."

It is a simple tale of life in an English village, the autobiography of Hope Trueblood, born in that village without the knowledge of a father and suffering the tortures which that stain applies to a sensitive soul in a narrow community. One gets but a glimpse of Hope's mother, but the sweetness of her personality is a dominating influence throughout the story. It is filled with a delightful mingling of humor and pathos, and it has the quality of apparent reality that is so remarkable in "The Sorry Tale." A tantalizing mystery holds the reader in suspense to the end of the tale. There are vivid sketches of scenes, and there is much characteristic beauty of thought and of diction.

Patience Worth Publishing Co., Inc.
31 Tiffany Place, Brooklyn, New York City.

TELKA

An Idyl of Medieval England

By
PATIENCE WORTH

AUTHOR OF "THE SORRY TALE," "HOPE TRUEBLOOD," "LIGHT FROM BEYOND" (SELECTED POEMS), "PATIENCE WORTH" (WITH SPIRIT PORTRAIT), "THE POT UPON THE WHEEL," ETC.

Edited with a Preface by
HERMAN BEHR

NEW YORK
PATIENCE WORTH PUBLISHING CO., INC.
1928
LONDON

TWO RESPECTABLE LADIES placed their hands lightly on the ouija board and waited – humbly hoping for some message from recently deceased relatives. It was May 1913, the town was St Louis in the southern United States, and the two ladies were a Mrs Hutchings and her friend, Mrs Pearl Curran.

The pointer of the ouija board began to move, apparently struggling to spell out a certain name. 'Pat-C, Pat-C, Pat-C . . .' it insisted, while the ladies turned the name over in their minds in bewilderment. Mrs Curran's husband John, who was also in the room, suggested that it might be a deceased Irishman. Come to think of it, Mr Curran went on (with perhaps just a hint of a twinkle in his eye), he had once known a Pat McQuillan. Immediately, the late Mr McQuillan seemed to take over the board for a time, cursing mildly to give plausibility to the character of a 'vivid Hibernian'.

However, Mr Curran, contemptuous of what he saw as the ladies' gullibility, had invented Pat McQuillan and was naturally amused to see his fictitious Irishman swear at them. But 'Pat-C', once unhindered by the pranks of Mr Curran, was to come through again – and establish herself as one of the most prolific post-mortem authors in the remarkable history of 'automatic writing'.

On 22 June 'Pat' returned and spelt out a pretty but obscure paragraph: 'Oh, why let sorrow steel thy heart? Thy bosom is but its foster-mother, the world its cradle and the loving home its grave.' Not the utterance of an imaginary Irishman this time, but it proved to be an auspicious beginning to a lengthy and, indeed, celebrated partnership between Mrs Curran and the unknown 'writer'. Pat announced herself quite clearly on 8 July, when 'the board seemed to possess unusual strength', as 'Patience Worth'.

At first Patience Worth was reluctant to give any information about herself or her past life on Earth – or, indeed, her present situation (a common enough phenomenon in the seance room). She merely contented herself with spelling out such quaint advice as: 'Thine own barley corn may weevil, but thee'lt crib thy neighbour's and sack his shelling.' Mrs Curran, fascinated by the phenomenon, was nevertheless bewildered by these rustic sayings and often spoke sharply to Patience, requesting understandable English and a clearer 'message'.

Eventually Patience Worth told how she had been born in Dorset in the 17th century. She had been raised as a good Quaker girl, humbly working in the fields and busying herself with domestic chores, until her family emigrated to America. Not long afterwards, Patience was killed by Indians.

A clearer picture was hard to come by, for

Above: American Indians attacking European settlers in the 17th century. Patience Worth claimed she had been born in Dorset in the 17th century, emigrated as a Quaker to the New World, and been killed by Indians. But if questioned further about her earthly life she was consistently reticent

Patience apparently enjoyed her life on Earth so little that she could hardly bring herself to recall it. Perhaps such a short and unfulfilling life was not worth remembering, especially as – now she had 'found' Mrs Curran – she had an opportunity to make up for lost time.

From 1913 until Mrs Curran's death in 1938 Patience Worth 'dictated' a colossal number of words, mostly of a quality that can fairly be described as 'literary'. Some of this output was in the quaint English that she had first used, some was in a more modern, readable style. Her speed was enormous: one evening she produced 22 poems. In five years she 'wrote' 1,600,000 words through the mediumship of Mrs Curran.

Psychic bestseller

If sheer volume of words were the most remarkable aspect of this case, we might never have heard about it. Yet more staggering were the variety and quality of what Patience Worth wrote. She composed poems, novels and plays. One of her full-length novels, *Hope Trueblood*, was published in England under the name 'Patience Worth', with no explanation of the bizarre circumstances surrounding its composition. It won acclaim from the totally unsuspecting critics and public alike.

Hope Trueblood was a highly emotional tale of the life and trials of an illegitimate child, set in Victorian England. The *Sheffield Independent* commented favourably: 'Patience Worth must command a wide field of readers by the sheer excellence of *Hope Trueblood*, which contains sufficient high-grade characters, splendidly fashioned, to stock half a dozen novels.' The *Yorkshire Post*, a little more ambiguously, remarked that 'the writer, whose first work this is, harks back to the time in which the Brontës wrote, in order to portray in a form so exactly appropriate the biography of a brat. . . .'

Patience's epic 'Golden Age' poem *Telka* contained 60,000 words and made astonishingly accurate use of Middle English phraseology. Her book *The sorry tale* told in 325,000 words the story of a contemporary of Christ whose life ran parallel to his and who ended by being crucified beside him as one of the thieves. *The sorry tale* was written extremely rapidly – in an evening's work of only two hours, Patience Worth could produce an average of 3000 words. In addition, no research was necessary. The details of social, domestic and political life in ancient Palestine and Rome, and the language and customs of Greeks, Arabians, Romans and several sects of Jews are rich and convincing. They could have been set down only by a highly knowledgeable scholar who had specialised in the history of the Middle East of 2000 years ago.

This could not have been Mrs Curran. She had been to Sunday School and that was the limit of her knowledge of the Bible lands.

Lavendar and lace

A purple sky; twilight,
Silver-fringed of tremorous stars;
Cloud rifts, tattered, as old lace,
And a shuttling moon – wan-faced,
seeking.

Twilight, and garden shadows;
The liquid note of some late songster;
And the scent of lavendar and rue,
Like memory of the day aclinging!

PATIENCE WORTH, 12 January 1926

(*'Lavendar' was Patience's own spelling*)

She was not fond of reading and had finished her school education at about 15 years of age. She had never been abroad and, indeed, had rarely left St Louis. Until the appearance of Patience Worth she had concentrated her energies on being a housewife and an amateur singer of some talent. She knew little poetry and the verses she composed as an adolescent were no worse – but certainly no better – than those of any other girl of her age and background. One such work, entitled *The secret tear*, was written when she was 15. It began (with her own spelling reproduced):

I heard a voice whisper 'go out and pray'
See how in the garden the fairies did play
So out I went in the fresh summer air
I spied a sweet rose and she was
passingley fair
But she hung her fair head, and her
bright carmean cheek
Could not have been equaled so far as
you'de seek

This is not the sort of juvenilia one would expect from the pen that was later to 'write' works described by the psychical researcher

Opposite: Mrs Pearl Curran, Patience Worth's amanuensis, who died in 1938. Though 'Patience's' books won critical acclaim, Mrs Curran's own literary abilities were negligible and her education limited. (She thought Tennyson's famous poem was called *The lady of Charlotte*, for example.) It seems impossible that Mrs Curran could have deliberately invented the ghostly Patience – but there is no evidence to show that Patience ever existed on Earth as she claimed

Henry Holt as 'very close to masterpieces'. One might make out a case for Mrs Curran being a late developer but this seems unlikely in view of the sheer volume of literature produced through her that was of better than passable quality.

Naturally enough, 'Patience Worth' was intensively investigated by psychical researchers as well as academics. In 1929 Walter Franklin Prince, the Executive Research Officer of the Boston Society for Psychical Research, wrote a book, *The case of Patience Worth*, in which he detailed the investigations to which Mrs Curran had been subjected.

Prince, together with Charles E. Cory of Washington University, one Caspar S. Yost and other members of the Society, searched Mrs Curran's house for books of esoteric knowledge that could have been incorporated, consciously or unconsciously, into such works as *The sorry tale*. They found none. They also noted that the few books of poetry in the Currans' meagre library were unthumbed, and in one the pages were uncut. (Mrs Curran firmly believed that Tennyson's famous poem *The lady of Shalott* was called *The lady of Charlotte*.)

The investigators tested Mrs Curran's ability to write in her own persona by asking her to produce short stories and poetry. These reveal a style that might be expected from a housewife unused to putting her thoughts on paper. Her personality shows through sufficiently to make any connection with the serious Quaker attitudes of Patience Worth seem positively ridiculous.

Other incidents concerning communications from Patience reveal significant gaps in Mrs Curran's education and reading. For

Above: a ouija board in action. This is similar to the one used, at first out of idle curiosity, by Mrs Curran in 1913. The letters of the alphabet, the numbers 1 to 10, and the words 'yes' and 'no' are inscribed on the board. The pointer is mounted on castors and one or more of the 'sitters' places a hand lightly on it. Questions are asked of the 'spirits' and almost every time the pointer moves – as if directed by an invisible force – and spells out messages. Although proper ouija boards are not much used these days, many people use an impromptu version with the letters, numbers and words on pieces of paper arranged in a circle on a table, and with an upturned glass acting as the pointer

The poet from the shadows

A phantom? Weel enough,
Prove thee thyself to me!
I say, behold, here I be,
Buskins, kirtle, cap and petty-skirts,
And much tongue!
Weel, what hast thou to prove thee?

This was Patience Worth's verse entitled 'Patience Worth', a wry comment on her unique status as the genius of the ouija board – the 'phantom' behind the poetry, plays and novels written through Mrs Curran which won major critical acclaim on both sides of the Atlantic.

Among numerous literary works she produced poems, plays and *The sorry tale* – an enormous novel of 300,000 words 'dictated' every evening over a two year period. This massive work (concerning the fate of another child born in Bethlehem on the same night as Jesus) revealed scholarly knowledge of Biblical lands and customs way above that of the medium. Professors of literature, poets, journalists and churchmen hailed the work as 'the Gospel according to Patience Worth', and gushingly complimented its ghostly author on its brilliance. But not everyone agreed. Some reviewers commented that they found her writing to be 'feverish, high-flown and terribly prolix'. Other reviewers compromised uneasily: 'but it is a wonderful book, well worth wrestling with, and the marvel is, who wrote it?'

For many people the mystery of its authorship was the book's main attraction, while others were prejudiced against it for the same reason, thinking it 'spooky' and distasteful. But Patience Worth – whoever she was – was compared to the Brontës, Keats, Browning, Milton and even Shakespeare. She was often invited to literary receptions, but sent her regrets.

example, a Roman Catholic archbishop in the St Louis area had been preaching that if spirits returned after death, they were 'emissaries of the Evil One'. Mrs Curran asked Patience her views on the subject:

> At once Patience had this to say: 'I say me, who became apparent before the Maid? Who became a vision before Bernadette? No less than the Mother; yet they have lifted up their voices saying the dead are in his [the devil's] keeping.' This last about the dead gave us the clue to what she referred, though we had no idea of what she meant by the rest. Looking up the matter the next day we found that Bernadette Soubirous was the Maid of Lourdes. . . .

Subtle impostor?

A fraud would readily acknowledge the need to look up a reference transmitted by a 'spirit' – ah, the reader would think, Mrs Curran had not even heard of Bernadette of Lourdes. But surely Patience's reference to 'the Maid' was not to 'the Maid of Lourdes' but to *the* Maid – Joan of Arc. Surely two visionary women, not one, were being cited to prove that 'spirits' were not always 'emissaries of the Evil One'. If Mrs Curran pretended to miss this point, she was a very subtle impostor.

But who was Patience Worth? Was she really a Quaker woman who emigrated from her native Dorset 300 years before to die a spinster in America? She has not been traced. But her quaint English has been analysed by linguists and apparently she used perfectly the language and idiom of her place and day. The linguists drew attention to the spelling of certain words that were spoken very differently in the 17th century than they are now. For example, 'boy' was pronounced *bwy*, 'with' and 'give' were *wi'* and *gi'e*.

But even assuming that Miss Worth had existed and returned to pour out her literary talent – denied fulfilment in life – to Mrs Curran, how could an uneducated Quaker girl know of the customs of ancient Jewish sects detailed in *The sorry tale*?

Did she perhaps gain this extensive knowledge after her death, at a kind of post-mortem university? Some Spiritualists would take this view. Other groups believe such knowledge is plucked from the 'Akashic records': in this case, either by Patience Worth, by Mrs Curran's subconscious mind or – who knows? – by both.

Celebrity brought recognition from public bodies. The States Capitol Commission of Missouri, which wished to decorate the walls of the new State House with inscriptions by local literary figures, called on Patience Worth, through Mrs Curran, to supply a short piece. It was to be no more than 120 letters long. Patience immediately produced, as fast as Mrs Curran could write:

> 'Tis the grain of God that be within thy hands. Cast nay grain awhither. Even the chaff is His, and the dust thy brother's.

Counting spaces, punctuation marks and letters, this adds up to 120 characters precisely.

The ouija board was soon found to be too slow and clumsy as a means for taking down Patience's dictation. Mrs Curran began automatic writing proper. This involves resting a pen or pencil, held lightly in the hand, on a piece of paper. If one is so gifted, the pen will begin to write of its own accord. But soon even this method became too restrictive for the prolific outpourings of Patience Worth, who began instead to communicate directly with Mrs Curran's mind. She 'spoke' her poetry through Mrs Curran, who at the same time witnessed beautiful, atmospheric visions. Mr Curran took down Mrs Curran's/Patience Worth's utterances in longhand, and they were then typed.

Patience admitted to having burning literary ambition – and also acknowledged that in some way she might be a messenger of God. Perhaps she was suggesting that the mysterious phenomenon she was causing could guide people to God and a belief in eternal things. She wrote: 'I weave not, nay but neath these hands shall such a word set up, that Earth shall burn with wonder.'

A daughter of the dead

If Patience had been a frustrated writer she remedied that easily through Mrs Curran. But her maternal instinct had also been frustrated, so Mrs Curran received her most bizarre instructions: that she should adopt a baby girl whom she would 'share' with the long-dead Patience. Patience gave Mrs Curran a description of this as yet unborn child: it must have red hair, blue eyes and be of Anglo-Scottish descent.

The Currans found a recently widowed pregnant woman who agreed that they could adopt her child if she happened to die in childbirth. She did indeed die and the child – fitting Patience's description exactly – became known as Patience Worth Wee Curran.

The child grew up, supervised by the ghostly Patience (who insisted on her wearing quaint Quaker-girl clothes) and later moved to California where she married twice. In 1938 Mrs Curran died and Patience fell silent forever. But in 1943, at the age of 27 and in good health, Patience Wee had a premonition of her approaching death. She began to lose weight and a very mild heart ailment was diagnosed. Then, just before Christmas, 1943, she died in her sleep. Many believed that her ghostly 'mother' had come for her own.

Above: Dr Walter Franklin Prince (1863–1934) an ex-Methodist minister and psychical researcher. He was particularly interested in the case of Patience Worth, believing it to be one of the most important psychic case histories of all time

The art of automatic writing

Only very rarely does automatic writing produce anything like literature. When a genius of Shakespeare's stature 'comes through', the results are bound to be fascinating. This chapter discusses the technique and examines the claims made for it

AUTOMATIC WRITING is still a matter of intense interest among psychologists and parapsychologists alike. Not all occurrences of automatic script are as difficult to explain away as the remarkable case of Patience Worth. A leading British psychical researcher and scientist, Professor Arthur Ellison, has said: 'I expect a third of the population of England could produce some form of automatic writing – but the results would be mostly gibberish.'

Anyone can try an experiment by resting a pen lightly on a blank page, diverting their attention from it and letting the pen do what it will. It used to be assumed that automatic script must be the product of discarnate entities, desperate to communicate and grateful for the opportunity to take command of a pen. The only question in believers' minds was: 'Is the communicator an Earth-bound spirit or a spirit sent by God?' But the scribbles produced in automatic writing can reveal a great deal, if not about the spirit world, then certainly about the subconscious mind of the pen-holder.

In the first three decades of the 20th century automatic writing was in fact used as a tool in diagnosing and treating mental disturbances. Dr Anita Mühl was a pioneer of this particular method of encouraging patients to express spontaneously their hidden conflicts.

Above: William Shakespeare and his contemporaries. In 1947 a medium named Hester Dowden allegedly communicated with Shakespeare (seated centre) and other Elizabethans through automatic writing. She was told that the plays attributed to Shakespeare were in fact a group effort. Among the contributors were Francis Beaumont (standing third from left), John Fletcher (seated third from left) and Francis Bacon (seated at the end of the table)

The beginner in automatic writing may have to be very patient (and suffer writer's cramp before a single word has been written), for it can take hours before the pen begins to move, seemingly of its own accord. Some people never achieve automatic writing; many get meaningless squiggles or jumbles of letters; but a very few get coherent, intelligent and apparently purposeful messages, sometimes in handwriting distinctly different from their own.

An ex-clergyman, William Stainton Moses, was a medium in the latter part of the 19th century who 'specialised' in automatic script, although he could produce these automatisms only while in a self-induced trance. From 1872 to 1883 he filled 24 notebooks with trance-inspired writings, mingled with 'spirit writings', some signed. (Mendelssohn allegedly appended his signature to a page of Moses's script.)

If one takes a sceptical view, certain 19th-century religious works were not directly dictated by angels or by God, as alleged, but were the result of automatic writing by the 'prophets'. *The book of Mormon*, for example, was purportedly dictated by an angel called Moroni to a New York State farm boy, Joseph Smith, in 1827. It was written in a style similar, but inferior, to that of the King James Bible. It is not necessary to believe that Joseph Smith was a liar to doubt that *The book of Mormon* is the word of God.

One early case of automatic writing that is still considered unique is that which involved William T. Stead, a leading British Spiritualist of the late 19th century, and a certain friend who communicated with him automatically through his pen. What is remarkable about this particular case is that the friend was alive at the time. The story goes as follows in Stead's own words:

> A friend of mine . . . was to lunch with me on the Wednesday if she had returned to town. On the Monday afternoon I wished to know about this, so taking up my pen I asked the lady mentally if she had returned home. My hand wrote as follows: 'I am sorry to say that I have had the most unpleasant experience, which I am almost ashamed to tell you. I left Haslemere at 2.27 p.m. in a second-class compartment in which there were two women and a man. At Godalming the women got out and I was left alone with the man. He came over and sat by me. I was alarmed and pushed him away. He would not move, however, and tried to kiss me. I was furious and there was a struggle, during which I seized his umbrella and struck him with it repeatedly, but it broke, and I was afraid I would get the worst of it, when the train stopped some distance from Guildford. The man took fright, left me before the train reached the station, jumped out and took to his heels. I was extremely agitated, but I kept the umbrella.'

Stead dashed off a sympathetic note to the lady, explaining the reasons for his solicitude, and – being a thorough investigator – asked her to call, bringing with her the broken umbrella as evidence. She replied in some perturbation, saying she had intended never to mention the incident to anyone. However, she added, one point in his account of her misadventure was wrong – the umbrella was hers, not her assailant's.

A great American psychical researcher of modern times, Dr J. B. Rhine, was inclined to dismiss automatic writings as spontaneous 'motor automatisms' or, as previously hinted, the outward expression of subconscious conflicts, obsessions or repressions. There seems little doubt that he and his like-minded colleagues are right in this appraisal of much automatic writing. But Dr Rhine admitted that some cases – that of Patience Worth, for example – are not so easily dismissed.

A provocative case of automatic writing occurred in 1947, through the mediumship of Hester Dowden, who had for many years been famous for the automatic scripts that she produced, even when blindfolded. Percy Allen, an author, sat with her while she held written 'conversations', allegedly with Elizabethan dramatists. As a result of these seances Mr Allen believed he discovered the answer to the tantalising question 'Who was Shakespeare?' Was he really Francis Bacon? Lord Oxford? Or perhaps was William Shakespeare just William Shakespeare?

Mrs Dowden claimed she received written information on the matter from those three gentlemen, and also from other Elizabethans involved in the writing or staging of plays. Mrs Dowden's communicators explained that the 'Shakespeare' plays were a group effort. Shakespeare and Lord Oxford were the principal contributors, while Beaumont and Fletcher, famous as the authors of many other plays, occasionally provided additional material. Bacon acted as a kind of stern script editor.

Each did what he was good at: Shakespeare created many of the stronger characters, both comic and tragic, such as Iago and Falstaff,

Above: American psychical researcher Dr J.B. Rhine, who believed that most automatic writings can be explained as the spontaneous expression of subconscious conflicts

Below left: William Stainton Moses, a 19th-century medium who claimed to have received numerous messages from the spirit world through automatic writing. One of his scripts (below), dated 1874, was 'signed' by Mendelssohn – who died in 1847

Below right: Edward de Vere, 17th Earl of Oxford. According to medium Hester Dowden, Oxford wrote the lyrical and romantic passages of 'Shakespeare's' plays, and was the author of most of the sonnets

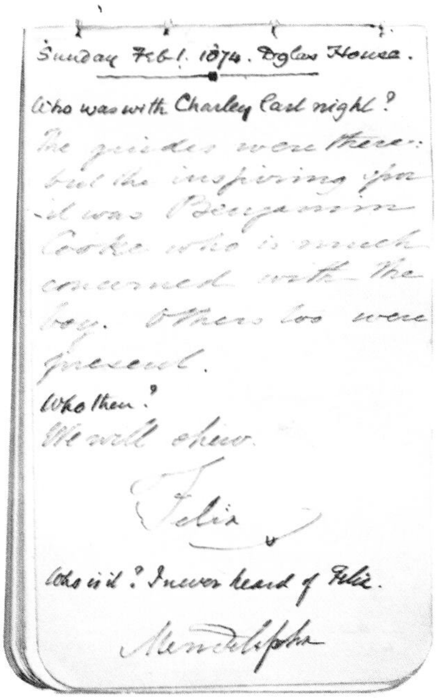

Above: a 19th-century engraving entitled 'Charles Dickens's legacy to England'. Dickens said that many of his characters simply appeared before him while he was dozing, almost as if they had a life of their own

and he had a talent for dramatic construction, which the others willingly used. Lord Oxford, on the other hand, created the 'honeyed Shakespeare' by writing the lyrical and romantic passages.

Mrs Dowden was similarly informed that it was Lord Oxford who penned the majority of the sonnets. He also 'dictated' three new ones to her.

Bacon reiterated time and again to Mrs Dowden that the body of literature that the world knows as Shakespeare's was a group effort. Will of Stratford himself allegedly told Mrs Dowden:

> I was quick at knowing what would be effective on stage. I would find a plot (*Hamlet* was one), consult with Oxford, and form a skeleton edifice, which he would furnish and people, as befitted the subject . . . I was the *skeleton* of the body that wrote the plays. The flesh and blood was *not* mine, but I was *always* in the production.

Of course, automatic literature may be a dramatisation of a deep or repressed creativity, finding expression through a means we can so far only guess at. After all, many writers and artists over the centuries have 'listened' to their 'muse'. Often whole plots, scenes or minutely observed characters have 'come unbidden' to writers, dramatists, poets. Often, when Charles Dickens was dozing in his armchair, a wealth of characters would appear before him 'as it were, begging to be set down on paper'. Samuel Taylor Coleridge dreamed the whole of his poem *Kubla Khan* and would have written it all down for posterity had not someone known to history only as 'a person from Porlock' called casually and put most of it out of his mind forever. Mary Shelley dreamed *Frankenstein*, Robert Louis Stevenson came to rely on his dreams for his stories, including the allegorical Dr Jekyll and Mr Hyde. When such a writer as Charles Dickens says a tale 'wrote itself', however, we can only assume he did *not* mean his pen shot across the paper inscribing, of its own accord, *Oliver Twist*. Inspiration is in practice very different from the process of automatic writing.

Somewhere between the two, perhaps, lay the strange case of Patrick Branwell Brontë. He was an unfortunate and unsympathetic character, famous mainly for his inability to hold liquor and laudanum, or to cope with sharing an isolated house on the moors with his eccentric sisters Charlotte, Emily and Anne. He had literary pretensions, which came to nothing. However, during one of his brief periods of humble employment (as a railway clerk) he discovered that he could compile the week's railway accounts with one hand, while his other, quite independently, began to scrawl. First the name of his beloved dead sister, Maria, appeared; then came other fragments – some prose, some poetry. He later claimed to have written an alternative version of *Wuthering Heights* by pure coincidence at the same time as Emily was writing a book of the same name.

However, this was the second version of the incident. He had previously stolen the opening chapter of Emily's book and read it to his cronies as his own work. It was only when he was disbelieved that he came up with the 'alternative version' account.

Left: Mary Wollstonecraft Shelley (1797-1851), creator of *Frankenstein*, one of the most famous 'horror' stories. The plot of the novel came to her in a dream

Literature of the dead

Above: 'Chico' Xavier, Brazil's foremost Spiritist writer, at one of his public automatic writing sessions

Inset: the frontispiece of *Parnassus from beyond the tomb* – allegedly written by no less than 56 dead poets

Can novels, poems and plays really be 'written' by the dead? If so, what do they tell us about the afterlife?

THERE APPEAR TO BE fashions in paranormal phenomena as in other aspects of life, and automatic writing seemed to have fallen from grace for a period, whether as an attempt to communicate with the dead or even as a party trick. Yet automatic scripts are being produced in vast quantities today. Possibly the world's most important and prolific psychic writer has largely escaped attention in Europe and America because he is a Brazilian, writing in Portuguese that is sometimes extremely erudite and technical.

Francisco Candido ('Chico') Xavier, now in his seventies, is certainly one of Brazil's most popular figures, devoting his life to helping the poor and producing edifying, entertaining and highly profitable best-sellers. He does not accept any money for these books, nor any credit. For, he says, he did not write them – discarnate Brazilian authors did.

For the past 50 years Xavier has spent at least five hours a day letting dead authors write through him. He has often given over his precious spare time for the spirits to use, for until his retirement in 1961 he also had a full-time (but humble) job in local government offices.

Best-sellers from beyond

One of 'his' best-sellers is a volume of poetry called *Parnassus from beyond the tomb.* It contains 259 poems (taking up 421 pages) in markedly differing styles, and is signed by 56 of the leading literary figures of the Portuguese-speaking world – all of whom are dead. The poems deal with many subjects – love, the hypocrisy of the priesthood, the nature of human evolution – and some contain jokes. One is a simple declaration of the poet's identity, entitled *Ego sum* (Latin for 'I am'). Translated by Guy Lyon Playfair, author of *The flying cow* and expert on Brazilian Spiritism, it reads: 'I am who I am. Therefore it would be extremely unjust if I did not declare myself; if I lied, or deceived you in anonymity, since I am Augusto.' And the poem is signed 'Augusto dos Anjos', a famous deceased Brazilian poet.

But nothing so far described offers anything like proof that the automatic scripts of Chico Xavier are not either conscious or unconscious frauds (although one would think a conscious impostor would eagerly accept the millions of dollars his books have made over the years).

It is true that Xavier is not entirely illiterate – he had an elementary school education (which, as Mr Playfair wryly points out, can be very elementary indeed in Brazil). But the vocabulary he uses is far above the heads of even educated people – he says he often cannot understand a word of it! This applies to the massive work *Nosso lar* (*Our home*), which totals no less than 2459 pages and was purportedly dictated to Xavier by the discarnate doctor Andre Luiz, a pioneer in tropical medicine. It is in fact a novel in nine books with a very simple plot – the hero dies at the beginning of the first book and the subsequent action takes place in the next world ('our home'). This, says Dr Luiz, is not the paradise that the priests tell of, but is much like our life on Earth. 'Death is merely a change of clothing,' he warns and adds that the hereafter is 'the paradise or hell we ourselves have created.' We have a noble purpose, even the humblest of us, says Luiz:

'We are sons of God and heirs to the centuries, conquering values from experience to experience and millennium to millennium.' Reincarnation, we are told, does take place but the rules governing it are much more complex than many living people, even those who believe in it, can guess at.

This massive sequence of novels discourses at great length on a variety of medical and technological subjects, discussing in detail, for example, the fertilisation of the human egg and the slow processes of evolution on Earth. On 2 February 1958 Xavier took down a lengthy passage containing this sort of phraseology:

> The existent hiatus, as noted by Hugo de Vries, in the development of mutationism was bridged by the activities of the Servants of Earthly Organogenesis, who submitted the *Leptothrix* family to profound alterations . . .

Hugo de Vries was a Dutch botanist famous for his work on the laws of heredity – a fact not very likely to be taught at a Brazilian elementary school at the beginning of the 20th century. (Once Xavier had complained to Augusto dos Anjos that he couldn't understand what he was 'writing'. 'Look,' came the reply, 'I'm going to write what I can, for your head can't really cope!')

The spirits dictate

By the mid 1970s he had produced 130 books, all bearing on their title page the phrase 'dictated by the spirit of . . .'. More than 400 discarnate authors are said to have written posthumous works through him, and they are certainly selling better, using Xavier as their 'agent', than they did in life. *Our home* alone had sold more than 150,000 copies by late 1980.

One of his more remarkable achievements – which some consider final 'proof' that dead writers are still working through him – was a bizarre incidence of co-authorship, very reminiscent of the case of the 'cross-correspondences'. *Evolution in two worlds* was psychically written by Xavier, in the small town of Pedro Leopoldo, a chapter a time – but *alternate* chapters, making no consecutive sense at all – and by Dr Waldo Vieira, who 'wrote' the interim chapters hundreds of miles away. But it was only when Xavier had finished his pile of disjointed and apparently unfinished chapters that his spirit guide told him to contact Dr Vieira. Of course then the whole project made sense. This was the first of 17 books they were to write in this way. As Guy Lyon Playfair points out, frequently one of Dr Vieira's chapters – written without any knowledge of the previous chapter 'written' by Xavier – takes up the story precisely where the other left off.

Now an old and frail man – nearly sightless in one eye – Xavier spends his days helping at the welfare centre 'his' royalties have financed, writing down spirit messages for individuals who need advice, signing books, shaking hands, handing out roses, greeting each new face as if he had been anticipating that very meeting with the utmost pleasure. His 'automatic' writing is often done in public, for perhaps three hours at a time, for anyone to watch. (He writes, said an observer, as if his hand were driven by a battery.) He types up his own psychically produced scripts, answers his own letters (usually over 200 a day, many seeking advice or prayers from him, others simply consisting of fan mail), and attends public Spiritist meetings.

He is widely regarded as a saint – even, by some of his followers, as the reincarnation of St Francis of Assisi. But he has his detractors, and his enemies. The Roman Catholic Church in Brazil believes him to be evil, even possessed by the Devil, and one leading Brazilian Jesuit has taken as his mission in life the utter destruction of Chico Xavier's reputation.

Europeans tend to discount even such well-attested cases as this when they occur in distant and exotic places like Brazil. Yet automatic writing flourishes in Europe today. The young British psychic Matthew Manning, although an accomplished automatic writer in the traditional way, has found that 'spirits' have taken it on themselves to do the writing. Notable amongst them is Robert Webbe, who built and lived in the Mannings' Cambridgeshire home in the 17th century and haunted it for some years. Over 300 names and short phrases in differing styles

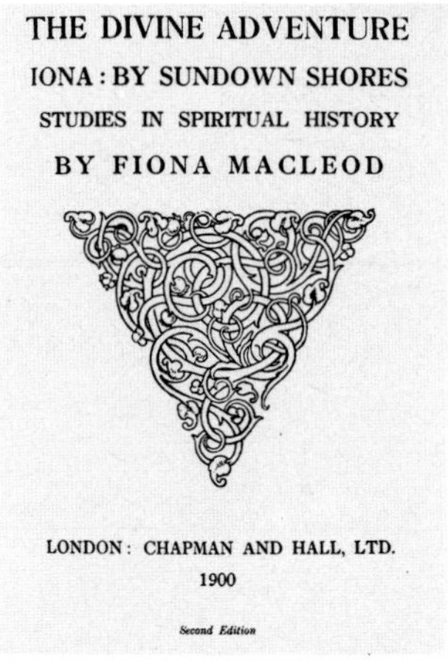

THE DIVINE ADVENTURE
IONA: BY SUNDOWN SHORES
STUDIES IN SPIRITUAL HISTORY
BY FIONA MACLEOD

LONDON: CHAPMAN AND HALL, LTD.
1900
Second Edition

Top: the Scottish poet and occultist William Sharp, who had a secondary personality known as Fiona Macleod. Both personalities wrote, but quite differently. Their work was published separately, as Sharp had no sense that Macleod's writing was his own

Above: the frontispiece of *The divine adventure* by Fiona Macleod, a mystical work about the Scottish Isle of Iona, published in 1900

of handwriting have appeared on Matthew Manning's bedroom wall. After each session of spirit graffiti a blunted pencil would be found on his bed, although during the time of the writings no member of the family had been in the room, or even, on many of the occasions, in the house.

In Scotland a publishing company has been set up devoted entirely to the works of a particular spirit writer – or rather, a pair of authors making up a double personality. One half of the double is William Sharp, a Scot and self-styled poet and occultist, who died at Il Castello di Maniace, in Sicily, in 1905, aged 50. Above his grave close to Mount Etna there is an Iona cross, bearing two epitaphs. One says:

> Farewell to the known and exhausted Welcome to the unknown and illimitable.

The other, more obscurely says:

> Love is more great than we conceive, and Death is the keeper of unknown redemptions. F. M.

So who was 'F.M.'? These are the initials of Fiona Macleod, his *alter ego*, his feminine side personified, whose name and works had inspired the 'Celtic renaissance' in late 19th-century Scotland.

The Paisley project

Dual, or even multiple, personalities are not unknown in the annals of psychiatric medicine. But what is so significant about 'Wilfion' (Sharp's own collective name for his two selves) is that he/she is allegedly communicating thoughts and poetic works from beyond the grave.

From the early days of 1970 an American expert on William Sharp, Konrad Hopkins, began to receive psychic scripts from many discarnate souls – including one 'George Windsor', better known perhaps as King George VI – but mainly from Sharp himself. In 1974 Hopkins met a Dutch sensitive called Ronald van Roekel and shortly afterwards they began a publishing venture in Paisley, Scotland, called Wilfion Books.

Meanwhile in Ventnor, Isle of Wight, a lady called Margo Williams was discovering her long-hidden gifts as a medium. By summer 1980 Margo had received more than 4000 psychic scripts, purporting to be dictated by more than 360 discarnate persons. The first was her spirit guide, Jane, and the second was someone called William Sharp.

The deceased Scottish poet clairaudiently informed Konrad Hopkins of the Margo Williams connection. A correspondence between the medium and the directors of Wilfion books sprang up and soon arrangements were under way for *The Wilfion scripts* – the Wilfion writings received through Mrs Williams – to be published in Paisley.

There are 92 verses and some prose that make up *The Wilfion scripts*. The verses are, on the whole, short, childish (some would say child-like) and bad. The introduction to the verses, by Hopkins and van Roekel, includes this curiously obscure apology for the low quality of the poetry:

> Sharp . . . admits that the verse is bad because he is trying to reach a confession of a truly horrific sight which he either saw himself or relived through his ability to pick up sensations at stone circles and it then haunted him the rest of his life.

But Mrs Williams generously ascribes to Wilfion 'a masterly economy of words'. On 12 December 1976 William Sharp dictated this through her:

> Observes scenes from the past
> Which impress and will last
> Scenes which survive throughout ages
> Make interesting reading on pages.

And, perhaps shrewdly summing up the feelings of many of his latest readers, Sharp had this to write on 19 January 1977:

> What a joke
> I can cloak
> Sharp by name
> But be same.
> Macleod be known by
> Until day I die,
> Write tales so strange
> Over a wide range
> Celtic verse
> Sounds much worse
> From intelligent being
> Little folk to be seeing,
> What a joke,
> Make men choke
> With laughter loud
> About Macleod.

In the jargon of parapsychology all these bizarre effects could be the products of 'telepathic psychokinesis', 'motor automatisms', 'repressed psychosexual creativity'. But is this not disguising the fact that we just don't know what is behind them?

Above: King George VI, who, as 'George Windsor' is said to have communicated posthumously with the American medium Konrad Hopkins. Hopkins was one of the partners who published *The Wilfion scripts*

Above right: Margo Williams, the medium whose many automatic scripts include poems from 'Wilfion'

The Victorian spirit

The surge of interest in spiritualism during the middle of the nineteenth century crossed barriers of class, nationality and economics. Many prominent Victorians became involved and some of the case studies remain among the most important in the field.

The women in white

Of all Spiritualist phenomena, materialisation is the rarest. Yet the young Victorian medium Florence Cook apparently found it easy to materialise 'Katie King' - or did she? This chapter investigates a controversy that continues to this day

IN THE LATE 19th century, the appearance of a young woman dressed in white was causing a sensation. Wealthy men paid dearly just to see and talk to her for a few minutes and journalists on staid daily newspapers waxed lyrical about their encounters with her.

The object of all this attention was the beautiful Katie King, but it was not her good looks that brought admirers flocking to see her. Katie was a spirit with the ability to materialise – that is, she could make herself solid in appearance and walk and talk like an ordinary human being.

Between 1850 and the mid 1870s Katie was a very popular spirit with mediums in England and the USA. Many claimed that she was making personal appearances at their seances: for Katie to drop in on psychic proceedings was like receiving the seal of approval from the spirit world.

Above: 'Katie King' manifests in Dr Glen Hamilton's Winnipeg circle in 1930

Below: Katie King and William Crookes in 1874

Since then Katie has turned up on photographs taken in 1930 in Winnipeg, Canada, by psychical researcher Dr Glen Hamilton. And in July 1974 the ubiquitous Katie emerged yet again from retirement on the 'other side' in order to materialise in front of 23 people at a seance in Rome.

There is no hard evidence that Katie ever lived on earth, but there is no shortage of accounts of her 'spirit return'. She claimed to be a pirate's daughter. Her father (known as John King in Spiritualist circles, where he also was much in demand) was said to be the buccaneer, Henry Owen Morgan, who was knighted by Charles II and appointed Governor of Jamaica.

According to Katie, her name when on earth was Annie Owen Morgan and she had married and had had two children. But she confessed to having committed many crimes, including murder, before her untimely death at the age of 22 or 23. Her spirit return, she explained, was to convince the world of the truth of Spiritualism: a task given to her to expiate the sins she committed in life.

Among the earliest seance appearances were one-night stands with the Davenport brothers, Ira and William, sons of a police official, who were among the first American Spiritualist mediums. They toured their own country and Europe demonstrating their alleged paranormal powers in theatres, but

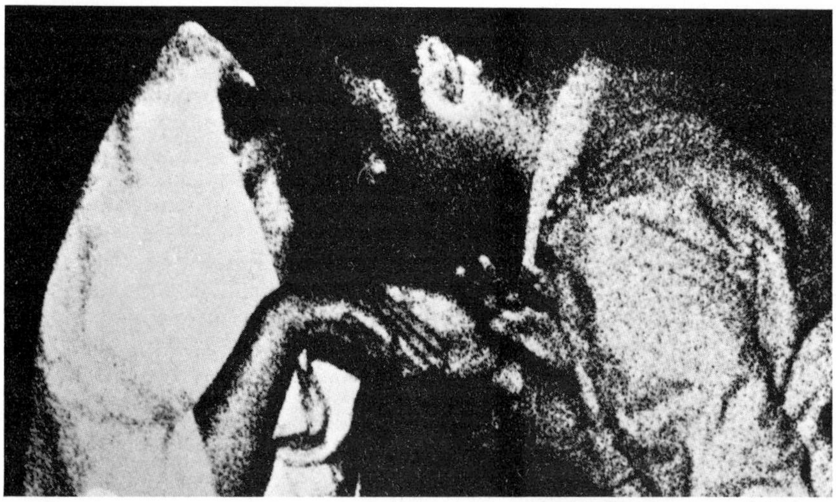

are dismissed by many critics as no more than clever magicians.

When she spoke at the Davenport seances, Katie King was far from spiritual. Her voice was described as shrill 'like that of a person of the lower walks of life', and she apparently prattled incessantly in what can only be described as very small talk.

But Katie's reputation improved when she crossed the Atlantic and began to manifest through the mediumship of a young east London girl named Florence Cook. Florrie had apparently seen and heard spirits from an early age but this was dismissed at the time as vivid imagination. Her mediumship blossomed at the age of 15 after she had taken part in a table-turning session with friends at a tea-party. The table had moved violently and Florrie was levitated.

Intrigued by this experience, she and her mother began holding seances at home and very soon young Florrie's hand was controlled by a spirit who wrote a message in mirror writing (it could be read only when its reflection was viewed in a mirror).

The spirit message told her to visit a bookseller who would introduce her to the Dalston Association of Spiritualists (in east London), and there she would make the acquaintance of the editor of *The Spiritualist*. This happened exactly as predicted, with the result that Florrie was soon giving seances to the society, and her mediumship was featured in the columns of that influential weekly newspaper.

The paranormal phenomena that occurred in her presence were sometimes an embarrassment to Florrie. On one occasion she is said to have been levitated over the heads of other sitters and then stripped of her clothes by invisible hands. When that happened her mother forebade further public seances, but she and her husband, together with Florrie and two other daughters (who also became mediums) and their maid Mary, began holding regular seances in the privacy of their Hackney home.

It was at these meetings that the spirit of Katie King made her presence felt, first by speaking through the lips of the entranced Florrie. Katie promised to stay for three years and reveal many strange things, as well as endeavouring to make herself visible. To make this possible, Katie asked Florrie to sit in a curtained-off recess (called a 'cabinet' by Spiritualists) to enable a white substance – or 'ectoplasm' – to be drawn from her body. Clothed in this, Katie King would be able to appear in physical form.

The mask of death

Katie King made her first attempt to materialise at the Cook home circle in April 1872 when a face like a death mask appeared between the curtains of the cabinet. When the face was examined it was found to be hollow at the back.

In time, the face filled out, the obscuring drapery surrounding her features became less abundant, and within a year the fully materialised form of Katie King, dressed in flowing white 'spirit robes', was able to step out of the cabinet.

News of Florrie's remarkable mediumship soon spread, and various visitors were able to attend the seances and meet Katie King. They included Charles Blackburn, a wealthy businessman from Manchester, who guaranteed an annual retainer for Florrie so that she could give her mediumistic services when required.

During this period Katie was seen in the Cook home almost daily, virtually becoming a member of the household. The family reported that she walked about the house, and even went to bed with Florrie. After Florrie married Captain Elgie Corner in 1874, he is reported to have felt that he had married two women and at times was not

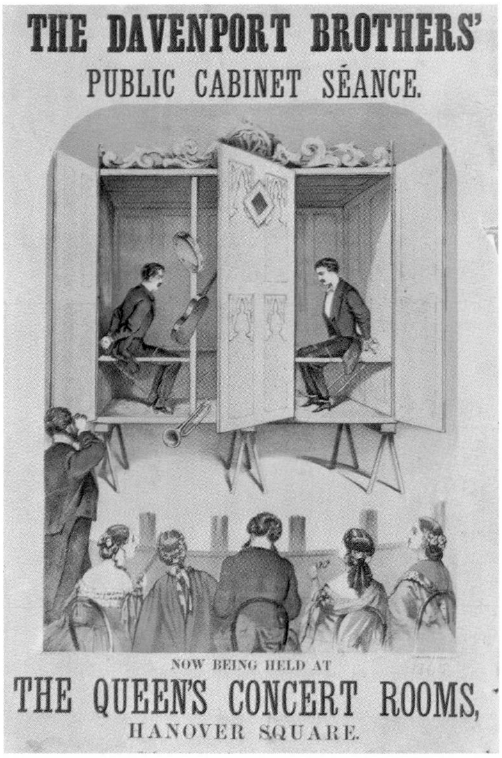
THE DAVENPORT BROTHERS'
PUBLIC CABINET SÉANCE.
NOW BEING HELD AT
THE QUEEN'S CONCERT ROOMS,
HANOVER SQUARE.

Top: 'Katie King' appears in a seance in Rome in 1974 – exactly 100 years after she was investigated by William Crookes in London

Above: the 17th-century buccaneer Henry Owen Morgan supervises the sacking of a Jamaican town. As 'John King', his spirit is said to be a frequent visitor at seances and his name is even associated with the SORRAT psychokinesis group of Rolla, Missouri, USA. Katie King claimed to be his daughter

Right: a poster advertising a public seance of Ira and William Davenport, famous American mediums of the mid 19th century. It was at one of their seances that Katie made an early appearance

Sceptics have frequently remarked on the extremely close resemblance between the medium Florence Cook (right) and the alleged spirit manifestation Katie King (below), although William Crookes and a few others noted dissimilarities. Katie herself is said to have bemoaned her resemblance to Florrie, saying 'I can't help it, but I was much prettier than that in earth life'

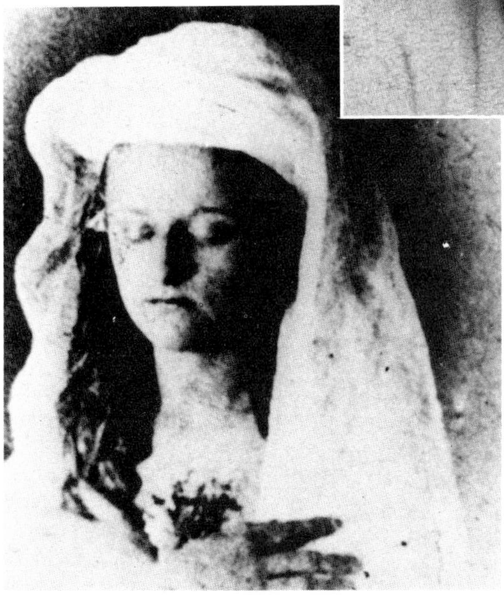

sure which was his wife. This is not too surprising, since medium and spirit were remarkably similar in appearance – a fact that served only to confirm the worst suspicions of the sceptics.

Even the believers were aware that the manner in which the spirit of Katie King appeared was highly suspicious, and so they often went to extraordinary lengths to ensure that the medium could not dress up as Katie. And some were privileged to see both medium and spirit together.

Novelist Florence Marryat (Mrs Ross-Church) had many seances with the Cook circle, and this passage is taken from her book *There is no death* (1891):

> I have seen Florrie Cook's dark curls nailed to the floor in view of the sitters, whilst Katie walked about, and moreover, I have seen both Katie and Florrie together on several occasions, so I have no doubt that they are two separate creatures. Sometimes Katie resembled Florence Cook in features; at others she was totally different. One evening Katie walked out and perched herself on my knee. I could feel that she was much plumper and heavier than Miss Cook, but on this occasion she resembled her in features, and I told her so.
>
> Katie did not seem to consider this a compliment, and said: 'I know I am. I can't help it, but I was much prettier than that in earth life. You shall see, some day. You shall see.' After she had retired that evening she put her head out of the curtain and said: 'I want to see Mrs Ross-Church.' I rose and went to her, and she pulled me inside the curtain, which I found was so thin that the gas from the other room made everything inside quite visible. Katie pulled my dress impatiently and said: 'Sit down on the ground', which I did. She then sat on my lap. Florence Cook meanwhile was lying on the floor in a deep trance. Katie seemed very anxious I should ascertain that it was Florrie.
>
> 'Touch her,' she said; 'take her hand, pull her curls. Do you see that it is Florrie lying there?' When I assured her that I was quite satisfied there was no doubt of it, the spirit said: 'Then look round this way and see what I was like in earth life.'
>
> I turned to the form in my arms, and what was my amazement to see a

Below Charles Blackburn, the businessman who paid Florrie – and after her, her sister Kate – a retainer to act as mediums. Kate and Florrie's husband became main beneficiaries in his will

woman, fair as the day, with large grey or blue eyes, a white skin and a profusion of golden red hair. Katie enjoyed my surprise, and then asked: 'Am I not prettier than Florrie now?' She then gave me a lock of her own hair and a lock of Florence Cook's. Florrie's is almost black, soft and silky; Katie's a coarse golden red.

On another occasion, Florence Marryat testifies, Katie King asked her to follow her into the cabinet 'and dropping her white garment, stood perfectly naked before me. "Now," she said, "you can see that I am a woman." Which indeed she was, and a most beautifully made woman too.'

A *Daily Telegraph* reporter who attended some of the Cook seances reported seeing a fully materialised spirit who identified herself as Katie King. He was able to take some photographs of her by magnesium light and declared that it could not have been Florrie Cook masquerading as Katie because the medium was still in her black dress, with her boots on and the knots securing her still sealed.

Another testimony to Katie King's reality comes from Alexander Aksakof, Imperial Councillor to the Tsar of Russia; he was invited to witness Florence Cook's mediumship by her father during a visit to England in the autumn of 1875.

Aksakof, a pioneer Spiritualist in Russia who had studied many mediums, satisfied himself that the 'cabinet' used by Florrie was no more than a curtain hung across a small corner of the room from the fireplace and that it did not contain a trapdoor or sliding panels. Florrie, dressed as usual in black, was tied securely in a chair.

The room was lit by a small lamp and, a quarter of an hour after the seance began, the curtain was drawn aside and Aksakof saw a human figure standing upright close to the curtain. It was dressed completely in white, a veil covering the hair and with bare hands and arms. It was Katie King, who talked for a while and then invited questions. Aksakof tells what happened next:

> Taking the hint, I asked her: 'Can't you show me your medium?' She replied: 'Yes, certainly, come here very quickly and have a look!' In that very instant I stood up from my chair, and drew back the curtain. I had only to take five steps to reach the curtain but the white clad figure had disappeared. In front of me, in a dark corner, the figure of the medium, clothed in a black dress, was sitting in an armchair.

However, he had not been able to see the medium clearly enough to be sure that it was Florrie. When Katie reappeared and asked

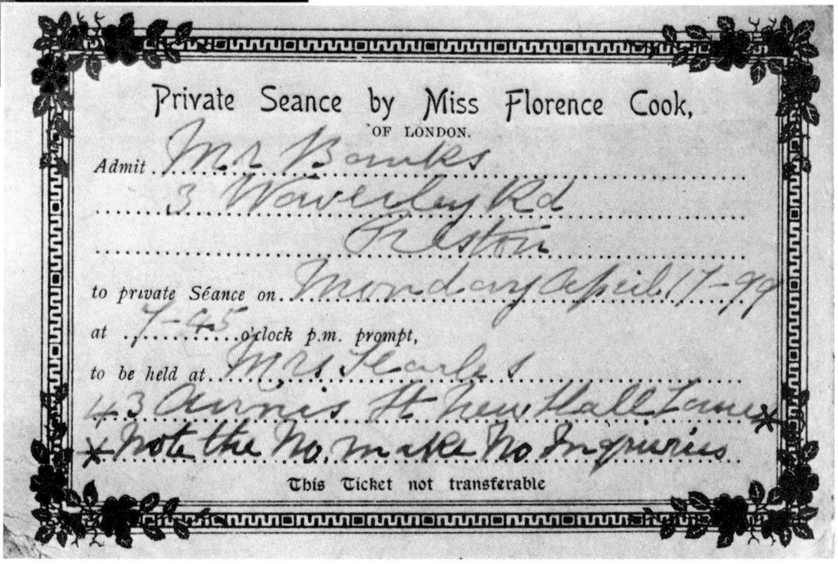

Private Seance by Miss Florence Cook,
OF LONDON.
Admit Mr Banks
3 Waverley Rd
Preston
to private Séance on Monday April 17-99
at 7-45 o'clock p.m. prompt,
to be held at Mrs Searle's
43 Annis St New Hall Lane *
* Note the No. make No Inquiries
This Ticket not transferable

Top: a contemporary illustration showing Katie King materialising at a seance in Philadelphia, USA, shortly before she began her association with the east London girl Florence Cook

Above: an invitation to one of Florrie's private seances enjoining the sitter to 'make no inquiries'. All her sitters were specially invited

Right: Alexander Aksakof, Imperial Councillor to the Tsar of Russia. In 1875 he testified that he had proved that Katie King and Florence Cook were distinctly separate girls

him if he was satisfied he said he was not.

> 'Then take the lamp with you and go and have a look immediately.' Within a second I stood behind the curtain, holding the lamp in my hand. Every trace of Katie had disappeared. I found myself alone and facing the medium who, in a deep trance, was sitting in a chair, with both her hands bound fast behind her back. The light, shining on the medium's face, started to produce its usual effect, i.e. the medium began to sigh and to awake.

After the seance Aksakof found all the bindings, knots and seals on the medium were still intact. In fact, Florrie's hands were so tightly bound that he had trouble getting the scissors under the tape in order to free her.

Too, too solid flesh

In spite of all the precautions that were taken to prevent fraud, some sitters found Katie King far too solid and 'human' to be convincing as a spirit. On the evening of 9 December 1873, one of the guests at the Cook home was a Mr W. Volckman. When his suspicions were apparently aroused by the appearance of Katie King, he decided to take matters into his own hands.

Suddenly, while Katie King was parading in front of the curtain in the dimly lit room, Volckman rushed forward, seized her hand and then her waist. Two of the medium's friends went immediately to Katie's aid and a struggle ensued during which Volckman lost part of his beard. Witnesses of this seance included the Earl and Countess of Caithness and Count de Medina Pomar.

Another guest was a barrister, Henry Dumphy, who testified that Katie appeared to lose her feet and legs and made a movement 'similar to that of a seal in water'. Katie, he testified, glided out of Volckman's grip leaving no trace of either her person or her clothes behind. Volckman saw it differently: he claimed that Katie was forcibly freed from his grasp and escaped into the cabinet – to become Florrie again.

Five minutes later, when the excitement had subsided and the curtains of the cabinet were drawn back, Florrie Cook was found in her black dress and boots with tape bound tightly round her waist, as at the start of the seance. The knot on the tape, sealed with the Earl of Caithness's signet ring, was still intact. When she was searched, no trace of white drapery was found.

Quite apart from any real doubts he might have had about the genuineness of Katie, perhaps Volckman had an ulterior motive in attempting to expose her as a fraud. Not long after this episode, he became the third husband of Mrs Samuel Guppy (née Nichol), a famous medium of the time who, we know now, was very jealous of Florrie Cook. It is more than likely that he set out to discredit Florrie at the instigation of his wife-to-be.

Although she had not been caught in fraud, the disturbance made Florrie ill and damaged her reputation – but not for long. Within weeks the public learned that Florrie's mediumship had been investigated by one of the country's leading scientists, William (later Sir William) Crookes.

Crookes had witnessed the materialisation of Katie and was about to conduct more experiments. When the results of those tests were published they caused a sensation, and they remain among the most astonishing and controversial seance room phenomena ever recorded.

During a seance at the Cook home on 9 December 1873 the materialised Katie King was seized by William Volckman, a Spiritualist, who was suspicious about the resemblance between Katie and Florrie. The unseemly scuffle that ensued was witnessed by the Count de Medina Pomar (left) and the Earl and Countess of Caithness (below and below right). Volckman lost part of his beard and was, he claimed, prevented by some of the others from rushing immediately into the cabinet. When he eventually looked inside, there lay Florrie with all the bindings intact – but, he said, she looked remarkably dishevelled

Guaranteed genuine?

When the eminent Victorian scientist William Crookes began investigating the pretty teenage medium Florence Cook – and her manifestation 'Katie King' – the gossips had a field day. What was Crookes's role?

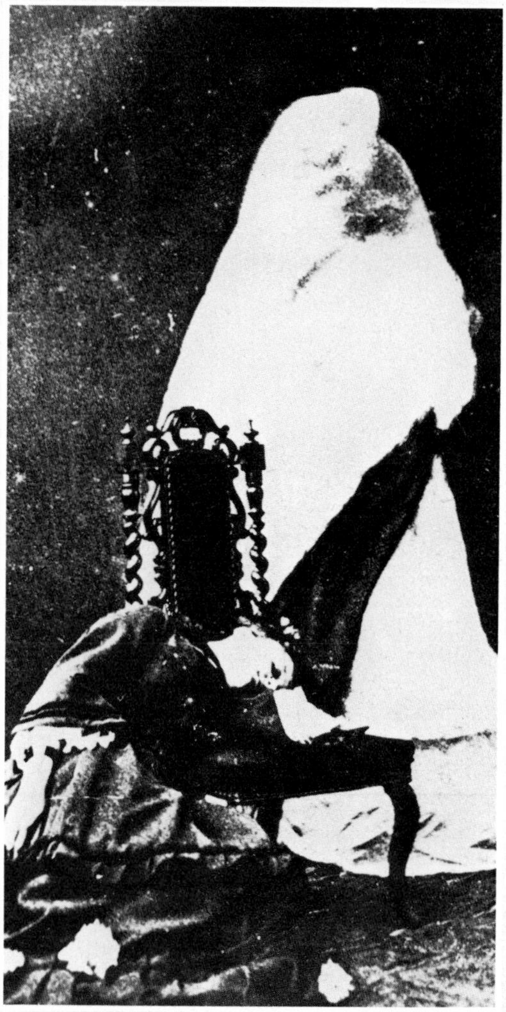

Left: one of the 44 photographs Crookes took of Florrie and Katie together. Unfortunately the drapery that is apparently blowing across Katie's face does little to dispel the critics' charge that, depending on the situation, Katie and Florrie were either one and the same person or that Katie was, in fact, Florrie's sister Kate. Sadly, many of the negatives were destroyed by Crookes shortly before his death in 1919, but of those that remain there is not one that indisputably shows that Katie and Florrie were separate people

Below: Mornington Road in north-west London, where Crookes investigated the mediumship of Florrie Cook in 1874. The road was bombed in the Second World War

THE CURTAINS that hung across the corner of a dimly lit basement in east London parted and a figure in white stepped out. Katie King, the good-looking daughter of a pirate, had left the spirit world once again in order to materialise on earth in the late 19th century.

The witnesses could see her bare hands and arms as well as her attractive face: the rest of her was enveloped in white robes. For two hours she walked about the room, talking familiarly with those present.

On several occasions she put her arm through the arm of a gentleman guest and they walked together around the room. The man in question was William (later Sir William) Crookes, one of the greatest physicists of the 19th century, and he testified that, as they walked arm-in-arm, 'the impression was conveyed to my mind that it was a living woman by my side, instead of a visitor from the other world. . . .'

That, sceptics say, was hardly surprising since Katie King *was* a living woman – Florence Cook, the young medium in whose presence the 'spirit' appeared. Florrie, after all, would sit behind the curtain before the seance began, then Katie would emerge and perform some minutes after the lights were put out, and would return to the screened-off cabinet at the end of the session. After a suitable wait the lights would be turned on,

the curtains opened and Florrie would be found, dressed in black and usually tied up in just the way she had been at the start of the session.

Non-believers saw it as an open-and-shut case of a clever medium masquerading as a spirit. Florrie and Katie even looked alike – suspiciously so. But science, in the impressive form of William Crookes, came to the rescue.

Crookes's first experience of psychic phenomena occurred in July 1869 and a year later, after the controversial American medium Henry Slade visited London, the famous scientist announced that he would conduct a thorough investigation of Spiritualist phenomena.

He began by studying one of the most famous mediums of all time, Daniel Dunglas Home, and was soon convinced that Home was endowed with a powerful psychic force. Many believed that Crookes would expose the phenomena he witnessed. But this rapid conversion to the ranks of believers surprised the public and shocked his scientific colleagues.

They were in for an even bigger shock when they learned, in 1874, that Crookes was on friendly terms with a pretty young female spirit. He made the revelation in the columns of a weekly newspaper, *The Spiritualist*, instead of the scientific press, and he did so, it seems, to restore public confidence in Florrie's mediumship following an unsuccessful attempt to expose her.

Being a medium in Victorian days almost guaranteed that one was the centre of attention – not all of it uncritical. Among the many American mediums who were lionised in Europe were Henry Slade (right) and the celebrated D. D. Home (above). Home was investigated by William Crookes and his phenomena were found to be genuine – shortly before Crookes began his more famous investigation into the mediumship of Florrie Cook

Left: the materialised Katie King stands in front of the curtained-off recess that served as the traditional medium's cabinet in Crookes's house in Mornington Road. The dark material at her bosom might be taken by some sceptics to be a glimpse of Florrie's customary black dress under the voluminous 'spirit robes'

Rising spirits

Aware that the sceptics believed Katie was really Florrie, the scientist gave his reasons for knowing that she was not. He described a seance at which he was sitting just a few feet from the cabinet while the materialised Katie King stood before him. At the same time, he could hear Florrie moaning and sobbing, behind the curtain, as if in pain. That did not satisfy the doubters. Perhaps Florrie was using an accomplice – or was employing ventriloquism. And a major criticism of the early seances that the scientist attended with this young medium was that they mostly took place in circumstances over which he had no scientific control.

The first time he saw both medium and spirit together was at the Cooks' home in Hackney, east London. Katie asked Crookes to turn out the gas light and, using a phosphorus lamp for illumination, to follow her into a room behind the curtain. Inside, the scientist found Florrie crouching on the floor.

> Kneeling down, I let air into the lamp, and by its light I saw the young lady dressed in black velvet, as she had been in the early part of the evening, and to all appearance perfectly senseless; she did not move when I took her hand and held the light quite close to her face, but continued quietly breathing. Raising the lamp, I looked around and saw Katie standing close behind Miss Cook. She was robed in flowing white drapery as we had seen her previously during the seance.
>
> Holding one of Miss Cook's hands in mine and still kneeling, I passed the lamp up and down so as to illuminate Katie's whole figure, and satisfy myself thoroughly that I was really looking at the veritable Katie whom I had clasped in my arms a few minutes before, and not at the phantasm of a disordered brain. She did not speak, but moved her head and smiled in recognition. Three separate times did I carefully examine Miss Cook crouching before me, to be sure that the hand I held was

Florrie had no accomplices. But time was running out: Katie announced that the three-year period during which she had promised to work with Florrie was nearly up. Before ending her association with the medium, however, the spirit girl agreed to participate in various experiments with Crookes and allowed him to take pictures of her.

In the week before her departure, Katie appeared almost nightly in Crookes's home and a total of 44 photographs were obtained, among which were, according to Crookes himself, 'some inferior, some indifferent, and some excellent'. During these sessions the scientist reported that the medium's head was covered with a shawl to protect it from the light. Frequently the seven or eight witnesses in the laboratory saw both spirit and medium when Crookes lifted the curtain. Crookes reported that:

> One of the most interesting of the pictures is one in which I am standing by the side of Katie; she has her bare foot upon a particular part of the floor. Afterwards I dressed Miss Cook like Katie, placed her and myself in exactly the same position, and we were photographed by the same cameras, placed exactly as in the other experiment, and illuminated by the same light. When these two pictures are placed over each other, the two photographs of myself coincide exactly as regards stature, etc., but Katie is half a head taller than Miss Cook, and looks a big woman in comparison with her.

The spirit's height was, he said, greater than the medium's, by between $4\frac{1}{2}$ and 6 inches (11 and 15 centimetres). And he noted other points of difference. Florrie's ears were

> that of a living woman, and three separate times did I turn the lamp to Katie and examine her with steadfast scrutiny until I had no doubt whatever of her objective reality.

But since all this happened in the Cook family home sceptics would be justified in asking if the seance room were specially prepared so that someone else could enter it, after the session began, to play the part of Katie – one of Florrie's sisters, perhaps.

Crookes much preferred to control the conditions under which he investigated mediums and he wrote of his early work with Florrie Cook: 'On a few occasions, indeed, I have been allowed to apply tests and impose conditions; but only once or twice have I been permitted to carry off the priestess from her shrine, and in my own house, surrounded by my own friends, to enjoy opportunities of testing the phenomena I had witnessed under less conclusive conditions.'

Eventually Florrie's parents agreed that their teenage daughter could give more seances at the Crookes's house in Mornington Road, north-west London. In this way, the scientist and his friends could be sure that

Above: Katie King proves that she is flesh and blood; this, however, was not the question debated by sceptics. To them it seemed that she was only too obviously solid flesh – in the person of either Florrie herself (swathed in white robes) or her sister Kate, acting as accomplice

Right: 105 Elgin Crescent, Notting Hill, where Florrie's patron Charles Blackburn lived with the Cook family from 1883 to 1887

pierced, Katie's were not. Florrie's complexion was very dark, Katie's was very fair. The spirit girl's fingers were much longer than Florrie's and her face larger. On one occasion Crookes observed: 'Katie's neck was bare last night; the skin was perfectly smooth both to touch and sight, whilst on Miss Cook's neck is a large blister. . . .'

When Katie King made her final appearance, at a seance held in the scientist's home, she invited him into the cabinet:

> After closing the curtain she conversed with me for some time, and then walked across the room where Miss Cook was lying senseless on the floor. Stooping over her, Katie touched her, and said, 'Wake up Florrie, wake up! I must leave you now.' Miss Cook then woke and tearfully entreated Katie to stay a little time longer. 'My dear, I can't; my work is done. God bless you,' Katie replied, and then continued speaking to Miss Cook.
>
> For several minutes the two were conversing with each other, till at last Miss Cook's tears prevented her speaking. Following Katie's instructions I then came forward to support Miss Cook, who was falling on to the floor, sobbing hysterically. I looked round, but the white-robed Katie had gone.

Dr Gully of Malvern takes Katie's pulse, which was said to differ markedly from that of her medium, Florrie. It has been said by Florrie's critics that hastening to don Katie's robes would alter one's pulse rate significantly. But several witnesses attested that Katie and Florrie were, indeed, very different individuals: one having pierced ears, the other unpierced; one (Katie) being taller by some inches and her face being broader than Florrie's

William Crookes was knighted more than 20 years later. The discoverer of thallium and inventor of various items of scientific apparatus, he became President at different times of the Royal Society, the Chemical Society, the Institution of Electrical Engineers and the British Association. In his scientific work he was used to people taking his word for the accuracy of his reports, and he must have been surprised that this did not happen with his accounts of Spiritualist phenomena.

A private view

Because of this hostile reaction Crookes abandoned his attempt to convince fellow scientists of the truth of mediumship. He also refused to allow the circulation of a photograph showing himself and Katie King arm in arm, realising, no doubt, that it would have been very damaging for his career. But he never changed his mind about his psychic experiments.

Crookes said in his presidential address to the British Association in 1898:

> Thirty years have passed since I published an account of experiments tending to show that outside our scientific knowledge there exists a Force exercised by intelligence differing from the ordinary intelligence common to mortals. I have nothing to retract. I adhere to my already published statements. Indeed, I might add much thereto.

And what happened to Florrie after Katie left her? The medium began a spirit association with Marie, a girl from the other world who liked to sing and dance at seances. But her performance was rudely interrupted on a cold January night in 1880 by Sir George Sitwell, who was among the sitters. He grabbed and held her tight. When the lights were turned on the 'spirit' was found to be Florrie Cook wearing only corsets and a flannel petticoat.

But did the young London girl really fool the greatest scientist of the time? It seems so unlikely that non-believers have come up with an alternative theory: Crookes was not fooled but was party to the fraud – to cover up the scandal of his affair with Florrie Cook.

Would Crookes risk his career by doing such a thing? It seems unlikely, but stranger things have happened. Whatever the truth, the existence of Katie King does not rest entirely on Crookes's experiments, however impressive. Many others are said to have testified to having seen her manifest in a way that would seem to have ruled out any suggestion of fraud.

genuine spirit, but it had usually been assumed that Crookes – despite his scientific training – had himself been duped by Florrie's clever trickery.

Hall, a chartered surveyor, magistrate and honorary vice-president of the Magic Circle, set out to demonstrate that Crookes was a party to this brazen fraud. In the course of his researches, using previously unpublished material, he could find no official record of Florrie's birth. Did this mean, he asked, that she had been born out of wedlock? This lack of a birth certificate, Hall suggested, enabled the medium to lie about her age, pretending to be a young teenager when she was, in fact, older.

Hall traced Florrie's possibly dubious career to 1874 when, paid a retainer by Charles Blackburn, her future as a medium seemed assured. Things went badly wrong, however, when William Volckman made a grab at the alleged spirit form of Katie King. As a result of this fracas Florrie's credibility suffered, and her patron threatened to stop sending her money.

Hall stated that, as a direct result of this incident, Florrie took herself off to William Crookes – who had announced his intention of investigating Spiritualist phenomena and was already working with D.D. Home – to offer her services. They were accepted.

Meanwhile, Blackburn's doubts about Florrie's mediumship were temporarily suspended and the money from his account continued to flow. What is more, Crookes was soon announcing that Florrie's phenomena were genuine and he began the series of intense studies culminating in a photographic session at which pictures of the materialised Katie King were taken.

Hall maintained that the seances were not genuine; moreover, that Crookes not only suspected them to be fraudulent – he actively colluded with the medium to stage-manage them. Hall based this conclusion very largely on Crookes's strange behaviour at the time.

Although his experiments were supposed to be scientific, Crookes announced his findings in the columns of *The Spiritualist* instead of scientific journals. He did not name the witnesses at the series of seances he conducted nor ask them for signed reports. The seances had a different, invited audience each night, so few people had the opportunity of seeing the trick performed more than once.

Crookes claimed that Florrie and Katie were physically dissimilar, even though most other observers insisted that they were apparently identical. He also wrote of having seen the materialised spirit and the medium together on many occasions, including the

Haunted by scandal

William Crookes's investigation of Florence Cook's mediumship either proved its authenticity beyond a shadow of doubt – or was a blatant attempt to cover up their illicit affair.

SIR WILLIAM CROOKES, the eminent Victorian scientist, was a liar and a cheat. That sensational claim was made by psychical researcher Trevor Hall following his detailed study of Crookes's seances with medium Florence Cook in 1874, at which the materialised 'spirit form' of Katie King was said to have walked and talked with witnesses, as described in the last chapter.

In *The Spiritualists* (1962), Hall accused the scientist of complicity with the medium to produce fraudulent paranormal phenomena. Many other psychical researchers had refused to believe that Katie King was a

Above: Katie King. Edward W. Cox, a contemporary researcher, said of her materialisations: 'If facts, their importance cannot be exaggerated – if frauds, their wickedness cannot be exceeded.' Even today there are some who believe that Katie King represented the modern proof of resurrection

final appearance of Katie King when she and Florrie had a long and moving conversation. However, no one else of any scientific standing was allowed to see them together.

While Katie King was performing, the curtain would be drawn back to show witnesses the entranced medium lying on the floor or sofa, but a shawl always covered her head. It was possible, in the dim light, that what the witnesses could see was no more than the medium's discarded clothes stuffed with cushions.

During the Crookes-Cook experiments a 'double materialisation' seance took place. A second young medium, Mary Showers, joined Florence Cook at the scientist's home. They both went into the curtained-off cabinet and after the usual delay of up to 30 minutes two spirits, Katie King and Florence Maple, emerged and walked arm-in-arm around Crookes's laboratory.

The problem, said Hall, is that Mary Showers later confessed to Crookes that she was a fraud. Now, if Katie King were a genuine spirit, what on earth was she doing parading up and down with a human being disguised as a spirit? And Crookes had acted as master of ceremonies for this extraordinary double bill.

The conclusion, Hall wrote, is inescapable – Florrie Cook was also a fraud. Therefore Crookes could not have seen her and Katie together, as he claimed in his reports of the seances. So why did he lie? Because, said Hall, he was having an affair with the medium. The seances gave him the cover he needed to see her frequently, have her staying in his own home for long periods (while his wife was pregnant with their tenth child) and even take her to Paris on occasions.

Support for this theory was first given to the Society for Psychical Research (SPR) in 1922 by Francis Anderson. He told the society's research officer that he, also, had had an affair with Florence Cook in 1893 during which she confessed to a sexual liaison with Crookes. She told Anderson that her seances were fraudulent and that Crookes had used them as a cover for their affair.

Right: Florence Cook in late life. She married Captain Edward Elgie Corner secretly during her investigation by Crookes in 1874, although why her marriage was clandestine is still a matter for conjecture. According to one Francis Anderson, Florrie confessed, many years after her collaboration with Crookes, that her mediumship had always been fraudulent – and that Crookes not only knew it but actively conspired with her to perpetrate the fraud. Anderson said the reason for this was simply that Crookes was infatuated with Florrie, and 'the materialisation trick' was employed as a cover for their affair

Below: 34 Ladbroke Grove, Notting Hill, in west London, where Charles Blackburn died in 1891 – surrounded by the Cook family. Kate (Florrie's sister) and Captain Corner became significant beneficiaries of his will – though Florrie herself was left very little

Anderson made a fuller statement in November 1949 and a further one in December of the same year, both of which were placed in the SPR's files and marked 'confidential' because Mr and Mrs Anderson were still alive. The Anderson statement, which Hall quoted in his book, included an account of how Florrie Cook (who was then Mrs Edward Elgie Corner) seduced him when he visited her at her home in Usk Vale, Monmouthshire.

Quite apart from the Crookes-Cook affair, Hall's book also exposed other unsavoury aspects of Victorian Spiritualism. The Cook family, it seems, were money grabbers. When, for whatever reasons, Charles Blackburn eventually stopped giving money to

A free spirit

An independent testimony to Florence Cook's mediumship comes from Count Louis Hamon, the celebrated palmist known as 'Cheiro' (left). The story was first published in *Fate* magazine in 1961 and was supplied by Hamon's widow who stated: 'Letters corroborating facts of this narrative are among the documents held in trust to prove the truth of the story.'

Hamon writes of an occasion when he was challenged by his friend Robert W. Macbeth, a Royal Academician of great talent, to prove that spirits could return from the dead through the active work of gifted individuals commonly known as 'mediums'. Hamon said:

'I thought of Miss Cook with her extraordinary power of causing materialisations to appear even in the light. I had such a long series of experiences with her mediumship that I felt justified in taking up her challenge.'

Count Hamon gave Macbeth Florrie's address, and he went outside immediately and hailed a cab to send for her.

'It was only the week before,' Hamon added, 'that General Sir Alfred Turner and I had been present in Sir William Crookes' house when not one, but several, spirits had materialised and walked about the room in full light.'

Within half an hour the cab returned with the medium, who agreed to give a seance under strict test conditions. Macbeth's wife took Florrie to her bedroom where she was asked to undress and put on Mrs Macbeth's dressing gown. Florrie returned and was tied to a chair, the knots being sealed with Macbeth's own seal. Her feet were then placed in a tub half filled with plaster of Paris, which came up to her ankles. They waited until it set, then Macbeth locked the door.

No curtain was used. The medium sat at one end of the room, in the dark, while the witnesses sat at the other, near a lighted lamp on the piano. After about 10 minutes, everyone saw something floating in the air.

'Slowly, but clearly and distinctly, there appeared the form of a young woman. The head, face and body as far as the waist became very clearly developed. There was no mistaking, the apparition was that of a young girl.'

Moving in front of Macbeth the apparition said in broken English: 'Monsieur, do you remember me?'

She then reminded Macbeth of a tragic incident in his earlier life that had taken place in Algiers, involving the murder of the young girl whose spirit this was believed to be. To the Macbeths and to Hamon this seance provided the ultimate proof of life after death – and of the authenticity of Florrie's mediumship.

Florence, her sister Kate suddenly developed mediumistic powers that were almost identical to Florrie's – and Blackburn soon started supporting her financially.

In time, the Cook family (with the exception of Florrie) lived with the old and ailing Blackburn, and he left them money and property in his will – a condition of which was that they looked after his mentally disturbed daughter, Eliza. Shortly before his death, when he was too ill to attend seances, Blackburn would write letters to Lillie Gordon, the spirit who 'materialised' at Kate's private home sessions. He addressed them to 'My own dearest Spirit Lillie' and ended with 'best Love and Kisses'. Her replies, written in pencil, were in similar terms. It seems likely that this 'spirit' correspondence considerably influenced the gullible old man in making his will and subsequent codicils.

One of those who benefited from the will, Hall wrote, was Florence Cook's husband, Edward Elgie Corner, a mariner. He had married Florrie on 29 April 1874, but this had been kept a secret from Crookes and Blackburn until June. After Florrie's death in 1904 and immediately following the introduction of the Deceased Wife's Sister Act in 1907, Corner married Kate Cook. All in all,

Right: a mass-produced poster used to advertise the stage magicians' version of seance-room phenomena, with space to insert details of individual acts. With the widespread popularity of Spiritualism in the late 19th century, illusionists were not slow to adapt their acts accordingly. And some mediums were, in fact, no more than clever magicians themselves; their exposure as fakes did nothing to enhance the reputation of the Spiritualist movement. In *The Spiritualists* (1962) Trevor Hall maintained that Florence Cook was a gifted confidence trickster who practised 'the materialisation trick' for personal profit

discussion of Crookes's researches.

Trevor Hall had earlier responded to some of the criticisms made of his theory with an article in the magazine *Tomorrow* in 1963. This resulted in a detailed rebuttal by another researcher, Mostyn Gilbert, which was serialised for three months in the weekly Spiritualist newspaper *Psychic News*. Gilbert began by saying that his own study of the published and unpublished material left him feeling that 'the inquiries by Crookes into the mediumships of Florence Cook, Mary Showers, *and* a Mrs Fay, indicate reasonable standards of scientific investigation to reflect the *probability* of non-fraudulent manifestations.'

Hall, who seemed by now to be tired of the controversy caused by his book, said his *Tomorrow* article would be his 'last word' on the Crookes-Cook seances. Others, however, were happy to continue the argument, and among those who have defended him was Archie Jarman, who answered criticisms made by Dr Robert Thouless in *Psychic News*.

But the controversy continues, although it is now impossible with any degree of certainty to come to any conclusions since over a century has elapsed and much vital evidence has been destroyed. Like Spiritualism itself, it depends largely on what one is prepared to believe.

The Crookes-Cook seances were either the most flagrant confidence trick – and juiciest scandal – in the history of Spiritualism, or the most convincing demonstration of life after death ever produced.

Hall's picture of the Cooks was distinctly unsavoury.

However, others were able to provide different and less damaging interpretations of the words and deeds of so long ago. For example, there was, in fact, no mystery about Florence Cook's birth. A search of public records by other investigators located her birth certificate without any difficulty. And it proved that the only lie she told about her age was to make herself out to be merely a month younger than she was. Strange though this may seem, it cannot be said to be sinister.

Francis Anderson's testimony was also torn to shreds. It was given, Hall's critics point out, 56 years after his alleged affair with Florrie. He was 79 when he made his statement to the SPR. Moreover, a visit to the house in which he claimed Florence had seduced him proved that his memory of its layout was totally wrong, even though he had declared: 'I can remember the scene of how it all started as if I saw it now.' So could his memory of his conversation with Florrie be trusted?

Two psychical researchers, R.G. Medhurst and Mrs K.M. Goldney, writing in the SPR's *Journal* in 1965, felt it was unfortunate that Hall had allowed Anderson's testimony to play such a disproportionate part in the

Above: William Crookes, arm in arm with Katie King

Right: Katie was said to be some inches taller than Florrie, but unfortunately this photograph looks as if the effect was achieved through the simple expedient of kneeling on a piece of furniture and arranging a length of skirt over it, so that it reached to the floor. Judging by this photograph alone Katie's legs were unnaturally long – and her dress extremely strange

Knock, knock-who's there?

The strange rappings in the home of the Fox family caused a sensation throughout America – for many people regarded them as proof that the living could communicate with the dead

WHAT HAPPENED TO Margaretta Fox and her sisters, if it was truly what it purported to be, should have been quite simply the greatest single event in human history. Conclusive proof that we can communicate with the spirits of the dead – which presupposes that the dead exist in spirit form to be communicated with – would mean that thousands of years of speculation were over; death would be positively established as being not the end of life, but a transfer of existence to another and superior plane; our stay on earth could henceforward be regarded confidently, not as a short-lived biological incident, but as part of a continuing process. This, and nothing less than this, seemed to have been established by what occurred in a small wooden house in the village of Hydesville in the state of New York on 31 March 1848. It was this 'breakthrough' that was to mark the beginning of the modern Spiritualist movement, whose adherents were to swell to millions throughout the world in the decades that followed.

There were seven Fox children in all, but only three were actively concerned in the events: Leah, aged 34 in 1848, Margaretta, aged 14, and Catherine, aged 12. The definitive account of the epoch-making incident was supplied by their mother, Margaret, in a sworn statement four days later, countersigned as accurate by her husband. She told how the house in which they were temporarily living had been disturbed by unaccountable shakings of the walls and furniture, by the sound of footsteps and knockings on the walls and doors. The family had 'concluded that the house must be haunted by some unhappy restless spirit'.

Tired by the disturbances, the family went to bed early on the night of Friday, 31 March. Margaretta and Catherine – the only two children still living with their parents – were frightened by the noises and had left their own room to sleep in another bed in

Below right: Catherine Fox who, together with her sister Margaretta (centre right), became the focus for paranormal rappings. These, the girls claimed, said that they had been chosen for the task of convincing the world of a life after death. When the girls travelled to Rochester to stay with their elder sister Leah (far right), the noises travelled with them and even manifested on board the steamer in the course of their journey

Below: the Fox family home in Hydesville, New York state, as depicted in a 1930s postcard. The original building was destroyed by fire; today an exact replica, built in the 1950s, stands on the site

their parents' room. No doubt it was the reassuring presence of their mother and father that encouraged the girls to respond so cheekily when the sounds recommenced:

> The children heard the rapping and tried to make similar sounds by snapping their fingers. My youngest child, Cathie, said 'Mr Splitfoot, do as I do!', clapping her hands. The sound instantly followed with the same number of raps. When she stopped the sound ceased for a short time. Then Margaretta said, in sport, 'No, do just as I do. Count one, two, three, four,' striking one hand against the other at the same time; and the raps came as before. She was afraid to repeat them. . . .

From this they proceeded gradually to more elaborate questions, using an alphabetical code by means of which it was established that the rappings were done by a spirit; eventually the entity identified himself as a pedlar, aged 31, who claimed to have been murdered in that very house, and his remains buried in the cellar.

Neighbours were called in to verify the proceedings; they too heard the raps, put questions of their own and received answers. Next day other visitors came and, in the evening, urged by the spirit, some men started digging in the cellar to see if the story could be substantiated; unfortunately the hole filled with water and the attempt had to be abandoned. Later reports suggest that parts of a body were indeed found, but Mrs Fox does not mention this in her statement of 4 April. She claims that when the noises commenced again on the Saturday evening there were some 300 people present who heard them: there were no noises on Sunday but they began again on Monday and were continuing when she made her statement on the Tuesday.

For the Fox family, then and there, it seemed to be simply a case of haunting. Stories in which the dead return to earth in order to pass messages or warnings to the living have been told throughout history; but in this instance a new element had been added – a two-way conversation between the living and the dead. Others perceived the significance of this and appreciated its implications: as a subsequent historian of the Spiritualist movement, Emma Hardinge Britten, observed, it implied that

> not only the supposed murdered pedlar, but hosts of spirits, good and bad, high and low, could, under certain conditions not understood, and impossible for mortals to comprehend, communicate with earth; that such communication was produced through the forces of spiritual and human magnetism, in chemical affinity; that the varieties of magnetism in different individuals afforded 'medium power' to some, and denied it to others.

Such subtleties were not at first realised, but

The Fox sisters' parents, Margaret (below) and John (bottom), documented the events of 31 March 1848 – the first day on which the rappings were heard. While they did not believe in 'haunted houses', they came to the conclusion that the noise emanated from a 'restless spirit', which in due course announced that it was a pedlar (above) who had been murdered in the house five years earlier

it was clear that the Fox sisters were in some way specially gifted to receive these communications: the raps occurred only in their presence, and furthermore occurred wherever they went. When, their lives disrupted by the publicity given to their experiences, the girls and their mother left Hydesville to stay with their sister Leah in Rochester, the rappings travelled with them. And although others were soon to discover that they, too, had some of this 'medium power', the spirits themselves confirmed that the Fox girls were specially endowed. Repeatedly, the messages insisted: 'You have been chosen to go before the world to convince the sceptical of the great truth of immortality.'

Had such messages come out of the blue to young and ignorant schoolgirls in a rural community, it might indeed have been convincing evidence that beings on another plane of existence were seeking to establish communication with us on earth. But the situation was not so simple, for such notions were current in the America of the 1840s.

In the previous century there had been some who considered the newly discovered mesmerism not as an altered mental state that could be accounted for in human terms, but as a process designed to enable communication with the spirits. The controversy had raged ever since. Two years before the happenings at Hydesville, a commentator noted that 'the newspapers and magazines are teeming with slashing discussions upon the subject of magnetism and clairvoyance.'

That commentator was Andrew Jackson Davis, a semi-literate American mystic and psychic, who while in a trance state churned out volume after volume of turgid revelations about life, the Universe, and everything. The fact that his account is full of errors somewhat dents his credibility, but at the time many accepted his heralding of a new era:

Above: Emma Hardinge Britten, a medium and author of *Modern American Spiritualism* (above right: the title page of the first edition). She helped to establish the new 'religion' in Britain

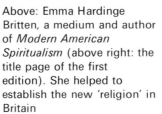

It is a truth that spirits commune with one another while one is in the body and the other in the higher sphere, and this, too, when the person in the body is unconscious of the influx, and hence cannot be convinced of the fact; and this truth will ere long present itself in the form of a living demonstration, and the world will hail with delight the ushering in of that era when the interiors of men will be opened, and the spiritual communication will be established such as is now being enjoyed by the inhabitants of Mars, Jupiter, and Saturn.

Dawn of a new era

Given such utterances, it is not surprising that Davis is often seen as the John the Baptist of the Spiritualist movement. His writings inculcated a mood of expectancy in America, and they explain why the public was so quick to seize on the events at Hydesville as signs of a new age.

Matters advanced with extraordinary rapidity. While staying with their sister Leah at Rochester, the girls were instructed by the spirits to hire the largest hall in the town and give a demonstration of their powers: this they did on 14 November 1848. Now at last the whole matter was out in the open; and it was quickly apparent that public opinion was sharply divided between enthusiastic adherents, who had been awaiting just such a revelation, and no less determined sceptics who saw these manifestations as imposture at best, at worst as the work of the Devil.

Feelings ran frighteningly high. The girls were widely ridiculed, frequently physically attacked: attempts were even made on their lives. When a committee investigated the phenomena and could find no evidence of trickery, its findings were discounted and a second, tougher committee appointed: when this, too, reported that it could detect no imposture, the girls' opponents were only made yet angrier. It became impossible for the Fox sisters to lead normal lives. They left Rochester for Troy, then for the state capital at Albany, and finally for New York, which they reached in June 1850.

The three sisters took New York by storm. The newspaper reporters descended on them, and on the whole treated them kindly; one account admitted:

> We saw none that we could suspect of collusion. . . . We came away utterly disbelieving in all supernatural agency, and at the same time unable to say how any human means could be used without detection.

While it is true that investigative procedures were primitive by present-day standards, it must be accepted that the New Yorkers who sat with the Fox sisters were not eager to be made fools of; hundreds of sitters went determined to be the ones who revealed to the world how the imposture was carried out

Left: monuments to the Fox sisters and Spiritualism: the obelisk at Rochester (above) where, on 14 November 1848, the girls gave the first public demonstration of their remarkable powers; and the interior of the family home at Hydesville (below), which was turned into a museum

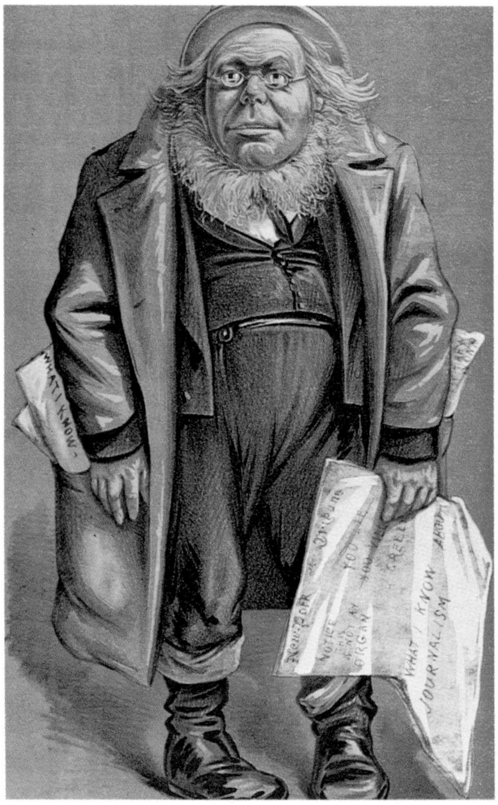

Right: a caricature of Horace Greeley, influential statesman and editor of the *New York Tribune*, from *Vanity Fair* (1872). Greeley gave valuable support to the Fox sisters. He came to believe that the phenomena were genuine, but retained an open mind as to their nature

Below: Andrew Jackson Davis, American mystic and psychic. He had no doubt that it was possible to communicate with the dead (left: an illustration depicting Davis himself receiving information from a 'spirit'), and in the early 1840s he stated that a demonstration of this fact would soon be given. To many Americans, Davis's prediction was fulfilled in 1848, when the Fox sisters' manifestations began, and he was acclaimed as the prophet of Spiritualism

– and emerged, if not persuaded that the message of the spirits was genuine, at least that the phenomena defied normal explanation. Horace Greeley, editor of the *Tribune* and one of the most influential men in the country, was persuaded of the girls' integrity and became their valiant champion.

By now other mediums were emerging in emulation of the Fox sisters, but none challenged their pre-eminence. The phenomena developed from rapped questions and answers to automatic writing and spoken utterances, culminating in direct voice communication in which the mediums were 'taken over' by the alleged entities. All kinds of physical phenomena accompanied the messages – movement of furniture, teleportation of objects, levitation of sitters or the medium herself, all kinds of noises and a wide variety of luminous phenomena. Time and time again the sisters were tested, perhaps most strictly when, while visiting England, Kate Fox submitted herself to the investigations of William Crookes. He vouched for her with persuasive insistence:

> For several months I enjoyed almost unlimited opportunity of testing the various phenomena occurring in the presence of this lady, and I especially examined the phenomena of these sounds. . . . It seems only necessary for her to place her hand on any substance for loud thuds to be heard in it, like a triple pulsation, sometimes loud enough to be heard several rooms off. I have heard . . . these sounds proceeding from the floor, walls, &c., when the medium's hands and feet were held – when she was standing on a chair – when she was suspended in a swing from the ceiling – when she was enclosed in a wire cage – and when she had fallen fainting on a sofa. . . . I have tested them in every way that I could devise, until there has been no escape from the conviction that they were true objective occurrences not produced by trickery or mechanical means.

But not everyone was so thoroughly convinced. From the outset, there had been sceptics who had claimed that the sisters were playing tricks. They had never succeeded in substantiating these claims, and their proposed explanations were generally ridiculously inadequate to account for the phenomena. But their claims were to receive unexpected support, first from the girls' family, then from the mediums themselves.

THE SISTERS FOX, THE ORIGINAL SPIRIT RAPPERS.

THE MISSES FOX.

Our readers, believers and non-believers in Spiritualism, will thank us for presenting them portraits of the "original rappers," the Misses Fox, of Rochester, who have made so much noise in the world. The likenesses are from a daguerreotype by Meade Brothers, of New York, and are therefore reliable. Since the origin of the rapping excitement in Rochester, in 1849, mysterious demonstrations of the nature of those of which the Misses Fox were the media have been signalized all over the world; they have given rise to books, pamphlets and newspapers without number, and the believers in their spiritual origin are numbered now by hundreds of tnousands. The phenomena exhibited by the media are so curious, that learned and scientific men have felt it their duty to investigate them, and various are the theories by which they are sought to be accounted for. One of the most elaborate works on the subject is that by Professor Mahan. Prof. Faraday, of England, has also given the subject his attention, and honored it with his theory. Congress has been memorialized to appoint a committee of investigation; but as yet our legislators have not seen fit to devote their time to spiritualism. Of the ladies, whose portraits we present, it may be sufficient to remark, that no imposture has been found upon them; and that committees composed of the cutest Yankees, both male and female, have failed to discover any secret machinery or fixtures, by which the sounds heard from and about them might have been produced.

Margaretta and Catherine Fox, the 'discoverers' of Spiritualism. To many, the girls' experiences signalled the dawning of a new era, in which the living could communicate at will with the dead. Others, however, saw the girls simply as clever tricksters and were determined to expose them; but, despite numerous tests and investigations, the sisters were never detected in a hoax

Confessions and confusions

When the Fox sisters admitted to fraud, the sceptics had a field day. But then the confessions were withdrawn. What is the truth about the acclaimed founders of Spiritualism?

THREE YEARS AFTER the epoch-making events at the Fox family home in Hydesville, USA, on 17 April 1851, a shattering statement was made at Arcadia, New York state, by a Mrs Norman Culver. She was a relative by marriage of the Fox girls, her husband's sister being the wife of their brother David.

She stated that for about two years she had been

> a very sincere believer in the rappings; but something which I saw when I was visiting the girls made me suspect that they were deceiving. I resolved to satisfy myself in some way; and some time afterwards I made a proposition to Catherine to assist her in producing the manifestations.

She claimed that Catherine welcomed her offer, and proceeded to demonstrate how the tricks were worked:

> The raps are produced with the toes. All the toes are used. After nearly a week's practice, with Catherine showing me how, I could produce them perfectly myself. At first it was very hard work to do it. Catherine told me to warm my feet, she said that she sometimes had to warm her feet three or four times in the course of an evening. . . . I have sometimes produced 150 raps in succession.

Such a statement, coming from so authoritative a source, cannot be lightly set aside, particularly as she demonstrated her ability to produce raps. It is impossible for us today to determine what motivated Mrs Culver's revelation. It may have been simple love of the truth, or there may have been some jealousy to inspire the statement. On the face of it, her revelations seem inadequate to account for *all* the phenomena associated with the Fox sisters; but they do show how *some* of them could have been effected. Clearly, trickery cannot be ruled out as a possible partial explanation.

At the same time, it is a fact that the sisters were tested and investigated time and time again, and that never once were they detected in flagrant imposture. As their champion, *Tribune* editor Horace Greeley, pointed out, it was indeed likely that many of their feats could be reproduced by stage magicians, but these were accomplished performers and the girls had none of their skills or training. Greeley was impressed as much by the Fox sisters' failures as by their successes:

> A juggler can do nearly as well at one time as another; but I have known the most eminent mediums spend a long evening in trying to evoke the spiritual phenomena, without a gleam of success. I have known this to occur when they were particularly anxious to astound and convince those who were present. . . .

'An absolute falsehood'

But the logic of their defenders and the favourable findings of investigators were forgotten when, on 24 September 1888, Margaretta (now Mrs Kane) told a reporter from the *New York Herald* that she intended to reveal that their mediumship had been a fraud from start to finish. Her younger sister Catherine (now Mrs Jencken) arrived from England to support her. On 21 October a huge crowd gathered in the New York Academy of Music to hear the confession:

> I am here tonight as one of the founders of Spiritualism to denounce it as an absolute falsehood from beginning to end, as the flimsiest of superstitions, the most wicked blasphemy known to the world.

The *New York Herald* described the reaction:

> There was a dead silence. Everybody in the great audience knew that they were looking upon the woman who is principally responsible for Spiritualism, its foundress, high-priestess and demonstrator. She stood upon a little pine-table with nothing on her feet but stockings. As she remained motionless loud, distinct rappings were heard, now in the flies, now behind the scenes, now in the gallery . . . Mrs Kane became excited. She clapped her hands, danced about and cried: 'It's a fraud! Spiritualism is a fraud from beginning to end! It's all a trick! There's no truth in it!' A whirlwind of applause followed.

It should have been the death-blow to the movement for whose birth Margaretta had been responsible. But though perhaps a majority of those present were convinced, others were not; and their reservations were justified just over a year later when first Catherine and then Margaretta took back their confessions. Margaretta told a reporter from *The Celestial City*, a New York Spiritualist paper:

> Would to God that I could undo the

Although Leah, the eldest of the Fox sisters, had not been involved in the original rappings at Hydesville, she was the first of the three to become a professional medium and, in the 1850s, held many private seances in the parlour of her New York home (right). She also cooperated in a wide variety of experiments, convincing the investigators that the sounds she created had nothing to do with the physical body and that 'the medium has no more power over the sounds than the investigators have'

In 1851 a group of researchers came up with an explanation for the rappings: when the Fox sisters' legs were held, the noises stopped; therefore the girls must be 'popping' their knee joints. Sceptics seized on this as proof of the mediums' deception – but still they could not account for the variety of noises or the levitation of tables that occurred at many of the seances

injustice I did the cause of Spiritualism when, under the strong psychological influence of persons inimical to it, I gave expression to utterances that had no foundation in fact.

She insisted that the charges she had made against Spiritualism had been 'false in every particular'. She refused to say who had put pressure on her, but mentioned that 'persons high in the Catholic Church did their best to have me enter a convent.' She had in fact been converted to the Catholic faith soon after the death of her husband, whom she had married at the age of 16 and lived with only briefly.

She also blamed her sister Leah, accusing her of having drawn Catherine and herself into the career of mediumship. It may well be the case that Leah encouraged her younger sisters, and perhaps, as the most practical and far-sighted of the family, she had taken upon herself the decision to commit the three of them to a course of life that could not but put great social and emotional stress on them all. But never at any previous time had there been any sign that this was resented by her sisters, nor that she was eager where they were reluctant.

Right: the Swedish singer Jenny Lind who, after attending a seance held by the Fox sisters, was convinced that the mediums were genuine

Below: Margaretta's husband, the Arctic explorer Elisha Kent Kane. His letters and verses contained many references to his wife's 'deceit' and implored, 'Do avoid spirits.' After Kane's death in 1857, Margaretta agreed to the publication of this damning evidence, thereby implying that she had – as accused – been guilty of cheating

What, then, was the truth behind the confessions made and withdrawn? Certainly one fact must be faced: if Margaretta could produce trick raps on the stage in demonstration of her ability to cheat, there is a strong presumption that those tricks had been used in the course of her mediumship – for why otherwise would she have developed the necessary skill?

The suggestion that she cheated, at least some of the time, is confirmed from an unexpected source: her husband. The eminent Arctic explorer Elisha Kent Kane had fallen in love with Margaretta when she was only 13; for three years, against his family's opposition, he courted and helped her, finally marrying her – only to die shortly afterwards, of illness, away from her in Cuba. Distracted by grief, Margaretta published the letters and verses he had written to her during those years: they contain abundant evidence that he believed her to cheat. 'Oh Maggie,' he wrote in one letter, 'are you never tired of this weary, weary sameness of continual deceit?' And in another, 'Do avoid "spirits". I cannot bear to think of you as engaged in a course of wickedness and deception.' His verses echo the same sentiments:

Then the maiden sat and wept,
Her hand upon her brow;
So long this secret have I kept,
I can't forswear it now.
It festers in my bosom,
It cankers in my heart,
Thrice cursed is the slave fast chained
To a deceitful art.

The fact that Margaretta allowed such incriminating documents to be published suggests that she was conscious of having used trickery; but if we accept the account she presented in 1888, of total deceit from start to finish, we find ourselves faced with almost as many difficulties as if we accept all as genuine. One of the many eminent sitters with the Fox sisters was the singer Jenny Lind, who perceptively distinguished between the physical and the mental phenomena: 'If it were possible for you to make these sounds, I know it is impossible for you to answer the questions I have had answered this evening.'

Reporters at the ready

Dozens of testimonials survive, recorded at the time by sitters who were convinced – often despite their previous scepticism – of the Fox sisters' psychic ability. If some visitors erred by excessive gullibility, others surely made up for it by implacable scepticism; and at all times there were reporters on hand, eager to seize on anything the least suspicious. All who investigated in hope of exposing the mediums as frauds came away frustrated.

This is not to say that the sisters' manifestations were accepted for what they purported to be. There were many, like Horace Greeley, who admitted the genuineness of the phenomena as phenomena, but retained an open mind as to their nature:

> Whatever may be the origin or cause of the 'rappings', the ladies in whose presence they occur do not make them. We tested this thoroughly and to our entire satisfaction. . . . The ladies say they are informed that this is but the beginning of a new era, in which spirits clothed in the flesh are to be more closely and palpably connected with those who have put on immortality; that the manifestations have already appeared in many other families, and are destined to be diffused and rendered clearer, until all who will may communicate freely with their friends who have shuffled off this mortal coil. Of all this we know nothing, and shall guess nothing; but if we were simply to print the questions we asked and the answers we received, during a two-hours uninterrupted conference with the 'rappers', we should be accused of having done so expressly to sustain the theory which regards these manifestations as the utterances of departed spirits.

It seems not merely charitable but reasonable to attribute the 'confessions' of the two younger sisters to the strains of their personal predicament. Both had been schoolgirls when the events started, and throughout the early years; both had been swept from a rural obscurity to a prominent position in one of the world's greatest cities. The tragic end of Margaretta's story-book love affair would have unbalanced a girl far less precariously situated; she took to drink and drugs, as did her sister Catherine before her own marriage to the lawyer Henry Jencken; though this brought her two children, it was also terminated by his abrupt and early death.

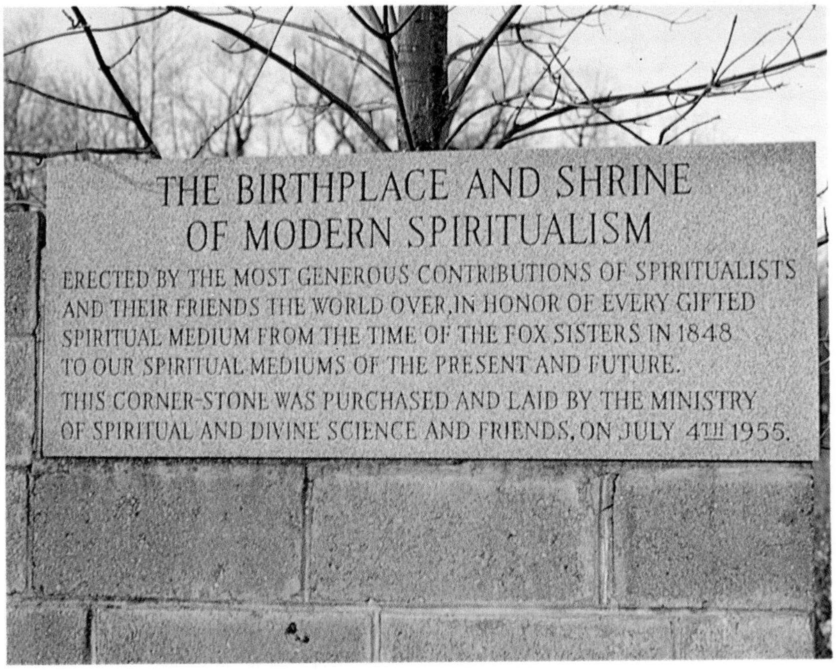

The cornerstone of a shrine to modern Spiritualism, which stands at the rear of the replica of the Fox cottage in Hydesville, USA. The building of the shrine started in 1955, but it was left uncompleted

In these circumstances, and perhaps influenced by the enemies of Spiritualism, it would not be surprising if the two sisters, neither of them notably intelligent at the best of times (Crookes was scathing about Catherine's intellectual limitations), reached a state of confusion in which the truth and the falsehood of their careers became inextricably confounded.

In 1904, when all the Fox sisters were dead, a wall of their old home at Hydesville collapsed: among the debris exposed there were found the remains of a body. Whose body it had been, it was impossible to determine: but it is a curious confirmation of the 'messages' that had been given to the Fox sisters half a century before. From this it does not necessarily follow that the information came from the spirit of the dead man, but it would demonstrate that the Fox sisters' careers were, at the very least, founded in truth.

Whether, as time went on and the pressure on them to produce phenomena to order increased, the Fox sisters 'helped out the spirits' by resorting to trickery, must be a matter for individual judgement; the girls were never detected in imposture, and the evidence for it is only circumstantial. But the presumption is there: and it is hard to believe that the Fox sisters could have been induced to make confessions that were totally false, without the least shade of guilt to provide a lever for those who sought to persuade them to confess. In its confusion of truth and falsehood, in its baffling ambiguity, the career of the Fox sisters seems to be a paradigm of Spiritualism itself.

Impressions of the afterlife

From spirit communications and reports of near-death experiences, we can draw a surprisingly cohesive picture of the nature of the world beyond the grave and the meaning of death.

What happens after death?

The one great certainty for everyone is death. Yet how many of us consider – let alone prepare for – this major trauma? What are the reasons for believing in an afterlife?

WHAT HAPPENS WHEN WE DIE? Nothing? Complete bliss – 'eternal life'? Or a vague, insubstantial something?

Materialists and atheists would answer 'nothing'. For them life is a purely biological process; when the body dies the personality dies with it, just as electricity stops being generated when a battery fails. To such people life cannot 'go somewhere else'.

These rationalists frequently point out that the age-old belief in an afterlife is merely a reflection of Man's terror of death, of personal oblivion. Throughout history he has either avoided the unthinkable or surrounded it with ritual and a childish optimism. The materialist believes this to be craven and intellectually dishonest – we ought to face 'the facts' – after all, it is true to say that the one fact of life is death.

What of the concept of 'eternal life'? Nearly all religionists have preached that we survive bodily death – in one form or another. It is probably true to say that the more sophisticated the religion, the more certainly it envisages *some* form of 'life everlasting' for some deathless element of the individual, whether in a kind of paradise or amid the torments of hell.

If the materialist is correct, no further enquiry need be made. If the religionists are correct, then it surely behoves each individual to look to his or her salvation. But in the context of religion, belief in the afterlife must remain a matter of faith, and only the experience of our own death can prove us right or wrong.

But what if neither of these rigid concepts is correct? What if something – some life-spark, vestige of the human personality – survives and enters a new kind of existence, not as a form of reward or punishment, but merely obeying a natural law? Today many

The plains of heaven by the English painter John Martin, 1853. Hosts of the blessed rejoice in a dramatic landscape worthy of the mid-Victorian Romantic poets. These angels, some of them winged, play the traditional harp

Far left: a reconstruction of the Fox family's historic home in Hydesville, New York, where the modern Spiritualist movement was born

Left: the Fox sisters, Margaretta, Catherine and Leah, from a daguerreotype taken in 1852. The strange rappings and table turnings in their home were taken by many to be the long-awaited proof of communications from the dead

psychical researchers feel that the balance of evidence suggests that 'something' does survive, not necessarily for very long after death, nor necessarily the whole personality. According to them, parts of an individual's memory-system and personality traits sometimes seem to survive for a time, enabling his disembodied self to be recognised by the living who knew him, but later perhaps to disintegrate forever.

The objective analysis of purported evidence for human survival is a major concern of the Society for Psychical Research (SPR), founded in London in 1882. But the founding of the SPR would probably never have happened but for events of a generation earlier, which themselves might never have happened but for the emancipation of Man's thought that began in the Renaissance.

Closed minds, closed ranks

As the horizons of knowledge expanded, the materialist position strengthened and by the mid 19th century a 'thinker' was generally reckoned to be someone who had freed himself from the trammels of 'superstition'. Religionists, feeling themselves under attack, tended to close their minds to facts that undermined their position, ironically adopting much the same attitude that some scientists take today when confronted with overwhelming evidence for certain paranormal events ('We don't believe in it, therefore it isn't true').

In the light of such hard rationalism, a faith with results that could be demonstrated was sought after. So when poltergeist activity occurred at the Fox family home in Hydesville, New York, in 1848 the general public was tremendously excited. Here at last was 'proof' of the survival of the spirit; an antidote to the bleakness of materialism. Spiritualism was born and has become a significant movement in the western world.

Spiritualists believe that their faith demonstrates incontrovertibly the existence of a life after death. They point to seances where, it is said, spirits move heavy tables, play musical instruments and introduce apports; where dead relatives and friends speak recognisably in their own voices of events known only to themselves and one or more of the sitters, and sometimes even materialise in their own appearances before them.

But scientists refused to investigate seance-room phenomena, while Spiritualists – and fundamentalist Christians – took refuge (though not as allies) in simple faith that regarded scientific discoveries as due to Devil-inspired cleverness.

It was in this climate of extremes that the SPR was founded. The founder members were a group of British intellectuals who objected to the entrenched positions of 'believers' and 'sceptics' and who felt that the objective assessment of unusual phenomena was long overdue. The material collected by the British SPR and similar societies in other countries provides the strongest clues for the serious enquirer into the question 'What happens when we die?'

The huge body of material collected since 1882 may be categorised as follows: phantasms; communications through mediums; cross-correspondences; 'drop-in' communicators; 'welcoming' phantasms seen by the dying; experiences of patients during 'clinical death'; out-of-the-body experiences; cipher and combination lock tests; appearance pacts; evidence for reincarnation; electronic voice phenomena.

Phantasms The SPR's first great achievement was a census of hallucinations. Seventeen thousand replies to a questionnaire about the prevalence of hallucinatory experiences were collected, and of these – after all possible explanations were exhausted – about 8 per cent remained as apparently genuine experiences of phantasms. These

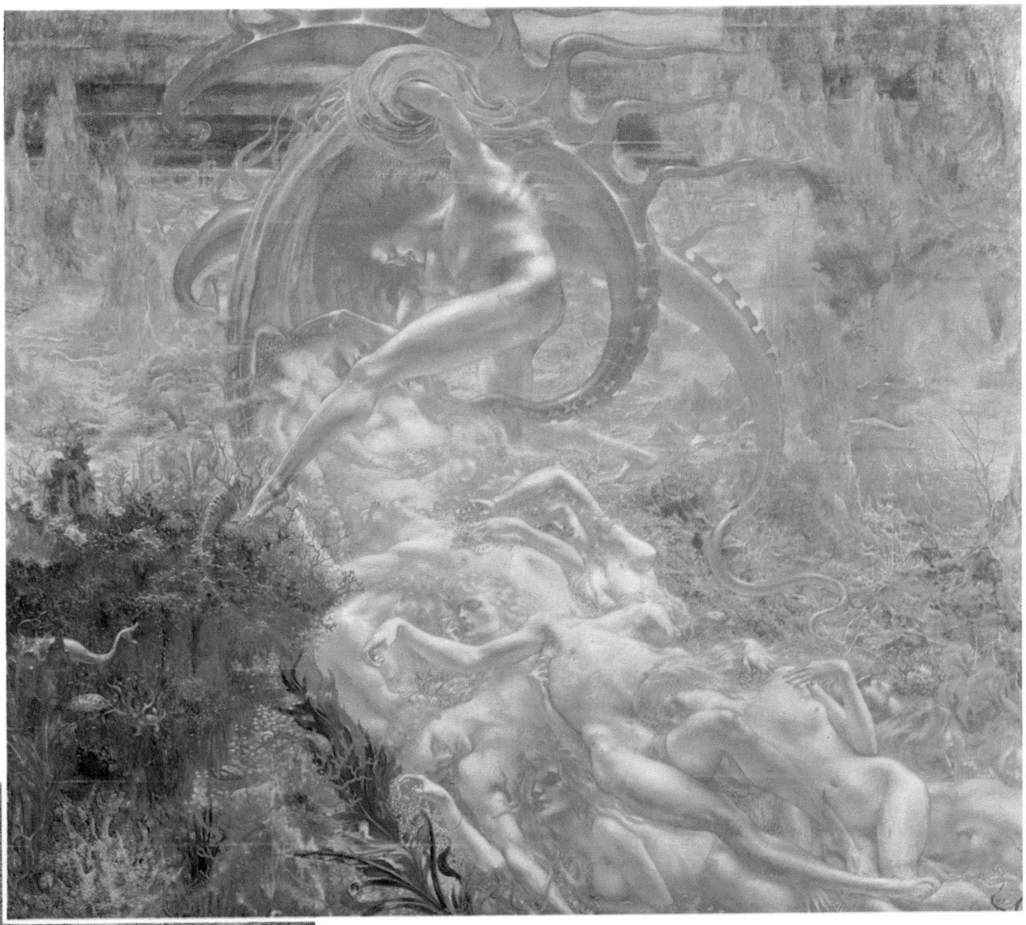

Left: *The treasures of Satan* by the late-19th-century French symbolist Jean Delville. Satan, flame-coloured as a sign of lust and of his fiery destruction of souls through degradations of the flesh, crushes his victims beneath him. Monstrous 'wings' of serpents flail about the tormented sinners

Below left: burial of the dead is not universal. Here a Red Indian brave visits the rotting corpses of members of his tribe. They have been exposed to the elements and birds of prey, on a hill set apart for the purpose. Their spirits were believed to spend eternity in the Happy Hunting Ground

were critically examined by the leading members of the SPR and upon the findings were based two volumes, *Apparitions of the living* and *Human personality and its survival of physical death.* Listed in the former were several apparitions of people said to have appeared up to 12 hours after their deaths. At the time the researchers felt that these might be due to thought transference from the newly dead individual to his living contacts, delayed perhaps until conditions were right for it to appear. Even so, a number of these cases would now still be classified as evidence of – at least temporary – survival.

Most parapsychologists who accept the evidence of phantasms at all agree that thought transference – which includes thoughts, feelings, and images both visual and auditory, and would today be classified as extra-sensory perception (ESP) – is a faculty of some human minds and could be used to explain phantasms of the living. It also seems to be confirmed by some individuals' claims that they 'think' themselves into paying 'astral visits' – travelling while out-of-the-body – to acquaintances. The claimants not only 'see' the rooms into which they project themselves mentally but report accurately such features as changes of furniture, of which their conscious selves were ignorant. Furthermore, they are often seen by the friends they 'visit' and are sometimes also accurately described by strangers.

However, some 6 or 7 per cent of the apparitions recorded in the SPR survey appeared too long after death for them to be explained as delayed telepathic communications. This small number of cases remained after all other explanations – hoaxing, exaggeration, mistaken identity, dreaming and so on – had been examined and found inadequate.

The cases that were classified as genuine apparitions or phantasms of the dead showed certain common features. In some, the apparition conveyed information previously unknown to the percipient. In others it showed a clearly defined purpose. In yet others it resembled a dead person unknown to the percipient who later recognised him from a portrait or photograph, or from some characteristic of the deceased unknown to him at the time. Sometimes different people at different times – independently of each other – saw the same apparition.

Some psychical researchers think that only those cases in which the apparitions indicate a specific purpose for their manifestation can be taken as significant evidence of survival and even then perhaps only as evidence of temporary survival. It could well be that, as a memory survives the event remembered, so a thought or anxiety to communicate something urgently to the living might continue to exist after the thinker's death until its purpose was fulfilled; then it, too, might die.

Since the early days of the SPR many astute

minds have studied and recorded evidence of survival provided by such apparitions. Some have believed that we live on, others not. It is safe to say that none of the researchers involved has been convinced of survival on the evidence of apparitions alone.

Communications through mediums. While phantasms were being investigated by the SPR so, too, were the activities of mediums – or, as they are better named, sensitives. These are people (more often women than men) who have unusual psychic talents, which they display in various ways. According to their specific gifts they are generally classified into 'mental' and 'physical' sensitives.

A 'mental' sensitive may go into a trance, in which a 'control' ('controlling spirit' or 'spirit guide') speaks through her, frequently in a voice entirely different from her own, and occasionally even giving her a different appearance, so that a European woman may temporarily take on the likeness and voice of, say, a Chinese man.

Through the sensitive the control may introduce other alleged spirits, recognisable by voice, gesture, or the nature of the private information they give to one of the sitters at the seance. Such so-called spirits may seem extremely convincing, though it must be said that those who want to believe will believe anyway. However, sensitives often have striking gifts of clairaudience, clairvoyance and other qualities of ESP. Sometimes they will communicate through the planchette board, like 'Patience Worth', for instance, or perhaps through automatic script, or they might draw in the style of recognised masters, or compose in the manner of famous musicians.

Another type of sensitive is the 'direct voice' medium, who does not, as a rule, go into a trance and from whose vicinity voices of both sexes and different kinds speak in various accents, and sometimes other, identifiable languages.

Communications from these sources vary enormously in quality. Much of it is trivial and curiously materialistic. It was a frequent gibe in the early days of Spiritualism that spirits seemed to spend their afterlife smoking cigars and drinking whisky. Yet this, and other similar 'materialistic' evidence would support the teachings of some Eastern religions that an early stage after death involves passing through a realm of illusion where the ego may indulge in anything and everything it wants.

Other communications, however, are of high ethical and literary standard. Yet frequently when challenged to give an unequivocal description of what awaits us on the other side of life, communicators reply (perhaps not unreasonably) that the spirit existence is indescribable. But some rare spirits are more forthcoming, and an uncannily consistent picture of the afterlife

Above: the 'Viking' galley is burned at the climax of the annual Up Helly A festival at Lerwick in the Shetland Isles, Scotland. The ancient Viking funerals combined cremation with dramatic spectacle, the dead being placed in a burial ship, which was set alight as it was pushed out to sea. It must have seemed to the mourners on the shore that the journey to Valhalla (the Viking heaven) was a very real one

Right: Peruvian Incas bury a chief, preparing him for an afterlife just as stylish and prosperous as his earthly life. Like many other pagan peoples, they buried food, treasure and weapons with their dead, believing the artefacts to be necessary for the dead to survive in the next world in the manner to which they were accustomed

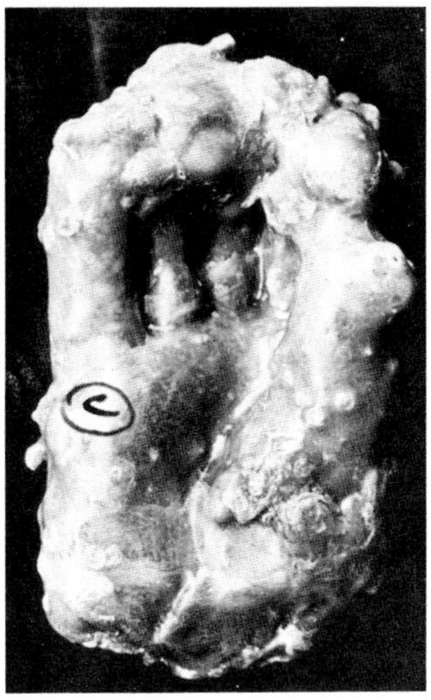

Very popular at Edwardian seances was the moulding of 'spirit' hands in paraffin wax (above); they were believed to dematerialise, leaving the moulds unbroken. But Harry Houdini, the great escape artist and scourge of fraudulent mediums, proved that it was a relatively easy trick to learn (top left)

Top right: an elaborate, pagoda-like cremation tower on the island of Bali

emerges through their communications.

'Physical' mediums are those in whose presence, whether they go into trances or not, physical phenomena occur. These may include loud raps from the seance table or from various points around the room; sometimes they seem to be in an intelligent code as if trying to convey some message. Also common are telekinetic phenomena (solid objects moving as if handled by an invisible person); levitation, of the sensitive and of objects; the playing of musical instruments by unseen hands, and actual materialisation of spirit forms.

Sadly, in the short history of Spiritualism, many of these phenomena have been faked, but there still remain many cases of genuine physical mediumship that defy 'rational' explanation. Many tests have been set up to try to trap the frauds, and, to a lesser extent, to determine the extent of the phenomena. One such was the provision of a dish of warm wax at a physical seance; the materialised 'spirit' hand dipped itself into the wax, which rapidly set. The hand dematerialised, leaving the mould unbroken.

But even such demonstrations of paranormal effects do not prove survival of death in themselves. The material accumulated by the SPR contains, so many researchers believe, far stronger evidence.

How can we possibly know if we survive death? Must it remain, as most people believe, a mystery? A surprising amount of evidence has been presented that seems to indicate there is indeed an afterlife

'The undiscover'd co

Above: a soul being ferried across the river of death – the Styx – in the 16th-century painting by Joachim Patinir. It reveals a blend of Classical and Christian beliefs: the Styx and its irascible ferryman, Charon, were believed by the ancient Greeks to carry the dead to their appointed place for eternity. The dead were buried with coins in their mouths so that they could pay the ferryman. Failure to pay resulted in damnation. However the Christian conceptions of purgatory, paradise and hell are shown on either side of the dread river

THE SOCIETY for Psychical Research (SPR) was fortunate enough in its early days to be able to call upon the services of highly intelligent, well-educated sensitives with open minds, whose names are still household words among psychical researchers: Mrs Piper, Mrs Thompson, Mrs 'Willett' (a pseudonym for Mrs Coombe-Tennant), Mrs Leonard, Mrs Garrett, among others.

Some of these were 'physical' mediums but most 'mental' – which may be significant, for physical mediums have become progressively rarer as methods of investigation have become more sophisticated. Cynics may leap to the conclusion that the likelihood of being caught as a fraud is so great these days that few dare attempt 'physical' mediumship. But an alternative view is that the very act of setting up the elaborate apparatus necessary for the investigation may inhibit the delicate, barely understood mechanism that produces the phenomena. There also seems occasionally to be an 'experimenter effect' whereby sceptical and even merely objective experimenters may have a dampening effect on the activities of the seance room.

Although the SPR's team of mediums produced some very convincing results, members of the Society were divided over the major question of proof of the afterlife. But they did agree that thought transference – including the communication of thoughts, feelings, images, sounds, even scents – had been proved beyond reasonable doubt. And although more than three decades were to pass before J. B. Rhine's work shifted the emphasis from psychical research (the scientific study of the paranormal) to parapsychology (treating psychic phenomena as expressions of little-known mental activity), extra-sensory perception, psychokinesis and general (super) ESP were already being taken as alternative explanations for the mediums' 'proof' of survival.

It is alleged that ESP explains all uncannily accurate information a medium might give a sitter, purporting to come from a dead relative. For by ESP a human mind can – almost literally – 'pick the brains' of others, without being conscious of doing so. And PK – 'mind over matter' – is the mysterious force exerted by certain gifted minds over inanimate objects. This would explain the so-called 'spirit' table turnings, rappings and so on in terms of a natural, if rare, function of the human mind. And the theory of general or super ESP is that some human minds can glean information not only from other human minds but also from any written,

printed or other kind of record (including presumably, microfilm), arrange it and produce it as a coherent account. Such a concept, if true, destroys any chance of proving survival as a fact, for any message from a deceased person – no matter how accurate or how personal the information given – could theoretically be the result of GESP. Put in Theosophical terms, this store of the sum of human knowledge is called the 'Akashic records' and there are certain sensitive people who have long been believed to have access to its 'files'. So it could be that, in some unknown way, the cross-referencing necessary for a medium to produce a convincing story of someone's life on Earth has already been done.

There are two other major arguments against evidence for survival as provided by mediums. The first is that a sensitive's so-called 'control' or 'spirit guide' may be no more than an example of the dissociated or multiple personalities that are occasionally discovered by psychiatrists. These seem to be personalities apparently formed by the splitting off of some mental processes from the mainstream of consciousness. If these 'other selves' come to the surface, they can take over completely and the condition becomes a serious illness. (There have been cases where over a dozen completely distinct personalities have inhabited the same body, either taking over in turns or fighting among themselves for possession.) And such manifestations have sometimes happened unexpectedly when apparently normal people have been hypnotised. So perhaps a sensitive, by her very nature, may be more susceptible to the development of secondary personalities than more down-to-earth, or openly sceptical, people.

ntry'

Left: Persephone and Pluto, in a detail from a Greek vase. Pluto was the ruler of Hades, or the realm of the underworld, believed by the Greeks to be a real geographical location that the dead souls reached through caves. It was a shadowy and sinister abode but not a place of active judgement or punishment. However, at a popular level there was a widespread suspicion that Hades was a much more fearsome place

The versatile forger

Add to this another extraordinary power of the human mind – *mythopoeia*. This is the extraordinary ability to create myths or detailed stories that are strikingly convincing and frequently surface during hypnotic regression as 'past lives'. It can also result in subconscious forgery, enabling some sensitives to imitate the voices, mannerisms, handwriting and even the style of musical composition or drawing of the (sometimes famous) dead. All this may be at second hand, drawn from the minds of others. Mythopoeia may also be responsible for the ability of people in trances to sing or pour out dramatically a flood of unintelligible language, known as 'speaking in tongues'. It is a theory that provides an alternative explanation for the many bizarre phenomena that have been taken as 'proof' of survival.

Cross-correspondences The deaths of the SPR's founder members, notably that of F. W. H. Myers in 1901, were followed by an extraordinary new phenomenon, that of the 'cross-correspondences'. These were fragmentary messages received at different times

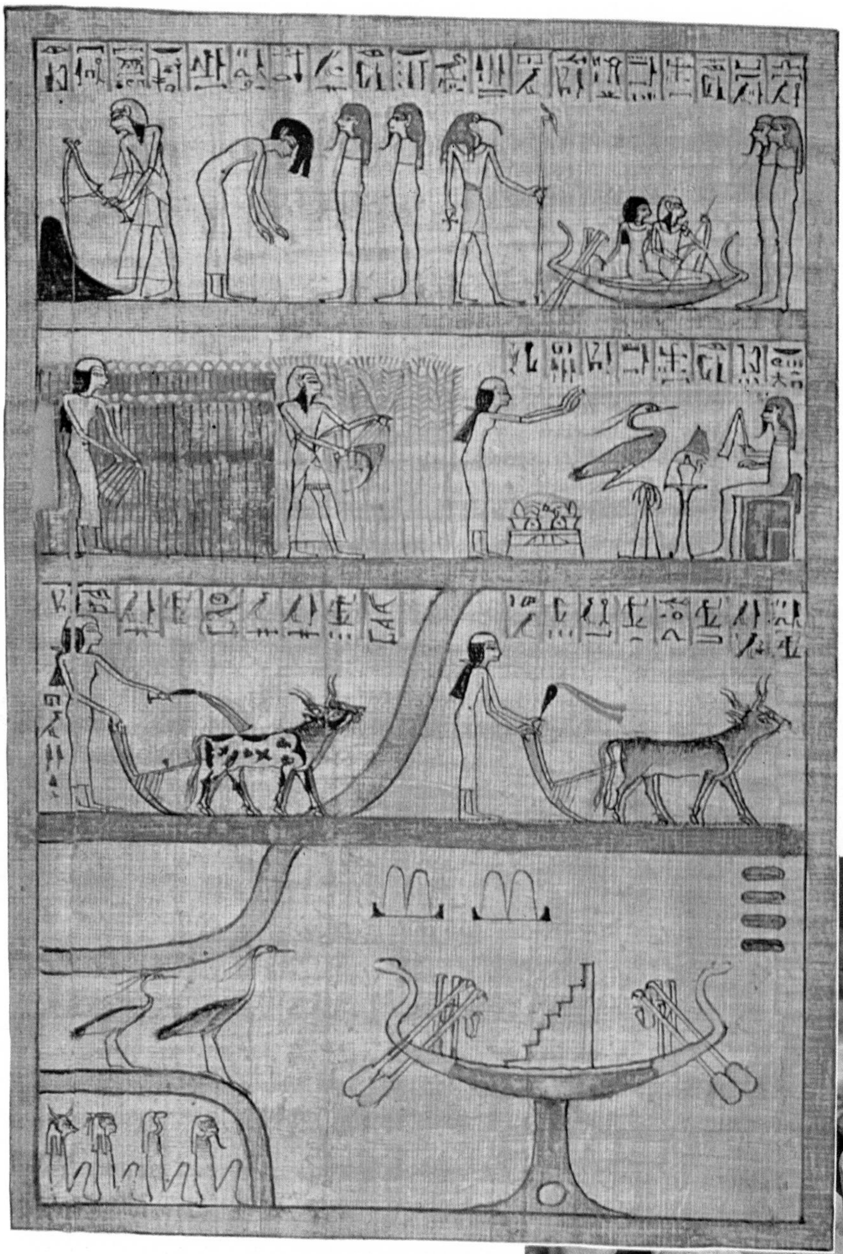

Above left: a soul farming in the Elysian fields. The ancient Egyptians believed the afterlife to be very similar to earthly life but more pleasurable

Above: funerary model of bakery and brewery slaves from an ancient Egyptian tomb. The model slaves were believed to assume real duties in the afterlife in the service of the master in whose tomb they were put

and places through two or more sensitives unconnected with each other. The messages, often apparently nonsensical taken separately, made perfect sense when fitted together. The compiling of the cross-correspondences took over 30 years. The timing of their beginning, coinciding as it did with the deaths of those whose main preoccupation in life had been to understand the mysteries of death, seems to many investigators to prove beyond doubt who was behind the experiment. It seemed as if the founders of the SPR had a meeting beyond the grave and said, 'Any normal message we send will be ascribed to thought transference. Let us devise a method of communication that will not be open to such an interpretation.'

Certainly no messages easily ascribable to thought transference had ever been communicated in fragments to different mediums before. And the subject matter of the messages – poetry and erudite classical allusions – was highly characteristic of the group of dead SPR members. Although to a certain extent GESP could account for much of the material of the cross-correspondences, many researchers believe that they are the best evidence yet of survival. But even so, all they do is attempt to convince us, in as many ingenious ways as possible, of the continued existence of certain individuals. (The dead Myers is alleged to have found the effort of communication trying, and 'endlessly presenting my credentials' frustrating in the extreme.) But even assuming its authenticity, this massive, painstaking experiment tells us little of what happens when we die except that we retain something of our earthly habits of thought and some traits of personality.

'Drop-in' communicators Some seances have been interrupted by 'drop-in' spirits who are unknown to anyone present, yet who give information about themselves that is later discovered to be substantially correct. Again, this phenomenon can be explained by GESP, but why should a sensitive pick up information about someone in whom no one present has any interest?

'Welcoming' phantoms Witnesses of the dying often report that dead friends and relatives are apparently seen by them just before death – coming to welcome them to the 'other side'. Perhaps these are hallucinations, a mechanism of nature to ease the passing from life. But this does not explain the cases where the dying have exclaimed at the 'visit' of a relative whose own death was unknown to them.

Clinical death Since the 1960s research has been carried out into the experiences of people who have clinically 'died' – often on the operating table – and who have come back to life. They nearly all report approximately similar experiences, whether they had previously believed in survival or not. They were conscious of leaving their

Right: an early 15th-century view of heaven as a peaceful garden. In days when life was short (and youth and beauty tragically brief), and Man very much at the mercy of the raw elements, an eternal period of relaxation in beautiful surroundings had an obvious, emotive appeal. Here the garden of heaven is shown peopled with young, healthy and attractive souls – among them a winged angel. They relax in each other's company, reading, picking choice fruits, playing musical instruments, and holding pleasant conversations. They are all dressed in the finest and most fashionable clothes. The wall suggests the exclusivity of heaven – and a sense of security after the fears of life

bodies and passing through a dark tunnel with a light at the end. When they emerged from the tunnel they were met by a radiant figure, often too bright to be seen clearly. This being they identified differently, according to their religious 'vocabulary'; for the Westerner he is usually taken to be Christ. They may also be aware of the presence of dead friends or relatives, and are filled with tremendous peace and joy. Yet they are told that their time has not yet come and they have to return. With the greatest unwillingness they re-enter their body. Significantly, people who have had this experience are never afraid of death again, seeing it as something to look forward to.

Out-of-the-body experiences Another mass of evidence that we exist apart from our physical bodies concerns out-of-the-body-experiences, sometimes referred to as OOBES. Many people have had the curious experience of finding themselves hovering over their sleeping – or unconscious – bodies:

Above: the medieval hell was a place of brutal torment, believed to be both 'physical' and spiritual. Although sophisticated theologians of the day argued that the real anguish of hell was the knowledge that one was eternally denied the presence of God, most ordinary people believed that hell was the proverbial fiery pit. Paradoxically, it was for them a world in which the physical pain of lingering tortures was the only sort of punishment, although it was admitted that one no longer had a physical body. Sinners suffered tortures of the most sadistic nature without any hope of mercy or cessation of their pain

frequently this happens in moments of crisis; during accidents, torture, or while undergoing an operation. Some people later astonish surgeons and nurses by telling them exactly what they had done and said while carrying out the operation. A few claim to be able to leave their bodies at will: and this, to them, is certain proof that they exist apart from their bodies and that this aspect of them will survive bodily death.

Ciphers and combination-lock tests A few tests have been arranged by the living so that, after their deaths, they might prove their continued existence by revealing, through mediums or friends, the solutions to puzzles. So far, none of these has been successful, though the number of the tests arranged may be too small to be significant.

Appearance pacts Lovers or friends have made pacts that the one who died first should appear to the other, perhaps under certain specific circumstances. Allegedly they have done so. But grief frequently produces hallucinations of the deceased – indeed, it seems part of the natural mourning process, acting as a comfort. Such appearances can also be categorised as crisis apparitions or similar manifestations of ESP.

Reincarnation Evidence for reincarnation not only indicates that we survive and are reborn (perhaps many times), but also offers clues as to why we are born at all. Hypnotic regression into 'past lives'; some children's spontaneous memories of being someone else; the 'far memory' of some adults; some *déjà vu* experiences; all these, though amenable to other explanations, point to reincarnation as

a possibility. Many people believe that we must submit to a string of different earthly lives until we have achieved near perfection of soul, then we become gods or progress on a purely spiritual plane of existence. Some think that not everyone is reincarnated but that we do not understand the rules governing the selection process involved.

Dr Ian Stevenson of the University of Virginia in the United States has made a detailed and scholarly investigation into the evidence for reincarnation. He has amassed hundreds of cases of alleged 'past lives' and came to the conclusion that 'a rational man . . . can believe in reincarnation on the basis of evidence.' However, for the majority of people such a belief will remain a matter of faith alone.

Electronic voice phenomena Since the 1960s tape recorders have allegedly been picking up voices of the dead. The phenomenon was discovered by the Swedes Jürgenson and Raudive and has since become something of a cult. However, all that can be said of it so far is that, whatever the source of the voices, they do not add to our information about the afterlife.

Despite the fast-growing interest in the paranormal and psychical research, it is true to say that the majority of believers in survival of the spirit belong to a religion, and for them, a belief in the afterlife is entirely a matter of faith.

Above left: Buddha sits in the midst of the blessed. Stylised lotus flowers (symbols of enlightenment), peacocks, pagodas, elegant shrubs and a decorative pool are reminiscent of the Christian conception of heaven as a garden

Above right: this ancient Chinese painting depicts the Buddhist seventh hell, where the souls of the condemned are chased by ferocious dogs and devils into a deadly river

Opposite page: the Indians of the northwestern coast of Canada wove elaborate myths about the nature of the hereafter and the journey from life into death. This mask represents Bokwus, the wild-man-of-the-woods and chief of the dead who lives in an invisible house in the forest eating rotten wood and grubs. He feeds hapless passers-by on what appears to be dried salmon, after which they die and join his ghostly retinue.

And this faith goes back a very long way; the oldest known burial customs show that ancient Man believed in survival. Even today, primitive religions take survival of bodily death for granted.

The world's more sophisticated religions, however, differ widely in their concept of Man's ultimate goal. Hindus and Buddhists teach that we escape from the miseries of earthly incarnations into a mystical and blissful unity with Brahma, the Supreme Principle, or entry into Nirvana, in which the self is lost in the infinite.

In the ancient world Greeks, Romans and Hebrews believed the spirit departed to an unsatisfactory existence in a shadowy Hades or *sheol*. Later Jews accepted the concept of the resurrection of the righteous to companionship with the patriarchs, but even today Judaism does not teach a certain doctrine of eternal life for everyone.

From ancient Egypt and Zoroastrianism the idea of judgement descended to Judaism, Christianity and Mohammedanism, with consequent doctrines of rewards and punishments, heaven, purgatory, limbo and hell.

But believer or atheist, philosopher or materialist, each one of us must die. And only then will we find out the truth for certain.

The journey of the soul

Do the souls of the dead live on? Do they go to heaven, hell, purgatory – or to some other, as yet unknown, plane of existence? And if they do continue to exist, how do we know about their experiences? This chapter surveys the evidence for the afterlife

EVEN AMONG PEOPLE who believe in some kind of an afterlife, alleged communications from the 'other side' are frequently regarded with suspicion. Perhaps it is natural to ascribe such accounts to the result of wishful thinking or to unjustified hopes and morbid fears. For this reason most people are unaware of the enormous amount of material purporting to describe the next world from people *who are now there*. But if, for a moment, we suspend our disbelief, what emerges from this material is not only evidence for an afterlife but an amazingly consistent description of what it is like to be dead.

Obviously these accounts cannot be checked, and examining them in an open, unprejudiced way is not easy. The basic issue is one of testimony: who are the witnesses – the communicators and the living people who receive their messages?

Bearing witness

Although there are many 'communicators' and just as many 'mediums' or sensitives, not all bear the marks of good witnesses. If the dead speak to us at all, their task cannot be easy; but this does not mean that we should feel obliged to accept any communication no matter how garbled or trivial. We are entitled to listen to only the best – the most balanced, consistent and rational – accounts. In England the Society for Psychical Research (SPR) and the College for Psychic Studies have accrued a vast amount of material, which seems to emanate from intelligent and honest sources, that has been given to reputable mediums over the past 100 years or so. In the end we ourselves have to judge the communications on their own merits and on the responses they awaken in us. But a good witness is worthy of a good listener. So what do the majority of these accounts tell us?

If we do indeed survive death, then by definition the surviving part of us must already be present within us during our life on earth. The first feature of the accounts is that we do indeed take with us the same memory bank, and the same emotions and mental concepts that we had before death. We start from where we left off. But which of us survives: the tired elderly man, or the one in vigorous prime, or even the one full of illusory youthful ideals? The answer, judging by the mass of evidence, points to our having available the private, inward contents of *all* these various 'past selves'; we can reside in them temporarily, or hold on to one aspect or the other. All these imperfect selves have made us what we are; we are said to meet them all in turn again after death, in order to understand them as they really were, and profit by re-experiencing them.

A good witness is Mrs Winifred Coombe-Tennant, known in psychic circles as 'Mrs Willett'. In life she was one of the first English women JPs and a delegate to the League of Nations. She also took part as a non-professional sensitive in the cross-correspondences, which form a highlight in the multiplicity of evidence collected by the SPR. After her death, medium Geraldine Cummins received an enormous amount of material (in the form of automatic writing) purporting to come from the discarnate Mrs Coombe-Tennant. Much of this describes the afterlife as she had experienced it. Of the 'many selves' enigma she says:

> A human being consists of a number of selves or aspects with a primary self, the total of a sum in arithmetic. . . . We only become unified in spirit on the higher level.

Dying, it seems, is not the absolute event most people fear; largely, it appears to be a state of altered consciousness. Evidence points to it being harder after death to get rid of the old earthly self than we had supposed. The same personal limitations continue until we resolve them. Death does not in itself change us; it gives us a different kind of opportunity to change ourselves.

In the seventh heaven

In spiritualistic communications, life after death is often described as a progress through seven spheres, each of a more rarified and spiritually invigorating nature than the last. The seven spheres – or mansions, or staging posts – basically represent levels of consciousness, and any of these levels is reached only by a widening and deepening of the moral nature. One is helped by teachers of superior moral stature who have progressed, so to speak, beyond the scope of recent arrivals, but who adapt themselves temporarily to make themselves understood. After death one must realise that life continues as a process of learning.

The great majority of communicators describe the death process itself as one of peacefulness and freedom from pain, even if, during the last hours, the physical body had shown every outward appearance of distress. Communicators often say this apparent pain

Left: *The garden of earthly delights* by Hieronymus Bosch. He saw the average man's ideal world as totally physical – and, ultimately, totally degrading

Below: the traditional Christian belief in a day of reckoning, as portrayed in Fra Angelico's *The day of judgement*

Bottom: T.E. Lawrence, better known as 'Lawrence of Arabia', who died in 1935. In life a brilliant yet difficult man, he was obliged to confront certain unappealing aspects of his character – 'the monk and the prig' – in the afterlife, in order to progress to higher planes

did not register with them. They say death is a gradual withdrawing, often accompanied by alternating periods of sleep or unconsciousness. Then they describe 'waking up' and being greeted by those they had deeply loved who had died previously – and also by others, familiar or not yet familiar, who will be found to know them intimately, even their secret selves. These are not angels sitting in judgement, but more highly developed spirits. Frequently an encounter with them is found to be disturbing. As one newly dead doctor of divinity is purported to have said of such a meeting:

> He evidently regarded my whole life on earth – which hitherto I have thought of as being so important – as mere preparation, a preliminary to the real work I have to do here. That has been one of the greatest surprises.

Experiences are, apparently, by no means uniform, and naturally enough are partly determined by old patterns of behaviour and thinking. This first plane of experience is

exactly – and literally – what you make of it. According to all communicators, the imagination is supreme; just by thinking of something it appears. Some have given this plane the term 'ideo-plastic', meaning creation through ideas alone. Some create around them past environments of home and possessions that they are unwilling to relinquish. The important key to understanding this plane is that matter is now reported to be of a finer texture, highly malleable to thought. Some, who had not believed in an afterlife, even fail to recognise they are dead. They feel they must be in a vivid dream.

But willing pupils in this environment – called the *summerland*, says the posthumous Frederic Myers – can create what they most desired on earth. But this is not 'heaven' as more enlightened communicators hasten to point out. Summerland in time shows that these 'dreams' are after all not wise enough, nor spiritual enough; they are gradually found to be too selfish and materialistic. People may find that they are seeking little more than a kind of perpetual summer holiday. Yet many accounts stress that the purpose of summerland is to enable its inhabitants to find that much of what they thought valuable is valueless.

But what sort of world does a man find around himself, if his life has been devoted to selfish gain, or if he has fallen prey to crime and violence? The habits of his mind remain the same and so, as in life, he finds he can contribute very little to his after-death environment. His self-absorption has cut him off from being able to enjoy any wider, disinterested feelings, which make up true companionship. As in the summerland his environment reflects himself – and his poverty of soul assumes an awful 'reality'. Many accounts tell of darkness, mist, bare earth and a hovel to live in. This is *winterland.*

In his continuing selfishness such a spirit often feels anger and indignation for his lot. Neither he nor others in that condition can please one another, for all are equally selfish. More unfortunately, he often treats with contempt those who enter his world from their own superior realms of freedom, who wish to help and teach him how to change. But frequently such a person is said to stop his ears, much as he often stopped them in life to the promptings of his conscience.

Yet it would be hard to find a man who is totally degraded, and each of these unfortunates who finds himself in winterland is there for only as long as he refuses to listen to the other, higher part of himself. Those who try to help him are really looking for this better self, however deeply overlaid. It is stressed that these individuals are not being 'punished'; their suffering stems only from their own nature as they have created it; and it is fully in their power to regenerate it. They can discover and build on their latent qualities, just as can those who find themselves in the summerland. And just as summerland is not 'heaven', neither is winterland 'hell'. Both states exist because of the individual's inner self. When he becomes more spiritual they are transcended.

Those who have outgrown the summerland state pass on to the *first heaven.* Here selfless ideals can be developed in a life shared with those who also wish to serve others. Its joys are not passive, however; they are certainly to be enjoyed, yet used strenuously to obtain growth of spiritual stature. But this level of consciousness is superior to that of the summerland. The soul is shown, step by step, its nature as it was when on earth. This self-knowledge includes the revelation and re-evaluation of all faults, errors and blindnesses – many of them, even at this stage, hard to accept. Faults easy to excuse on earth, or to hide from oneself, now show up in their true shape.

The prophet Mohammad journeys to the seven heavens, as depicted in an early 16th-century Persian painting. The idea that the afterlife is a continuing process, involving the soul's ascent through various stages of enlightenment, is a belief common to many different religions

As others see us

This process is usually named the *judgement.* It is widely reported by communicators that the judgement is not made by God (as in the popular idea of 'the day of judgement'), nor by some superior being sitting in condemnation, but is in some way self-induced. To see, and then to have to condemn oneself, is painful, the more so since many faults now revealed were formerly unsuspected. The posthumous T.E. Lawrence is said to have recognised the monk and prig in himself, which had led him to reject women's values, and brought about what he now says is a travesty of the man he could have been. The judgement shows what one has made of oneself, and it is more often than not a painful experience. But once recognised these faults can be transcended, creating a different self.

The judgement usually extends over a considerable period of experiences and adjustments; it also of course includes recognition of those qualities and actions that are worthy – in this sense life in the first heaven is part of the judgement. Though judgement is carried out by oneself, loving companions are there to explain, support and give guidance for necessary corrective steps. W. V. Blewett, a former agricultural scientist, is believed to have said, 'Here we receive absolute justice, such as can never be possible on earth.'

Motive is shown to be paramount. Hence one's actions are shown as they really were, not as one preferred to think them; and whatever joy or suffering they brought about in others is now exactly felt and experienced oneself. This can be very painful without the deadening effect of the physical body, in the same way that emotions felt in dreams – love, fear, disgust – are sharply defined as if suddenly in focus, whereas the same emotions felt in our everyday lives are muffled by the demands and stimuli of the outside world. Here there is no 'outside world' – it is all 'inside', all experienced with the awful, or beautiful, clarity of dreaming.

From what we can piece together, the various 'stages' of the afterlife can be experienced one after the other – and most frequently are – but sometimes the discarnate spirit can work at several tasks at the same time or go from one to the other alternately. There seems to be no rigid plan to which every person must adhere; as on earth, all people are individuals with different needs, and these are allowed for.

Above: a Hindu statue of an *apsaras*, who is believed to gratify men's sexual desires in paradise. Most ancient religions – with the exception of puritan Christianity – imagine paradise, or heaven, to comprise endless feasting, drinking, idleness and sex in scented gardens. The indications are that the first stage of the afterlife is indeed a place where one's dreams come true

Left: William Blake's illustration for Robert Blair's *The grave*, 1813, showing the newly freed spirit rising from the shrouded corpse, keys in hand, to open the way to a blissful future

But most communicators express difficulty in conveying to us that their surroundings, seemingly much as on earth, are actually part of a wonderful mental world, and are much more malleable to thought than dense earth matter. All is permeated by the thoughts, feelings and beliefs of those at a common level of consciousness. The mental-emotional environment to which one belongs is not isolated, however; it is also influenced or 'played upon' by the consciousness of those at higher levels, in a way that is as sustaining and invigorating as sunlight.

How far and how much we can see is, as always, bounded by our own limited consciousness; being played upon from higher levels is aimed at helping us gradually to enlarge our vision, somewhat in the way we learn on earth from a teacher's entire personality and not merely from the facts he passes on. But exactly what is learned on this plane is difficult for us to imagine. It can hardly be of a mechanical or practical nature for physical objects no longer exist. And it is unlikely, in the circumstances, to entail philosophical discussion about the 'nature of life'. Learning must be confined to lessons of a moral or spiritual nature, as indeed many communicators describe. But such a formidable course of study begins only when the student is ready – and eager – for it.

Each succeeding level is shut off from us until we are in a fit state to appreciate it. It is possible that some souls never rise above the 'summer holiday' plane of the summerland. It seems more likely, however, that everyone progresses to higher planes, but at his or her own pace.

These events – life in the summerland, winterland, the first heaven, and the process of the judgement – form what is meant by the 'astral' or 'desire' world of consciousness. Each man now begins to learn that it is necessary to leave this plane behind, to shed it in order to win the freedom to dwell in the most spiritual parts of himself.

Surrender of the self

The experience that many believe now awaits him is known as the *second death*. Each must now gradually become as willing to yield up his present values as, in very many cases, he was ready in the end to shed his earthly body on death. His desires in the astral world, however much they have included love of others, good fellowship and companionship, have also, as he now begins to see with certainty, really largely centred upon himself. Even when he loved others, much of this was for his own emotional satisfaction. Now in the second death he sheds all he has valued; his achievements and all the things he has won in the desire world (of which earth too is a part) have now to be given up. His gifts no longer exist for him but for the glory of God. Conan Doyle, in describing his own posthumous experience, calls this transition 'terrible and marvellous', adding that 'there are no trimmings on a man after the second death.' Yet this traumatic experience prepares the student, shorn of his most dearly held pretensions, for the next stage in his progress. Through this he can begin to find his 'true self'; a larger, more complete being – one, he discovers, for which he has always been searching.

The purpose of death

Far from resting in peace, it is claimed that the dead lead a strenuous and purposeful existence; in fact that they are more 'alive' than we are. What is the meaning of the afterlife?

IF DEATH IS NOT the end of man's personality, but rather the beginning of a sort of 'pilgrim's progress' as many psychical researchers claim, then what are the stages of this adventure? The discarnate spirit, after meeting the loved ones who had died before him, lives first in summerland or winterland, both of which he creates from his own habits of thought, good or bad. These are both on the *ideo-plastic* plane and seem to serve to break him of his earthly preoccupations and make him yearn for the benefits of higher, more spiritual faculties. But he must first undergo the judgement and the second death, processes that hold a mirror up to the person he was, mercilessly stripping him of his illusions about himself and making him realise – by momentarily *becoming* other people in his life – what his actions and words had done to them.

Through experiencing the shattering but ultimately rewarding process of the second death the spirit 'earns' his entry into the *second heaven*. What has been shed in the trauma is only, he discovers, his outer self, his personality, which had seemed so essential in his earth life. Personality is derived from the Latin *persona*, meaning 'actor's mask'; having cast this away during the second death he can emerge as his real, 'undivided self'.

The purpose of the second heaven is, apparently, to enable the questing spirit to grow and develop. The process takes place in what many accounts call 'the great silence'. During this period one's former identity dissolves away and one experiences a sense of great peace. One no longer knows who or where one is, but this is not in any way distressing, any more than it is 'distressing' for a butterfly to undergo the natural process of emerging from its cocoon.

Above: the Hindu deity Vishnu reincarnates for the second time – as a turtle. Belief in the transmigration of souls, or reincarnation as man or animal, is still common in the East. But, according to the alleged evidence for the afterlife, man is always reincarnated as another human being

Right: the ninth hell as described in Dante's *Inferno* and illustrated by Gustave Doré. In this wasteland of ice and desolation, the damned soul is frozen forever, unless he confesses his sins to the superior souls who visit him

Kinship of the spirit

At this point the spirit loses contact with all those he had known during his earth life. This is a temporary phase but apparently essential if he is to concentrate his energies on coping with the new, immeasurably broader landscape he now faces. There are now highly significant meetings with others, men and women with whom one feels a deep spiritual link and an intimate familiarity. This is reported as being like meeting old friends on earth with whom one has shared profound experiences. However, the spirits on this plane, although they are indeed old friends, belong to relationships formed over many lifetimes. And this one fact is central to the understanding of the whole nature of the afterlife. With those friends from long ago the spirit relives ancient memories, memories to which his immediately previous personality had no access. Together the members of the reunion relive past events they had shared, and as they do so they begin to see a distinct purpose and meaning emerge

Most ancient cultures believed in a supernatural deity whose sole task was to preside over the dead. Part custodian and part judge, he is usually shown as a terrible figure, such as Yamantaka, Tibetan lord of the dead (above) or the Totonac god of ancient Mexico, Mictlantecuhtli (right)

from the apparently disparate and fragmentary personalities they had been in the past. Each soul has been reincarnated many times.

They now see that their lives are in no way arbitrary; they form part of a pattern and purpose that are still being worked out. Each is slowly awakening towards recognition of, and participating in, what is named his *causal self*. This carries within it the seeds of each former life but also contains hints of what is to come in future incarnations. The second heaven is both retrospective and prospective; a plane of insight into both past and future. As the posthumous Frances Banks, a former Anglican nun, is claimed to have said, it is 'the initial stage of a journey into light, during which the surviving entity is gradually reunited with the whole soul.' And now he sees his past earth life in its true perspective; not, as he perhaps thought as he was actually living it, that it was the 'be all and end all', but that it was only a tiny fragment of a much larger prospect.

The past life is only the latest chapter in a long book, the 'story' of which can stretch back over many earth centuries. As the spirit begins to witness the unfolding panorama of his lives he will inevitably realise that much in his past life was the direct consequence of actions from other, previous incarnations. Nothing is meaningless – now at last he knows the answer to the question every person asks at some point: 'Why me?'

There are many incarnations for most spirits, for almost everyone needs many chances to learn all the necessary lessons. All the opportunities will be there over the centuries for everyone. Not everyone will profit by his experience or learn at the same rate but there are many chances to put right mistakes made or opportunities lost. Perhaps the failures of the last life are similar to those experienced before, or perhaps at last the spirit has overcome a lengthy pattern of mistakes. Frances Banks said, 'It is still a continuation, a sequel. There is a definite continuing thread.'

This enrichment of the soul through the revelations of the past is the first step in the process of reassessment carried on in the second heaven. There are two other, equally important steps.

The first involves advice from wiser beings on how to deal with one's future earth life. The second step clarifies the true nature of the spirit's relationship with his peers, those 'old friends' with whom he has just been reunited. He now realises that they are all bound together for all eternity, united with the same overall purpose. Together they form part of a highly important unit known as a *group soul*. It is said that to be with its members is to feel a deep spiritual homecoming.

The members of an earth family may be spiritually close or they may simply be genetically linked – effectively strangers on

The statue of Justice that stands above the Old Bailey, Britain's foremost criminal court. The scales and the sword she carries represent the two aspects of justice: mercy and retribution. Absolute justice, however, is said to be found only in the afterlife – where motives are seen for what they really were in life. During the judgement the soul suffers the pain and humiliation he once inflicted on others. He learns for himself – the hard way – the effects of his every word and deed. But his kindnesses are also relived and rewarded

any deeper level. Their spiritual 'family' is elsewhere. Such people are said to be the true foundlings. But in the afterlife there are no such random or loose ties; the group soul comprises only members who are totally committed to their particular long-term spiritual assignment under the leadership of one who can perhaps best be called an elder brother. The individual members of each group are responsible to each other – and to the world – in order to fulfil the special task assigned them when their group was created.

Life goes on

If these narratives that claim to describe conditions in the afterlife – and, indeed, the purpose of life itself – are true, then our individual lives on earth can be seen in proper perspective, as part of a much greater plan. And although these accounts seem basically in harmony with the conventional Christian belief in purgatory, hell and heaven, the approximately similar states exist, not as final punishments or rewards for a single earth life, but as stages in a continuing education. Each has to redeem those parts of himself that are bound by the chains of his own creation. Even in the second heaven the processes of self-cleansing and selfless service continue. Here the spirit learns that there are further states of bliss, but these are too intense for it yet.

It becomes plain that life on earth and life between incarnations simply provide different opportunities of 'growing up'. Each spirit will pass from hard work to refreshment and from refreshment to further tasks – and although on the planes beyond the surroundings are said to be more pleasant than on earth, basically the work is just as strenuous. It takes enormous effort for each spirit to make any lasting progress, but he is not alone and can expect the kind of help, advice and inspiration that would have been impossible on earth. Encouraged and inspired, the individual can progress towards his own ultimate maturity.

The destiny of each soul will be fulfilled, say the communicators, only when that of the

The man who would be king

Death is said to be 'the great leveller' and nowhere is this shown more clearly than in *A Tudor story* by the late Canon W. S. Pakenham-Walsh. This purports to tell the tale of the Canon's relationship – through several mediums – with various members of the Tudor court from the early 1920s to his death at the age of 92 in 1960. Pakenham-Walsh found that his main spiritual mission was to aid Henry VIII himself, who was angry, lost and clinging pathetically to a crown he no longer possessed, and could therefore make no progress in the afterlife.

One medium had to remind 'Henry' that he was king no longer. He was furious, saying 'I am a king. I carry royal birth and death in my hands. . . . A king does not commit acts for which he is sorry.'

The Canon enlisted the help of the 'spirits' of Anne Boleyn and Elizabeth I among others, while also praying for the King's soul himself. For a time Henry vacillated between apparent repentance and humility and outbursts of regal temperament. The breakthrough came when he was allowed to meet his sons – including the baby who had been stillborn, now grown up. Henry's last communication was: 'Know that Henry, once King of England, did repent.'

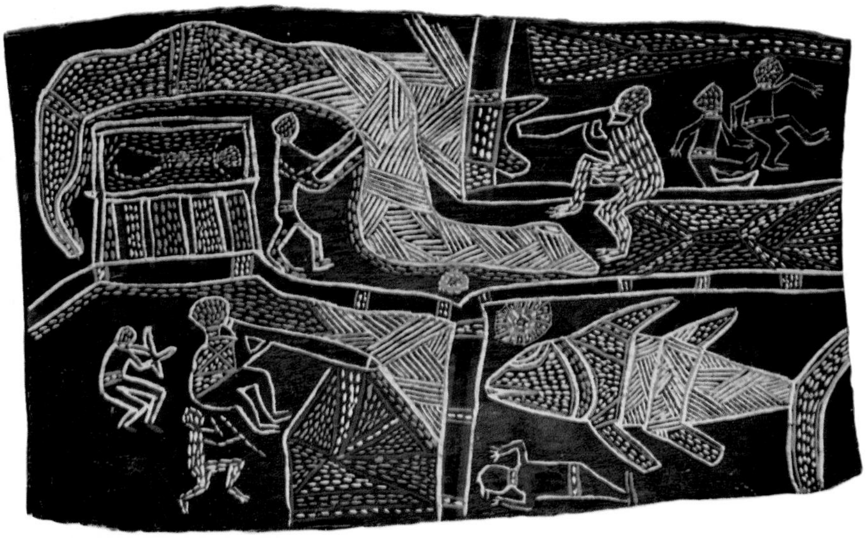

group soul is completed. This may take aeons. There are many group souls, said to range from comparatively few members to many hundreds. Frequently a person's inner urge on earth is a reflection of the quest of his group soul, his equivalent of the Holy Grail. Everyone retains his free will to depart from the group soul's set path, but the promptings of his own inner nature will, it is believed, eventually lead him back to it.

During his stay in the second heaven the spirit learns from the 'replay' of his past lives to discover his true potential and what steps he should take to fulfil it. Strengthened by the insight and love of his companions he is now ready for a yet further expansion of his consciousness, which takes place in the *third heaven*. This is, however, too intense an experience for many spirits to endure for very long, although it is open to them for precisely as long as they can endure. Although almost impossible for us to understand, communicators tell us that in the third heaven a spirit comes to the limits of his consciousness. After a brief glimpse of this plane he finds he cannot go further into it than his nature allows. Faced with his limitations he has no choice but to return to earth.

Other lives, other worlds

However, if his next incarnation goes well and he grows spiritually as a result, he will find that he can then proceed deeper into the third heaven. This in turn will enable him to make more of his succeeding earth life, for it is in the third heaven that the true nature of the group soul's task unfolds as consciousness expands in the individual members.

But what happens when a person has little more to learn from earth? Most accounts agree that a choice awaits him. He can take a leap into the great unknown, leaving this planet and its successive incarnations altogether, and begin again somewhere else. Communications are vague on this point, but they do seem to imply a new cycle of physical lives on another planet. Few, the posthumous F.W.H. Myers says, are sufficiently strong to go the first time the chance arises. Most spirits prefer to wait, helping others if needed, even if it means being reincarnated on earth yet again. A group soul will move on only when every member is ready to go. No one will be left behind.

People frequently deplore the injustice of 'life', meaning their earthly existence. But if the accounts of the afterlife summarised above are substantially true, then there is such a thing as absolute justice, there is cause for hope, there is free will and ever-expanding consciousness. The narratives purporting to come from people in the after-life can be examined by anyone – religious beliefs and pious hopes aside – as evidence. Perhaps the last words of Mary, Queen of Scots, 'In my end is my beginning', express the literal truth for everyone.

Above: a bark painting by the Australian Aborigine artist Bunia, showing the afterlife

Right: an early 15th-century representation of St Peter receiving three souls at the gates of heaven. In the traditional Christian view, admission to heaven was in itself a kind of judgement, although the dreadful day of judgement was still to come

Below: a wall painting at Tepantitla, Mexico, dating back more than 1000 years. It is believed to show the rain god's paradise

'Come back, my child...'

A small girl, dangerously ill, 'died' for a quarter of an hour – and, according to her own account, went to a new world in the stars, met long-dead relatives and had an interview with God. Her father tells her astonishing story

LATE IN THE AUTUMN of 1968 Durdana, the younger of my two daughters, then about two and a half years old, 'died' for around a quarter of an hour. She had been ill for some months, getting progressively worse. She began to become paralysed, and later developed episodes of vomiting and blindness. I was an army doctor in those days, posted to a small unit high in the foothills of the Himalayas; we took Durdana to the military hospital, some miles away, for examination, but investigations proved inconclusive. A suggestion was made that the symptoms might be the after effects of a viral encephalitis that had claimed the lives of some dozen children in the area some time before.

I was busy in the medical inspection room one morning when my orderly came running to tell me that my wife was calling me – something had happened to baby Durdana.

My living quarters were a large hut in the station compound, adjacent to the inspection room. Durdana had been very bad the night before and, fearing the worst, I hurried home. My wife was in the garden, standing beside the child's cot. A hurried examination revealed no sign of life in the little girl. 'She's gone,' I said. With a look almost of relief, for the child had been in extreme pain, my wife gently lifted the limp little form from the cot and carried her inside. I followed. Certain emergency measures are mandatory under army regulations, and one of my staff, who had followed me from the inspection room, hurried off to get the requisite equipment.

My wife carried the child to our bedroom and laid her down on my bed. After another examination I began to carry out the prescribed emergency procedures, rather half-heartedly, knowing that they were unlikely to have any effect. While doing so, I found myself repeating, half unconsciously, under my breath, 'Come back my child, come back.'

As a last resort, my wife poured a few drops of the nikethamide – a respiratory stimulant – we had given Durdana the night before into the child's mouth. They trickled out of her lifeless mouth and down her cheek. We looked sadly on – and then, to our amazement, the child opened her eyes and, making a wry face, gravely informed us that the medicine was bitter. Then she closed her eyes again. Quickly I examined her – and, as I watched, signs of life began to reappear, albeit very faintly. Gradually they grew stronger. It is difficult to say, but I think she had been 'dead' for around a quarter of an hour.

One day soon afterwards – when Durdana had somewhat recovered from her 'death' and my wife from her shock – mother and daughter were in the garden. 'Where did my little daughter go the other day?' asked my wife. 'Far, far away, to the stars,' came the surprising reply. Now Durdana was an intelligent and articulate child – and whatever she said had to be taken seriously, or she would become annoyed. 'Indeed,' exclaimed my wife, 'and what did my darling see there?'

'Gardens,' said Durdana.

'And what did she see in these gardens?'

'Apples and grapes and pomegranates.'

'And what else?'

'There were streams, a white stream, a brown stream, a blue stream, and a green stream.'

'And was anyone there?'

'Yes, my grandfather was there, and his mother, and another lady who looked like you.'

My wife was greatly intrigued. 'And what did they say?'

'Grandpa said he was glad to see me, and his mother took me in her lap and kissed me.'

'Then?'

'Then I heard my daddy calling me, "Come back my child, come back." I told Grandpa that Daddy was calling me and I must go back. He said we should have to ask God. So we went to God, and Grandpa told

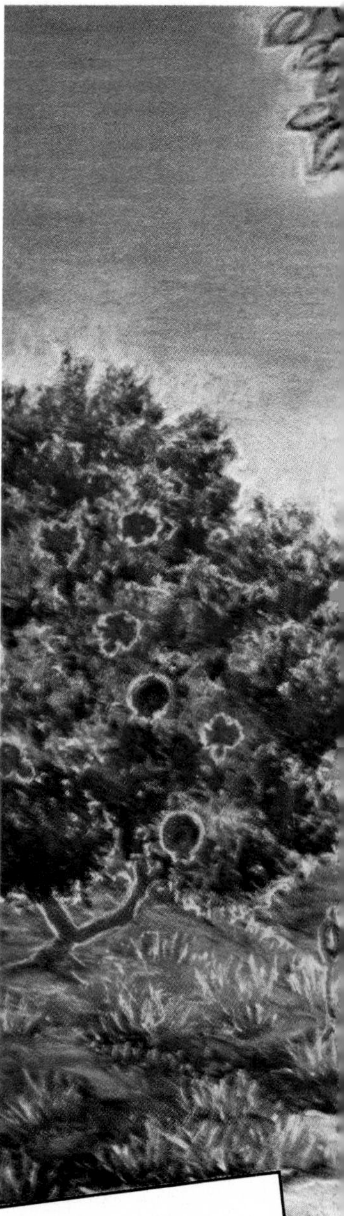

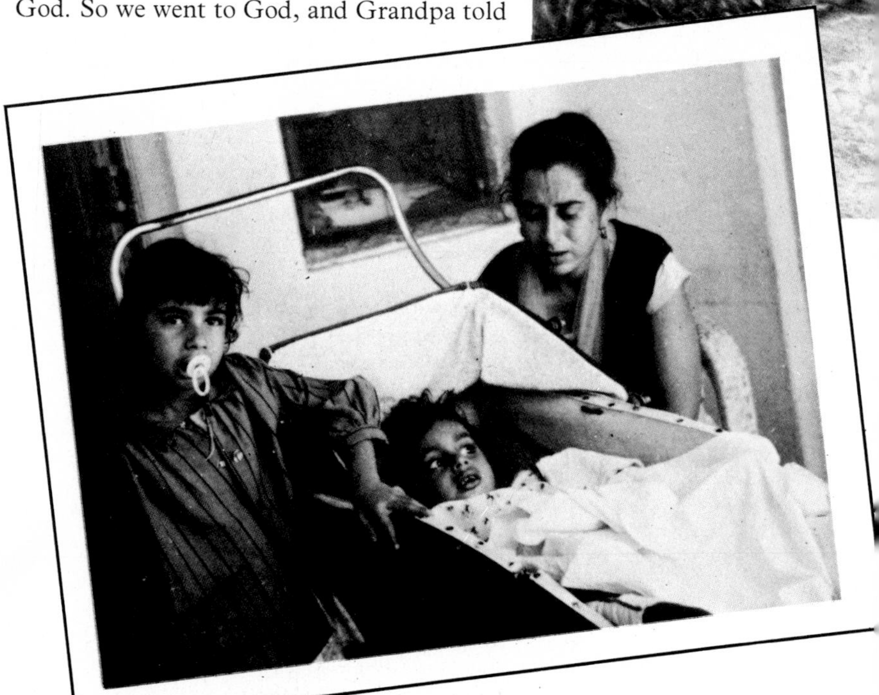

Left: Durdana's impression – painted in 1980 – of what she saw on her visit to the 'stars'. She found herself in a garden with four streams – white, brown, blue and green. The white stream is shown in this painting. Subtle differences showed Durdana that she could not be on Earth: there appeared to be no Sun – everything shone with its own faint luminescence – and physical objects seemed to have no substance. Durdana has painted this picture (below) to show what the scene would look like on Earth

him that I wanted to go back. "Do you want to go back?" God asked me. "Yes," I said, "I must go back. My Daddy is calling me." "All right," said God, "Go." And down, down, down I came from the stars, onto Daddy's bed.' This was more than interesting. Durdana had indeed 'come to' on my bed – an unusual place for her to find herself, for the children slept or played in their own beds or their mother's, never in mine. And when Durdana regained consciousness she was in no state to know where she was. But my wife was more interested in Durdana's interview with the Almighty.

'What was God like?' she asked.

'Blue,' came the startling reply.

'But what did he look like?'

'Blue.'

Try as we might, then and later, to get the

Left: Durdana, aged two and a half years, with her mother and older sister, on her way to recovery after having 'died' for a quarter of an hour as the result of a neural illness. Once she was well enough to speak, her parents asked her where she had gone during that quarter hour. 'Far, far away, to the stars,' was Durdana's disconcerting reply

Left: Durdana's impression of God. Questioned soon after her experience, she said that she had heard her father's voice calling her home – and had gone to ask God's permission to return to Earth. When asked to describe what God looked like, she could only say 'blue'

child to describe God in more detail, she could only repeat that he was 'blue'.

Soon afterwards, we took Durdana to Karachi for treatment at the neuro-surgical department of the Jinnah Post-Graduate Medical Centre. After a complex operation on her skull, Durdana gradually began to recover. I returned to duty, while my wife stayed in Karachi with the convalescent Durdana. Before they left to rejoin me, they visited several of our relatives and friends in Karachi. While visiting the house of one of my uncles, as they sat chatting over a cup of tea, Durdana wandered about the room, holding onto pieces of furniture for support – for she was still unable to stand unaided. Suddenly she called out 'Mummy, Mummy!' My wife ran to her. 'Mummy,' said Durdana excitedly, pointing to an old photograph on a side table, 'this is my grandpa's mother. I met her in the stars. She took me in her lap and kissed me.'

Durdana was quite right. But my grandmother died long before Durdana was born; only two photographs of her exist, and both are in the possession of this uncle of mine. Durdana was visiting his house for the first time in her life, and in no way could she have seen this photograph before.

We later moved to London, and Durdana's story began to attract interest from the media. The BBC featured Durdana in a 1980 *Everyman* programme on survival of death and, before the filming began, the producer,

Angela Tilby, came to visit us. She admired a number of paintings by Durdana that were hanging on the walls. Durdana had become a gifted landscape painter, and had received many awards and prizes for her paintings. Mrs Tilby made the interesting suggestion that Durdana should try to paint what she saw when she was in the stars.

'I've been to this place . . .'

Durdana was later featured on the BBC programme *Pebble Mill at one* – and her paintings of the stars were shown and discussed at some length. The day after the programme had been broadcast, I received a telephone call from a Mrs Goldsmith, one of my patients – a very intelligent, well-read German-Jewish woman. She said she had seen Durdana on the television the day before, and expressed the wish to meet my daughter personally and to see her paintings again. It turned out that Mrs Goldsmith had had an experience of near death similar to Durdana's. 'I nearly jumped out of my chair when I saw this picture on the television,' she said about one of the paintings. '"My God," I said, "I've been to this place. . . ."'

Listening to her speak, I felt that she seemed a little over-excited – until I realised that what she was trying to tell us was not that she had been to similar gardens, but that she had visited the actual spot that Durdana had painted. It appeared that she had seen more of the place than Durdana had – I had called Durdana away too soon! Mrs Goldsmith recognised everything that was in Durdana's picture, and described things that were not in the picture. They sat and talked about what was round the bend in the stream that Durdana had painted, and about the location of the other streams that Durdana had described to her mother.

Below: Durdana and her father with one of Durdana's paintings of the scenes she saw during the time she was apparently dead. One of Durdana's father's patients, a Mrs Goldsmith (right), saw the paintings when they were featured on the BBC television programme *Pebble Mill at one* – and immediately recognised the landscapes as those she had seen during a near-death experience. Mrs Goldsmith, however, had seen more than Durdana had

What of Durdana's feelings during her experience? They are strikingly similar to those reported by Mrs Goldsmith – and by many other people who have gone through near-death experiences. She was very happy in the stars, and returned only out of a sense of duty, because her daddy was calling her. She had a feeling of freedom: she felt she was everywhere at once, and could reach wherever she wanted to. There was no source of light, and hence no shadows. Everything was visible through its own luminescence. There was no sound, and no animals – at least, she saw none. Physical objects were ethereal images: they seemed to have no substance, no weight. She felt she knew everything and everybody.

I have presented Durdana's story as simply as possible, as it happened. But what does it imply? Where was it that Durdana spent her quarter hour of 'death'? Durdana herself believes that her experience somehow reflects her own expectations: 'If I had been a Martian, perhaps I would have been sent to a replica of Mars. There perhaps, God would have appeared red.' And yet Durdana's experience must be more than a dramatisation of her own imagination – for Mrs Goldsmith recognised the very same place.

Such questions must be left for experts to decide. This is merely an account of the experience of one little girl – an experience that is strange, thought-provoking and not a little awe-inspiring.

Index